D1342524

The Global Business Guide for the successful use of Coaching in Organisations

2013 Edition
by Frank Bresser

IMI
Library

2 8 NOV

Sandyford Road, Dublin 16
Telephone: 01 2078513
Email: knowledge@i⌐
http://ww
.om

© 2013 by Frank Bresser/

Herstellung & Verlag: Bo⌐
Coverdesign: Bresser Con⌐   easyCover BoD
Coverbild (gelbe Weltkarte): © Pixel Embargo – Fotolia.com
Übernommenes Design von 1. Edition: depunkt
Graphische Textänderungen für 2. Edition: bloomotion

ISBN 978-3-8482-5378-4

Bibliografische Information der Deutschen
Nationalbibliothek:
Die Deutsche Nationalbibliothek verzeichnet diese
Publikation in der Deutschen Nationalbibliografie;
detaillierte bibliografische Daten sind im Internet über
www.dnb.de abrufbar.

2nd Edition

The 1st Edition was published in 2010 by:
Frank Bresser Fachbuch, Fridolinstr. 13, Cologne, Germany
Design and Production: depunkt, M. Holz, Cologne
(Ebook)
www.frank-bresser.com

About the author:

FRANK BRESSER

received for his work the Global HR Excellence Award 2011.

Together with his team, he is helping companies design, implement and optimise tailor-made coaching programmes suited to their organisation-specific needs and generating business success. He pioneered the development of systematic and strategic design, implementation and improvement of coaching programmes as a distinct discipline and is a regular keynote speaker on national and international conferences.

He holds an MBA with Distinction in International Management from the University of East London (dissertation topic: Implementation of coaching in business) and has (co-)written over 30 books and articles on coaching. Bresser Consulting also publishes the Global Coaching Survey, which examined the situation of business coaching across the globe in each continent, region and country (covering 162 countries).

Frank is based in Cologne, Germany, and can be contacted at: info@bresser-consulting.com

www.bresser-consulting.com

About the editor:

AMANDA BOUCH

heads **abc (Amanda Bouch Consulting)** a management consulting and coaching business working with organisations of all sizes up to global and across a range of industries and government and works as a Senior Consultant at Bresser Consulting. Amanda has an MBA with Distinction from Manchester Business School (dissertation topic: Performance Management) and is an Accredited Coach with the Association for Coaching (AC).

She was created Honorary Fellow of the Association for Coaching for her services to the AC and the coaching industry in the UK. Amanda was active on the Board of the AC from 2003 and was Vice Chair of AC in UK from its launch in 2009 to end 2011.

She has authored a number of articles on leadership/management and coaching and speaks (and blogs) on these topics.

Amanda can be contacted at: amanda@amandabouchconsulting.co.uk

www.amandabouchconsulting.co.uk

Foreword to the 2013 Edition

Coaching is one of the fastest growing business phenomena in the world. It is increasingly used as a professional business tool and becoming more and more ingrained into organisational life in various ways. Organisations and academics have now widely recognized the value of coaching and the number of people engaged in coaching, either professionally or as part of their role, is rising significantly. The challenge for organisations is *how to implement and optimize coaching successfully.*

The good news is: A growing number of impressive coaching success stories can be found in enterprises today. Companies have started to think through their coaching initiatives in a more systematic and strategic way and to increasingly tailor the use of coaching to their specific context and business goals. The spread of the Bresser management tools for the successful use of coaching in organisations is rising continuously, and we are now seeing the beginnings of what we call 'coaching programmes of the second generation' (Coaching Initiatives 2.0). These systematic and strategic coaching programmes are the future of successful coaching in organisations.

At the same time, the bad news is: The average quality of coaching programmes in businesses today is not high. Many enterprises are not applying the management tools for the successful use of coaching in companies yet, but stick to a rather sporadic, ad hoc use of coaching and/or miss key aspects even though they are trying to take a systematic approach. This corresponds to what we call 'coaching programmes of the first generation' (Coaching Initiatives 1.0). In particular the following five critical areas can be identified in the current poor coaching practice in many companies:

1. Poor qualifications of implementers
2. Lack of real coaching plans/concepts/definitions
3. No or very low strategic integration of coaching
4. Lack of understanding of the real potential of coaching
5. Insufficient financial and staff resources

So there is still a lot of work to be done: the overall practice of the professional design, implementation and optimization of coaching programmes in companies is still in its infancy.

Companies today are at the crossroads, i.e. on the verge of moving from first to second generation coaching programmes.

This 2013 Edition, available as paperback as well as ebook, provides a complete set of 7 effective management tools for the optimal design, implementation and optimization of coaching programmes and confirms the implementation of coaching in organisations as a distinct discipline. It is the ideal toolkit to make Coaching Initiatives 2.0 a reality. The management tools are as cutting-edge as ever, yet at the same time already well-proven; first published in 2005, our tools now have a history of successful application.

This book addresses beginner, advanced as well as master levels regarding the use of coaching in companies. Wherever coaching is right now in your organisation (or in the organisations you work for/with), the Global Business Guide will help you take coaching to the next level(s).

Sincerely

Frank Bresser, January 2013

How to best approach this book

In this publication, you will find 7 leading-edge frameworks for the successful implementation and improvement of coaching in business/organisations as well as over 20 up-to-date company case studies on coaching from across the globe.

We suggest different approaches for reading this book depending on your level of experience/knowledge in the field of coaching (see below) and your time available (see next page):

According to your current level of experience/knowledge:

This book is addressing beginner, advanced as well as master levels regarding the use of coaching in companies.

for Beginners

You have no or hardly any experience/knowledge in implementing and optimizing coaching in an organisation.

See the first framework (i.e. the key success factors framework) as a separate book which best meets your needs. It is a great introduction for you and at the same time already addresses all key issues in detail. Be prepared that some sections may be very challenging for you, and so do not expect to understand everything right from the beginning. Proceed to Framework 2 (or other frameworks) only when you really feel ready for it or are particularly interested in getting to know more about it. However, do also have a look at Framework 6.

for Advanced

You have some experience/knowledge in the implementation and improvement of coaching.

Focus on Frameworks 1 and 2 (i.e. key success factors framework & coaching value chain framework) at first. Both are great learning for you and will include very challenging sections. Then, feel free to choose from and

start to explore some or all of the remaining frameworks, depending on which seem most relevant, appealing and interesting to you. Do have a look at Framework 6.

for Masters

You have a lot of experience/knowledge in the implementation and improvement of coaching.

We suggest you aim to understand and be able to use all frameworks given in this book. Also have a close look at the coaching pyramid model in the introduction explaining the context and essence of all coaching forms and frameworks. A number of sections may still be quite challenging for you. When reading, be aware that Framework 1 is the base – not least because all key issues are addressed there in detail. Also have in mind that Framework 7 integrates all other frameworks and finally puts you on the path to excellence. Choose from and explore the 7 frameworks in the order most appropriate to you – depending on which ones seem most relevant, appealing and interesting to you.

for All Levels (Beginners, Advanced and Masters)

- Do read the introduction of this book, which already provides substantial information and input: It gives an overview of all frameworks and explains the coaching pyramid model setting out the context and essence of all coaching forms and frameworks.
- Whenever you like, take a look at the practical company case studies on coaching spread throughout the book. These give a great insight into the current practice of the use of coaching in firms across the globe.

According to your time available for reading this book

Quick Overview

If you want to get a quick overview of the frameworks, just read the introduction at the beginning, and the first pages of each framework chapter (where you will find visual representations of each framework). If you have even less time available, have a look at the brief and the detailed table of contents to get a first idea. (Here you also find the complete list of company case studies and extra boxes included in this book.)

Detailed Reading

This publication contains 7 leading-edge frameworks for the implementation and improvement of coaching as well as over 20 company case studies on coaching. You will find this book is comprehensive and in depth. To facilitate greatest pleasure, effectiveness and efficiency in your reading, please see the suggestions for approaching this book according to your current level of coaching experience/knowledge (beginner, advanced, master) as set out above.

Specific Reading

If you want to look up specific issues or other particular information in this book, first have a look at the short and detailed table of contents (which also includes the complete list of company case studies and extra boxes included in this business guide). The straightforward structure of this publication with 7 consecutive frameworks facilitates easy reading and information finding. What is more, Framework 1 – the key success factors framework – addresses all key issues in detail.

Brief Contents

	Page:
About the author and the editor	2
Foreword to the 2013 Edition	3
How to best approach this book	4
Brief Contents	6
Detailed Table of Contents	8
Acknowledgements	19
Foreword	20

> **WITH OVER 20 COMPANY CASE STUDIES ON COACHING, SPREAD THROUGHOUT THE BOOK**
> (listed on the next page)

Introduction — 21
A complete toolbox: The **7 frameworks** for the successful implementation and improvement of coaching

PART I	The coaching success factors framework	36
PART II	The coaching value chain framework	246
PART III	The coaching capacity building framework	273
PART IV	The coaching change dynamics framework	299

= CORE FRAMEWORKS

PART V	The coaching growth and maintenance framework	319
PART VI	The coaching guidance and support framework	333

= EMBEDDING FRAMEWORKS

| **PART VII** | The coaching integration framework | 348 |

= ACTIVATING FRAMEWORK

Conclusion and future perspective	362
Your Notes	363

www.frank-bresser-consulting.com

LIST OF COMPANY CASE STUDIES FROM ACROSS THE GLOBE

all written by managers/directors responsible for coaching in their organisation

Case Study 1 : **SAP, Germany:** Internal coaches – the development of coaching competences in the organisation at SAP (p.45)

Case Study 2 : **PPI Adhesive Products, Slovakia:** Coaching for people development (p. 50)

Case Study 3 : **Borusan Lojistik, Turkey:** Coaching travel on the way of change (p.70)

Case Study 4 : **Debut Image Consultants, Kenya:** Overcoming obstacles in our sales team through coaching in times of organisational growth and change (p. 73)

Case Study 5 : **X-Bank, Mediterranean country/Europe:** Introducing coaching into our bank culture (p. 85)

Case Study 6 : **X-Optics, Hong Kong & P.R. China:** Building a coaching culture for excellence (p. 102)

Case Study 7 : **NASA, USA:** How NASA integrated coaching throughout the learning process (p. 104)

Case Study 8 : **Baker Tilly Ukraine, Ukraine:** Growth and development through in-house coaching (p. 116)

Case Study 9 : **Wüstenrot, Austria:** Certificate coaching program drives cultural change at Wüstenrot (p. 121)

Case Study 10 : **MTN, Uganda:** Coaching for performance – the case for MTN Uganda (p. 126)

Case Study 11 : **X-Bank, Africa:** Team coaching at work (p. 133)

Case Study 12 : **UNIQA, Serbia:** Coaching at UNIQA (Serbia) (p. 141)

Case Study 13 : **Pepsico, Portugal:** Effective leadership development by combining 360° feedback and one-to-one coaching (p. 146)

Case Study 14 : **Ramada Hotel, Costa Rica:** Coaching for team collaboration and strategy alignment (p. 182)

Case Study 15 : **BBC, United Kingdom (UK):** Creating an in-house coaching service at the BBC (p. 212)

Case Study 16 : **Atieh Roshan Consulting, Iran:** Coaching in Iran (p. 234)

Case Study 17 : **Calouste Gulbenkian, Portugal:** Coaching for self-awareness and leadership (p. 236)

Case Study 18 : **T-Mobile International, Europe:** Coaching drives skills development in T-Mobile (p. 242)

Case Study 19 : **Avea, Turkey:** The coaching program in Avea (p. 270)

Case Study 20 : **Nordea Bank, Estonia (East-/Northern Europe):** From good to great through coaching (p. 296)

Case Study 21 : **EOS Matrix OOD, Bulgaria:** Building resilience in the process of organizational transformation (p. 313)

Case Study 22 : **Front Row Venture Limited, Kenya:** Recovery coaching for optimal team performance (p. 329)

Case Study 23 : **CSOB, Czech Republic:** The CSOB Coaching centre (p. 331)

LIST OF EXTRA BOXES

Extra Box 1 : **The 12 dimensions of coaching** (p. 41)

Extra Box 2 : **The state of coaching across the globe: Results of the Frank Bresser Consulting Global Coaching Survey 2008/2009** (p. 221)

Detailed Table of Contents

	Page:
About the author and the editor	2
Foreword to the 2013 Edition	3
How to best approach this book	4
Brief Contents	6
Detailed Table of Contents	8
Acknowledgements	19
Foreword	20

Column for company case studies
and extra boxes in this book:

INTRODUCTION	21
A complete toolbox: The 7 frameworks for the successful implementation and improvement of coaching	21
1. Overview of the 7 frameworks	22
• The 4 core frameworks	22
• The 2 embedding frameworks	25
• The 1 activating framework	26
2. Company case studies and extra boxes	28
3. Setting the context properly: The coaching pyramid	28
• Dynamic appropriateness	29
4. Final note	35

THE 4 CORE FRAMEWORKS	36

PART I	
The coaching success factors framework *(also called: The 10 key success factors* *framework)*	36

Page:

Key success factor 1:   39
Develop an organisation-specific
understanding of coaching
   1.1. The core of coaching   39
   1.2. Organisation-specific definition   39
                                          41
                                        45

Key success factor 2:   49
Adopt a systematic approach
                                        50

Key success factor 3:   53
Choose an adequate level of organisational
penetration of coaching
   3.1. People coaching forms   54
       3.1.1. Self-coaching   55
       3.1.2. Peer coaching   55
       3.1.3. Classic one-to-one coaching (by
              external or internal coaches)   55
          • External versus internal coaches   56
          • Stages of any 1:1 coaching intervention   58
             1. Availability of suitable coaches
                 (building coach pools)   59
             2. Request for coaching   62
             3. Matching coach and coachee   62
             4. Contracting   63
             5. Coaching process   68
             6. Evaluation   69
                              70
                              73
       3.1.4. Team coaching   75
       3.1.5. Coaching in groups   75
       3.1.6. Manager as coach of direct reports
            (Be very careful!)   76
       3.1.7. Coaching leadership style (or coaching
            management style)   78
          • Implementation and development   82
          • Clear distinction from other   83
            coaching forms   85

Extra Box 1:
The 12 dimensions of coaching

Case Study 1:
SAP, Germany

Case Study 2:
PPI Adhesive Products, Slovakia

Case Study 3:
Borusan Lojistik, Turkey

Case Study 4:
Debut Image Consultants, Kenya

Case Study 5:
X-Bank, Mediterranean country/Europe

Page:

3.1.8. Coaching culture   87
  • Coaching communication style   89
  • Coaching attitude   89
  • Coaching mindset   89
  • Coaching principles   94
  • The process of building a
    coaching culture   97
                                                         102
                                                         104
3.2. Organisation coaching forms   106
  • Coaching of organisations
    (coaching consultancy)   108
  • Coaching interfaces   108
  • Coaching facilities   108
  • Coaching operations   109
  • Coaching processes   109
  • Coaching structures   109
  • Coaching organisation   110
  • Coaching business model   110
3.3. Technology & Tools coaching forms   112
  • Coaching HR tools   113
  • Coaching (other) tools   113
  • Coaching technologies   114
Summary and closing note   114
                                                         116

Key success factor 4:   119
Involve the top
  4.1. Get the support of top management   119
  4.2. Begin with the implementation at the top   120
                                                         121

Key success factor 5:   125
Promote coaching as a positive developmental tool
  5.1. Coaching for excellence   125
  5.2. Branding and marketing   125
                                                         126

Key success factor 6:   129
Create an optimal win-win value for all stakeholders
  6.1. Benefits of coaching   129
  6.2. Pitfalls and guidelines   131
                                                         133

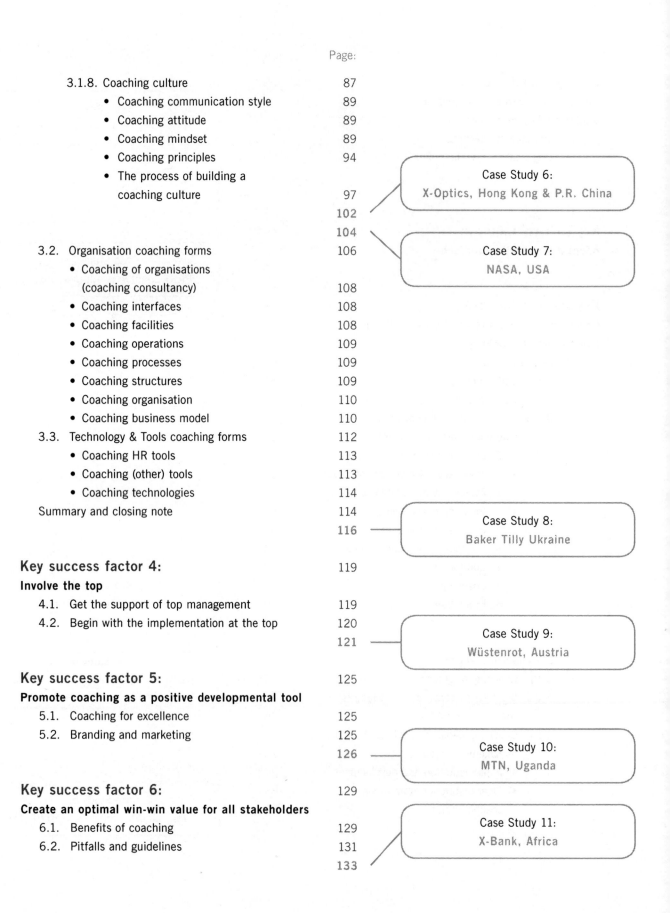

Case Study 6:
X-Optics, Hong Kong & P.R. China

Case Study 7:
NASA, USA

Case Study 8:
Baker Tilly Ukraine

Case Study 9:
Wüstenrot, Austria

Case Study 10:
MTN, Uganda

Case Study 11:
X-Bank, Africa

FRANK BRESSER CONSULTING & ASSOCIATES

EXCELLENT COACHING SOLUTIONS ↗

www.frank-bresser-consulting.com

Page:

Key success factor 7:   135
Achieve full consistency of coaching with
business strategy
   7.1.   Strategic use and positioning of coaching   135
   7.2.   Creating optimal consistency   138
          141

> Case Study 12:
> UNIQA, Serbia

Key success factor 8: **Ensure complete**   143
transparency of the whole coaching concept
   8.1.   Conceptual transparency   143
   8.2.   Driver transparency   144
          146

> Case Study 13:
> Pepsico, Portugal

✳ **Key success factor 9:**   149
Evaluate effectively and carefully
   9.1.   The nature of the evaluation of coaching   149
   9.2.   The current practice of coaching evaluation   150
   9.3.   Effective evaluation   151
       • A clear coaching concept/plan   151
       • Take an evaluation perspective right
         from the beginning   155
       • Develop a detailed coaching
         evaluation plan   155
   9.4.   Careful evaluation   169
       • Impact of confidentiality on evaluation   171
       • Relationship between people's commitment
         and evaluation   174
       • Impact of volunteering/compulsion
         on evaluation   176
          182

> Case Study 14:
> Ramada Hotel, Costa Rica

Key success factor 10:   185
Ensure high integrity and quality at all levels
   10.1. High integrity   187
       • Suitable integrity standards   187
       • Optimal integrity compliance   193
       • Integrity of organisational structures and
         technology & tools   197
   10.2. High quality of your coaching programme   197
       • Suitable quality standards (and profiles)   197
       • Optimal quality assurance   205

Page:

- Quality of organisational structures
  and technology & tools   210
                                                            212 ——— Case Study 15:
                                                                     BBC, United Kingdom

Underlying factor 1:   216
Impact and importance of culture
    - The impact of culture on your   216
      coaching programme
    - Embracing all cultures   217   Extra Box 2:
    - Varying cultural openness to coaching   218   The state of coaching across the globe
    - Culture-specific   218
                                                            221
                                                            234 ——— Case Study 16:
                                                                     Atieh Roshan Consulting, Iran
                                                            236

Underlying factor 2:   239
Continuous learning process
                                                                        Case Study 17:
                                                                 Calouste Gulbenkian, Portugal

Underlying factor 3:   240
Implementation and improvement intelligence

Summary: 241
Coaching Success Factors Framework
                                                                        Case Study 18:
                                                            242 ——— T-Mobile International, Europe

PART II

The coaching value chain framework   245

    1. The Input   248
        1. Coaching   248
        2. Further inputs   248

    2. The Output   249
       Benefits at the individual, team, organisational
       and social level

    3. From input to output:
       The Core Value-adding Process   251
       Step 1:   Filtering   251
       Step 2:   Implementing/Optimizing suitable
                 coaching forms   251

www.frank-bresser-consulting.com

Page:

Step 3:   Building coaching capacity   253
Step 4:   Achieving higher dynamic appropriateness
              (better fit)   253
Step 5:   Realisation of the output (chain of benefits)   254

4. The Primary Activities   255

1.   Put coaching on the radar screen   255
2.   Acquire coaching literacy   255
3.   Make a needs analysis   256
4.   Identify potential areas of application   256
5.   Develop the coaching concept   256
6.   Ensure the availability of required resources   259
7.   Prepare carefully   260
8.   Introduce coaching/the coaching
         programme properly   260
9.   Enlarge the coaching initiative step-by-step   261
10. Manage and maintain the programme   261
11. Evaluate effectively and carefully   261
12. Develop the concept and measures further   262

5. The Support Activities   263

1.   Company-specific implementation/improvement   263
2.   Systematic and careful planning   263
3.   Keeping a realistic view   264
4.   Promoting coaching as positive,   264
         developmental tool
5.   Involving the top   264
6.   Alignment with business strategy and ensuring
         optimal win-win   265
7.   Communication and transparency   265
8.   People involvement and co-creation   265
9.   Ensuring high integrity and quality   266
10. Considering the cultural dimension   266
11. Continuous learning & development
         of intelligence   267
12. Making relevant 'make-or-buy' decisions   267

Summary: 269
Coaching Value Chain Framework

270

Case Study 19:
Avea, Turkey

Page:

PART III

The coaching capacity building framework   273
(also called: The high performance coaching culture framework)

Starting point: What is coaching capacity?   276
- Ability to achieve better fit/higher dynamic appropriateness   276
- Tacit knowledge/skill   276
- Other terms: Coaching culture/capability/ intelligence   276

Underlying basis: Key principles for building coaching capacity   277
- Cyclical (progressive) growth of coaching capacity   277
- Using the scalability of coaching capacity initiatives   277
- The coaching capacity triangle   278
- The 10 key success factors (and their underlying factors)   278
- The coaching value chain   278

Step 1: For what purpose do you want to build coaching capacity?   279
- Your company-specific objectives   279
- Scalability of objectives   279
- Envisaged chain of benefits   280

Step 2: What kind of coaching capacity do you need?   281
- Possible coaching capacity dimensions   281
- Emphasized coaching principles   281
- Nature of coaching capacity   283
- Scope of coaching capacity   284
- Degree of coaching capacity   285

Step 3: How to actually develop and build coaching capacity?   286
- Acknowledging the key principles   286
- Making use of scalability in terms of objectives, principles, scope and degree   286

Page:

- Time   286
- Budget   287
- Means (coaching forms)   288

**Step 4: Making it happen, evaluating and
developing the programme further**   293
- Continuous learning process   293

Summary: 294
Coaching Capacity Building Framework

                                                296 ──

> Case Study 20:
> Nordea Bank, Estonia

PART IV

The coaching change dynamics framework   299

**1. Where is your coaching programme
on the time line?**   301

2. Identify the coaching design variables. 302
- Choice and thinking in continuums   302
- List of 30 classic variables   303
- Relationship between variables   305
- Importance and variability   305

3. Identify the internal influences.   306
- General internal influences   306
- Coaching-specific internal influences   307
- Coaching programme itself   307
- Importance and variability   307

4. Identify the external influences.   308
- General external influences   308
- Coaching-specific external influences   308
- Importance and variability   309

**5. Configure your variables in
accordance with the influences**   309
- General guidelines   310
- Typical configurations   310

www.frank-bresser-consulting.com

Page:

6. Reconfigure your variables on a
   continuous basis over time   311
   • Dynamic process of adaptation   311
   • Continuous learning process   311
   • Increasing coaching intelligence   311

Summary:
Coaching Change Dynamics Framework   312
                                                  313

REVIEW:
The Core Frameworks (Frameworks 1 to 4)   317

Case Study 21:
EOS Matrix OOD, Bulgaria

THE 2 EMBEDDING FRAMEWORKS   319

PART V

**The coaching growth & maintenance
framework** *(also called: The coaching   319
gardening metaphor framework)*

Starting point: The organisational garden   321

1. Why grow coaching?   321

2. Who are the coaching gardeners?   322

3. What number and kind of coaching
   trees to plant where?   323

4. How to cultivate your coaching trees?   326

5. Harvest (and harness) your
   fruits properly   326

6. Prepare for the next cycle of growth   327

7. Review the gardening process and
   learn continuously   328

www.frank-bresser-consulting.com

Page:

Summary:
   Coaching Growth and Maintenance Framework   328
                                                      329

331

Case Study 22:	Front Row Venture Limited, Kenya

Case Study 23:	CSOB, Czech Republic

PART VI

**The coaching guidance and support
framework** *(also called: The coaching*
lighthouse metaphor framework)   333

Starting point: The coaching lighthouses   334
   Distinguish management from delivery

1. Assess your level of existing
   coaching literacy honestly   335

2. Analyse the gap between your current
   and needed coaching capability   336
   • **Question of analysis competence**   336
   • **Compare your existing with the needed
     coaching capability**   337
   • **Find optimal ways of filling your
     identified gap(s)**   338

3. Identify your exact needs for
   external guidance and support   340

4. Identify and select suitable external
   guidance and support in the market   342

5. Contract properly   344

6. Learn continuously from your
   collaboration with the externals   344

7. Evaluate properly (and re-contract
   accordingly)   345

8. Reduce the need for external guidance
   and support on the same issue over time   346

www.frank-bresser-consulting.com

Page:

Summary: 347
Coaching Guidance and Support Framework

THE ACTIVATING FRAMEWORK   348

PART VII

The coaching integration framework   348
(also called: The coaching microchip and powerhouse framework)

Starting point: The high-power coaching microchip   350

1. Choose the main components of your microchip   351

2. Activate it!   353

3. Spin it!   354
    3.1. Conceptual and practical integration   354
    3.2. Application in your company   356

4. See the effect of (and on) your spinning microchip becoming a powerhouse   357

5. Continuously optimize your microchip/powerhouse!   360

Summary: 361
Coaching Integration Framework

CONCLUSION AND FUTURE PERSPECTIVE   362

Your Notes   363

Acknowledgements

This book is the result of many years of great effort and hard work to develop a comprehensive, systematic framework for the successful implementation and improvement of coaching in businesses/organisations.

Being able to present you this book is a blessing, not to be taken for granted. Therefore, I want to take this opportunity to thank the following individuals and institutions for their enormous support:

- my family, with special thanks to Lia, my aunt, my brother, my parents and Nina

- my friends, with particular thanks to Constantine, Matthias, Frank and Joana

- my friends and colleagues, with special thanks to Amanda (who is also editor of this book and did an excellent job), Lutz and Katherine

- my whole consulting team and network of partners and colleagues

- my clients/client organisations

- the coaching, HR and other associations around the globe, who have supported my work, with particular thanks to the AC

- the HR, OD and L&D managers & directors who took the time and effort to write the case studies for this book

- the many, many organisations, experts, coaching practitioners and academics who have contributed to/participated in my research projects

- people I worked for in the past who believed in my potential and from whom I learnt a lot, with special thanks to John

- the schools, universities and institutes I visited, with special thanks to the UEL and to my tutor Klaus at the RFH

- depunkt for the great design of the first edition; bloomotion for the graphical adjustments for the 2013 Edition

- all other people and institutions, who supported me in one way or other on my journey

- myself for keeping focus and completing this book.

Dedication

This book is dedicated with love to my daughter Lia.

Foreword

by Amanda Bouch

The number of books on coaching is increasing all the time, but there are very few books out there which specifically address the questions of how to implement coaching in organisations. That is the significant contribution to the coaching industry that this book brings. It is written for the implementer – Directors or Managers in Human Resources, Learning & Development or Organisational Development departments, though, of course, coaches and those running coach training can also gain a lot from reading this book.

Frank has written a very thorough guide to implementing and improving coaching in organisations, covering all aspects in some depth. He addresses aspects of coaching, such as coaching tools & technology and coaching organisation that will be new to many, as well as the well-known aspects such as how to choose the appropriate coaching form, design and planning of coaching interventions and how to evaluate.

The models and frameworks he has developed provide comprehensive structures to support the design, planning and implementation of coaching in organisations. These helpful overviews of what is needed allow the implementing manager to easily check and cross-reference their plans and then to pick out the sections of the book that will help them in their understanding and to develop the best possible solution for their own organisation.

This book is a treasure trove of ideas, models, frameworks, examples and case studies from around the world and to support your learning, there are practical exercises for you to try out. There are no assumptions about what the reader may know and therefore those new to this field can find the guidance they need, while more experienced readers can dip into the sections they want to understand better. Whatever question you may have about implementing coaching, you will find answers in this guide. Frank doesn't do your job for you, he acknowledges that each organisation is unique and has its own context and challenges, what he does is provide you with the steps you need to take and asks you to apply these in your organisation.

In editing this book, I have sought to maintain Frank's style of writing, whilst ensuring its readability. In working together with Frank he encouraged me to challenge him on the concepts and principles he was developing, and we enjoyed many open debates on the topics. All these discussions, I'm sure, led to a better end result.

The collaboration has resulted in a truly comprehensive guide to implementing coaching that will be of value to coaching managers the world over and support them in achieving high quality coaching practice in their organisation.

Addendum to the Foreword
Since publishing the tools, we at Bresser Consulting have used all 7 frameworks to great effect with our clients and these have provided structure and detail to our discussions. Clients have been most complimentary about how the frameworks have supported them in planning the coaching initiatives, preparing the business case and monitoring the implementation. In particular, it is the strategic fit of the design of the coaching initiative that has helped the HR, L&D and OD managers to achieve board approval and helped boards to get people's buy-in top-down.

www.frank-bresser-consulting.com

INTRODUCTION

Coaching is one of the fastest growing business phenomena in the world. It is increasingly used as a professional business tool and becoming more and more ingrained into organisational life in various ways.

Now that organisations and academics have widely recognized the value of coaching and the number of people engaged in coaching, either professionally or as part of their role, is rising significantly, the challenge for organisations is how to implement and optimize coaching successfully.

In this regard, there has long been a lack of well-grounded tools and literature in the market. Now, by the publication of this book, that gap is finally closed.

A complete toolbox:

The 7 frameworks for the successful implementation and improvement of coaching

This book provides you with 7 cutting-edge management tools to structure the implementation and improvement of coaching in its various forms in organisations.

Learning and Development (L&D), Human Resources (HR) and Organisational Development (OD) managers, concerned with the implementation or optimization of coaching pro-grammes in their organisation, will find this guide an inva-luable resource for their daily work in this area. Also CEOs, board members, directors, coaching providers and consul-tancies involved in coaching programmes will benefit from reading this book.

This business guide is written in a practical, easily acces-sible and straight-forward way; yet the management tools are based on very extensive research and experience. Also, the book's depth allows for solutions and answers to detailed aspects and questions in the field.

The book covers all existing coaching forms in the business context (e.g. one-to-one coaching, peer coaching, team coaching, coaching as a leadership and management style, the development of coaching cultures, coaching as a business model) and enables you to understand, choose and make proper use of any of these as appropriate.

This guide critically examines and identifies the most suitable ways of using coaching, rather than promoting and assuming a specific coaching form as the only correct one or naively assuming the value of coaching under all circumstances.

The next pages will give you an overview of the 7 frame-works in this book and properly set the context of coaching in business.

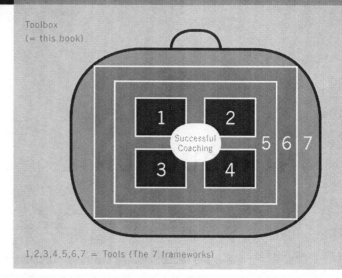

Toolbox
(= this book)

1,2,3,4,5,6,7 = Tools (The 7 frameworks)

Figure: The complete toolbox

1. OVERVIEW OF THE 7 FRAMEWORKS

This book is a complete toolbox for the successful implementation and optimization of coaching in organisations – containing 7 leading-edge tools:

It is highly sophisticated and provides optimal choice and guidance rather than fixed off-the-shelf solutions. The 7 frameworks included are the following:

1. **Coaching success factors framework**

2. **Coaching value chain framework**

3. **Coaching capacity building framework**

4. **Coaching change dynamics framework**

= **CORE FRAMEWORKS**

5. **Coaching growth & maintenance framework**

6. **Coaching support & guidance framework**

= **EMBEDDING FRAMEWORKS**

7. **Coaching integration framework**

= **ACTIVATING FRAMEWORK**

As with all toolkits, you may need and want to use just one, more or all of the tools included in it. Each framework can also stand alone and be used separately.

THE 4 CORE FRAMEWORKS

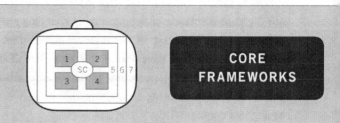

CORE FRAMEWORKS

These are the most comprehensive ones, each one gives very clear and concrete guidance on the process of implementing and optimizing coaching. Framework 1 is a particularly important one, as all recurrent key issues encountered in all frameworks are addressed here in detail (and only here in detail – in order to avoid repetition in later frameworks). However, Framework 1 is in principle the most general and high-level one among the four. The following three frameworks are like looking through a magnifying glass or microscope with increasing precision and exploring in more and more depth the previous one(s).

COACHING SUCCESS FACTORS FRAMEWORK

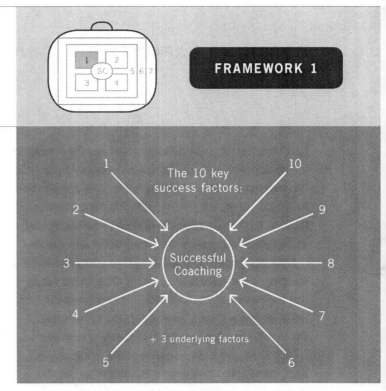

FRAMEWORK 1

The first of the management tools – also called the "10 key success factors framework" for the implementation and improvement of coaching – will give you an overview of the most important aspects to take into account when planning, executing and optimizing coaching initiatives. As the first framework in the book, it will also set out all recurring key issues found in the following frameworks. It is therefore by far the longest chapter in this book. It covers the 10 key success factors as well as the three underlying factors:

Framework 1: Coaching success factors framework
(simplified version)

COACHING VALUE CHAIN FRAMEWORK

FRAMEWORK 2

The second management tool provides you with a complete step-by-step guide to achieve best practice in coaching. It sets out all the chronological steps towards the successful implementation and improvement of coaching programmes. In this way, it will enable you to fully think through the whole coaching initiative and gain/keep absolute clarity on the process and how coaching adds value.

This framework explains the input into the coaching value chain, its output (the coaching benefits), the core value-adding process from input to output, the 12 primary activities and the support activities:

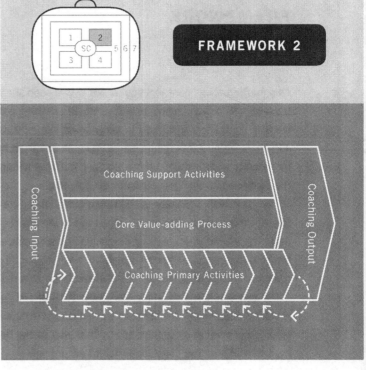

Framework 2: Coaching value chain framework
(simplified version)

www.frank-bresser-consulting.com

COACHING CAPACITY BUILDING FRAMEWORK

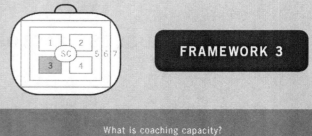

FRAMEWORK 3

This third tool focuses on an integrated and deeper approach to implementing and optimizing coaching, by emphasizing the common aim of all coaching forms: developing or enhancing coaching capacity/capability in the company. Whether this is as a means to achieve something else or as an explicit asset and skill to have in the organisation.

From this perspective, you will gain a greater understanding of the essence of coaching, its dynamic nature and the human and cultural factors in any coaching initiative. You will learn more about how to make use of the scalability and adjustability of coaching programmes.

This framework addresses what coaching capacity is, what the key principles around building it are, and the steps towards making it a reality.

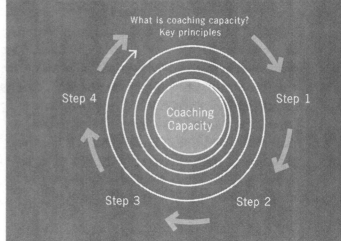

Framework 3: Coaching capacity building framework (simplified version)

COACHING CHANGE DYNAMICS FRAMEWORK

FRAMEWORK 4

This fourth management tool equips you with a sophisticated framework to design, configure and refine all coaching programme parameters accurately in accordance with existing and changing business requirements. It emphasizes the need for mobility and flexibility of any coaching initiative within the continuously changing business environment.

This framework increases your awareness of existing (or future) influences and helps you adjust and make effective decisions around your coaching programme on a continuous basis. It explores in depth the scalability and adjustability of coaching initiatives as well as their dynamics and complexity.

The tool covers the coaching design variables of any coaching programme, the possible influences (internal and external; general and coaching-specific) as well as the best ways to configure the coaching variables accordingly.

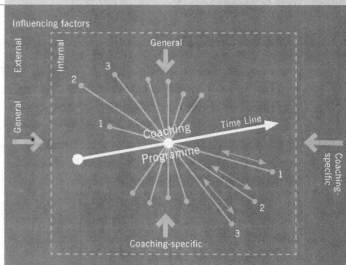

Framework 4: Coaching change dynamics framework (simplified version)

www.frank-bresser-consulting.com

THE 2 EMBEDDING FRAMEWORKS

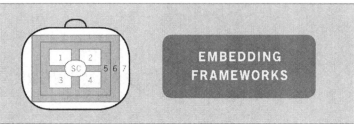

Frameworks 5 and 6 are more general than the previous four core frameworks. They provide you with an overall idea of how to make effective use of coaching in your organisation. While, in part, they embed the application of the previous frameworks, they can also stand alone and be used separately.

COACHING GROWTH AND MAINTENANCE FRAMEWORK

FRAMEWORK 5

This fifth tool will give you a different perspective on the implementation and improvement of coaching: Through a coaching gardening metaphor, this framework enables you to get a deeper sense for the right balance between organic and control management of coaching programmes. You may also improve your systems thinking regarding coaching and better understand the requirements of continuous management of coaching initiatives and the need for patience and calmness. Finally, the gardening metaphor addresses the emotional part of your brain and will help you integrate and see more links and complex relationships.

Speaking within the metaphor, this framework leads you through the process of planning your organisational garden, being and/or choosing good gardeners, and growing and cultivating thriving coaching trees successfully.

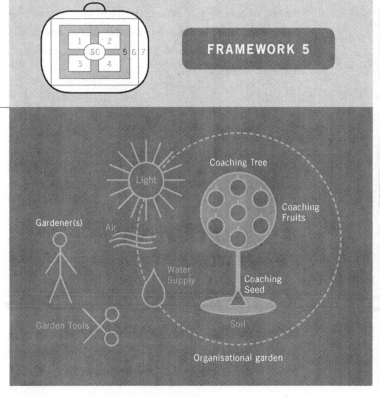

Framework 5: Coaching growth and maintenance framework (coaching gardening metaphor) (simplified version)

COACHING GUIDANCE AND SUPPORT FRAMEWORK

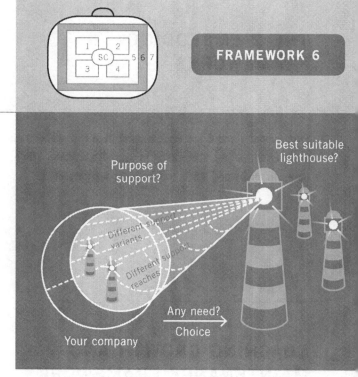

FRAMEWORK 6

This sixth management tool provides you with an easy-to-use framework to assess your own limits of coaching literacy, identify your exact needs for further external input (beyond this publication), make appropriate 'make-or-buy' decisions and get adequate external guidance and support on the implementation and optimization of coaching in your company, if required.

Through the use of a coaching lighthouse(s) metaphor, this framework helps you reach higher precision, confidence and assertiveness in identifying and sourcing external support on the use of coaching. It addresses how to identify and arrange your needs, when to use external support (and when not), what kind of support is available in the market, and how to achieve the best fit.

Framework 6: Coaching guidance and support framework (coaching lighthouse metaphor) (simplified version)

THE 1 ACTIVATING FRAMEWORK

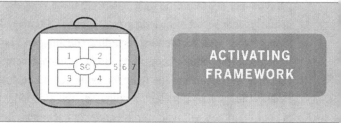

ACTIVATING FRAMEWORK

The final management tool aims to fully activate and integrate all previous frameworks and unites them. However, you may apply the core idea of it to any other context or coaching approach you want to integrate. This framework can also stand alone and be used separately, i.e. independently of the previous ones.

www.frank-bresser-consulting.com

COACHING INTEGRATION FRAMEWORK

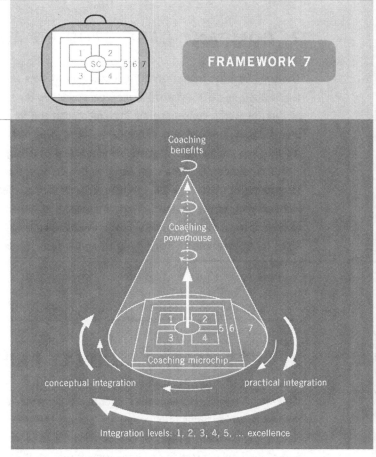

FRAMEWORK 7

This tool equips you with a synergizing framework helping you bring any (or all) of the previous frameworks into optimal flow and make them one. You will find that the various tools will become much more manageable, clear and easy to use, as they will transform into one integrated toolkit.

This last framework provides you with a still deeper understanding of the effective use of coaching in organisations. The integration of the various frameworks will put you on the path to excellence and produce the best results. Leveraging the full potential of this framework for optimal coaching implementation and improvement is the master discipline of this book.

Through an energetic coaching 'microchip and powerhouse' metaphor, the framework sets out how to bring the frameworks into real movement, how to achieve increased conceptual and practical integration of them, and what levels of integration are needed to achieve true excellence.

Framework 7: Coaching integration framework (coaching microchip & powerhouse metaphor) (simplified version)

Further remarks on the 7 frameworks

You may choose to acquire or use just one, some or all of the tools included in the toolbox – depending on what you need.

The tools are complementary, providing different perspectives, building on each other in different ways and constitute an integrated toolkit. So the more tools you are able to use and combine, the better. The ability to use all seven perspectives in a coordinated, complementary manner will produce the best results for your organisation.

The structure of the book is designed for ease of understanding: working through the coaching success factors framework first serves as an ideal foundation and orientation; you will then find it easy to work with the coaching value chain framework. After familiarising yourself with the value chain framework, you will find the coaching capacity building framework easy to use, and so on.

However, do find the right pace and approach for yourself, to enhance your knowledge of coaching implementation and improvement. It is always better to use one framework properly than all frameworks poorly. Quality of application is much more important than quantity.

In this spirit, revisit the first page of this book ("How to best approach this book") where you find useful suggestions on how to approach this book according to your level of current coaching literacy. There is no doubt, coaching in organisations is a continuous, evolving learning process.

2. COMPANY CASE STUDIES AND EXTRA BOXES

The book includes more than 20 practical case studies written in 2010 by L&D, OD and HR managers/directors from all over the world, concerning the implementation and improvement of coaching in their company. These give great insights into the current, international practice of coaching.

This publication is also a book partly written by organisations for organisations and you can refer to those case studies independently of the chapters. A set of questions at the end of each case study will provide you with extensive opportunities for further reflection and for applying the tools learned in this book.

Please note, that the authors of the company case studies are responsible for their content. These don't necessarily represent the Frank Bresser Consulting opinion.

Additionally, you will also find side boxes in the text providing you with supplementary information on specific themes, e.g. on the current state of coaching across the globe (the results of the Frank Bresser Consulting Global Coaching Survey).

3. SETTING THE CONTEXT PROPERLY: THE COACHING PYRAMID

While the 7 frameworks embrace and critically illuminate all relevant coaching forms in business, the process of defining coaching and choosing the right coaching form is already part of the implementation and improvement process itself.

Having said this, it is important to set the context of this book properly and identify the common element and essence of all coaching forms and frameworks, as this is what this book is all about: the use of coaching (in its various forms) in organisations.

As you will see in a minute, it is 'modern, dynamic appropriateness' that lies right at the heart of any coaching approach and programme. However, do not expect a simple one line definition of coaching or anything similar that would immediately capture everything. Instead, on the following pages, we will develop step-by-step a complete model – the three-sided coaching pyramid – that sets out the context and essence of coaching.

This model is not meant to be the one right or final explanation of coaching, but a helpful orientation and tool at your disposal. It doesn't say that you should now give up your definition of coaching, but that there are different tenable and appropriate ways of defining coaching in different contexts. This model enables you to understand, explain and put all of them in context.

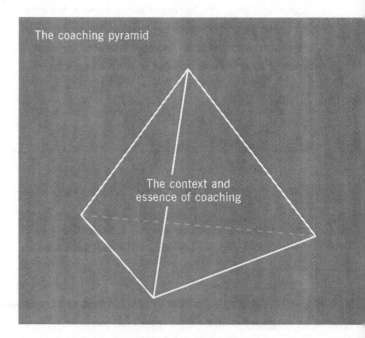

The coaching pyramid

The context and essence of coaching

Be prepared that the following may stretch your thinking and be quite challenging at first. It makes people think beyond their current, probably more specific, understanding of coaching. This exactly **is** the purpose of this model.

The pyramid consists of various layers within. Let us build these up one at a time:

Dynamic appropriateness

At the very centre of the pyramid and thus of all coaching forms stands modern, dynamic appropriateness. It is about fit: what fits best where and how.

This understanding of appropriateness is eclectic and fosters thinking in continuums rather than in extremes of right and wrong.

There is no absolute appropriateness: What is appropriate in one case, may not be appropriate in others. What is appropriate now, may not be appropriate at a later date. Any appropriateness is relative depending on perspective and choice of priority.

The meaning of appropriateness here is thus a modern one and may differ from more traditional, rather authoritarian approaches to appropriateness. Traditionally, appropriateness was judged by rational considerations only, based on a pre-fixed set of given rules and values. The new, modern way of seeing appropriateness is proactive, pluralistic and dynamic, embraces all kind of considerations (e.g. also emotional and intuitive ones), is eclectic, based on continuum thinking and open to all values as appropriate. It is simply about what fits best where and how. This modern approach is actually much better suited to today's requirements.

In times of increased globalisation, a faster changing business environment, a more pluralistic and diverse society, of

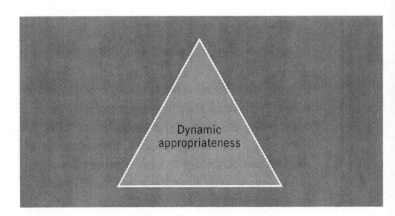

rising questioning and break-up of traditional values and systems, of increasing complexity in all aspects of our work and life, this principle of dynamic appropriateness gains in significance and becomes a universal principle with high validity.

In our view the term 'coaching' perfectly carries this spirit of what we call 'dynamic appropriateness' and fills it with lifeblood in the workplace (and beyond). In fact, coaching is the continuous process and practice of exactly this dynamic appropriateness.

While 'process' means the search for highest possible appropriateness, 'practice' refers to its realization and maintenance once you have identified an appropriate approach or solution. Finding a balance between the process on the one hand and the practice on the other hand is key and also a fundamental part of the process itself.

Integration of organisation, people and technology & tools

As a direct expression of dynamic appropriateness in business, at the next level coaching is also integrative and balancing: it is concerned with the dynamic process and practice of continuously bringing together people and business requirements in an optimal win-win way to achieve organisational (and people) performance and excellence.

Actually, there are three pillars of any organisation and its performance. These are …

1. Organisational strategy, structures, processes
2. People
3. Technology & Tools

Coaching is about integrating and bringing together the requirements of these three pillars in the most appropriate

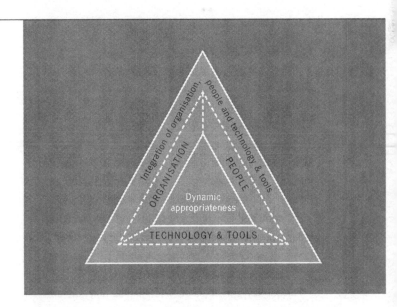

way. The exact focus will differ depending on each coaching intervention.

www.frank-bresser-consulting.com

Integration of external and internal requirements

Building on the above, at the third level coaching also implies the continuous and dynamic process and practice of integrating and combining external and internal requirements – be it from an organisational, team, individual or other relevant perspective or a mix of perspectives. The actual focus will vary according to the kind of concrete coaching action taken.

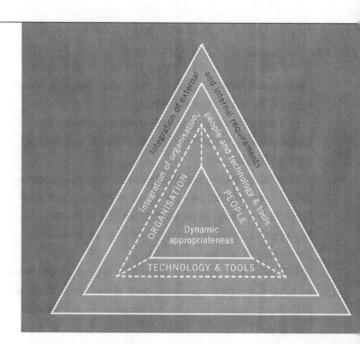

The three levels above already constitute the **core of the coaching pyramid.** We will build more layers setting out the **application** of it and so, to keep things simple, we substitute the above core layers with the following graphic:

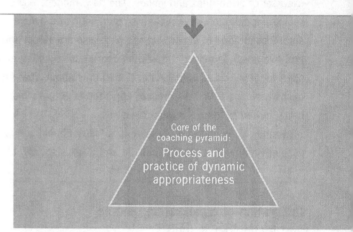

Now we come to the further pyramid layers.

The coaching principles

Many coaching principles have emerged in the coaching industry and in business. These all turn out to be applications of the core of the coaching pyramid.

Fundamental coaching principles you may encounter in today's coaching industry are high performance and excellence, growing people and performance alike, purpose, awareness, responsibility and self-belief.

Further key principles of coaching you may find are those like empowerment, ownership, self-directed and life-long learning, the learning organisation, trust, open communication and feedback, daring to make mistakes

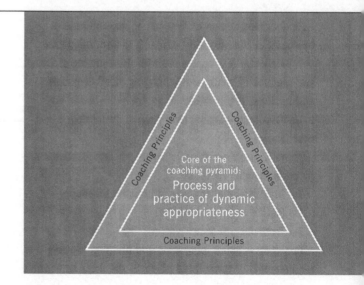

(no blame-culture), collaboration and information sharing, mutual support, on-the-job staff development, respect and seeing people in terms of their future potential.

Finally, there are new emerging coaching principles that are increasingly present which are principles like whole

systems thinking, natural systems thinking, sustainability and corporate social responsibility.

Depending on context, perspective, purpose and school of thought, different coaching principles may gain or lose relevance and get more or less promoted in different settings.

The coaching forms

Many different coaching forms exist in business today. These, in turn, all represent applications of any of the above coaching principles and of the principles included in the core of the coaching pyramid.

The most well-known of all coaching forms is one-to-one coaching, followed by coaching as a management and leadership style, coaching cultures and team coaching. This is only part of the whole range of existing coaching forms.

We may distinguish between three main categories of coaching forms, depending on whether they focus on people, organisation (strategy, structures and processes) or technology & tools.

These are different possible entry points for coaching in a company. Naturally there is great overlap between the three, and each one will have immediate, direct impact on the other two in some way.

1. People coaching forms mainly embrace the following: self-coaching, peer coaching, one-to-one coaching (by external or internal coaches), manager/leader as coach, coaching management/leadership style, coaching communication style, coaching attitude/mindset, coaching culture.

2. Organisation coaching forms mainly include the following: coaching business model, coaching organisation, coaching strategy, coaching structures, coaching processes, coaching facilities, coaching interfaces and professional coaching of organisational systems.

3. Technology & tools coaching forms contain coaching HR tools, coaching (other) tools and coaching technologies. The question here is how sophisticated, customized and tailored they are, i.e. how appropriate for their purposes.

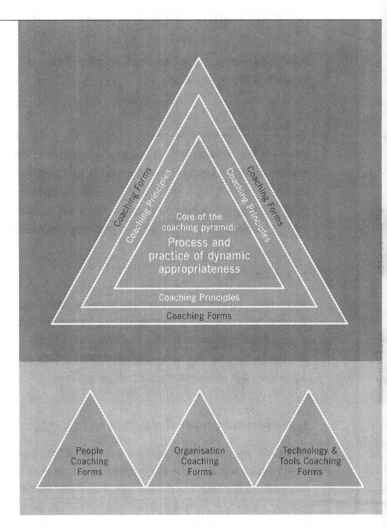

(This is only a short overview. You will get detailed explanations on each of the various coaching forms later in Framework 1 under key success factor 3.)

For clarification, it is your choice what your definition of coaching is and whether you want to use the term coaching in all the above areas (or dismiss it). The point here is to acknowledge that all the above coaching forms do exist in some way and they do make sense to some organisations in some way.

The following box provides more detailed background information on the coaching forms.
To go directly to the next layer of the pyramid, just skip this box and see the next page.

Background information: Coaching forms

Appropriate, possible levels of under-standing a coaching form

A coaching form (e.g. the coaching leadership style) can have very different meanings:

1. A question

Some will see a coaching form just as a question like: What role can coaching play in a specific area? (E.g. coaching leadership style: What is the most appropriate leadership style? What does coaching mean in the context of leadership?) It is simply a question without providing any answers.

2. A discipline

Others may understand by a coaching form the discipline of coaching in that area (e.g. the coaching leadership style is the discipline of leaders using a coaching approach). This means opening and accepting an interesting field of exploration, but still without providing any answers.

3. A driver and enabler of real choice

Others will see a coaching form as the explicit affirmation of real choice and as a true application of dynamic appropriateness in the area, i.e. the encouragement and invitation to seek, create and identify a whole range of options and choose the most appropriate ones. (E.g. a coaching leadership style means the permission to consider all existing leadership styles and choose the ones for oneself that are most appropriate.) This understanding actively promotes choice and dynamic appropriateness, but doesn't give any answers on what options are finally the most appropriate.

4. A best practice recommendation

This view is a suggestion of what is classically most appropriate in the respective area, given the contemporary

challenges in business today. This understanding still embraces the whole range of options, but makes concrete best practice recommendations by giving more emphasis on some options than on others (e.g. a coaching leadership style may mean a recommendation to have and use a proper mix of leadership styles, but with an emphasis on a more empowering leadership style these days).

5. A specific option

Some will understand by a coaching form a very specific way of doing things in that area (e.g. the coaching leadership style is just listening, asking questions and giving and receiving feedback as a leader at the workplace). This view highlights a specific option, rather than addressing the question of selection, i.e. what is the most appropriate option.

All above five perspectives have their role to play and may complement each other. However, do avoid the following:

Inappropriate possible ways of seeing a coaching form

1. A panacea (it is not)

Where people overemphasize or overvalue a coaching form and blindly see it as a response to everything. This actually limits real choice and appropriateness and produces inappropriate behaviours and results. Coaching needs to be well-grounded and clearly linked to reality.

2. The only right way (it is not)

Unfortunately, it does sometimes happen that people become all too dogmatic about coaching, make their understanding an absolute, and stigmatise any behaviour and characteristic that doesn't fit their understanding. When someone says their specific coaching form is the only right way to behave,

www.frank-bresser-consulting.com

Background information: Coaching forms

be alarmed! Coaching is about widening options to achieve higher appropriateness, not about narrowing them at the cost of appropriateness.

Many sub-forms within each coaching form

There are lots of different coaching methodologies, techniques, models (e.g. GROW), tools (e.g. psychometrics), procedures and approaches that have been developed and put into practice. You find a lot of debate on what are actually the most appropriate ones for what purpose and context (e.g. directive versus non-directive coaching; external versus internal coaches). So a great variety of sub-forms within each coaching form exists.

Further development of coaching forms

The internal and the external environments change continuously and require adjusted and new approaches and solutions. The existing coaching forms and their sub-forms are therefore in a steady flux of development. Useful elements need to be maintained. New approaches may need to be created. Obsolete ones may undergo change or disappear.

(The same is also true for the coaching principles above, though less strongly. Even the core of the coaching pyramid, to some degree, requires steady adjustments. So there is a lot of dynamism in the whole coaching field.)

Whether coaching terminology is actually used or not in every case, is not of central importance. It is above all the appropriateness of a tool as such that counts.

We now come to the next layer of the coaching pyramid.

Coaching transformation

By the proper application of the above coaching forms and principles, change and transformation towards optimal fit do actually happen. A truly transformative process towards higher dynamic appropriateness is initiated and executed.

The ability to practise and make this kind of transformation a reality on a continuous basis is what we commonly call 'coaching implementation and improvement intelligence', 'coaching capacity' or 'coaching capability'. A more metaphorical way to describe this phenomenon is the image of coaching as a 'tacit intelligence glue' or 'DNA' of a company. Again others call it 'flow' continuously working towards and bringing about optimal fit.

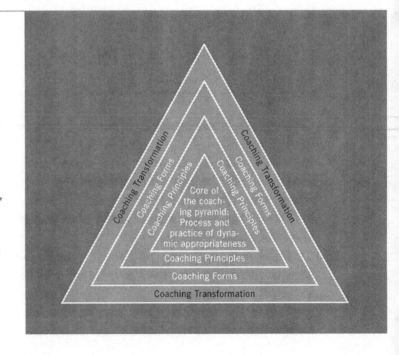

Coaching vitality

This last layer of the coaching pyramid refers to the challenge of really living coaching. Theoretical knowledge of the above is something very different from actually putting it into practice and using it in an integrated, intuitive manner.

The question here is: What is the level of liveliness and interconnectedness in the process and practice of dynamic appropriateness? Also, is this level sustained at a healthy level on a permanent basis, as coaching is a continuous learning process and requires constant activity?

Some may know a lot about the theory, but just don't fill it with sufficient lifeblood to achieve the expected results. Others may know very little, but are able to outweigh this partly with high vitality and achieve remarkable results with what they know. As stated above, do find the right pace and approach for yourself to do a quality job.

The coaching pyramid is now complete. Coaching vitality is the outside and last layer of it.

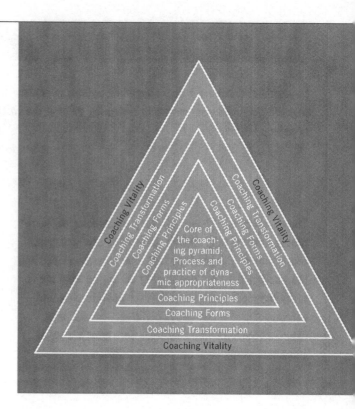

Concluding remarks on the pyramid

The coaching pyramid is an implicit part of all the 7 frameworks presented in this book and may serve as a helpful orientation and central reference point. It sets the context and acknowledges dynamic appropriateness as the heart of any coaching programme.

Using the model facilitates making sure your coaching initiative provides best results, is well-grounded and linked to business reality at any time.

In the end, all coaching principles, coaching forms and coaching frameworks centre on optimal dynamic appropriateness. It is the core of any coaching initiative in business – consciously or unconsciously.

Be aware that this pyramid model may take some time to settle. So don't necessarily expect to fully understand it immediately. You can refer back to it whenever you like and deepen your understanding.

The higher your level of coaching implementation and improvement intelligence, the more you will discover and understand the enormous reach, relevance and usefulness of the coaching pyramid.

A continuous self-check while reading this book

The pyramid, for instance, can help you as a kind of self-measurement and self-check at any time. Here are examples of useful, basic questions derived from the pyramid. You need not answer these right now, but may find these very valuable and helpful in the following:

- Is your coaching initiative/programme appropriate?
- In what way is it appropriate/inappropriate?
- What is it an appropriate answer to?

- Does it adequately take into account organisation, people and technology& tools requirements?
- Does it properly bring together internal and external requirements?
- Are your coaching principles appropriate?
- Are your coaching forms appropriate?
- Is the application appropriate?
- Does your coaching programme have appropriate vitality?

Now, you are very well prepared for moving on to Part I of the book, which will set out Framework 1 (coaching success factors framework) in proper detail.

4. FINAL NOTE

I very much hope and believe that this book will add real value to the implementation and improvement of coaching in businesses and other organisations. I welcome any feedback on this book, any stories about how your firm is applying the tools, as well as any enquiries about working together to implement and improve coaching successfully in your organisation.

THE 4 CORE FRAMEWORKS

The 4 core frameworks

The first 4 frameworks in this book are the most comprehensive ones each giving very clear and concrete guidance and support on the process of implementing and optimizing coaching:

Framework 1: **Coaching success factors framework**

Framework 2: **Coaching value chain framework**

Framework 3: **Coaching capacity building framework**

Framework 4: **Coaching change dynamics framework**

PART I

THE COACHING SUCCESS FACTORS FRAMEWORK

(also called: The 10 key success factors framework)

This first management tool for the implementation and improvement of coaching will give you an overview of the most important aspects to take into account when planning, realizing and optimizing coaching initiatives. Being the first framework presented in the book, it sets out in detail all recurrent key issues also encountered in other frameworks (in order to avoid repetition in other framework chapters). It includes coverage of the 10 key success factors as well as their underlying factors.

A very short outline of the history of this framework attests to its enormous degree of solidity, reliability and validity:

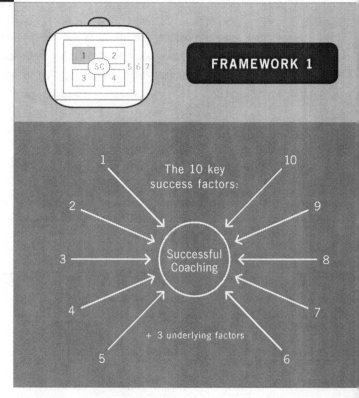

FRAMEWORK 1

*Framework 1: Coaching success factors framework
(simplified version)*

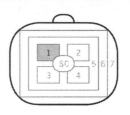

FRAMEWORK 1

The earliest version of the coaching success factors frame-work was initially developed in 2005 as an outcome of the Frank Bresser Consulting Coaching Research Project 2005 on the implementation and improvement of coaching in organisations. This project was and has remained leading-edge in the field and contained the analysis of about 150 relevant literature sources, a worldwide coaching survey, a Transatlantic coaching pilot project as well as a series of in-depth interviews with leading coaching experts and managers/directors responsible for the use of coaching in their organisations. Through further very extensive research and experience, Frank Bresser Consulting has continuously developed this framework and now, in 2010, it is a much more advanced framework than ever.

The coaching success factors framework has helped develop and formulate international standards in the implementation and optimization of coaching and is being used and applied by companies worldwide. Just to give one figure – the execu-tive summary on the 10 key success factors has already been downloaded about 10,000 times from the official Frank Bresser Consulting website.

Remarkably, while our clients and many other companies have given extremely positive feedback on the framework, no adverse feedback has been received so far.

The Framework

According to extensive research and experience, managers and directors responsible for the implementation and im-provement of coaching in their companies need to have the following ten key success factors (as well as their under-lying factors) in mind for coaching in organisations to be successful. These Success Factors can be considered as a "must know" for everybody actively involved in coaching programmes.

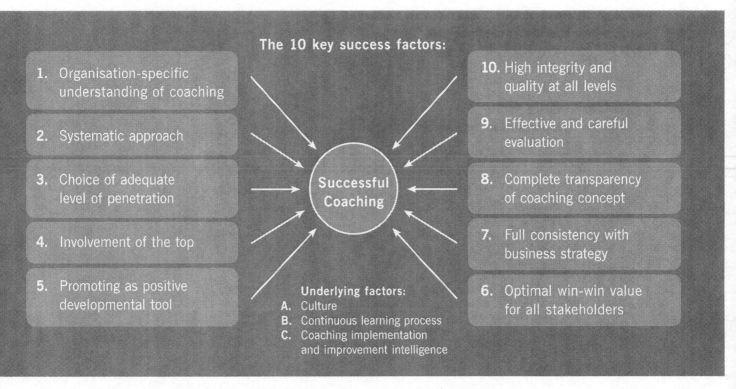

The 10 key success factors:

1. Organisation-specific understanding of coaching
2. Systematic approach
3. Choice of adequate level of penetration
4. Involvement of the top
5. Promoting as positive developmental tool

Successful Coaching

Underlying factors:
A. Culture
B. Continuous learning process
C. Coaching implementation and improvement intelligence

10. High integrity and quality at all levels
9. Effective and careful evaluation
8. Complete transparency of coaching concept
7. Full consistency with business strategy
6. Optimal win-win value for all stakeholders

Framework 1: Coaching success factors framework (The 10 key success factors framework) (full version)

www.frank-bresser-consulting.com

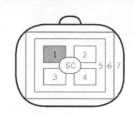

The 10 Key Success Factors:

1. Develop an organisation-specific understanding of coaching.
2. Adopt a systematic approach.
3. Choose an adequate level of organisational penetration of coaching.
4. Involve the top.
5. Promote coaching as a positive developmental tool.
6. Create an optimal win-win value for all stakeholders.
7. Achieve full consistency of coaching with business strategy.
8. Ensure complete transparency of the whole coaching concept.
9. Evaluate effectively and carefully.
10. Ensure high integrity and quality at all levels.

The 3 Underlying Factors

have impact on the application of all key success factors and thus form some kind of their underlying base. They are as follows:

A. Culture
B. Continuous Learning Process
C. Coaching implementation and improvement intelligence

There are two main ways of making use of this management tool: On the one hand, it may serve you as a central thread and starting point to plan, design and implement new coaching programmes. On the other hand, you may use it as a measure and means to review and optimize existing coaching initiatives. Either way, you will find it an invaluable tool to support achieving outstanding results through coaching.

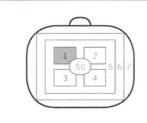
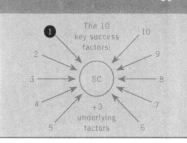

KEY SUCCESS FACTOR 1

DEVELOP AN ORGANISATION-SPECIFIC UNDERSTANDING OF COACHING

It is crucial to understand that the process of defining coaching is already part of and fundamental to the implementation and improvement of coaching programmes. So you need to make a distinction between what is common to all existing forms of coaching (the core of coaching) on the one hand, and the way you define it for your own organisational context specifically on the other hand.

1.1. The core of coaching

Recall the coaching pyramid model (see again the book introduction), which sets out the context and essence of all existing coaching forms in the business environment. This corresponds to the core of coaching.

A subsidiary, less integrated and less explicit way of identifying the limits of the core of coaching are the 12 dimensions of coaching (see Extra-Box 1 below at the end of key success factor 1) which have also influenced the international debate on coaching. These give an overview of the common elements as well as the diversity and controversies in the understanding of coaching.

There is indeed extensive debate in the coaching industry on what coaching actually is. The term "coaching" may thus mean very different things to different people and organisations.

(In this book, if not specified otherwise, the term "coaching" is used in a broad, inclusive sense. This is, once again, to explicitly acknowledge the existing diversity of coaching approaches: each of them has a role to play in some way or another. The challenge is to know which one fits best where and how, i.e. what kind of approach to choose when. You will find detailed guidance on finding the right choices in this book.)

1.2. Organisation-specific definition

There are several tenable ways of understanding and defining coaching. So it is up to you to find (or develop) the coaching definition that best suits your company's needs specifically. We encourage you to take the time you need for this and have the confidence to make up your own mind and define coaching autonomously for your context. It will pay off tremendously.

Some (arbitrarily chosen) examples of possible organisation-specific coaching definitions are:

- "a way of communication at all levels of our organisation to create a learning organisation"
- "one-to-one coaching for our senior executives in specific areas only"
- "an offer for our high potentials to support their career planning and development"
- "a sounding board for any executive in our organisation desiring it"
- "a specific tool to foster team building and enhance team motivation in our business"
- "a means to expand the portfolio of our executives´ leadership skills"
- "a measure to facilitate effective knowledge-transfer after trainings"
- "the binding glue for change management in our company"
- "a way we act towards our customers to best satisfy their needs"
- "an important vehicle to foster creativity in our organisation"

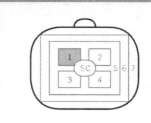

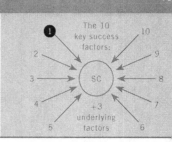

- "a specific set of values we widely share and live in our firm"
- "our whole business model"
- "the way we define, design and use our tools and technology"
- "a principle around empowerment"
- "appropriateness"

How you can best develop a specific understanding of coaching for your own firm is dealt with in detail in later sections of this book. As a general statement for now: Research your organisational needs, acquire proper coaching literacy (e.g. by reading this book) and finally bring both together by developing a clear and comprehensive coaching concept. As a first warm-up, the 12 dimensions of coaching in Extra Box 1 (see next page) may give you an overview of existing key alternatives and debates around the understanding of coaching.

At this very early stage of reading this book, however, the vital point is to become fully aware of the great importance of reflecting carefully on this issue.

If you stick to a specific understanding of coaching too quickly, or adopt the definition of coaching from another company or consultancy without carefully thinking through whether it applies to your organisation, you run the risk of reducing (and sometimes even negating) the potential of coaching for your company.

Organisations fundamentally vary in their characteristics and business environments, and accordingly require different kinds of coaching measures. There is no one-size-fits-all coaching programme. A key task for the manager/director concerned with the implementation or improvement of coaching programmes is to find out what is the best coaching approach for their organisation in their situation. This process may take some time, but is necessary to produce genuine and sustainable benefits from coaching programmes.

As organisations change over time, it is necessary to review the coaching definition on a regular basis. After all, it is not about finding a coaching definition that sounds particularly trendy or intellectual, but one that really fits and has relevance in the light of organisational needs.

For example, it took a global company about 18 months to develop the following definition of coaching: "Coaching is business coaching for executives". Now, this seemingly "simple" definition is based on central decisions as a result of thorough reflection processes:

1. The company decided to implement and use one-to-one coaching only (at this stage).
2. Any coaching would have a strong business focus.
3. The target group for coaching would only be executives.

This understanding was fully appropriate for the organisational purposes at that time.

Of course, defining what coaching is for your company, also means saying what it is not, what are its limits and what are its relationships to other disciplines and tools.

In particular with regard to one-to-one coaching, there is, for example, a need to distinguish coaching from therapy. There are various ways of doing this. One tenable standpoint is to say 1:1 coaching is based on the already functioning self-management of the coachee and only accelerates the coachee's progress, but doesn't address serious dysfunctions or any other illness and doesn't provide a therapeutic diagnosis. Coaching is forward-focused and based on the coachee's full ownership of the process and his or her self-responsibility.

www.frank-bresser-consulting.com

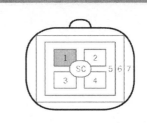

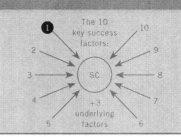

The 12 dimensions of coaching

Developed by Frank Bresser Consulting, the 12 dimensions have influenced the international debate. They are included in chapter contributions to "Excellence in Coaching: The Industry Guide" (2006, 2010) (London/Philadelphia) and "Executive Coaching and Mentoring" (2008) (Hyderabad, India). This version is the updated, most recent one and constitutes a significant, further development of the previously published ones.

This set of dimensions illuminates coaching from various perspectives and gives a first overview of common elements as well as of the diversity and controversies in the understanding of coaching.

The 12 dimensions are terminology, history, goals/benefits, fundamental coaching principles, coaching relationship, coaching models and techniques, target groups, relationship to other disciplines, qualification, levels of implementation, culture and specific coaching experience.

1. Terminology

A great variety of coaching definitions exist, and the term coaching is used to describe a wide range of approaches and interventions. Some welcome the absence of a legally binding definition and that everybody is free to call anything coaching. According to this standpoint, a binding definition would only limit and narrow the potential of coaching being a work in progress. Others take the opposite view that the term actually does have a clear meaning which shouldn't be blurred by an inflationary use of it. They (partly or widely) regard today's wider use of the word as an abuse.

2. History

A number of people argue that coaching has existed since the dawn of civilisation. A contrary approach presents this discipline as a new invention of the second half of the 20th century. A middle position, reconciling both views, contends that although single coaching elements may always have existed, the recently attained high quality and visibility of coaching (i.e. by the recent development of models and their use in workplace environments) represent a new and innovatory move forward in the 20th/21st century.

3. Goals/Benefits

Commonly mentioned benefits of coaching include enhanced personal and organisational performance, higher motivation, better self-reflection, optimized decision-making and improved change management. The concrete benefits vary from case to case and coaching allows win-win situations for all stakeholders.

One question remains the subject of on-going debate with regard to one-to-one coaching specifically: whose goals – those of the coachee or the sponsor organisation – should be primarily pursued, when these start to diverge? Some argue that it is in the very nature of coaching to serve

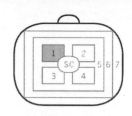

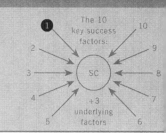

Extra-Box 1: *The 12 dimensions of coaching*

the coachee's goals (and this will in turn also benefit the organisation in the long run), others emphasize the sponsor payment and organisational context as dominant elements and prioritize the interests of the sponsor organisation.

A middle view regards coaching as collaborative in nature, serving both parties equally, and stresses the importance of professional contracting and common efforts to keep the win-win situation in place at all times.

4. Fundamental principles

Many coaching principles have emerged (e.g. awareness, responsibility, self-directed learning, appropriateness, empowerment, ownership). Depending on context, perspective, purpose and school of thought, different ones are actually emphasized and promoted. For example, with regard to 1:1 coaching, confidentiality and voluntariness may gain central importance. When thinking through any coaching principle, it is dynamic appropriateness that is at its heart and common to all principles. (See the coaching pyramid model in the book introduction.)

Debate continues in particular about the interpretation, the practice and the limits of the principles. What actually fits best where and how? How to handle possible conflicts of interest? Think of one-to-one and team coaching in particular: How can the coach be resilient towards external pressures? How does the coach most effectively deal with his or her own blind spots? Etc.

5. Coaching relationship

There are different kinds of coaching relationships such as coach – coachee; manager using a coaching management

style – direct report. A broad consensus in the area of one-to-one coaching exists, that coaching requires a coaching contract as the fundamental basis for a good coaching relationship. The coachee retains responsibility and ownership of the outcomes and is in control of the coaching process, whilst the coach tailors the coaching around the coachee's needs. This relationship is commonly described as an equal one, neither participant being superior or subordinate to the other.

In this context, there is debate on the questions of how directive a coach is allowed to be, and whether and to what extent executives can be coaches of their own direct reports, because of the conflicts of interests which may arise. Other questions concern the impact using HR and internal coaches has on the relationship, and whether and when the involvement of the coachee's manager in the process is appropriate. Different views also exist regarding the question of what kind of coaching relationships are required in other coaching forms (e.g. peer coaching, coaching management/leadership style, coaching culture).

6. Coaching models, methods and techniques

The techniques of listening, questioning and giving and receiving feedback are generally seen as essential. However, what models, methods and techniques are admissible and how these may be applied, is subject to debate – and also dependent on each coaching form. There are many different coaching approaches and schools of thought.

With reference to one-to-one coaching, the eligibility and pros and cons of alternatives to face-to-face communication, such as telephone, e-mail or videoconferencing, are open to dispute.

www.frank-bresser-consulting.com

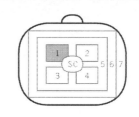
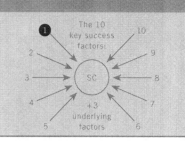

Extra-Box 1: *The 12 dimensions of coaching*

7. Target groups

A debate persists over whether and to what extent coaching is equally applicable to all target groups and what impact the choice of a specific target group has on the nature of coaching.

Some coaching forms, by their nature, tend to address a wider target group than others (e.g. high performance coaching culture targets all; one-to-one coaching targets individuals). Within professional 1:1 coaching, however, the target group may vary from all people to those in very specific niches or situations (e.g. executives; sales people; high-flyers; promoted managers; problem or valued employees). What is more, coaching may apply to people both inside and outside the company (e.g. customers, suppliers).

8. Relationship to other disciplines

Depending on how widely or narrowly coaching is actually understood by people, its relationships to other disciplines will differ accordingly.

In particular within 1:1 coaching, there is definitely a need for a clear distinction between coaching and therapy and for making transparent how coaching is linked to other services (e.g. consulting, mentoring, counselling).

Where coaching and another service are mixed, some maintain that this is not coaching; others argue that the term 'coaching' encompasses every service that includes any element of coaching. A middle view demands that for a service to be called 'coaching', the main emphasis must be on coaching.

9. Qualification

Depending on each coaching approach and form, different coaching skills may be required. However, skills around listening, questioning and giving and receiving feedback are seen as basic and essential in all types of coaching.

There is plenty of debate on what are most appropriate quality requirements in coaching and how to assess these. Also accreditation in the field of coaching and the main source of coaching proficiency (talent/natural ability, learning/training, experience or a combination of these) are topics for controversy.
In 1:1 coaching in particular, there is the key issue around whether (and to what extent) the coach needs expertise in the field he or she is coaching in – and what role this management or sector knowledge of the coach may play in the coaching process. Some argue that coaching is fully content-free and non-directive and therefore such expertise rather impedes the coaching process. Others contend that the coach must be an expert or that it is essential to have at least some expertise and understanding of the coachee's background to be accepted by the coachee. A middle view maintains that specific expertise is not required, but can be integrated in a non-directive way where it exists.

10. Levels of implementation

That coaching is a professional service provided by professional coaches, is commonly accepted. Whether it is preferable that such coaches are external (from outside the company) or internal (own staff) is a matter of debate.

There is no doubt that companies are now increasingly starting to make use of coaching forms beyond the one-

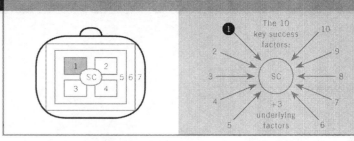

Extra-Box 1: *The 12 dimensions of coaching*

to-one coaching paradigm as well (e.g. team coaching) and also ingrain the coaching principles at the workplace (e.g. the coaching leadership and management style, high performance coaching cultures).

But the importance of each level is assessed very differently depending on the school of thought. (A minority opinion even questions the existence of any coaching form beyond external 1:1 coaching.)

One distinction that is highly useful to be aware of is between managers who coach their direct reports and managers who demonstrate a coaching leadership style. While the first category are acting like professional coaches and giving formal sessions, the latter maintain their role as leaders and integrate coaching elements, such as listening, skilful questioning and empowerment, into their everyday methods of leadership. It is advisable to be very reluctant and careful about using the first category due to the inherent likely conflicts of roles.

11. Cultural view

Coaching extends across various cultures at the global, regional, national, organizational and individual level and is a worldwide phenomenon today (see also Extra Box 2: Results of the Frank Bresser Consulting Global Coaching Survey). There is a lot of debate over how far coaching is universal and can be applicable to all cultures and to what extent different cultures require different coaching definitions.

12. Specific coaching experience

Each person's (and company's) unique coaching experience shapes their individual understanding of coaching. People and organisations may see and define coaching in a certain way simply because of how they coincidentally came across it for the first time. Reflection on and acknowledgement of one's own history and subjectivity regarding coaching is key to maintaining sound detachment and proper context.

Summary

Coaching is still work in progress. The 12 themes illustrate the common elements as well as the many issues that are part of the ongoing debate around coaching. The diversity of existing, tenable approaches may provide a rich source of choice for you while developing and formulating your own organisation-specific definition of coaching.

www.frank-bresser-consulting.com

Geographical focus: *Germany*

CASE STUDY 1	SAP, GERMANY

Company:	*SAP AG*	Author:	*Ralf Kronig*
	(Global provider of business software)	Function:	*HR Consultant, SAP*
	www.sap.com		

Internal coaches – the development of coaching competences in the organisation at SAP

In recent years, we have developed a pool of internal one-to-one coaches at SAP in Germany. We wanted colleagues to support colleagues, which is why we chose to build our in-house coaching capacity.

Defining coaching

Our understanding of coaching may be described in the following way(s):
- Coaching is a form of goal-oriented, individual consulting.
- Coaching is an individual learning and development process aimed at enhancing the coachee's personal success as well as achieving business goals.
- Professional and results-oriented coaching strengthens the self-reflection and personal growth of the coachee and helps raise energy, develop solutions and implement new perspectives and behaviour.
- Coaching is explicitly not only aimed at removing or reducing deficits (remedial), but also means specific preparation for new challenges/roles.
- Coaching is a solution-oriented and thus future-oriented consulting approach.

At a coaching day in our company, most participants answered the question "What is coaching for you?" with "colleague's help for self-help", which may thus be seen as a common basic understanding of coaching.

Coaching objectives

The aims of our internal coaching program are:
- Personal development to accomplish the business goals and meet the challenges of the coachee's professional role in an optimal way
- Building awareness of one's personality and inner personal attitudes
- Targeted reflection on personal strengths and weaknesses through concrete goals/questions
- Generating options in behaviour by changes in perception and attitudes and consequently, also by changes in behaviours that haven't proven to be successful in the past

Prevailing coaching issues in recent years have been the following:
- Career and professional perspective
- Understanding personality and personal development
- Life balance und health
- Gender, family and social environment

Designing and implementing our coach training

In our initial concept of basic coach and consultant training (lasting several days) for a first pilot group in 2003, the training and practice workshops focused on the acquisition of coaching methods and the development of a coaching

www.frank-bresser-consulting.com

SAP CASE STUDY: *Internal coaches – the development of coaching competences in the organisation at SAP*

attitude. Both practice and theory/reflection were central elements of the training.

Soon the participants discovered that a professional coach had to learn more than a set of coaching tools, but also had to develop a coaching mindset. Therefore, we also provided a second part to the training which particularly took this aspect into account.

The two-part division of the training is very helpful in ensuring our professional coach quality. At the end of part 1, the participants receive individual feedback from the trainers, and as a result, some trainees may not continue with part 2.

The coach trainings embrace learning, experience and practice as three key dimensions. Very consciously, we allow the use of a diversity of models and methods as appropriate, and didn't decide in favour of a specific single coaching methodology.

The external coach trainers pay particular attention to the participants' skills and give them regular feedback for continuous development. Trainees also get coached or take over practice coaching sessions themselves, which is seen as a particularly important training element. From the beginning, learning partnerships have been organized. These, later on, were also complemented by work in triads: an experienced coach is available as an observer of self-organised coaching practice.

Qualitative feedback shows the value of the professional coach training: "I particularly like the mix of and variation between theoretical inputs and practical exercises. You can immediately practice the relevant, theoretical content and discover that this is not all that easy." "Especially the well

designed exercises help me improve my coaching approach." "Questioning techniques, questioning techniques, questioning techniques – here I can really practice effectively."

The coaching practice and further development

After being certified, our internal coaches take on three coaching assignments per year on average. We have one-day "coach-the-coach" workshops, in which they reflect on coaching situations, acquire new methods, exchange their experience and learning, and bring new insights. Additionally, many coaches also attend further professional training that they finance themselves, or organize meetings for shared learning.

After 6 years, the coach pool in Germany today comprises more than 70 internal part-time coaches (i.e. coaches who work as a coach besides their main role/activity) coming from all levels of hierarchy and functions.

In 2008, more than 150 conversations with potential coach training participants took place. In 2010 the 16th group starts the coach training. The high interest is consistent, be it on the part of the coaches or the coachees.

All coaches and people interested in coaching – our "coaching-community" – receive at least 8 times per year the "Coaching-Monitor" newsletter with worthwhile information and tips on coaching. Also, each month, internal and external experts share interesting facts and insights in coaching-forums of 2-3 hours' duration. Once a year, the "coaching-day" with over 100 participants takes place as a highlight: Besides presentations and workshops, everybody may connect and expand their coaching networks.

In order to ensure the company coaching methodology makes a valuable contribution, we have sought, integrated

Geographical focus: *Germany*

SAP CASE STUDY: *Internal coaches – the development of coaching competences in the organisation at SAP*

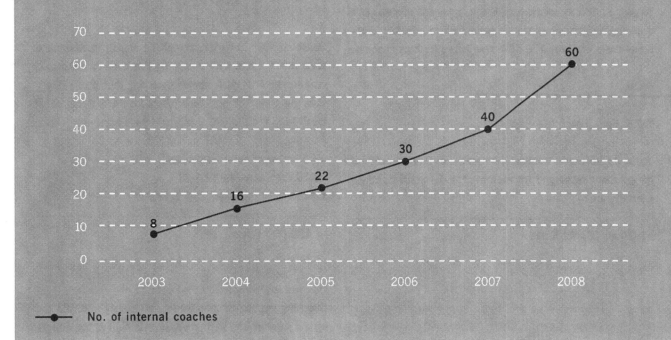

No. of internal coaches

and implemented many ideas and much feedback over the years.

We have also encountered critics saying "it is not possible that a colleague works as an internal professional coach – for this there are external coaches". Now, we have been able to disprove these statements. We have shown that professional internal coach training (including continuous further development in the following) can be an appropriate basis for solution-focused, developmental coaching within a company.

For us, defining quality standards (e.g. the guidelines for the coach training and certification) and monitoring them, as well as a professional intranet presence seem to be key in times of resource scarcity and high business dynamics. From our experience, coaching can be successfully intro-

duced in an organisation only in a slow and careful way – but, if done so, can also become a valuable part of the firm's corporate culture.

We have observed that particularly in times of crisis, the demand for our internal professional coaches increases. This demand may also be seen as success resulting from our perseverance and continuous development.

The ROI of coaching

The return on investment of coaching can be enormous, especially in the context of project management. The following feedback may illustrate this point: "Coaching helped us prevent a potential project loss of at least Euros 100,000, because an excellent project lead found a way to manage tremendous task overload for almost one year."

Geographical focus: *Germany*

SAP CASE STUDY: *Internal coaches – the development of coaching competences in the organisation at SAP*

To give another example, here is a cost-benefit analysis of a coaching assignment in another project where potential, additional costs of Euros 120,000 were saved through coaching:

Costs

7.000 Euro (coach training)

+

about 2.500 Euros = about 30 hours (i.e. time investment for internal coaching: 15 hours coach + 15 hours coachee) x hourly rate

────────────────

maximum 10.000 Euros

Benefits

Coaching made the exchange of the project head unnecessary, which would have meant an extension of the project duration by at least 6 weeks. Coaching thus also helped save the potential, additional costs for the external people involved in the project, that would have occurred:

10 (number of external people)
x 500 Euro (day rate/person)
x 24 (4 days per week, over 6 weeks)

────────────────

= 120.000 Euros

Our key learning/Recommendation:
Coaching implementation works particularly well with the strong support and permanent involvement of the company management. When making professional use of coaching, its benefits far outweigh its costs.

Questions and exercises for further reflection and to integrate practice and theory:

1. What is the business case for coaching in this case study?

2. What is the company-specific definition and understanding of coaching?

3. How has this informed the process of implementing and improving coaching?

4. What are the pros and cons of having internal coaches?
   (The question of external/internal coaches will also be addressed in Key Success Factor 3 in detail.)

5. What are the key benefits/outcomes so far?

6. What is your key learning from this case study?

www.frank-bresser-consulting.com

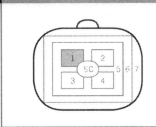 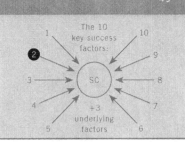

KEY SUCCESS FACTOR 2

ADOPT A SYSTEMATIC APPROACH

Start by developing a systematic, comprehensive coaching plan, covering the various stages of the programme – such as preparation, introduction, step-by-step enlargement, maintenance and evaluation. Make sure that the goals, objectives and responsibilities are clearly set, as well as the rules governing the different coaching measures. Establish the links between the programme and other activities in the organisation well, and embed the programme in the overall organisational development strategy.

Why? Simply because planning and thinking through coaching programmes thoroughly in advance significantly improves the functionality and quality of the coaching measures taken. It is also vital for you to develop a clear idea of the whole coaching initiative.

Ad hoc solutions and improvisation may cover the lack of systematic planning for a while. Sooner or later, however, the point will come when these fail and more systematic planning needs to be put in place. The question then is: How much damage has already been caused by not taking a systematic approach right from the beginning? In the worst case observed, a badly planned programme led to underperformance and very high distrust among staff members in coaching initiatives. Huge efforts are then necessary to build up new trust again.

The larger the size of a coaching programme, the more critical is the need for systematic planning. But also in very small coaching initiatives, the number and complexity of issues to be addressed may be extensive. Never underestimate the requirements of planning a professional coaching programme.

A systematic approach calls for genuine commitment on the part of your organisation to take coaching seriously and to ensure the best professional conditions in order that coaching succeeds in the long term. This normally implies some kind of structural change in the organisation, e.g. a coaching champion is appointed with responsibility for coaching in the company and with proper organisational authority to ensure systematic planning.

Develop a coaching plan that allows for balance between rigour in achieving the coaching programme and flexibility in making necessary adjustments. Adjustments may become necessary due to changes in organisational context or needs emerging from the evaluation results of the coaching programme.

How do you plan systematically? What are all the different issues you need to address to make your coaching programme excel? It is the 7 frameworks included in this book that give the answers. They are cutting-edge and provide you with the needed guidance and support.

Geographical focus: *Slovakia*

CASE STUDY 2   **PPI ADHESIVE PRODUCTS, SLOVAKIA**

Company: *PPI Adhesive Products s.r.o.*

(manufacturing of sophisticated adhesive materials and laminates for electronics and electrical segments)

www.ppiadhesiveproducts.com

Author: *Radoslav Marko*

Function: *Sales Manager Central Europe*

Coaching for people development

PPI Adhesive Products CE is an Irish company for Central and Eastern Europe. Our Slovakian unit is small, but effective. Since competition in our segment is high and we want to be better than our competitors, education and training of our people are a priority. In practice, we do a lot of outsourcing in this area.

Our people development system contains different methods and starts with the assessment of each employee's skills and performance. As we are a sales company (the production takes place in Ireland, not here), we mainly have sales people and customer service. Being good at sales indeed requires a lot of training and education. In addition, we also use coaching methods – mostly ad hoc depending on each situation and personal needs.

We assess people every quarter, and at the end of the evaluation process, they get a development plan to work on in order to improve their skills and foster their career. We may recommend to them some courses which they can attend. Beyond this, as head of the company, I do team building twice a year aimed at improving the atmosphere in the company, resolve communication problems and optimize our processes. Our company makes new books on management and sales available and supports self-directed study for our team members.

Beginnings of coaching in our organisation

How did we get to coaching? Management handbooks speak of coaching as an effective, positive way of impacting employ-

ees and team members. When I came across a course called systemic coaching in Slovakia, I didn't hesitate and immediately decided to attend it.

Coaching captivated me owing to the fact that it did not present a fixed way/solution that had to be observed, as other professional courses I had undergone before had done, but developed people from the inside out. It encouraged everyone to look for his or her natural way of achieving goals.

This made great business sense to me: When people find solutions that truly fit, this is more effective and much better for the person as well as for the company, than trying to push someone into a system (created by someone else) the person is not really committed to.

Our coaching practice so far

How do we use coaching techniques in our organisation?

Once a month I discuss with each sales person his or her business plan by asking coaching questions about their perspectives, performance and customers (we speak mainly about issues of communication, organisation and outcomes).

While all sales people have a sales plan and thus know what we expect from them, they are also encouraged to assess themselves in a self-directed way and try to find best and

---

FRANK BRESSER CONSULTING & ASSOCIATES

Geographical focus: *Slovakia*

PPI ADHESIVE PRODUCTS CASE STUDY: *Coaching for people development*

new ways to optimize their business themselves. In addition, one-to-one coaching by an external coach is made available to them ad hoc as needed to widen their perspective regarding behaviour, attitude and performance.

Enthusiastic about systemic coaching, I also started to "coach" two of my people myself:

Case 1

The first person that I coached had good trade results and was a true professional/specialist in the application of our products. Customers honoured him due to his deep technical knowledge and his ability to apply it well in practice. He was an open personality who liked people and trying out new things. However, his areas requiring further improvement were unstable work enthusiasm, evasiveness when talking with customers about problems, low self-confidence and weak negotiation of product prices.

When I assessed him in a quarterly evaluation, we not only identified goals and development targets for him for the next quarter, but I also offered him regular systemic coaching by me. He liked the idea and we agreed on three development targets to work on step-by-step. In addition, he could and also did make use of an external coach paid by the company to work on these goals as well. So both – the external coach and I – coached him for the next 2 months.

Please note that this person had already undergone several courses paid by us to improve in those areas. Although he had been satisfied with these courses and his enthusiasm had risen after them, this enthusiasm hadn't lasted long and he always had returned to his routine again after a short time.

Now, already after the first coaching sessions, I found that he had higher enthusiasm and effectiveness as well as

greater self-confidence when communicating with customers. He finally reached the set goals and we ended the coaching process.

But what would happen subsequently – would the variation in work effectiveness and reduced motivation occur again?

After half a year I was really surprised to see the man still so highly motivated and enthusiastic at work. Coaching had aroused in him a genuine interest in further self-education and -development. He was able to find out for himself what he needed and what approach was most suitable to him. He is still like this today bringing more productivity and profit to the company.

It was also interesting to observe the change in his communication towards people in problem situations: He started to use the techniques of systemic coaching at work himself. For example, he asked people questions around what they intended to achieve in a discussion.

Case 2

After this very positive result, I suggested giving regular systemic coaching conversations to another employee. He was highly self-confident, customer-oriented, made many trips to customers and knew how to win a customer's favour. However, what required further development was his work system, an insufficient sense of detail and an ineffective ratio between numbers and results of meetings. Together, we made up his development plan, and coaching again followed over two months by me and an external coach.

But in this case there wasn't any positive change coming up. No progress was made – neither in my coaching conversations nor in the external coaching sessions. Our evaluation results suggested that one reason for this was that there

www.frank-bresser-consulting.com

Geographical focus: *Slovakia*

PPI ADHESIVE PRODUCTS CASE STUDY: *Coaching for people development*

was internal resistance to develop and change. It seems the employee was not really open to try out new things in coaching, and he gave the impression that he believed he already knew everything the best. So this was an opposite experience to the first very successful one.

In spite of this, I continue to apply coaching techniques and elements vis-à-vis my employees. I also had a very good response in the customer service with positive impact on the company results.

Generally speaking, coaching arouses in our people (including myself) development, creativity, open-mindedness and a positive approach to problems. I find it widens my perspective and I learn to be even more tolerant and find new, more suitable ways of management and leadership.

Our key learning/Recommendation:
There is never only one way, but more ways to reach a goal. It is thus important to encourage every person to find the most suitable and joy-bringing way for him or herself. Coaching supports this process very well and leverages the skills that lie inside a person.

Questions and exercises for further reflection and to integrate practice and theory:

1. What is the business case for coaching in the organisation?

2. In what ways has coaching actually been used?

3. What are the benefits?

4. What are possible or the actually encountered problems?

5. How may a more systematic implementation and improvement of coaching in the future help better ensure optimal benefits and help avoid (and solve) these kind of problems?

6. What is your key learning from this case study?

www.frank-bresser-consulting.com

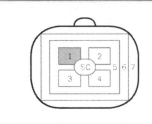

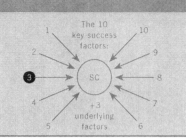

CHOOSE AN ADEQUATE LEVEL OF ORGANISATIONAL PENETRATION OF COACHING

Determine to what level of the organisation coaching will apply. This key success factor is commonly seen as one of the most valuable and important ones by L&D, OD and HR managers. Why? Because it clarifies what kind of levels and forms of coaching exist, what their characteristics are and how they relate to each other. It gives an integrated overview of the different levels of organisational coaching and raises awareness of the possibility of implementing coaching gradually and in various ways. In short, it gives you clarity, awareness and real choice.

The term "penetration" here means the degree to which coaching is used in an organisation in terms of depth (quality) and breadth of organisational scope/number of people

(quantity). As was already set out in the introduction, we may distinguish between three main groups of coaching forms, depending on whether they focus on people, organisation (strategy, structures and processes) or technology & tools.

As all three dimensions only show different sides of the same coin, we are talking here only about the different, possible entry points of coaching in a company. So naturally there is a great overlap between the three, and each one will have immediate, direct impact on the other two in some way.

Let us have a closer look at each of these one-by-one. We start with the people coaching forms which are clearly the most well-known and widely used ones today.

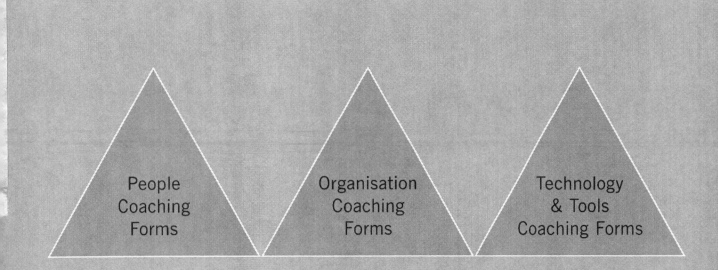

People Coaching Forms

Organisation Coaching Forms

Technology & Tools Coaching Forms

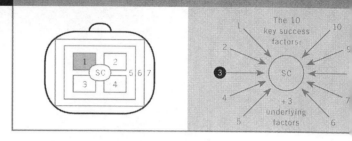

3.1. People coaching forms

Possible designs for coaching programmes with a people focus as the entry point range from the simple contracting of one external coach to creating a whole coaching culture and coaching leadership style in a global company. The figure below gives an overview of the main existing forms and levels of coaching with regard to people. Generally, it can be said that the closer you get to the centre of this figure, the higher the degree of organisational penetration:

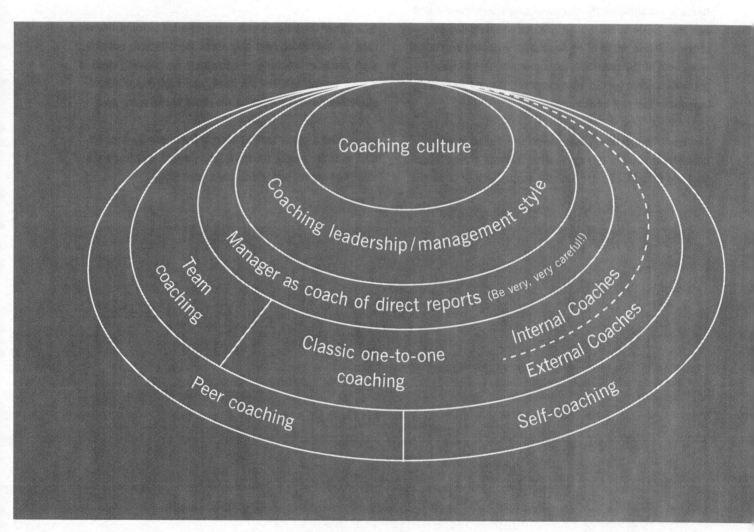

Figure: The different main forms and levels of coaching related to people

Let us have a look at and illuminate each of the levels.

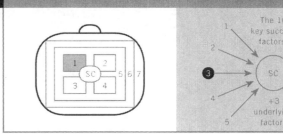

3.1.1. Self-coaching

is about coaching oneself. This form of coaching invites and encourages people to reflect by listening to themselves, ask questions and empower themselves to facilitate their own development and improvement in performance. Ways of implementing self-coaching in organisations may take several forms, such as literature recommendations, integrating the idea in training and providing online learning resources. Self-coaching is normally embedded as part of a wider initiative.

3.1.2. Peer coaching

is a form of coaching in which colleagues have coaching conversations to support each other, however normally without being professional coaches. It can be a one-way or a mutual service and as both colleagues have a similar background, this is a good base for mutual understanding and exchange of ideas. Possible methods of implementing peer coaching are the creation of an informal "buddy" coaching system, or the integration of peer coaching as a standard part of a wider training programme (e.g. managers coach each other on specific individual issues emerging from the training, in between the training modules). Peer coaching can also be a formalized programme in organisations.

3.1.3. Classic one-to-one coaching (by external or internal coaches)

is the form of coaching most people know: a professional coach, paid by the organisation, coaches a staff member in a confidential one-to-one setting. This highly individualized service gives the coachee time, space and support to develop and work on their issues and goals. The coaching sessions operate within a professional code of ethics, such as those developed by coaching associations.

Coaching may be **face-to-face and/or by phone.** The latter is particularly helpful where geographical distances are making face-to-face coaching very difficult or even impossible to realize. While face-to-face coaching may still be seen as the most classic, well-known and accepted

communication form here, phone coaching has definitely caught up and is also a fully accepted, valid 1:1 coaching communication form in its own right these days.

Both communication forms have their pros and cons: While face-to-face allows for highest quality communication and rapport at all levels (e.g. also body language, sharing relevant materials, presence in the room), phone coaching is reduced to the voice only, dependent on the quality of the phone connection (this latter point may be a problem with very long geographical distances and in internet phoning), and may raise questions of safety from interception. At the same time, phone coaching can take place anywhere

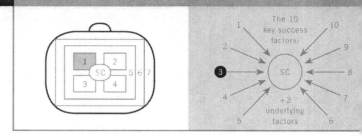

in the world and can be arranged spontaneously. The focus on the voice, which still tells a lot about one's inner state, may have a very positive effect: The dialogue is reduced to the essential – so there may be more focus and goal-directedness in it. The fact that the coachee is not seen by the coach, gives some people a feeling of great comfort, ease and security supporting the coaching process. In the end, which option is the most appropriate, often depends on the personal preferences of coach and coachee. Some take the most out of face-to-face, others out of phone coaching.

Email coaching and online coaching portals with materials, forums, questions, etc. have also emerged, but are rather seen as a complement to the above options. Video conferencing finally represents a new form of coaching communication in the middle way between face-to-face and phone. Internet services and programmes are making this increasingly possible and popular, as it can be done from the individual's PC/laptop/tablet.

Place, time and duration/regularity of coaching sessions may differ enormously: As appropriate, 1:1 coaching may take place indoor or outdoor, in the company facilities or elsewhere. Also shadow coaching where the coach accompanies the coachee on the job during the day is possible. Coaching sessions may be scheduled as needed (e.g. 1 hour, 2 hours, half a day, full day) and take place once, a few, many times or on a regular basis.

The next coaching session may be agreed upon only at the end of each coaching session – or you can have complete coaching packages agreed upon right upfront (e.g. providing 1:1 coaching support for the next 3 or 6 months or so).

It is possible to narrow the **focus** of 1:1 coaching down to specific themes (e.g. coaching on leadership/transition & change management/multicultural/career planning/self-management & work-life balance) or to keep it very broad (e.g. provide executives with a reflection space/sounding board they can use just as needed for their role).

Also, you can have a very broad target group (all people in the organisation that request it) or a more narrow one with regard to specific niches and situations (e.g. executives; sales people; females; high-flyers; promoted managers). The target group may even include people also from outside the organisation (e.g. customers, suppliers, managers from sister organisations).

One-to-one coaching may be implemented as a separate coaching programme (e.g. a pool of coaches provides one-to-one coaching for any executive in the organisation requesting it), or as **part of** a wider programme (e.g. a training programme for managers contains a number of one-to-one coaching sessions for the participants, or anybody receiving 360 degree feedback in the organisation gets a standard coaching session afterwards to review the results and make plans for appropriate action).

You can have all 1:1 coaches work on the basis of (one or more) specific **coaching models, approaches and techniques** that you have developed or identified as the most appropriate for your company and therefore see as fixed. Or you can emphasise finding out from each coach individually in what way their coaching approach is actually appropriate for your company purposes. As a third way, you may choose a combination of both approaches.

External versus internal coaches

External coaches (coaches from outside the organisation) are seen by some as "the only real and true coaches". Their classically mentioned advantages are: neutrality, objectivity, no involvement in internal politics, confidentiality fully assured, bringing in new and fresh perspectives from the outside.

Internal coaches (coaches being staff members of the organisation) have their strengths in other areas: they may understand the company culture and background better,

www.frank-bresser-consulting.com

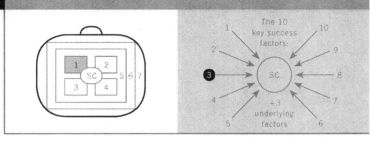

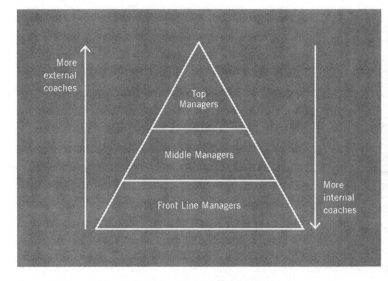

are generally less costly and can schedule coaching sessions more easily with the coachee at the workplace.

Therefore, both types of coach have a role to play and the right choice depends on the specific situation and the needs of your organisation. Generally speaking, it is recommended to consider combining the advantages of both types by building a coach-pool containing external as well as internal coaches. This may enable your organisation to best serve the whole range of different coaching requests coming in.

The following rules of thumb provide some further guidance on how to make your choice:

* The higher a coachee is in the hierarchy of your organisation, the more you may take into consideration the possibility of contracting an external coach (see figure). This is because a more senior person might tend to refuse internal coaching due to an increased desire for confidentiality and a resistance to share personal matters with a coach who is likely to be at a lower level than the coachee him or herself.

* The bigger the size of an organisation, the more appropriate it is to consider internal coaches. This is simply because, with internal coaches in small organisations, confidentiality issues can quickly become a serious problem. External coaches seem to be the better alternative here. But the larger an organisation is, the more unlikely it becomes that coach and coachee see each other on other occasions in the organisation and the advantages of external coaching diminish.

* The more experience an organisation has with coaching, the more realistic and promising it becomes to have internal coaches: The reason is that running an internal coach pool requires a high degree of coaching expertise. Therefore organisations with little or no experience normally start with external coaches. Then, later on, they upgrade and develop an internal coach pool to add to their external one.

Figure: External/Internal coaches along the hierarchy

* Where the organisational culture is open to external solutions, the option of using external coaches is often more appealing. The opposite applies for organisations which prefer internal solutions.

* Where the credibility of the L&D/HR department is high, the option of building a credible internal coach pool is more attractive, as the standards of managing organisational development have a strong influence on how the coaching is perceived.

Hybrid forms of external and internal coaches

Consider the following statement: The specific way you design and manage coaching measures will have a huge impact on the degree to which coaches are really external or internal.

Where, for example, you choose external coaches who have a close relationship to your organisation, come from the same background or have a very similar mindset to people in your organisation, those coaches may be strongly influenced

www.frank-bresser-consulting.com

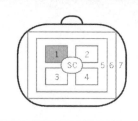
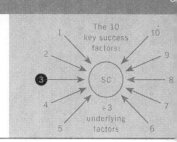

by the organisation. How objective and neutral can they be? Or, where external coaches have already worked for your company for many years, how unbiased can they be? This explains why some external coaches are sometimes perceived as internal coaches by people in the organisation. On the other hand, an internal coach is not necessarily biased or highly involved in internal matters in the organisation. For example, a pool of internal full-time coaches can be located separately and independently in the organisation (e.g. by creating a coach-pool in the Learning & Development Academy of a large company). The internal coaches in such a pool can then work highly independently and keep a great deal of neutrality. As a result, they are sometimes even perceived as external coaches by people in the organisation.

So make sure you not only pay attention to the question of whether your coaches are external or internal, but also how you position them and what your selection process is for them.

Internal full-time versus part-time coaches

Keep this important distinction in mind: internal full-time coaches concentrate on coaching only and therefore have some kind of neutrality and independent status within the organisation. In contrast, internal part-time coaches who also fulfil other functions in the organisation when not working as a coach (e.g. senior line manager), are clearly involved in the operational management of the organisation themselves. As a result, they need to be particularly clear on their exact role and task as a coach. Additionally, they may encounter the coachee during the course of their work outside the coaching sessions and this naturally leads to an increased risk of role conflict and breech of confidentiality.

For this reason, plan carefully when considering using internal part-time coaches. The following recommendations might help your planning to achieve optimal results:

1. Only make use of internal part-time coaches when you have a good plan/concept.

2. Give your coaches extra training/briefing/education to make them sensitive to the possible risks associated with this coaching form, and prepare them well to deal with them.

3. Include provisions in the coaching plan on how the various parties are to behave if a risk scenario occurs.

4. Make it most unlikely that coach and coachee see each other outside the coaching relationship (e.g. by ensuring that they come from different organisational divisions).

Stages of any 1:1 coaching intervention

In order to be successful, any one-to-one coaching intervention should be based on and designed around the following six stages, each requiring thorough planning and management:

1. Availability of suitable coaches (Building coach pools)
2. Request for coaching
3. Matching coach and coachee
4. Contracting
5. Coaching process
6. Evaluation

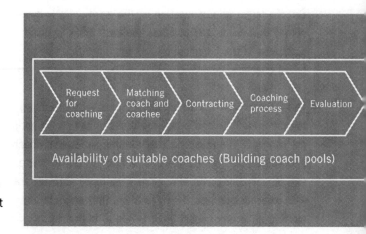

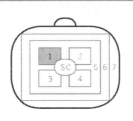
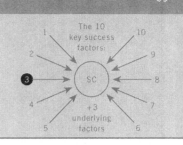

1. Availability of suitable coaches (Building coach pools)

Without proper coaches, there is no effective 1:1 coaching. So you need to scan the external as well as internal environment in terms of professional coaches – and manage the recruitment, quality and familiarisation of suitable coaches in order to build up an appropriate coach pool for your company. Also, you have to make sure that all coaches get proper support, supervision and training as needed to keep standards high. This is an ongoing process requiring permanent adjustment and refinement.

In order to find the right coaches with the best coaching approaches for your organisation-specific purposes, it is essential that you develop a **coach profile** as precisely as possible, setting out the most important quality and selection criteria (and the weighting of each of these). This will help you get optimal clarity and focus in your search for suitable coaches, and also give the coaches a clear picture of what is expected by you. This will help save you as well as the coaches a lot of time and energy and will bring about the most appropriate coach pool for your specific needs. (You will find more detailed information on coach profiles and quality requirements in key success factor 10.)

Classic **recruitment methods** (approaches to identifying suitable coaches in the market) are:

- reviewing the coaches you already know
- word of mouth/references/networking
- ask coaches to get in touch and apply through public advertising/a public bid
- using coach/accredited coach lists and search engines from coaching associations, other accrediting bodies, magazines, business registers, other independent portals, large coaching providers and others
- visiting coaching conferences and congresses
- tracking authors of relevant coaching models and literature
- coach and coaching provider websites

- other research (internet and beyond)
- using external support for recruitment (e.g. consultants)

Often used **selection methods** to actually choose and find out whether coaches do fit within the coach profile are:

- Application form (including CV, qualifications, experience, coaching approach/methodology, publications, references, etc.)
- Interviews with each coach
- Live Testing: a live coaching session (face-to-face or by phone, ideally on a real case)
- References (checking these in terms of facts and character)
- Coach Assessment Centres
- Other kind of tests (e.g. on business understanding)
- Making use of external experts/consultants to support the selection

Keep the recruitment and selection process effective and straight-forward at any time. The benefits of the process must always outweigh its efforts and costs – for you as well as for the coaches themselves. Be aware that any overload or lack of transparency of the process may discourage professional coaches (especially the very good ones) from applying.

Also keep in mind that being selected is only the first step for the coach. After an induction and familiarisation phase, the coach, when becoming active in the company, will undergo **permanent further assessment and evaluation**, in order to continue to prove his or her suitability. Also the organisational needs may change over time, or your coaching literacy may evolve and lead to different selection criteria. The aspect of further assessment of coaches is the more important, as only in practice will you actually find out how credibly and effectively a coach really works.

So the selection process continues after initial selection. The coach pool always needs to remain transient in some way: You may select new coaches to join it and formerly

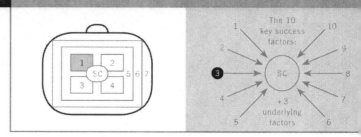

selected coaches may leave it. So there is no way for coaches to rest on their laurels. Keep your coach pool up-to-date and fresh at any time.

In this spirit, it is also essential to make sure that all coaches get proper support, supervision and training **(continuous professional development)** as needed to keep standards high. This is an ongoing process requiring permanent adjustment and refinement. Your company can either provide this to your coaches itself – or require from the coaches to seek CPD autonomously themselves and testify it to you in regular intervals (or have a combination of both ways).

Also consider developing and establishing an **internal accreditation scheme for coaches** (external and/or internal ones) in your company. This may look quite similar to existing external accreditation schemes provided by coaching associations for example, but has two main advantages for your firm:

1. You can fully tailor it around your company-specific needs – and change and adjust it any time as needed.
2. Your organisation has full ownership of the scheme and demonstrates credibility in and commitment for coaching. (This can also enhance your employer attractiveness overall).

Of course, developing and launching such a scheme requires a rather high level of coaching implementation and improvement intelligence. Therefore, beginners should definitely stay away from such an undertaking – or, as an alternative, seek proper external support to realize it.

Also consider developing and having a **standard frame contract** for all coaches working for your company. This contract will contain the general terms and conditions for coaching, the fee structure and any important provisions to be observed by any of the parties. This doesn't refer to a concrete coaching request yet, but just lays the basic fundament for later coaching assignments. As appropriate,

you may keep this frame contract more or less flexible and concrete.

In terms of **fee structure**, you may either decide to have a fixed pricing policy with clear provisions on what you pay to coaches, or you choose to keep it open and negotiate case-by-case. Also, you can combine both ways and have a clear range of possible fees within which you may still negotiate with each coach case-by-case.

1:1 coaching can be invoiced on an hourly, half-day, full day or package basis. (A package may be for example a coaching assignment for 3 or 6 months including maximum 24 hours of coach work.) In any case, it is important to make clear what time is included or invoiced (only the actually delivered coaching sessions, or also the preparation and travel time).

Generally speaking, the fees for coaches may differ significantly, mainly depending on the qualification and reputation of the coach, their target group (e.g. whether the coachee is a top executive or a front line manager), your type and size of organisation (e.g. profit versus non-profit organisation, global versus local company) and the local coaching prices in the respective region/country.

You may also find the practice of performance- or outcomes-related payment (or of elements of it) in particular cases at the top level in the market. For example the external coach may get a certain percentage of the increased company profit caused by coaching the CEO. However, be very cautious in using this approach in your organisation as it raises many concerns: firstly around undermining the coachee's ownership and self-responsibility in coaching, secondly around the difficulties to verify what outcomes can actually and only be attributed to coaching. So, use this approach, if at all, only very singularly, and do have a double-check whether it is really appropriate.

While coaching fees may be volatile and, like any other service, follow the dynamics of demand and supply and

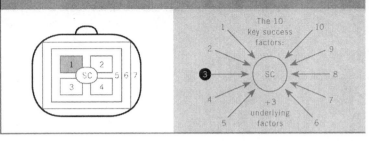

adjust to the current economic situation, discounts as such are not very widespread in coaching today. Instead, the extent of coaching programmes and their services is rather cut down to make them fit the budget.

Where you work with larger coaching providers offering a pool of coaches, you may have a different standard frame contract and fee structure (bigger packages leading maybe also to some kind of discount). However, it is recommended to assess, select and contract each coach individually, and to check thoroughly the quality of large coaching providers – in particular their internal quality assurance systems and the quality of the relationship between them and the coaches they list.

The **overall size and composition of your coach pool** will depend on various factors: On the one hand, its diversity and the range of coaching models and techniques covered by the coaches need to reflect the diversity of your target group and their issues to be coached on. On the other hand, the number of coaches in your coach pool must remain manageable and relative to the level of actual coaching demand in your company. In business today, you may encounter all sizes of coach pools – ranging from 1 or 2 coaches to many hundreds.

The following guidelines may help you make proper decisions in this regard while also keeping optimal flexibility:

1. The analysis of your organisation-specific coaching needs, your coach profile and quality and selection criteria determine what kind of coach pool to build and maintain.

2. The higher the number of coaching requests in your company, the larger your coach pool is likely to be.

3. The more diverse the coaching target group, their requirements and their issues are, the more diverse your coach pool is also likely to be.

4. Consider developing and maintaining a fixed, flexible and/or dormant coach pool: The fixed coach pool is your

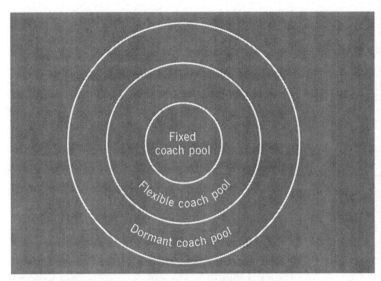

Figure: The fixed, flexible and dormant coach pool

official core team of selected, qualified coaches whose coaching services are needed on a continuous, regular basis. (This may also imply having standard coaches for standard requests.) The flexible coach pool is the wider group of coaches you have checked and selected, but which are on hold and only become active on specific demand and request. The dormant coach pool includes all coaches you have potential access to (directly or through intermediaries/coaching providers), which may become relevant for your purposes: You can quickly assess and select these on demand in specific cases, where there is a request for coaching that the coaches in the fixed and flexible coach pool do not cover and cannot serve adequately.

Consider both external and internal (full and part time) coaches in this regard. Internal full time coaches are always part of the fixed coach pool, otherwise you wouldn't need them. Internal part-time coaches are classically in the fixed or flexible coach pool. External coaches can be in the fixed, flexible as well as the dormant coach pool.

5. Structure and arrange your coach pool in terms of important categories such as key themes (e.g. leadership,

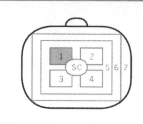 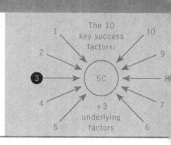

transition), target groups (e.g. executives, high flyers), geographical coverage (e.g. global, local, national), coaching methodology/approaches (e.g. niche expert coaching versus more content-free coaching/directive versus non-directive coaching), coach personality/background (e.g. top management experience, psychologist).

6. Differentiate between "must have" and "good to have" coverage of coaching requests. Make sure you have coaches in your fixed or flexible coach pool for the "must have" requests.

7. For optimal coverage of relevant requests coming in, think about the right balance between coaches who are specialising in a specific area on the one hand (i.e. niche/expert coaches: these mostly tend to be more directive and bring in their own expertise on the issue to the coaching sessions) and generalist coaches who work in a highly non-directive, rather content-free manner on the other hand (i.e. pure coaching process experts: these mostly tend to focus on supporting the self-reflection and self-directed learning of the coachee only). While the first only have a specific target group and area in which they can and want to coach, the latter can in principle coach on any issue with their approach. What is the best mix between the two depends on your specific coaching needs and people's receptiveness towards one approach or the other.

8. Always make sure that the size and composition of the coach pool is relative to the staff and resources deployed to manage it. Otherwise you very quickly get a great problem around quality assurance. What is a coach pool of 50 or 200 coaches for, if the person responsible for it doesn't have sufficient time to properly manage it – and can only remember 5 of them (and also actually makes use of these 5)? So it is important to fill any coach pool with real lifeblood. It is definitely better to have a small, but good and vivid coach pool, than a big, but poorly managed, inactive one.

2. Request for coaching

Your target group of the 1:1 coaching programme clearly identifies the kind of people who may be potential coachees. These may ask to be coached and thus are entitled to be the initiator of coaching requests. (You may consider providing a formalized request form in some way to facilitate the process.)

However, it is important to see that also you as HR, L&D or OD manager may suggest coaching to a person from the target group where appropriate. In addition, the coachee's line manager may also play an important role in recommending coaching or suggesting the possibility of being coached to the direct report.

Finally, 1:1 coaching interventions can also be an integrated part of wider programmes in the company (or a standard measure). In this case, a formal request specifically for coaching is replaced by the event of entering the wider programme (or being in the target group of the standard measure).

It is true that the higher the commitment of the coachee to be coached, the more promising the coaching success. Therefore, make sure that all request forms best support this commitment of the coachee. However, it is a widespread myth and inappropriate to require that coachees would always have to ask for the coaching voluntarily – in some cases, it is more the fact that the coaching programme is compulsory that best enhances the coachee's commitment. What levels of voluntariness are possible and in what specific cases compulsoriness may even be more appropriate, will be explained in detail in key success factor 9 on careful and effective evaluation of coaching.

3. Matching coach and coachee

The matching process is a very important step and concerned with the question what coach best suits the coachee and his or her issue. This requires a clear analysis of the

www.frank-bresser-consulting.com

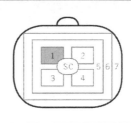

coachee's needs and the identification of suitable coaches (in terms of content and personal chemistry).

The more advanced you are in building and maintaining your appropriate coach pool (see above), the easier you will find this task, as your pool is already highly tailored and a good match for your target group overall. The step to follow here is only the concrete matching in each individual case. The enormous value created by not only good, but excellent matching cannot be overemphasized.

There are several ways of how and by whom the matching is actually done. What approach is most appropriate, will vary depending on each case:

1. The coachee may look for a suitable external coach in the market him or herself (and the organisation pays for it).

2. The coachee chooses a coach from a whole range of coaches or coach profiles presented by the company for example on a conference, in a coaching booklet or in the company intranet. Three main ways within this option are possible:

   a) The coachee immediately chooses a final coach for his or her request.
   b) The coachee may have a chemistry meeting/testing session with the coach of his first choice, and, if not happy, may still change the coach and try another one.
   c) The coachee chooses two or three coaches at the beginning and has chemistry meetings/testing sessions with all of them, before making a decision.

3. The company and the coachee are both involved in the matching process: In a first step, you (the company) identify the two or three coaches from your coach pool with the best fit – and only send their profiles to the coachee. In a second step, the coachee can then choose only from these (in either of the ways set out in 2 a to c above).

4. You (the company) choose and allocate the coach with the best fit to the coachee. There is no choice of coaches for the coachee. The company does all the matching.

Where the matching is mainly done by the coachees themselves, it is important to educate them on coaching upfront to enable them to make well-informed decisions.

4. Contracting

Any 1:1 coaching intervention requires a specific coaching contract which is the base for any coaching session and its evaluation. It may contain the following **main contract elements/provisions:**

- Name of coachee
- Name of coach
- Type/scope of coaching (e.g. executive, leadership, sales coaching)
- Goals/objectives/purpose of the coaching intervention
- Duration, regularity, place, time, etc. of coaching sessions (also with a clear end)
- Outline roughly the coaching methodology and coaching techniques to apply (as well as any other specific tools, e.g. 360 degree feedback or MBTI)
- Confidentiality in the coaching process
- Setting the limits of coaching (e.g. identifying the specific areas to coach on and excluding the others; possible or not to talk about leaving the company; no therapy)
- Provisions on how to behave if problems occur (e.g. regarding the chemistry coach – coachee; issues of confidentiality; breeches of the contract of any kind)
- Opt out provisions (when it is possible or required to end the coaching process earlier than planned)
- Provisions on the possibilities of re-contracting, where this need emerges during or at the end of the coaching process (e.g. because of a significant change in the workplace of the coachee, there is a desire to adjust

www.frank-bresser-consulting.com

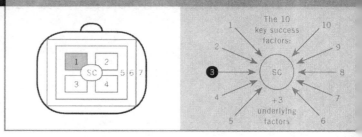

the goals of coaching accordingly; the agreed coaching sessions have all taken place, but there is a need for another 2 or 3 sessions)

- The role of all stakeholders involved (coachee and coach, the HR/OD/L&D manager and/or the coachee's line manager)
- Payment/fee provisions (if not already covered sufficiently by an existing coaching frame contract between the company and the coach)
- Any other important provisions to abide by for any of the parties/stakeholders
- Methods of evaluation (and how and when exactly these are to take place)

You may consider developing and having a (more or less) **standardized coaching contract** form that best fits your coaching programme and that the contract parties just have to fill out and sign. This may facilitate the whole contracting phase and make it very effective.

There are **different kinds of coaching contracts** depending on who is actually involved in contracting and how. The most important potential stakeholders of a coaching process are classically the coachee, the coach, the manager/director responsible for coaching in the company and the line manager of the coachee. The main options are as follows:

1. You (your company) and the coachee may agree on a contract that allows him or her to look for a suitable external coach in the market, make a separate contract with that coach and get reimbursed by the company for the expenses. This option thus gives the coachee most latitude and freedom:

2. Your organisation and the coachee may agree on a frame contract that allows him or her to choose any coach from your coach pool and make a standard contract with that coach without any further involvement by you (sometimes even without giving notice that a coaching is contracted and will take place). As you will also have a general frame contract with the coach, there now actually exist three separate contracts:

3. The above contracting approach only slightly changes where coach and coachee are (mostly or completely) matched by you (the company), and where you leave it to coach and coachee to contract themselves autonomously within the given assignment frame.

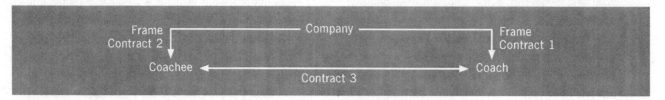

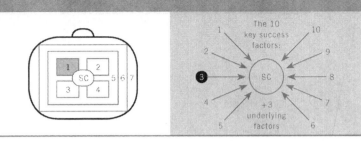

4. Another important approach to contracting is the triangle contract. Here you have three contract parties (organisation, coachee and coach) which come together and agree on one main contract for the coaching intervention. In addition, depending on your coaching programme, you may also have general frame contracts with the coach (e.g. on the fees) and/or the coachee (on how to use coaching in general).

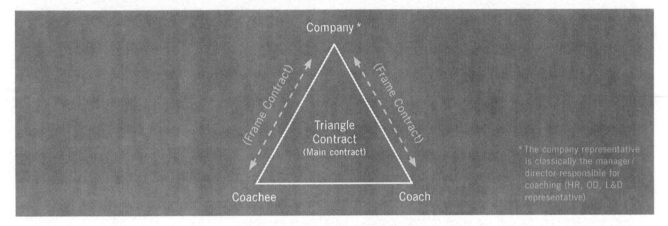

So in this approach, all main stakeholders get involved in the main contracting, can learn from each others' perspectives and make sure there is a real win-win. Coaching is thus more integrated. At the same time, the coachee's latitude in the use of the coach as well as the level of confidentiality are more limited.

The company representative for coaching is classically the manager/director responsible for coaching in the firm (/an HR, OD, L&D representative):

5. The coachee's line manager may also play an important role in contracting. In fact, he or she may get involved in mainly three ways:

a. The coachee's line manager is asked to join the contracting phase in order to share his opinions and perspectives only to support the contracting of the others. He or she is part of the round table, but not a contracting party:

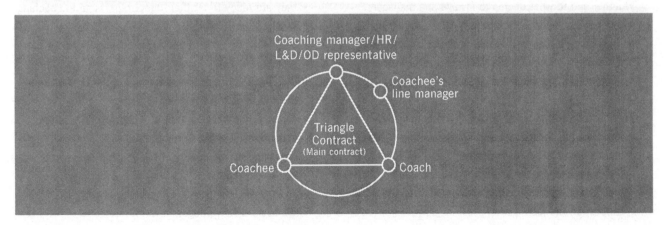

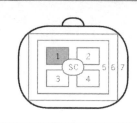

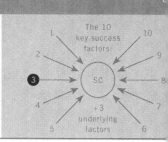

b. The line manager is also a true contracting party and rights and duties for him or her will emerge from the coaching contract:

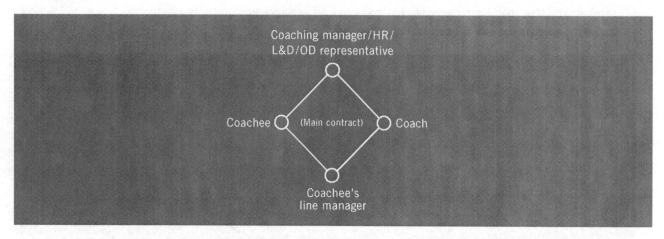

c. Finally, in some cases, you may find that the line manager is the main company representative and the HR/OD/L&D manager/director only the advising and supporting round table member:

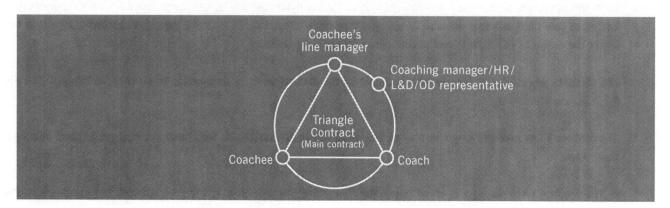

Whether and to what degree to involve line managers, will depend on various factors (e.g. type of coaching and coaching issue, relationship between coachee and line manager, coachee's and manager's receptiveness, management style, business culture).

The classic advantages of involving line managers are:
- improves the acceptance and understanding of coaching and its benefits by line managers
- the line managers better understand the learning needs of their direct reports and can provide additional support on-the-job

- they are ready to let their direct reports go to coaching sessions
- they learn from the round table conversations for themselves
- the coachee doesn't have the feeling he or she would need to keep the coaching hidden
- supports the development of a learning culture and collaboration in the firm
- may improve the quality of relationship between manager and direct report

The classic disadvantages in turn are:

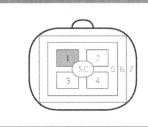
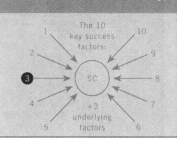

- coachees may refrain from using coaching because of insufficient confidentiality
- coachees may not be frank and open, but hide their inner thoughts and issues in contracting
- the line manager may get too much information on the coachee and use it to the disadvantage of the coachee at work (e.g. giving no promotion)
- insurmountable conflicts of roles may arise where the issue of the coachee is related to his or her line manager (directly or indirectly)
- too much business focus may distract from what is actually needed by the coachee personally
- creates additional time pressures on the line manager to arrange such a meeting
- decrease of acceptance of coaching in the company, where unmotivated line managers come, but perceive it as waste of time, and/or where the coachees feel uncomfortable

There is not one right or wrong way, but you need to find out what is most appropriate in your case.

In business today, you find that all variants of the above coaching contracts and all levels of involvement of the coachee's line manager may work very well, if used in the right context.

Make sure there is **no ambivalent or hidden agenda** in the contracting context. Pay attention to the consistency of all contracts – including the more general frame contracts as well as the specific, individual coaching contracts. Transparency is key, and in this spirit, also all evaluation methods to apply must be made transparent and agreed upon at the outset.

While 1:1 coaching must always be based on confidentiality, there are **different degrees of confidentiality** that you may choose from. What these are and what effect this choice has on evaluation, will be set out in detail below (see key success factor 9 on careful and effective evaluation).

It is crucial to set the **goals/objectives/purpose** for the coaching appropriately and include them in the contract. Goals may be formulated in a wide or narrow way: You may have very specific coaching in order to achieve a very specific outcome (e.g. sales coaching to increase sales by X%) or you may find it is adequate to just state a general purpose of the coaching in the contract (e.g. the purpose of the coaching is to provide the senior executive x with a useful space for self-reflection on current issues around leadership and self-management). It will depend on the design and purpose of your coaching initiative as well as on your company culture and evaluation requirements as to how precisely you break down and fix the objectives of the 1:1 coaching in the contract (see also key success factor 9).

As business and the coaching process can be very dynamic, you may need to review your goals from time to time and adjust them accordingly – and also consider re-contracting if the current coaching contract doesn't cover the needed adjustment.

A very important distinction around goals is the one between **public and private goals**. Public goals are those officially agreed upon by the organisation and the coachee and are known by all stakeholders involved. Private goals are those set within the coaching sessions by the coachee with the support of the coach only in order to achieve the public goals. These private goals remain confidential.

1:1 coaching is about **win-win**, i.e. about pursuing individual as well as organisational goals at the same time. So it should be made absolutely clear, that neither coachees nor coaches may (ab)use 1:1 coaching to the disadvantage of the company. The firm is paying for the coaching, and so it should go without saying that there needs to be a win-win for the coachee and the organisation. As soon as this is no longer the case, the coaching must be stopped. So while 1:1 coaching is indeed highly tailored around the coachee's needs, this definitely doesn't mean, it is only about the coachee's agenda. It is about the coachee's and the com-

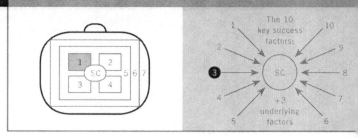

pany's agenda. If the coachee is only interested in his or her own agenda, he or she is free to look for a suitable external coach in the market and pay for it on a private basis. The same is also true for the coach: Where the coach starts to pursue his or her own agenda at the cost of the coachee's or the organisation's agenda, or where he or she starts to pursue the coachee's agenda only and ignore the organisational one, the coach becomes unprofessional and may need to be replaced.

Unfortunately, a great number of bad experiences made by businesses suggest there is a need to make this very clear at the beginning and include provisions on this in the contract.

Now, you may sometimes encounter **grey zones** where it is not that clear whether a win-win situation is still in place. For example, imagine a career development coaching where a coachee starts to explore and plan the option of seriously leaving the company. Is this then still in alignment with the organisational agenda and the coaching contract? Now, the more precisely you formulate the scope of the coaching and include related provisions in the contract upfront, the less uncertainty and ambivalence there will be. For example you could address the above issue in one of the following ways:

1. You say you want to keep all your coachees as employees and thus include a provision like: "This career development coaching covers the coachee's career development within the company only."

2. Or you take the view: if coachees, in the coaching sessions, come to the conclusion that they should leave the company, this is also advantageous for the company, as we only want and need employees who really fit within our organisation. So this is fine, and you may include a provision like: "This career development coaching also serves the purpose to allow the coachee to seriously check his or her own commitment for working in this company."

3. Finally, you may go a middle way: "When the coachee starts to seriously consider leaving the company, coach and coachee need to give notice to the HR/OD/L&D manager who will then decide how to proceed on the merit of each case."

As a final note on contracting, a particular approach to payment worth mentioning here (however still very rarely found in business today) is that the organisation and the coachee both pay a percentage of the coach's fee. This is a direct reflection and confirmation of this win-win nature of coaching. (It definitely isn't meant as permission for the coachee to just pursue his or her agenda!)

5. Coaching process (coaching sessions)

The coaching process actually implements the coaching contract. Depending on the coachee's needs and the coach's style, different coaching models, approaches, tools and techniques will apply in accordance with and in fulfilment of the contractual agreements.

The coaching sessions may be structured in very different ways: On the one hand you may have each single coaching session start with the question "What issue do you want to talk about today?" and a free flow of self-reflection and conversation. On the other hand, the coaching sessions may be highly structured and follow a very clear sequence of steps like building the relationship/rapport, setting (sub-)goals, gap analysis (current/desired state), considering options, deciding on a course of action and developing an action plan, implementation, evaluation and improvements and final measurement of success.

While listening, asking questions and giving and receiving learning feedback may be seen as the key behaviours displayed by coaches in the coaching sessions, some coaches will also work with more methods and techniques. Now, any method or tool may apply, as long as the coach

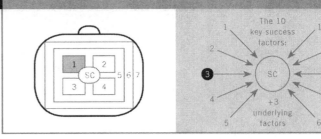

uses it in a coaching style, i.e. as long as it is appropriate and properly applied (and covered by the contract). This also requires from the coach to explain and make transparent the appropriateness of everything he or she does to the coachee (and to anyone else with a legitimate interest).

So every model, approach and technique may have its place and role to play, but the coach who applies them must know where these fit best when and how. A coach may have plenty of great tools and still be poor, while a coach just listening and asking questions may be absolutely excellent, nevertheless.

Also the overall way of how the coach supports the coaching process may vary enormously: Some coaches work in a highly **non-directive**, rather **content-free** manner, whereas others work in a highly **directive, advice-giving** manner. There is also a way in between. For example coaches may stay rather non-directive while giving input/advice by explicitly **asking the coachee for permission** to share their opinion, experience or expertise. Then, if the coachee affirms this, the coach may formulate the input in a careful, suggesting way, so that the coachee is totally free to pick it up or not.

All approaches may have a role to play; they are in principle all permissible, as long as they are in fact appropriate, properly applied in each case and in accordance to your coaching contract. What is most appropriate depends on many factors like the coaching topic, the coachee's preferences and specific needs, the company culture and so on.

By the way, the terms non-directive and content-free need to be put into right perspective: It is a myth to think non-directive coaches are not directive at all. A professional coach, however non-directive his coaching approach may be, will know that he or she is also directive in some way. This is because for example asking a question in a coaching session is also giving direction. It is implicitly saying "Think about my question!" or "This question may be worth con-

sidering". A coach may ask thousands of questions, but he or she chooses the one question only in that moment. The coach could also act in many other ways (e.g. give advice or just continue listening), but asks that one question only. By asking the one question, the coach thus gives input (i.e. content), be it directly or indirectly. So there is no fully content-free coaching. And there is also no fully non-directive coaching.

However, the distinction in terminology continues to make good sense to differentiate between more and less directive coaches and between coaches giving more or less advice. But it is, with this perspective, now only a question of degree, not of yes or no.

By developing your own organisation-specific understanding of coaching (see key success factor 1) and building up your coach pool on the basis of your proper coach profile, you will already develop and have a clear picture of how you define coaching and what models, approaches and techniques may be adequate and permissible in the coaching sessions for the coachees in your company.

During the coaching process, it will be your task to support the process from outside, to intervene promptly where problems occur (e.g. in case of contract breech) and to make sure the coaching also ends properly.

6. Evaluation

Monitoring and evaluating the 1:1 coaching intervention appropriately will help identify the coaching outcomes, improve and develop further the whole coaching programme and raise the acceptance and support by the top.

Coaching evaluation needs to be careful and effective at the same time. The possible and most appropriate ways of doing this will be set out in detail in key success factor 9 on evaluation below.

Geographical focus: *Turkey in Europe/Asia*

CASE STUDY 3

BORUSAN LOJISTIK, TURKEY

Company: *Borusan Lojistik*

(A logistics company which operates in 4 continents and is centered around two strategic business units: Port Management and Third Party Logistics Services)

www.borusanlojistik.com

Main Author: *Tugba Pasali Karacan, Istanbul, Function: Human Resources*

Co-author: *Dilek Yıldırım Akgün, ILGI Coaching*

Coaching Travel on the Way of Change

Competition has become increasingly fierce both here at home and around the world. It has become easier to imitate technology, products and services and we know that "the human factor" is the only resource we have that can create distinction.

Since 2006, we have been pursuing our objectives with the support of coaching, a brand new concept in Turkey. The first reason for implementing coaching was to ensure the professional development of our managers at every level. In the last 4 years, we have deployed the entire range of coaching practices from one-to-one manager coaching to in-house coaching.

In 2008, Borusan Lojistik obtained the Investors in People (IIP) certificate, which recognizes the importance of coaching as a personal development tool.

Basically we needed to adapt to a new, fast growing company culture and increase effectiveness within a changing organizational structure, as well as enhancing performance, leadership, management, team building skills, employee satisfaction and loyalty.

In the implementation of coaching, we decided to receive external consultancy from a professional internationally accredited coach and consultant, with the aim of internalizing different visions and approaches, and importing professional and objective support from outside.

The managers who would receive coaching determined the objectives of this practice according to their performance targets and their development needs as soon as they began working with their coaches.

When we look at the targets, we can see that they fall into three general fields.

Coaching for Performance focuses on the executive's effectiveness in his or her current position. Frequently it involves coaching on one or more management or leadership competencies, such as communicating vision, team building and team management.

Intercultural Coaching provides significant support for managers who have been transferred to Borusan Lojistik from other companies, appointed from one region to another, or who have come from different companies and started to work in a different culture and/or industry.

In order to ensure that newly employed or rotated managers add value to the company as soon as possible and to

---

www.frank-bresser-consulting.com

Geographical focus: *Turkey in Europe/Asia*

BORUSAN LOJISTIK CASE STUDY: *Coaching Travel on the Way of Change*

accelerate their adaptation to their new positions, we are also applying On boarding Coaching.

Our coaching program addresses all team managers, and we manage the process as follows:

- Managers who receive coaching first get "Coaching in Management" training before beginning their coaching sessions.

- Then the professional coach and the manager get together and determine the goals of their practice by using the 360° competency outputs.
- After this, the professional coach, the manager and the person to whom that manager reports come together to share their goals and give/receive feedback on the objectives.

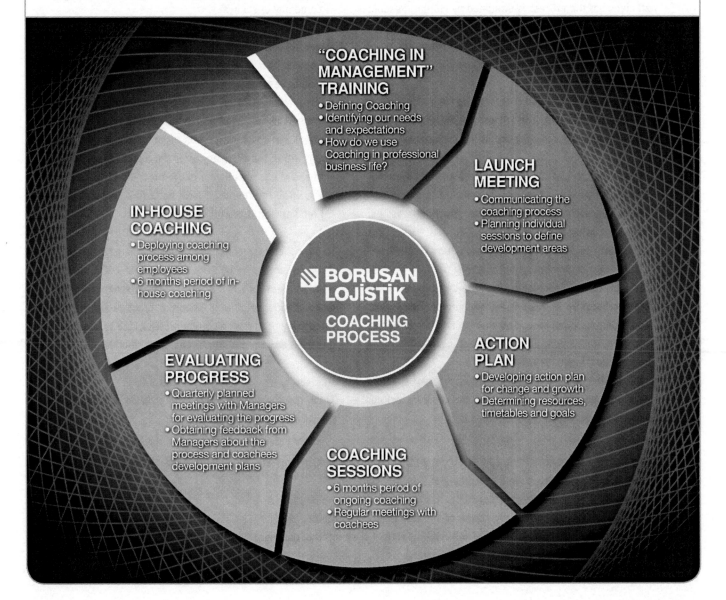

"COACHING IN MANAGEMENT" TRAINING
- Defining Coaching
- Identifying our needs and expectations
- How do we use Coaching in professional business life?

LAUNCH MEETING
- Communicating the coaching process
- Planning individual sessions to define development areas

ACTION PLAN
- Developing action plan for change and growth
- Determining resources, timetables and goals

COACHING SESSIONS
- 6 months period of ongoing coaching
- Regular meetings with coachees

EVALUATING PROGRESS
- Quarterly planned meetings with Managers for evaluating the progress
- Obtaining feedback from Managers about the process and coachees development plans

IN-HOUSE COACHING
- Deploying coaching process among employees
- 6 months period of in-house coaching

BORUSAN LOJİSTİK COACHING PROCESS

www.frank-bresser-consulting.com

Geographical focus: *Turkey in Europe/Asia*

BORUSAN LOJISTIK CASE STUDY: *Coaching Travel on the Way of Change*

- While receiving 18 hours of coaching over a 6-month period, the managers work on their goals (and are trained as potential manager in-house coaches).
- After the first 9 and 18 hours, the professional coach, the manager and the person to whom that manager reports gather and evaluate the progress within the process.
- At the end of the 3rd month and of the program, the efficiency of the process is evaluated by Human Resources via surveys, as well as feedback obtained during interviews. Remedial actions related to the process are taken for fields that require development.

Besides the use of external coaching, we have also built up an in-house coach pool. The following is the way how we practice and deploy coaching within the company:

- In order to conduct the process effectively and systematically, in-house coaches are first selected from among employees who have completed their coaching sessions. They have to be volunteers.
- We review the 360° competency evaluation results and assess their competencies for coaching, and we also ask the professional coach's opinion. The coaching competencies we focus on in this process are: strong questioning and listening, clear indication that he/she is monitoring the current situation, appreciation and acknowledgment, support and feedback skills.
- While matching coaches with coachees, we take special care to avoid choosing people from the same departments and those who report to each other.

- Here in Human Resources, we pay close attention to possible incompatibility between the coach and the coachee, as well as problems, like the inability to allocate the necessary time.
- In the middle and at the end of the process, our coach managers and a professional coach come together to discuss the process to enhance it, improve it and to overcome any obstacles.

Some of the employee opinions are:
- I believe that it helps people to set accurate targets for themselves.
- My relations with my clients and teammates improved. I was more motivated and more efficient in solving problems.
- I think the coaching process began to play a more prominent role within the company after the organizational changes.
- I believe this experience is the most effective and impressive of all the training I have had in my professional life. I recommend it heartily to everyone.

In our coaching process, the employee satisfaction score in 2008 has improved by 20% compared to 2007, increasing from an index rank of 75 to 89. The personnel turnover rate was reduced as well. Coaching practice also increased the quality of in-house communication due to the positive impact it had on our employees' performance.

Our key learning/Recommendation:
Think thoroughly about how to internalize and deploy the practice of coaching!

Questions and exercises for further reflection and to integrate practice and theory:

1. What is the business case for coaching at Borusan Lojistik?
2. What kind of coaching/coaching forms has the company implemented?
3. What is the design of the key stages of the coaching intervention?
4. In what way does the company ensure high quality of their internal coaches?
5. What is your key learning from this case study?

www.frank-bresser-consulting.com

Geographical focus: *Kenya*

CASE STUDY 4	DEBUT IMAGE CONSULTANTS, KENYA

Company:	*Debut Image Consultants Limited*	Author:	*Grace Musyoka*
	(Corporate Communications)	Function:	*CEO, based in Nairobi*
	www.debutconsultants.com		

Overcoming obstacles in our sales team through coaching in times of organisational growth and change

Background information

Our company had just moved from offering international media management services to a general focus on corporate communications. The associated transition, while necessary, caused us to suffer greatly, both due to the economic recession and also due to increased competition, as we entered a field dominated by plenty of well known names.

The sales team was hit the hardest, since they had to sell local media and get value-added-signups at the same time. There was a lot of moaning about the 'good days', and the economic recession didn't make things easier.

As a result we decided to implement a four-week coaching program (around block removal coaching) aimed to overcome our sales people's resistance to change and unlock their full potential.

Coaching of the sales team

Together with the coach, the sales team worked out and identified the areas that they felt were affecting their output, and pinpointed what their desired, ideal situation would look like. In addition, they asked people from other areas in the organization what their feelings and perceptions were regarding the sales team. The results "shocked" the team in a positive way: The members realized that – contrary to their previous expectations – they were actually appreciated and even envied for their jobs. This already caused a different atmosphere and better feeling in the team that the coach could capitalize upon in the following programme.

Role playing was encouraged to allow the whole sales team to experience and reflect on what individual team members experienced in their daily work. In the end, it was observed that the daily challenges were rather similar.

In order to enhance the team morale and also avoid people channelling any anger to the least-selling colleagues, we worked mainly on two exercises: how to manage disappointment in sales and how to become a better sales person.

In the context of these issues, we also worked on time management and having a "hobby" or an exercise to do – everyday – beyond working and meeting clients. We also put in a 'sales person of the month' competition to foster healthy competition. In addition, we discussed further education as a way to become a better sales person. As a result, the team was requested to sign up for courses

www.frank-bresser-consulting.com

Geographical focus: *Kenya*

DEBUT IMAGE CONSULTANTS CASE STUDY: *Overcoming obstacles in our sales team through coaching in times of organisational growth and change*

related to proposal writing and project management to improve their sales.

Coaching was done on a team basis after every sales meeting, where slide shows and motivational quotes were also shown and discussed. The coach also set aside the last five minutes asking for a success story – by any member – that could be directly attributed to the current coaching initiative. This helped the rest of the team realize there was direct output from actively applying the new learning in their lives and, more importantly, in sales.

We also developed a new Information Management System to deal with the new sales policy. Finally, it became increasingly clear that, at the end of the day, we would be able to achieve much – both individually and as an organisation –, the more we could remove stereotype thinking and hidden fears while making our professional and personal calls. This also contained questions of personal boundaries and of not just building, but also sustaining open-mindedness in our daily work.

Additional, individual support

To address personal requests and issues, the coach also met with each team member (maximum three times) to provide individual support and give specific tasks based on their performance. A self-analysis chart was developed together by the individual and the coach to help the person achieve corporate as well as personal milestones related to their work.

This opportunity created space for those having unique issues affecting the person's and group's success, and enabled them to address these in a constructive manner. Sales is often a lonely job and this aspect was important in helping to raise performance.

Outcomes

Working on both fronts – at the team and the individual level – has turned out to best serve our purpose for the coaching intervention. There has been a general improvement in results per individual and, accordingly, through the whole team.

However, the sales team is still in the initial stages of the application of what has been learned. Our celebrations, though overdue, will not be until we will meet our envisaged group sales target.

Our key learning/Recommendation:
It is possible to unblock limitations in output through coaching by openly addressing important issues – in particular closed thinking and stereotypes in teams which can grow into group think, if not addressed early on.

Questions and exercises for further reflection and to integrate practice and theory:

1. What is the business case for coaching in the company?
2. What coaching form(s) and approaches are they using?
3. What are the main differences between team coaching and individual one-to-one coaching?
4. What is your key learning from this case study?

www.frank-bresser-consulting.com

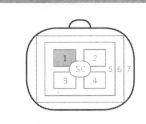
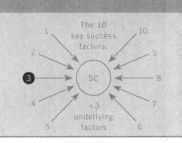

3.1.4. Team coaching

is a form of coaching in which a group of people operating as a team are coached by one or more professional coaches. In general, what is valid for one-to-one coaching is also applicable to team coaching.

However, as teams normally aren't as strong a unit as are individual human beings, more direction in leading the team through the whole coaching process is often required when coaching a team compared with one-to-one coaching.

There is also an additional dimension to the question of confidentiality that requires special attention upfront: In team coaching, by its nature, the level of confidentiality is lower than in a one-to-one coaching session, as the other members of the team are not professional coaches.

Also, commitment and voluntariness may mean very different things in team coaching. Do all team members need to be committed, only the majority or even only the manager of the team? Similarly, who may initiate the coaching request and make the coaching contract? Does the manager need to be included in the team coaching or not? What kind of hierarchy applies in team coaching?

The most adequate answers to these questions may vary depending on the circumstances of each case.

Team coaching may also mean team building, if the group wants to come together to work on it.

Like one-to-one coaching, team coaching can be a single intervention as well as part of a wider programme.

3.1.5. Coaching in groups (coaching workshop)

is an emerging form of coaching where one or more professional coaches and a group of people come together to "coach" each group member one by one on his or her individual issue. It is a hybrid form of peer coaching, one-to-one coaching and team coaching.

For this coaching intervention to work, it is particularly important to pay attention to the composition of the group, to create a trusting atmosphere and to ensure there are absolutely clear and adequate rules for all group members (e.g. regarding process, communication and confidentiality).

It is worth highlighting that each coaching form follows its own rules and dynamics and serves a different perspective and purpose within the scope of the overall coaching umbrella. Research and experience strongly suggest that, depending on the circumstances of each case, each form has a role to play and can be appropriate. So becoming familiar with all forms of coaching will enable you to really get the big picture, make well-informed decisions and implement the forms that best suit your organisation. However, be highly cautious with the next one:

www.frank-bresser-consulting.com

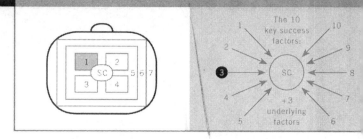

3.1.6. The manager as coach of direct reports (Be very careful here!)

is a form of coaching in which the manager gives formal coaching sessions to his or her subordinate as a (professional) coach. During the time of the session, the manager takes off the superior hat and puts on the professional coach hat. That he or she normally is a "superior", in possession of information about the performance of the coachee and provided with the power to direct him/her, is put into the background during the coaching.

For good reasons, this is seen as the most problematic variant of an internal part time coach in an organisation: the degree of the coach's potential bias and own involvement is enormous here. In particular, the manager may not be able to focus on the coachee's agenda sufficiently, because the personal concern about his or her own agenda as superior and manager in the organisation may prevail.

Accordingly, in this form the advantages and disadvantages of an internal coach come through in a very extreme way: on the one hand, the manager knows his or her reports and their workplace very well and can give additional support to the employee as a coach and/or as superior. On the other hand, the risk of role conflict and breech of confidentiality couldn't be higher. The manager is in continuous danger of mixing the two roles. Even if the manager can separate both roles properly, is the employee also able to do so? It is most likely that the coachee won't speak as frankly in the coaching session as he or she would with an external or a dissociated internal coach. This is also because, if he or she did, this might lead to a situation where the manager has too much information about and power over the employee, impairing the latter's self-autonomy and personal development.

Acknowledging the fact that the manager as coach of direct reports cannot really be an independent, dissociated coach for the coachee, helps identify the realistic limits of this coaching form regarding content and confidentiality: Only very exceptional circumstances are imaginable in which this coaching form may seem appropriate at all. So be very careful here. As long as you are not absolutely skilled and prepared to use the manager as coach, better keep your hands away! Before and while actually using the manager as coach, make sure you adhere to all of the following 10 guidelines:

1. Only make exceptional use of this coaching form. Do not implement it on a broader scale.

2. See it as one of many options within your pool of coaches aimed to meet the diversity of emerging coaching requests. Never implement only this form.

3. Only consider this coaching form, where the coach's knowledge of the coachee's workplace, and on-the-job support for the coachee are especially important.

4. Consider it only in cases where there is a very low risk of role conflict (e.g. improvement of very specific, well-defined, technical skills with no personal or political sensitivity).

5. When you use it, set very strict time boundaries by making sure the number of coaching sessions/hours per month is very low. In this way you avoid that the coach/ coachee relationship distorts the daily work relationship.

6. It is important that the coaching sessions have a minimum duration of time of, say, 15 minutes, so that they are also actually perceived as sessions. Coaching just for a minute here and there blurs the limits. Additionally, useful rituals to signal the behaviour and start a coaching session are: "I'd like to run a proper coaching session now." "I am putting my coach's hat on now." "I am going to operate as a coach now." Ideally coach and coachee distinguish the coaching session by booking it specifically in the diary.

www.frank-bresser-consulting.com

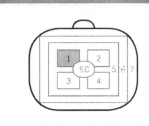

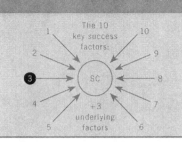

7. Only consider this coaching form, where there is a high trust relationship and good chemistry between the manager and the direct report, and the full willingness and commitment of both to work together as coach and coachee. At the same time both parties must be able to keep detachment and build up a professional coaching relationship in the sessions.

8. Treat the manager as coach of his/her direct reports like any other professional (internal or external) coach. Make it a requirement that they need to have the same qualifications and follow the same procedures as any other professional coach:
   • Before managers coach any of their direct reports, they should go through the same training and assessment as any other professional coach and, additionally, have received a supplementary briefing or training on the specific risks associated with their coaching form.
   • Don't give them a blank cheque to coach any direct report they want to, but, as with other managers, require that they report any interest of an employee in coaching to you. You can then, together with the interested employee and also the manager, find out what is the best option for the employee on the merit of each case. Maybe it is the manager as coach, maybe not.
   • Support, monitor and evaluate their work in the same way you do with any other professional coach. Provide them with supervision and further training.

9. Speak frankly about the limits and risks associated with the manager as coach of his/her direct reports in your organisation. Include clear provisions in your coaching plan on how the various parties are to behave if any of the risk scenarios occur, and also communicate these clearly in your company. Address emerging problems immediately.

10. Before using this coaching form in a concrete situation, check thoroughly whether other coaching forms – in particular classic one-to-one coaching, and adopting a coaching leadership style (see below) – are more suitable here.

If you observe all these guidelines, it is possible to use the manager as coach of his/her direct reports as a useful supplement to your portfolio of coaching measures. But, again, it should only play a very limited role in your overall coaching programme, if at all.

It seems appropriate to mention here that in the past many companies who tried to implement this coaching form outside the scope as outlined in this section, made very painful experiences. In particular in the cases, where the strategy was to make out of every manager in the company a coach of their direct reports, the programme didn't work. Employees saw the programme more as an attempt to manipulate them. Performance went down and distrust strongly increased in the organisation.

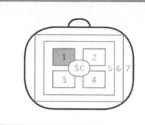
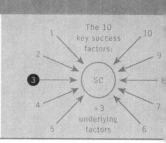

3.1.7. *The coaching leadership style (or coaching management style)*

is the form of coaching where leaders/managers naturally integrate the coaching principles and coaching techniques into their daily leadership and/or management style.

This coaching form, as opposed to the ones before, is not to be seen as anything separate from normal work – it is fully ingrained in organisational life. The leader/manager is not asked to be a coach and give formal coaching sessions on the basis of a coaching contract here, but to remain a leader/manager all the time.

Using a coaching leadership/management style, therefore, is not a time-consuming process. Most interventions may just take a minute or less: asking the right question in the right moment or listening actively when most needed, can be all it takes to make a difference. Listening, asking high impact coaching questions and giving (and receiving) effective learning feedback are classic key behaviours regularly displayed by a manager/leader applying a coaching leadership/management style.

There are mainly three different ways of understanding and defining a coaching leadership/management style that are set out in the following. These need to be distinguished very clearly, but in the end may complement each other very well:

1. *Dynamic appropriateness in leadership/ management overall*

This is the broadest understanding of the coaching style. It means choosing from the wide range and portfolio of existing leadership and management styles the one(s) that are most adequate for each person in each situation. This approach is an enabler of making best choice, rather than an upfront suggestion of a specific answer.

So here, the coaching leadership/management style embraces all existing (traditional as well as new) styles as possible, equivalent options.

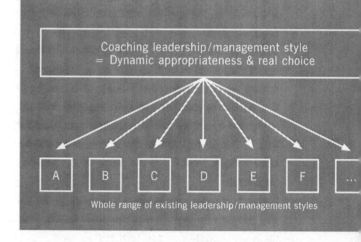

2. *A suggested, most appropriate mix of leadership/management styles*

This approach is already an application of general dynamic appropriateness and suggests a response to the question what style(s) is (are) in principle most appropriate given the contemporary challenges around leadership/management in business today. So the coaching leadership/management style here

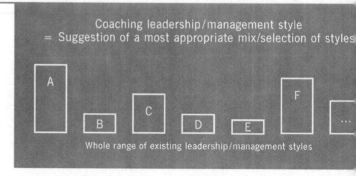

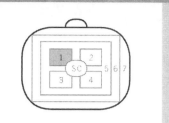
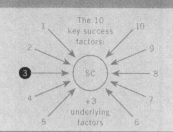

is a recommended best practice selection and prioritisation of the styles considered to be the most suitable ones these days.

This understanding thus embraces the whole portfolio of existing leadership/management styles, but makes concrete choices by giving more emphasis on some styles than others.

Specifically, the main focus in a coaching leadership/management style today is classically put on a more **empowering style of leadership/management** that promotes high performance and excellence, grows people and performance alike and raises people's awareness, responsibility and self-belief. Here listening, asking effective questions, delegating and giving and receiving learning feedback are the displayed behaviours.

This style can be seen as a currently favoured ideal way to lead/manage in organisations and there are good reasons for this. On a side note, these reasons may equally explain the recent rise of coaching cultures (see below) in organisations today:

Reason 1: Fast changing business environment

Globalisation, new technologies, instant communication, environmental, social and ethical issues pose completely new challenges to organisations today and are fundamentally changing the way we do business. In the 21st century, more than ever, companies need to be able to adjust to the market very quickly. Leaders need to be able to empower and develop their people to be leaders and take (and delegate) responsibility. In a fast changing business environment change is not just the responsibility of the top, but of all levels in the organisation. Also, leaders/managers increasingly need to lead/manage others who have better knowledge in some areas than they do. So working through others, rather than telling everyone what to do, becomes a key success factor.

Therefore, traditional methods of leadership and management which are less and less able to face these challenges,

are becoming abandoned. Instead, more modern leadership styles that ensure both high performance and flexibility in the company are being emphasized.

To illustrate this point, think of the following comparison: In the past it was highly possible for the top to lead and manage an organisation like a cox with a megaphone and a hand on the rudder in a rowing boat in flat waters – just shouting "1,2,3 … more to the right … 1,2,3, … more to the left …" to the line of rowers in front of him with their heads down and their back to the front.

Today, business is like canoeing in wild waters. Everyone in the canoe team needs to take on part of the responsibility and be highly sensitive to what all the others do. There may still be one main person appointed to lead and give key commands, but success is a team effort where everybody contributes and is equally dependent on the others to be able to adjust to the changing circumstances of the rapids.

Reason 2: Need for interpersonal skills

Teamwork, communication, information sharing and relationships are critically important in business. An ideal way of developing these interpersonal skills in organisations is through the adoption of a coaching management style (creation of a coaching culture). It is an interpersonal skill itself and brings about effective on-the-job staff development for both the manager and the people he or she works with.

Reason 3: Higher staff expectations and "war for talent"

Today, employees make increasing demands on employers. Companies need to offer employees an exceedingly attractive work environment to be successful in staff recruitment and retention. These people increasingly look beyond income and career for other aspirations like team spirit, personal fulfilment and a match of values in the workplace. A coaching leadership style (and coaching culture)

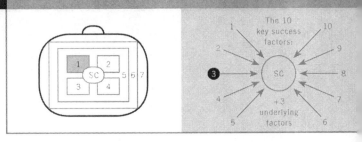

creates this kind of positive working environment that grows people and performance alike. In particular, it also clearly gives companies a competitive advantage in attracting and retaining the best talent out there in the market.

Reason 4: Latest findings in learning psychology

This modern coaching leadership/management style (as well as the creation of coaching cultures) reflects and integrates the latest findings and insights of today's learning and performance psychology. It is based on principles that demonstrably enhance people's learning and performance at the workplace. For example, giving people the possibility to find solutions themselves by asking effective questions, verifiably activates their brain in a much more intensive way, which leads to better and more sustainable skills development.

Given these reasons, the fast growing importance and increasing spread of a more empowering leadership style in businesses is hardly surprising.

But of course, this empowering style is still only one key element of the whole story. All other styles remain part of the portfolio and are valid options that still may have a significant role to play. The overriding principle here remains dynamic appropriateness for each case.

Think for example of traditional, authoritative leadership/ management styles. There are many situations, where **telling and command-and-control** may also be appropriate and even be more compatible with the coaching principle than listening or asking a question in the spirit of empowerment. For example, telling and command-and-control elements may be highly suitable and sometimes even better raise people's awareness, responsibility and self-belief where …

- hierarchical structures are needed to allow for effective decision-making and proper management.
- people need more input, education and guidance to cope with business requirements.
- some have expertise, information or tacit knowledge that others seek/need and where sharing information is simply the best and quickest way (e.g. this book).
- people do not have the skills to manage themselves yet and require strong leadership.
- quick, authoritative action is required in a case of urgency/crisis.
- it is a business requirement that everything is done in the same way (e.g. consistent assurance of quality standards).
- time and energy can easily be saved by not reinventing the wheel over and over again.
- people, who do not observe rules voluntarily that are vital for business success or the respect of law and

Whole range of possible leadership/management styles:

Traditional leadership/management style
(Principle: Authority/Hierarchy)

Coaching leadership/management style
Principle: Dynamic appropriateness

Listening
Asking
Empowering

range in between

Directing
Telling
Command

FRANK BRESSER CONSULTING & ASSOCIATES

EXCELLENT COACHING SOLUTIONS ↗

www.frank-bresser-consulting.com

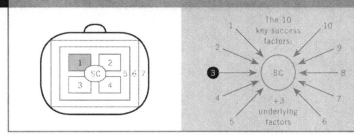

fundamental ethics, are not receptive to approaches that foster their insight and self-responsibility.

Having said this, be aware that people often all too quickly assume telling would be appropriate in situations, but when thinking it through they find a more asking style would have been more appropriate.

Also, where telling and command-and-control elements are adequate, they can and may often need to be combined

with elements of empowerment and dialogue (e.g. listening, asking questions and giving and receiving feedback).

In summary, the coaching leadership/management style suggests that both styles are important – the empowering style as well as the more traditional telling and command-and-control style. However, given today's business challenges, the overall tendency and balance should be more towards empowering/asking rather than directing/telling (see also the figure on the previous page).

3. *One specific, fixed way of leadership / management*

This is the narrowest understanding of the coaching leadership/management style. Here it only means a specific way of leadership/management that is seen as fixed and represents one option among many to choose from, rather than being an umbrella approach or enabler of choice at the meta-level.

Here, the coaching style is one specific method of leadership/management that simply complements the portfolio of other leadership/management styles.

Most often, it is used as a synonymous for this empowering leadership/management style as set out above, where listening, asking effective questions, delegating and giving and receiving learning feedback are often displayed behaviours.

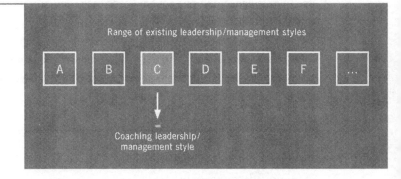

But you may also find other very different, specific fixations of a coaching leadership/management style in business – in particular in models setting out different types of leadership where the coaching style is included as one of them (e.g. the coaching style within situational leadership models/Goleman's EI leadership styles).

When using this narrow understanding of a coaching leadership/management style, be aware that it is only part of the whole story in coaching.

It is important to distinguish the above three understandings of a coaching leadership/management style, as they represent different types of dynamic appropriateness. Actually, they complement each other very well (see the figure on the next page).

The first understanding is most dynamic and is an overall enabler of appropriateness and choice. The second is half-dynamic and a recommendation of what are classically the best choices in terms of dynamic appropriateness. The third is fixed and in

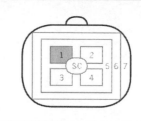 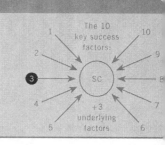

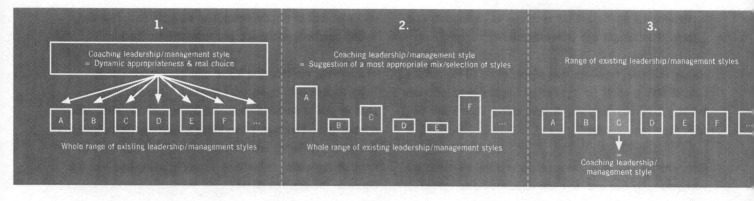

1.

Coaching leadership/management style
= Dynamic appropriateness & real choice

| A | B | C | D | E | F | ... |

Whole range of existing leadership/management styles

2.

Coaching leadership/management style
= Suggestion of a most appropriate mix/selection of styles

A   B   C   D   E   F   ...

Whole range of existing leadership/management styles

3.

Range of existing leadership/management styles

| A | B | C | D | E | F | ... |

Coaching leadership/
management style

itself not dynamic, but one option among many and so you need to check when it is most appropriate (which then leads you to the first understanding).

In any case, always make sure you properly appreciate all existing leadership and management styles at any time. Do not stigmatise any leadership/management styles, but leverage their potential. Coaching is about what best fits where and how, and all styles have their role to play.

Implementation and development of coaching leadership/management styles

Adopting a coaching style is an evolving process and in principle open to all managers and leaders in the organisation. As was said before, the leader/manager is not asked to be a coach and give formal coaching sessions on the basis of a coaching contract, but to remain a leader/manager all the time. He or she only integrates the coaching principles and coaching techniques in his or her daily leadership/management style.

So, as opposed to coaches who normally need to go through an extensive training before they may coach someone professionally for the first time, managers and leaders aiming to develop a coaching style in their everyday work can start with this immediately and improve further through practice and feedback received in the workplace day-by-day.

Accordingly, this coaching form can, at least in principle, be implemented and improved in a very straight-forward and highly scalable manner in the whole organisation (or parts of it) through specific coaching skills training for managers/leaders: You design and make this coaching skills training as extensive and regular as required, and you provide it for as many leaders/managers as needed for your company.

The degree to which you may aim to implement this coaching form in your company is equally highly scalable, depending on your organisational needs and culture:

• You may want to choose to make it the (or one of the) prevailing leadership/management style(s) in the whole organisation (or in parts of it). This may imply and mean a real shift in the leadership model and – more or less – also the creation of a coaching culture.
• Alternatively, you may choose the coaching leadership style only to complete and expand the classic portfolio of existing management and leadership skills in your company (or parts of it). In this case, there is no real paradigm shift. It would just mean an update and extension of existing skills with less impact on the overall organisational culture.

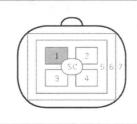
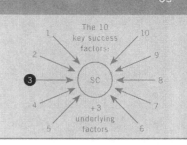

• Sometimes, you may find that people already use some kind of a coaching leadership or management style in your company, and you just want to reinforce and develop this style further. The existing coaching culture is then strengthened.

In order to be successful, any coaching leadership/management style initiative should be designed around the following seven key stages each requiring thorough planning and management:

1. Identify the exact kind and degree of coaching leadership/management style needed.

2. Develop a specific coaching skills training concept for the targeted managers/leaders.

3. Make sure very clear boundaries are set towards other coaching forms (in particular towards internal coaches/the manager as coach of direct reports).

4. Recruit and familiarize suitable, qualified trainers/training providers (external or internal ones or a combination of both: e.g. first externals, then increasingly also internals).

5. Train the targeted leaders/managers.

6. Provide continuous follow-up support for the trained leaders/managers to develop their skills further and keep standards high (e.g. building peer support networks; delivering advanced training; making relevant literature and other resources available).

7. Evaluate and continuously improve the measures.

One possible and often used way to support the whole process effectively and foster a coaching leadership/management style is to provide your managers with one-to-one coaching. In this manner, they may experience coaching personally and, as a result, may want and find it easier to apply the principles in their workplace.

You may also consider developing and establishing an internal certification scheme for your leaders/managers applying a coaching style in order to give them a proper forum to develop further, demonstrate and have officially testified and acknowledged their achieved levels of skills in this field.

The implementation and improvement of a coaching leadership style can take place through a separate leadership development initiative or as part of a wider programme (e.g. a big leadership or culture change programme).

Clear distinction from internal coaches/the manager as coach of direct reports

There may be many pitfalls to avoid in the implementation and development of coaching leadership/management styles (e.g. poor analysis of needs, lack of quality of trainers, neglecting the cultural dimension, etc.). But clearly the biggest and most frequent pitfall organisations fall into here is a poor quality concept, and in particular the lack of understanding of the distinction between the coaching leadership/management style on the one hand and internal coaches/the manager as coach of direct reports on the other hand.

As a reminder, the leader/manager only applying a coaching style is not a coach. He or she keeps the hat of the leader/manager on at all times (i.e. the leader who is applying a coaching style still leads). All he or she does is integrate the coaching principles in their daily work. This is also why this leader/manager doesn't need to be trained as a professional coach, only in the coaching principles and skills.

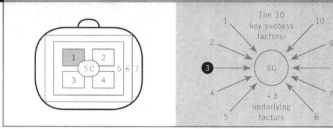

The internal coach and the manager as coach of direct reports (see above), in contrast, are coaches and need to abide by all rules that apply to professional one-to-one coaching.

It is crucial to understand this difference and, when implementing either of the mentioned coaching forms, also to communicate this clearly in the company. Unfortunately, this is often not done in organisations, which may result in high confusion, resistance, unsatisfying results and failures of coaching initiatives.

There are mainly three pitfall scenarios that are imaginable (and can be encountered in many organisations) that require prompt action from your side:

Scenario 1:

Coaching as a professional service and coaching as an integrated part of a leadership/management style are (totally) mixed up. There is no (or hardly any) awareness of the distinction at all in the organisation. The limits are highly blurred, and coaching isn't used properly. In this case, review your whole coaching programme and make sure the distinction gets well integrated into it and is communicated adequately in the company.

Scenario 2:

You do find a formal distinction (in terms of terminology) in the coaching programme between the coaching style and the professional coaching forms, but the two are still treated the same in terms of content and practice. One classic example to illustrate this is where the agendas of both trainings are exactly the same. The effect is that the trained managers/leaders are confused and overloaded with things that they will never or hardly use and, what's more, that prevent them from adopting a real coaching management/leadership style at their workplace. For example contracting in coaching, structures of longer coaching sessions, professional codes of ethics for coaches, etc. are issues primarily addressing coaches, not leaders/managers. In this case, change, amend and refine your coaching programme and make sure the characteristics of each single coaching form are properly reflected in their specific implementation.

Scenario 3:

There is a general understanding and awareness of the differences of the coaching forms in terms of content and practice, and this is also reflected in the specific coaching skills training agenda for managers/leaders, but the company does use misleading terminology. For example, terms like "leader as coach" or "manager as coach" to describe a coaching leadership/management style programme may raise wrong expectations in the company (e.g. in terms of levels of confidentiality given). Using more accurate terminology instead like "coaching skills training for managers/leaders" or "coaching leadership/management style training" can immediately build and restore full clarity and transparency and avoid any misunderstandings. So review your language and terminology at regular intervals and change it accordingly as needed.

Geographical focus: *Mediterranean country, Europe*

CASE STUDY 5	X-BANK, MEDITERRANEAN COUNTRY, EUROPE

Company: *X-Bank*
(company name changed/made anonymous)
(a full service commercial bank headquartered in the Mediterranean region with global subsidiaries, having won several awards)

Author: *Anonymous, Training and Development Department, HR Division, X-Bank*

Introducing coaching into our bank culture

In an attempt to further improve the focused training provided to managers in our bank, it was decided in mid-2006 to look into the possibility of introducing coaching as a means of management training and development. This led to the formulation of our strategic goal of 2007: Incorporating coaching as an integral part of the culture of the Group in order to support core principles of people management supported by the Group such as decentralization and empowerment, continuous individual growth and development and teamwork.

From this resulted the introduction of the following three key activities:

* Seminar for managers titled 'Principles of Coaching – Key to effective leadership'
* Enhancement of the role of Management Development Counselor
* Development and introduction of the X-Bank Coaching and Mentoring Network

Below is a detailed description of each of these elements as well as its impact on the achievement of the strategic objective that had been set.

1. 'Principles of Coaching – Key to effective leadership'

The purpose of the seminar is for managers to learn to implement a structured approach to coaching as part of their leadership style, so that they are in a better position to inspire others and encourage achievement of high levels of performance.

The coaching process used was that of Ken Blanchard. A member of our management training and development team was sent on the training for trainers program for this specific approach. After completion of the training, an internal seminar was formulated and implemented. It was delivered for the first time in late 2007. By the end of 2008, 50 managers had participated in it.

Currently the impact of the seminar is being assessed using a structured ROI approach. The results have been encouraging however without having the impact that we would have liked. Specifically, managers have become more participative in their management approach on the one hand with very positive impact on the overall performance of their team. They have also shown greater awareness and commitment to personal development activities, without however providing as much direct coaching as we would have liked. They feel strongly that they do not have enough opportunity to implement the structured coaching approach that they had learned.

2. Enhancement of the role of Management Development Counsellor

Managers that participate in the Management Development Centers are assigned a personal Management Development

Geographical focus: *Mediterranean country, Europe*

X-BANK CASE STUDY: *Introducing coaching into our bank culture*

Counsellor who has the responsibility to provide assistance with the creation and implementation of a personal development plan based on the findings of the Development Center.

This role was extended to also include the provision of coaching, so as to support and strengthen the development process. Individuals taking on this role were trained extensively in the coaching approach used and have been able to implement it with great success. Managers participating in the Development Center have reported that they have found the coaching provided by Counselors as extremely useful, often acting as a breakthrough to deeper self-awareness and focused action.

3. Development and introduction of the X-Bank Coaching and Mentoring Network

This Coaching and Mentoring Network is a complementary opportunity for development, going beyond on-the-job coaching offered by managers to members of their team as described above (see 1.).

The coaches and mentors of the network are executive level managers and key specialised personnel from the Training and Development department. The core goals of the network are:

* Increasing the quality and standard of performance of key staff members
* Provision of an alternative means of development of leadership talent
* Knowledge sharing within the Group
* Increased engagement of key management staff

Specifically, its aim is to provide coaching both in person and/or via long distance (e.g. telephone) to individuals with specific development needs in areas such as career planning, problem solving and change management.

The network was first implemented in 2009 and is still in its infancy. Although initial efforts have shown positive results, the main difficulty has been to get executive managers to commit sufficient time – and participate in formal coach training.

All the above activities are just the beginning of an effort that will continue to be at the core of our strategic objectives in the context of management training and development in the future.

Our key learning/Recommendation:

Always have a clear picture of where you want to go and the purpose of your endeavor. Ensure that key executives are fully aligned and committed to this journey. Measure, measure and measure again!

Questions and exercises for further reflection and to integrate practice and theory:

1. What is the business case for coaching in the company?
2. What kind of coaching forms have been implemented? And with what success?
3. What are the key differences between classic one-to-one coaching, the manager as coach of direct reports and a coaching management/leadership style (see 3.1.6. und 3.1.7.)?
4. Identify the problems that have occurred in the implementation of coaching. What might be the reasons for this? How could they overcome and solve these problems?
5. What is your key learning from this case study?

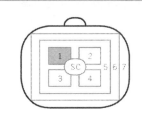
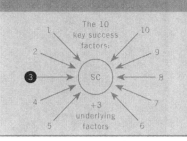

3.1.8. The coaching culture

is the form of coaching where people in the organisation naturally integrate the coaching principles into the way they are – their way of being – in the workplace.

It may apply to everyone in the firm and affect all communication and interaction in (and outside) a company – upwards, downwards and sideways. It is about developing a coaching attitude, a coaching mindset, a coaching way of communicating with and treating others in the organisation and beyond (e.g. customers). Coaching becomes the way business is done in a company (or in parts of it) – how things are perceived, approached and realized by its people.

In this way, classic coaching behaviours like active listening, effective questioning and giving and receiving learning feedback are increasingly ingrained into organisational life and facilitate empowering and connecting conversations throughout.

Coaching cultures may apply to potentially everyone and all contexts in the company. Therefore, they can have a much wider reach than the coaching leadership/management style set out above. The latter applies to leader and manager roles specifically, but, of course, also significantly shapes the way people are in the workplace. It is thus also very closely related to the coaching culture form and may constitute an important part of it.

With regard to the professional coaching forms, coaching cultures, like the coaching leadership/management style, are not to be seen as anything separate from normal work – they are fully ingrained in organisational life. People are not asked to be a coach and give formal coaching sessions on the basis of a coaching contract here, but simply integrate the coaching principles into their daily work. Having said this, any professional coaching form may be part of coaching culture initiatives. This is because you can see a coaching session facilitated by a professional coach also as a specific, separate space that gives the coachee explicit permission

and opportunity to live and practice a coaching culture. It is a useful laboratory and safe place to try out, experience, develop and internalize the coaching principles in a way that they can then be transferred to their daily work.

Likewise, self-coaching and peer coaching are included in the possible portfolio of elements in coaching culture programmes. In principle, it is possible to use any coaching form as a tool and means to build a coaching culture. This is simply because any coaching form, by its nature, is based on coaching principles and is an expression and ambassador of a coaching culture in some way or other.

Coaching is more than a simple external behaviour or superficial technique, it is (also) an attitude. Any coaching form lacking the link to this will miss a vital ingredient and may underachieve or fail.

In practice, bigger coaching culture programmes do typically include at least a number of different, if not all coaching forms. Which coaching intervention(s) to choose, will depend on the specific needs and situation of each company.

You can also turn it around and say: every implementation and improvement of whatever coaching form is already – deliberately envisaged or not – a kind of coaching culture initiative. It spreads and promotes the coaching principles among people in the organisation in some way.

Seeing it from this perspective, taking the cultural dimension into account is important for the successful use of any coaching form – all coaching forms require some kind of culture management/change in the end. For example, one key task of the HR or L&D manager, responsible for the implementation and improvement of 1:1 executive coaching in their firm, is to manage and support any culture change needed to allow coaching to thrive (e.g. towards a learning, no-blame culture among executives, towards a positive un-

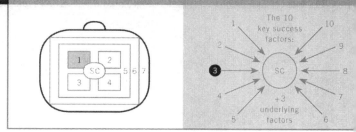

derstanding of coaching). This means building a supportive coaching culture in your organisation may be a precondition for your envisaged coaching programme.

To say it in different words: Even if you plan to implement only one of the other forms of coaching, you will also have some kind of a coaching culture plan to make coaching work in your organisation.

Coaching cultures are in fact more than a separate coaching form or level of implementation of coaching. The coaching culture approach may provide an integrated, comprehensive concept for coaching overall in the organisation, embracing all kinds of coaching forms. It may be seen as an overarching coaching umbrella, and it allows for excellence in the implementation and improvement of any coaching form in your company:

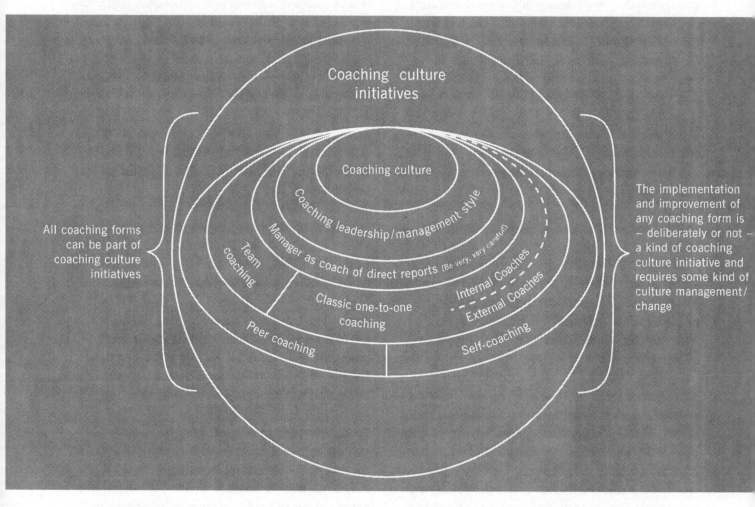

The coaching culture form lies at the heart of all coaching forms and is the most far-reaching coaching form. Creating a strong coaching culture throughout a company represents the highest possible level of organisational penetration of coaching with regard to people. At the same time, the coaching culture concept is highly adjustable and scalable, and coaching culture initiatives may have very different sizes and shapes.

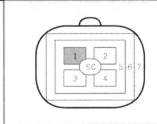
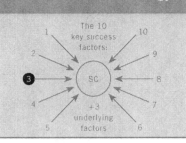

Within the discipline of building coaching cultures, there are three sub-forms worth mentioning here. These can also be seen as coaching forms in their own right and may stand alone:

The coaching communication style

is the form of coaching where employees naturally integrate the coaching principles and coaching techniques into their daily communication and interaction with others. What was said above in the context of developing a coaching leadership/management style, is also applicable here for every employee communicating with others.

The coaching attitude

is the form of coaching where people internalize coaching principles in such a way, that these become an integrated part of their attitude(s), be it in specific areas only or more generally. It is about inner thoughts and principles, rather than external behaviour and techniques, though of course, attitude always influences people's behaviour. So a coaching communication style, a coaching leadership style, or the ability of a professional coach to coach all need to have a coaching attitude as a driver. Attitudes may be very specific, though, one person may have various, very different attitudes on different points.

The coaching mindset (or coaching personality)

is the form of coaching where people naturally integrate and ingrain the coaching principle(s) into their overall mindset and personality. This goes one step deeper than attitude which, without a corresponding mindset, may still rather easily change and/or be replaced. With a coaching mindset, coaching really becomes part of a person's whole personality, his or her way of thinking and being. It shapes and characterizes a person's beliefs, values and overall mentality. You

may have different attitudes (which is always depending on topic and perspective), but only one mindset (which is about that state and structure of your mind, as it is). Coaching at this level thus gets even more integrated and rooted in people.

When people have (or develop) such a coaching mindset, they will, sooner or later, automatically demonstrate a coaching attitude and coaching behaviours (e.g. in communication, leadership, management) and thus be a true ambassador of a coaching culture. Where an increasing number of people in an organisation develop or have a coaching mindset, a corporate coaching culture may naturally emerge with positive effects on performance and the inner state of the company.

By integrating all coaching forms previously mentioned, we may refine and develop the basic model further and get a more advanced and complete version (see next page).

Besides being more comprehensive and precise, this model also better depicts and differentiates between the coaching forms that are in principle available to everyone and the forms that require professional coaches. The latter are marked in grey.

This advanced model focuses attention on the area where the biggest future potential of coaching is expected to lie: the coaching forms concerned with ingraining the coaching principles into organisational life (i.e. coaching culture, coaching mindset, coaching attitude, coaching communication style, coaching leadership/management style) is dedicated more space here.

Please note that "coaching in groups" as a coaching form in its own right is now included in the model. Also, the model more explicitly highlights the important point that the "manager as coach of direct reports" is just a very specific sub-form of professional, internal coaching: It shouldn't be implemented on a broader scale and should only be used very carefully.

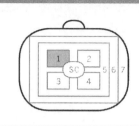

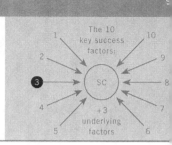

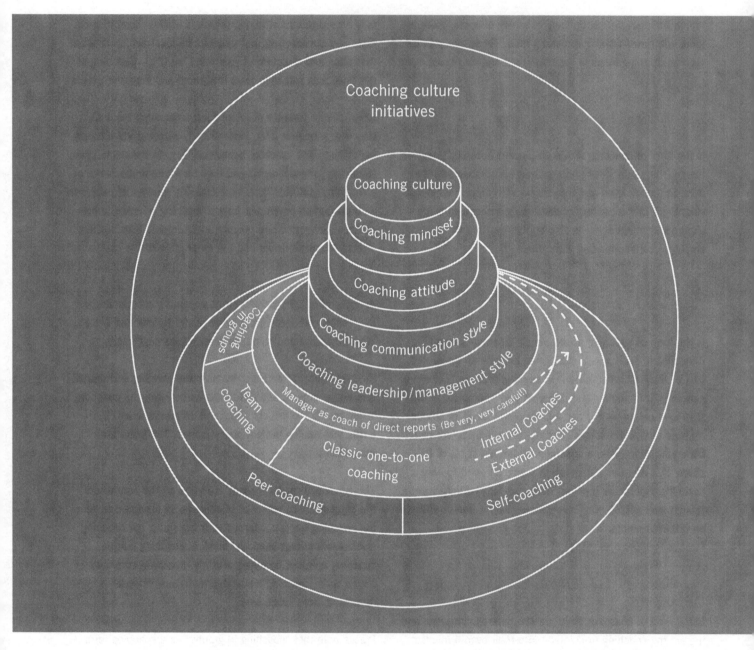

Figure: Detailed model on the various forms and levels of organisational coaching (regarding the people dimension) that may all be part of coaching culture initiatives

But what does a coaching culture actually mean in terms of content? – Quite similarly to the coaching leadership/management style above, there are also mainly three ways of understanding a coaching culture. These need to be distinguished very clearly, but complement each other very well:

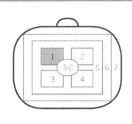

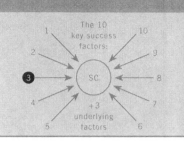

1. Dynamic appropriateness overall in the way of being (culture)

This is the broadest understanding of the coaching culture. It means an explicit choice from the wide range of existing ways of being (cultures/cultural elements) of the one(s) that are most suitable in each situation for each level: the individual, team, functional, business-unit and firm level.

This approach is an enabler of making the most appropriate choices around culture, rather than an upfront suggestion of a specific answer to which one is most suitable:

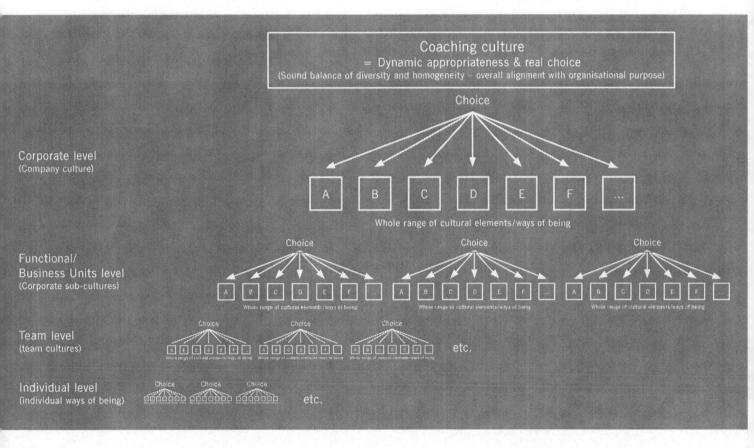

Here, the coaching culture embraces all existing ways of being and cultural elements as possible, equivalent options. It is a full acknowledgement and appreciation firstly of the enormous diversity of possible cultures/ways of being, secondly of the inherent, existing diversity and variety of cultures within one organisation (sub-cultures, etc.) and thirdly of the existing possibility to choose one's way of being and cultural orientation at least to some degree.

It is not possible to see choosing culture like selecting clothes or a specific tool to use or not in the moment, but there are areas that can evolve and thus can be changed. This is a highly evolving process, and it is about people's attitudes and mindsets. So any coaching culture needs to emerge and develop from within the people. In order to build sustainable coaching cultures, it is therefore necessary to have strong elements of co-creation. Having said that,

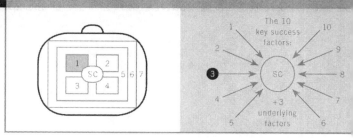

you *can* do a lot to encourage, foster and develop a certain cultural element or way of being among your people.

The choice of the most suitable cultures to develop will depend on your organisation-specific needs, your people's receptiveness and what is already there in your company. Work towards optimal, overall alignment of all cultures/ways of being with your organisational purpose and a balance between diversity and homogeneity. Too much homogeneity may lead to a lack of creativity and multi-perspective. Too much diversity may lead to a lack of mutual understanding and alignment. Go for a sound balance and optimal integration which also allows for great unity in diversity.

Instead of discussing very theoretically, whether and to what extent culture can be changed or not, let us just acknowledge that people and organisations may develop and evolve in their ways of being and cultural elements over time. There are areas that they may find quite easy to change, and there are other areas that they may find quite hard or even impossible to change. This is reflected in the following graph:

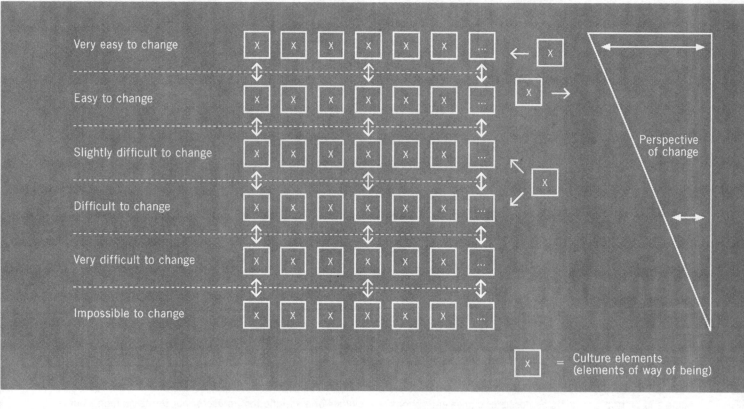

Please note that the limits between the levels and the elements included in each may evolve and change over time. The reasons for ease or difficulty of change may be a matter of ability and/or desire. If there is lack of ability, you need to provide skills and tools and the right conditions to enhance it. If it is a matter of desire, you need to take measures that increase the person's commitment to the envisaged change.

Any coaching culture programme needs to work around this. The more difficult something is to change, the more reduced the realistic perspective of change. You will need to find out

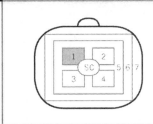

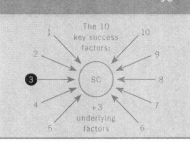

what kind of culture and ways to achieve it (e.g. balance of push and pull, support and challenge) are most appropriate for your company.

This understanding of a coaching culture already shows the impact of any coaching culture initiative on the whole system of an organisation. For example, if you only want to change the culture in a certain team, you need to think about what effect this has on the whole organisation, the business unit culture or the individual ways of being. Is this all compatible and consistent? Are there any friction points or resistance to expect that you need to address? And so on. Coaching culture initiatives do require systemic thinking.

2. *A recommendation for considering particular cultural elements*

This approach is an application of the above more general, dynamic appropriateness and suggests a response to the question of what cultural elements (elements of ways of being) are particularly worth considering given the contemporary challenges in business today. These may apply to the corporate, functional, business-unit, team and individual level alike. So here the coaching culture is a selection of best practice company culture elements considered to be particularly appropriate.

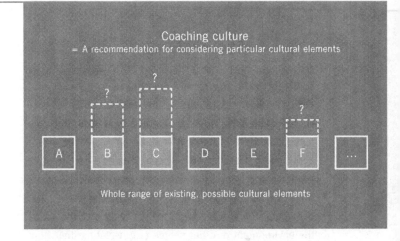

This understanding still embraces the whole portfolio of potential culture elements (ways of being), as all other culture aspects are still valid and may be highly appropriate depending on each case.

The coaching culture, approached in this way, can be seen as the currently favoured ideal business culture elements today. As already set out above in the context of the coaching leadership/management style, there are good reasons for this: Developing a coaching culture helps companies in particular to ...

- be versatile, adjust to changes very quickly and ensure high performance and optimal flexibility at the same time.
- develop and keep excellent interpersonal skills among the workforce.
- respond to increasing staff expectations and offer the best talent an attractive work environment.
- keep up-to-date and integrate the latest findings of learning and performance psychology.

Specifically, **the elements classically emphasized for consideration** are the **coaching principles**. In a coaching culture, these principles may become commonly shared and lived values within the organisation (or parts of it) and characterize its culture and inner state. The terminology and priorities of these and other elements, however, may differ according to the specific needs and situation of each company.

While the commonly found coaching principles have already been mentioned above, here are more detailed explanations on the meaning of each of them (except for the first three ones that were already covered in the coaching pyramid model in the introduction). The principles are presented in the order of their importance (top down):

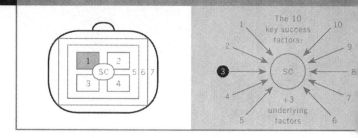

a. Core coaching principles

• **Dynamic appropriateness (and the process and practice of it)** (= what fits best where and how)

• **Integrating people, organisational and technology/ tools requirements**

• **Integrating external and internal requirements**

b. Basic coaching principles

• **High performance and excellence**
These are key orientations for any organisational activity. High Performance is performing at a high level, but excellence is more than this – it is about peak performance, about going the extra mile. It also implies a certain style, elegance and integrity in achieving performance. Organisations may be high performing, but where the employees burn out, or where the performance is done at the costs of the environment or other people (e.g. violating their human rights), this is not excellence. So excellence may be defined as the sustainable form of high/peak performance with integrity. (The coaching culture therefore definitely doesn't mean sugar-coating or "just about being nice to each other". In contrast, coaching cultures are about support and challenge together – and help accept and actively address even tough realities in a best possible, high-performing way.)

• **Growing people and performance alike**
It is a decisive factor for business success that the employees can grow – professionally and personally – in the workplace and also get adequate active support from the company in this regard.

• **Purpose, awareness, responsibility and self-belief**
Very generally speaking, purpose is about clarity in mission and goals, awareness about seeing and understanding reality, responsibility about identifying appropriate options and

making proper decisions, self-belief about commitment, the will and confidence in one's behaviour. For example, leadership and communication in the company may enhance these by active listening, asking high impact questions and giving and receiving effective learning feedback. But any style (e.g. also telling) may increase these as appropriate, depending on each case. These principles may affect everybody in the organisation.

c. Key coaching principles

• **Empowerment and ownership**
Employees in the organisation are asked to take on responsibility in their roles and to make their own decisions. Leaders should also work towards empowering their people to take responsibility and develop leadership skills themselves. As a result, often organisational structures may get flatter, i.e. less hierarchical. Having said this, the basic need for hierarchies in organisations to allow for effective decision-making and management is not put in question.

• **Self-directed and life-long learning**
Staff members are encouraged to develop solutions themselves and to understand their professional and personal development as a permanent, life-long learning process. This enables them to keep abreast of change and sustain and enhance their performance.

• **The learning organisation**
The company and its workforce are in a continuous learning process. This also implies that all its structures and working processes are more and more designed in such a way that the organisation constantly develops, learns and adjusts to the market requirements.

• **Trust, open communication and feedback**
An atmosphere of trust and openness in the organisation is desired. Learning feedback, whether positive or negative, is welcome throughout the company – upwards, downwards

www.frank-bresser-consulting.com

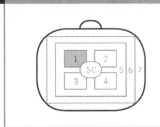
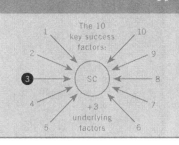

and sideways. It is seen as an opportunity for personal growth and performance improvement for everyone involved. This stands in contrast to 'traditional' approaches to feedback given only during performance reviews, which is often perceived as past-oriented criticism rather than future-oriented, constructive help and support. (Sometimes, in the coaching industry, you also find the term feedforward instead of feedback to emphasize this aspect.)

• **Daring to make mistakes/no blame culture**

Mistakes are considered as a natural part of any development and learning process. Often, it is only by failures, that we gain new insights and clues to improve our performance. Therefore, in order to ensure business success, employees are encouraged to seek new ways, accepting that mistakes are inevitable. Where mistakes are made, they are dealt with in an open, positive and constructive way. People still have to take responsibility for the mistakes they could have avoided (e.g. when they make the same mistake more often). For clarification, this principle is about encouragement to dare to make mistakes, not encouragement to actually make them.

• **Collaboration and information sharing**

Organisational success is by definition the result of people working together. In this spirit, a collaborative approach is encouraged within the company as well as in relation to customers and suppliers and, where appropriate, also to others operating in the same field. The performance principle, the principle of fair competition (internally as well as externally) as well as the principle of constructive controversy and criticism remain fully valid.

• **Mutual support and on-the-job staff development**

An atmosphere of mutual support in the company is key to success: line managers see one of their tasks as giving their co-workers good support and opportunities for on-the-job development. In a coaching culture, human resources development is not the exclusive task of the HR department (HR managers may the main champions, though), but is al-

so the responsibility of all levels and of everyone in the organisation.

• **Respect and seeing people in terms of their potential**

The way people see their co-workers is characterised by respect and the stance that in every single person may lie more potential. Everybody is given permission to be successful, have self-esteem and discover und unleash their full potential (i.e. to 'shine'). There is a sense of positive intent, joy and humour in the workplace, and diversity of people and their skills is seen as an asset to be leveraged.

d. Emerging coaching principles

• **Whole system approach**

The company and its environment are seen in a holistic way, as an integrated system. Accordingly, all working processes need to be integrated. Measures are not taken in isolation, but systemically, i.e. bearing in mind the whole system. Decision-makers are ready to acknowledge that everything is connected and take this interdependence into account.

• **Natural system approach**

Where possible and appropriate, leaders aim for organic development of the organisation. Processes can be initiated top down as well as bottom-up. There is an appreciation for authenticity and being natural. You find an explicit commitment and effort to create an organisational work environment where employees needn't hand in their personality at the entrance, but can be as they are in the workplace. It is not seen as a taboo to talk about one's emotions, intuition, inner voice, power, passion, wisdom and purpose of life or individual spirituality. People actively use all senses to understand situations and their complexity.

• **Sustainability and corporate social responsibility**

In planning for the long term success of a company, decision makers take into account environmental

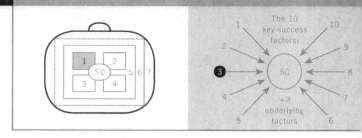

sustainability and corporate social responsibility. There is a commitment to contribute to the community and to help save the environment.

These are the principles that are especially worth considering as cultural elements for your firm. You may also choose not to give them particular importance.

The overriding principle remains dynamic appropriateness. So you need to consider all relevant cultural elements – for example any kind of tradition and/or cultural elements like command-and-control and high authority – as these may form part of the portfolio and are options that may have a significant role to play.

So in practice, the emphasis and level of adoption of the principles will differ significantly depending on each case. Companies clearly need to adjust their culture and behaviours according to their specific needs and situation. Within the organisation, you may have very different priorities regarding the principles depending on the function, business unit, team or individual. No principle is absolute, each value needs to be seen in context and appropriately balanced with other values.

3. *One specific type of culture (way of being)*

This is the narrowest understanding of a coaching culture. Here it means a specific culture (way of being) that has certain characteristics. It just represents one fixed type of culture among many possible ones, rather than an enabler of choice around culture at the meta-level.

Classically, the term coaching culture, in this understanding, is often used as synonymous with a company culture where listening, asking effective questions, delegating and giving and receiving learning feedback are dominant elements and displayed behaviours. So it is a specific culture that can be quite easily recognized from outside by an observer of people's behaviours.

It is also often used as a fixed term and synonym for a culture with a specific focus on one (or more) of the above prin-

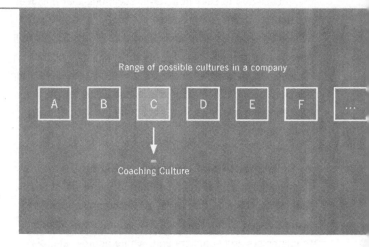

ciples (e.g. coaching culture = a trust culture/learning culture/feedback culture).

Therefore, when using this narrow understanding of a coaching culture, be aware that it is only part of the whole story in coaching.

It is important to distinguish the above three understandings of coaching cultures, as they represent different types of dynamic appropriateness. Actually, they complement each other very well (see next page).

www.frank-bresser-consulting.com

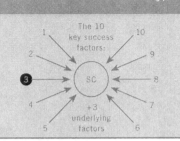

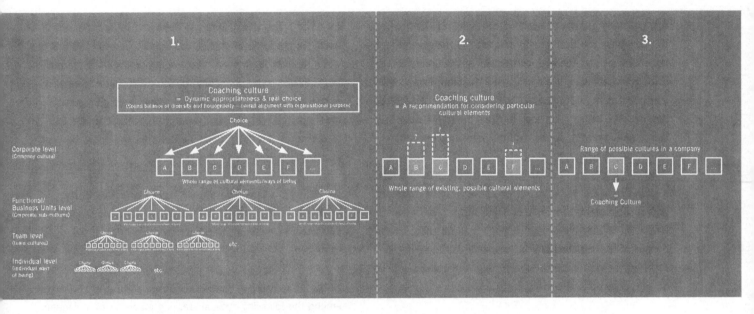

The first understanding is most dynamic and is an overall enabler of appropriateness and choice around culture at the various levels of a firm. The second is semi-dynamic and a recommendation for cultural elements that are seen as particularly worth considering in terms of dynamic appropriateness today. The third is a specific application, fixed and in itself not dynamic, but one option among many regarding culture – so you need to check when and where it is most appropriate (which leads you back to the first understanding).

In any case, always make sure you fully appreciate all existing cultural elements (ways of being). Do not stigmatise any cultural element or way of being, but leverage the potential. Coaching is about what best fits where and how, and all elements may have their role to play as and when appropriate.

The process of building a coaching culture

Developing coaching cultures is an **evolving process** that requires strong elements of co-creation in order to have a sustainable effect: As it concerns people's mindsets, it needs to emerge and develop from within the people, as each employee needs to make the decision whether or not to adopt a certain attitude. Therefore, there is a highly organic, interactive element here. However, you can do a lot to encourage, foster and develop a certain cultural element or way of being among your people.

Recall the full **complexity** of the issue of building a coaching culture that needs to be acknowledged: There are areas of culture that may be quite easy to change, and others that are quite hard or even impossible to change. The more difficult an area is to change, the more resistance you will encounter and the more limited the realistic perspective of change. Additionally, the areas may differ tremendously depending on each individual team, function and business unit in a company. Also bear in mind that small culture changes in small parts of the company may have an impact on the whole system.

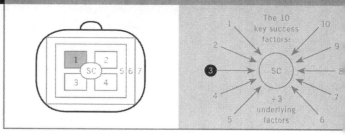

Any coaching culture programme needs to work around all this and have the flexibility to address the many existing uncertainties and the high complexity of the undertaking. Effective coaching culture initiatives therefore evolve and learn over time and will adapt to circumstances to achieve best results, rather than seek to force through a plan that is not well received. It is a **cyclical learning process.**

However, this doesn't mean that you should abandon having a plan. Key success factor 2 (see above: Have a systematic approach) clearly confirms this need. In fact, you need a long term strategy, you need a rough plan for the possible phases of the initiative and in particular you need detailed planning for the next time window (e.g. the upcoming phase). So yes, develop and communicate a plan.

However use it flexibly, don't emphasise planning at the expense of the process. Remain open for the process and

for what is actually required to make the initiative a success. Be prepared to change your plan, even fundamentally, when required by the new learning emerging from the process. Evaluate on an ongoing basis and respond to what is needed. Observe carefully and reflect emerging requirements instead of going through a bureaucratic preset list of measures. Creating coaching cultures is a lively, dynamic, evolving process.

Accordingly, a balance between **rigour and flexibility** of your coaching plan and its implementation is required. You need a systematic approach and flexibility at the same time.

Successful coaching culture initiatives are normally designed around the following cyclical learning process with a sequence of eight iterative stages each requiring thorough planning and management:

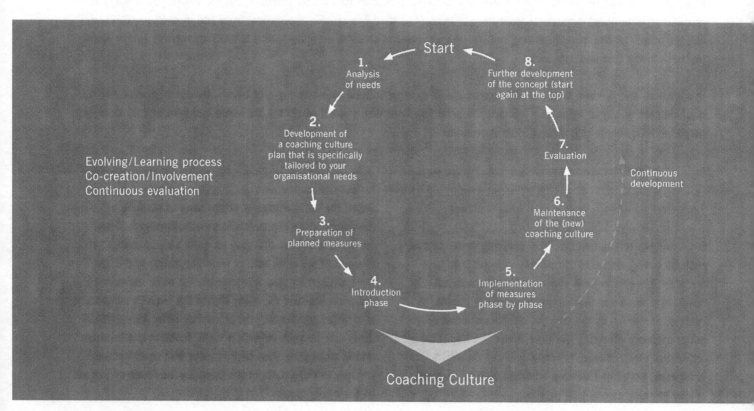

Figure: The 8-step-cycle for building coaching cultures

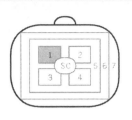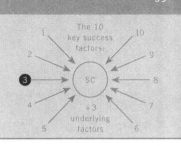

In order to develop a suitable company-specific coaching culture plan, you may work through the following **four key questions:**

a. For what purpose do you want to have or build a coaching culture in your company?
b. What kind/shape/form of coaching culture is needed in what context for your firm?
c. How to actually develop and achieve this kind of coaching culture?
d. What is the best way to evaluate the programme?

Also make sure you review these questions on a continuous basis.

What kind and degree of coaching culture actually needs to be developed by what means and at what pace in your company depends mainly on your organisation-specific needs, your people's receptiveness towards coaching and what is already there (i.e. where your organisation is already on its way towards a best fit culture).

During the whole process, think about keeping a **balance** between push and pull, support and challenge, being directive and non-directive, involving and determining. Too much direction may make people feel uncomfortable, manipulated and patronized. Too little direction may make people feel overstrained, confused and left alone. It is about continuously finding an optimal degree and mix of elements here.

For example, in order to enable people to find solutions for themselves, this may require an initial phase of input and direction from you. So identify the most appropriate level and degree of co-creation at any time: If it is most appropriate to let your people develop a complete coaching culture plan from scratch themselves, do this. If it is more suitable that you (as HR/L&D/OD manager or director responsible for coaching) develop the whole coaching culture plan yourself, do that.

In either case, asking for feedback on a continuous basis and also having a pilot upfront may help ensure the following programme will be a success. Generally speaking, the more uncertain things are, the more carefully you should proceed and the more feedback you should ask for in order to minimize uncertainty and make sure there is truly a good fit.

You need both the ability and the buy-in of your people to develop towards the envisaged coaching culture. Therefore provide them with the necessary tools, skills and conditions to enhance their ability and the support, information, incentive and business case to get their buy-in. Where you encounter resistance, deal with it constructively and learn from it.

There are some areas you can change, some areas you cannot change. The art is to know when to continue to try to change and when to stop. Assuming inflexibility too quickly will narrow the potential of your coaching culture initiative without good reason. Wrongly assuming change-ability, in turn, can mean you hit a dead end and generate resistance. Be aware that the way you proceed to effect the desired culture change will significantly determine and influence what you actually will be able to change or not. The more appropriate your approach, the more change may actually occur.

What may coaching culture programmes look like in more concrete terms? – **Possible designs for coaching culture initiatives** may range from massive long-term programmes aimed to build a complete coaching culture in a whole global company, to very small short-term programmes just introducing or reinforcing a certain coaching culture element in a little part of the organisation at a particular time.

In extreme cases, it may even happen that you have a coaching culture initiative where you do not even use the term "coaching culture" or "coaching" at all (at the beginning). Also, you may just use a coaching culture initiative to mitigate existing disadvantages of an existing company culture, rather than really going for a coaching culture.

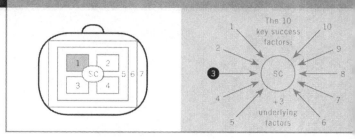

The kind of measures to be taken in coaching culture initiatives may vary enormously depending on each case. There is no exhaustive list of possible measures. What is appropriate may be included.

However, there are **classic types of possible measures:**

- Programmes around one, more or all of the previously mentioned people coaching forms: self-coaching; peer coaching; one-to-one coaching by external/ internal coaches; team coaching; coaching leadership/ management style; leader/manager as coach (with very limited scope only); coaching communication style; coaching attitude; coaching mindset
- Workshops (and other formats like board meetings) to discuss the existing and desired/needed culture, and/or develop a way to achieve a best fit culture (can explicitly refer to coaching terminology or not)
- Redesigning organisational processes and structures (e.g. decision-making processes, performance measurement systems, reward/appraisal systems, levels of hierarchy) in order to support the envisaged culture change
- Integrating coaching elements into already existing programmes (e.g. including more questioning techniques in traditional communication training)
- Other training on relevant topics like change, emotional intelligence (EQ), diversity, personal development, social skills, etc.
- Other, more informal means (e.g. spread the word, coaching success stories, networking, use of intranet and web 2.0; open days; events)
- Additional tools (e.g. mentoring programmes; 360 degree feedback, MBTI)
- Recruit/Bring in new employees with a coaching mindset
- etc.

The coaching culture is thus in no way a fixed, narrow concept, but a **dynamic, flexible and highly scalable** coaching form and level of coaching implementation. Depending on each case, you can set the objectives of your coaching culture initiative very narrowly or very broadly. The cultural focus may also differ and evolve over time tremendously. Equally in terms of scope, you can build a coaching culture in your entire business or at a specific level only, for a selected target group, in a certain business unit, division, department, area, group or team – these are then only 'pockets' or 'islands' of coaching cultures within a company. It is even possible to create simply little 'service islands' of coaching cultures that can be visited and used (e.g. peer coaching forums; one-to-one coaching offering; online coaching-culture forums).

Likewise, the coaching culture degree is flexible – you may start with developing a very low degree only and then enhance it as the process evolves. Equally, time (duration and pace) and budget are fully scalable. So are the means to achieve and maintain the culture.

When creating a coaching culture in your firm, you should make sure your coaching culture initiative already **role models** the change you want to see in the organisation and is a **living demonstration of coaching.**

You may, consciously or unconsciously, be caught in your company's culture and way of doing things yourself. This raises the question of how a person who is part of the system can still credibly and reliably bring about the needed change? This dilemma can, at least to a large part, be solved by contracting external consultancies which specialize in coaching in organisations and can bring in new, fresh perspectives from outside.

So as with most change initiatives, the change ideally starts with you. The higher your own coaching capacity and coaching implementation and improvement intelligence, the more credible and successful your coaching culture programme will be. Therefore, continuously work on yourself to be a good role model and living demonstration of the change and culture you want to see in your company. It is equally important to ensure that all other leaders and

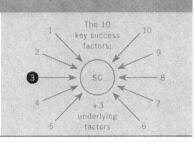

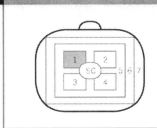

ambassadors responsible for and involved in the coaching culture initiative have appropriate qualifications and integrity to represent it credibly. Deciding who is responsible for building a coaching culture in an organisation and continuous

quality assurance are indeed key issues in any coaching culture initiative (also see key success factor 10: ensure high integrity and quality at all levels).

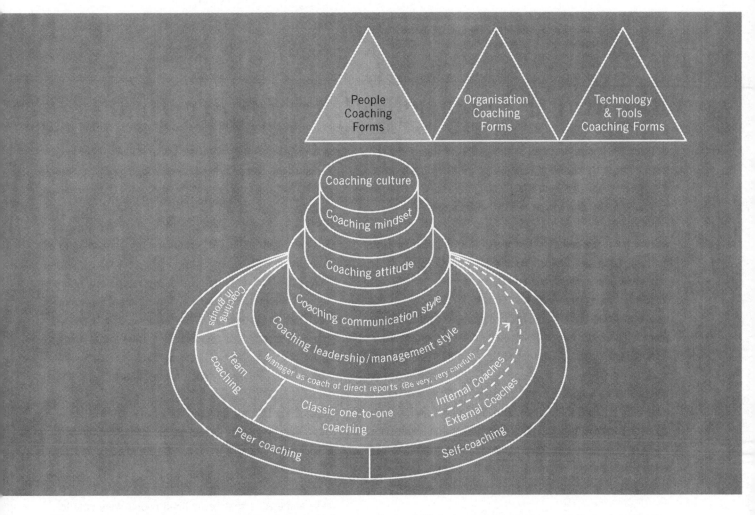

We have now looked at all people coaching forms, which are by far the most highly used and well-known coaching forms today. After the following two company case studies on coaching cultures, we will proceed to the next coaching group – the organisation coaching forms.

It is worth highlighting here that coaching can be infectious within a company, i.e. it may spread beyond the layer where

it was initially implemented. For example, an organisation that is implementing a massive classic one-to-one coaching programme may find after some time that a coaching leadership style and coaching culture has evolved in the organisation as a result of it. So, when implementing, improving and managing your coaching programme, also consider influencing the direction and control of this spread of coaching.

www.frank-bresser-consulting.com

Geographical focus: *Hong Kong & P.R. China*

CASE STUDY 6	X-OPTICS, HONG KONG & P.R. CHINA

Company: *X-Optics*

(company name changed/made anonymous)
(developer, producer and supplier of optical devices, with facilities in Hong Kong and P.R. China)

Main Author: *Anonymous, Chief Operating Officer (COO) X-Optics*

Co-author: *Charlie Lang, Managing Partner, Progress-U Limited*

Building a coaching culture for excellence

In 2006, X-Optics (founded in the late 90s) was in many ways a rather typical Hong Kong based company. Its founders, a number of siblings from Hong Kong, were veterans in the optical industry drawing on over 30 years experience each.

At that time, the company had about 200 employees based in Hong Kong and Shenzhen, and the growth in the first years had been strong. The management found that in order to sustain strong and profitable growth, X-Optics would need to aim at world-class standards in the way it operates and, more importantly, how it develops its most important asset – its people.

Most company employees are knowledge workers, and the management realized that for sustainable, optimal performance, it needed to maximize people's capabilities and engagement. In order to achieve this, they found they would need to develop a world-class corporate culture. Building a coaching culture was identified as the most appropriate approach.

Therefore, X-Optics searched for an external coaching company that would be able to assist them in transforming its culture accordingly – and found a suitable one with a proper mix of global expertise in coaching combined with a thorough understanding of the local culture.

X-Optics finally underwent the following steps to develop a coaching culture:

- A two-day workshop with the senior management team to redefine the company vision, mission, strategy, corporate values and the elements of the desired X-Optics coaching culture
- An internal image campaign with multiple activities to communicate the new direction and understanding to all employees
- Relocation and refurbishment of the Hong Kong office to support the culture change by this different environment
- 360 degree assessment (TrueProgress 360LS) and Harrison assessment (personality profile) for all managers at X-Optics
- Executive coaching for most managers at the 2nd and 3rd level
- A coaching training program for all managers to learn basic coaching skills (a two-day workshop for senior managers; a one-day workshop for supervisors and leaders of small teams)
- A recruitment workshop to improve the recruitment process and ensure that newly hired people were able to adopt and support the new, unique culture
- Modification of reward systems to reward wanted behaviours
- 1:1 executive coaching for selected new-joiners and ongoing 1:1 coaching for selected top talents to prepare them for more senior positions
- Wellness coaching & psychological counselling made available to senior managers

www.frank-bresser-consulting.com

Geographical focus: *Hong Kong & P.R. China*

X-OPTICS CASE STUDY: *Building a coaching culture for excellence*

* Encouragement of all employees to do charity work in the local community, with special focus on eye care services for the needy.

One of the challenges in implementing these measures was the fact that in traditional Chinese companies the leadership style is rather directive. So changing to a more coaching-oriented leadership style was at first difficult for the management. Also, the employees were initially somewhat resistant to take more ownership and responsibility. It was therefore important that the managers built trust and allowed a certain error tolerance (within boundaries). In addition, managers were encouraged to explain to their direct reports that, when these took more ownership, this fostered their development towards their desired next career level.

As a result of the measures taken, X-Optics noticed significant improvements in engagement levels and has developed a quite distinct culture over the past few years. In 2008, the company also received a prestigious HR Award for excellence in people management. Meanwhile, the firm size has grown to over 300 employees despite a difficult economical environment during the financial downturn.

In late 2009, X-Optics decided to launch the '2nd Wave' to further develop its culture. It includes the re-assessment (both 360 degree and personality assessments) of the senior management teams and targeted interventions like ...

* 1:1 executive coaching for the senior management team
* intensive coach training for two top executives (90 hours program)
* EQ training for selected senior managers
* 1:1 executive coaching for selected talents
* other specific interventions as appropriate

The expected outcomes of this '2nd Wave' are:
* Ensuring successful succession
* Preparing X-Optics for the next level of excellence
* Further strengthening the corporate coaching culture
* Stronger role models of coaching at the top management level
* Identification of new talents to ensure a healthy talent pipeline

X-Optics, though still a rather small player, stands out due to its rigorous attention to people development and uncompromising, continuous approach of building a coaching culture for excellence in order to deliver best services and innovations to its customers in Europe and North America.

Our key learning/Recommendation:
Developing coaching cultures may not only help large, but also smaller companies become world-class.

Questions and exercises for further reflection and to integrate practice and theory:

1. What is the business case for building a coaching culture in the company?
2. What coaching forms were implemented as part of the coaching culture initiative?
3. What other measures were taken as part of the initiative?
4. What are the benefits gained and the issues/problems encountered on the way?
5. What is your key learning from this case study?

Geographical focus: *United States (USA)*

CASE STUDY 7	NASA, USA

Company: *National Aeronautics and Space Administration (NASA)*

(U.S. Government aerospace agency engaging in space travel, scientific discovery, aeronautical advances and breakthrough technology development)

www.nasa.gov

Author: *Christine R. Williams*

Function: *Director, Systems Engineering Leadership Development (based in Washington, DC)*

How NASA Integrated Coaching Throughout the Learning Process

NASA, like many organizations, faces the challenge of ensuring a steady stream of qualified leaders ready and able to take on the challenges of the future. For NASA a key skill necessary for mission success is the chief systems engineer who works with thousands of complex technical and people variables and brings them together to achieve mission success.

In 2008, NASA leadership saw a number of factors shaping the Agency's ability to fill critical systems engineering leadership positions and decided to develop the Systems Engineering Leadership Development Program (SELDP) to accelerate the development of high-potential mid-level systems engineers. First-year results revealed an unprecedented 80 percent of participants transitioning into challenging positions that utilized their learning within four months of returning to their home centers. Within six months, 33 percent were promoted.

In studying the factors that led to this program's success a number of items were identified including the use of a variety of coaching methodologies. In SELDP coaching was ubiquitous and methodologies included:

• One-On-One Coaching: Each participant received one-on-one coaching from a master certified coach. As part of

this process coaches held discussions with participant's supervisors and mentors to ensure participants were insync with their management's needs and goals.

• Group Coaching: Coaches facilitated group coaching sessions during workshops where participants learned by observing each others' coaching interactions. One participant explained it this way: "Watching how others used their coach and how they were being coached, helped me see how I could more effectively improve my own coaching experience."

• Classroom Coaching: During program events and workshops consultants, coaches and program leaders provided in-the-moment observations and coaching.

• Peer Coaching: Participants were encouraged to observe each other and trained to give each other one-on-one peer coaching. This became an essential part of every classwide event which not only improved their feedback skills but caused some of the greatest shifts for participants. One participant noted: "Hearing the same feedback from my peers, really hit home. I realized that this was something I needed to act on."

www.frank-bresser-consulting.com

Geographical focus: *United States (USA)*

NASA CASE STUDY: *How NASA Integrated Coaching Throughout the Learning Process*

• Transition Coaching: Finally, participants were provided with an additional twelve hours of one-on-one coaching after they graduated from the program to help them effectively transition back to their organizations.

Great care was taken to develop a trusting and safe environment because in many cases coaching was performed in the classroom in front of the other participants so that the entire class could learn from the individual's experience and insight.

The coaching framework for SELDP was based on the results of a 360 degree assessment instrument that was specifically designed for NASA systems engineers by studying the behaviors that made highly skilled chief engineers successful. Because SELDP coaching was based on behaviors that were proven to work in the NASA culture, it gave the coaching process an added element of credibility with the participants, which led them to be more open to the coaching process. Along with creating this connection to the specific skills needed to be an effective systems engineering leader, another key cultural connection was made by selecting coaches who

understood and had experience working in the NASA environment. These alignments made participants more receptive to the coaching process. Participants were more willing to learn about themselves and make the changes necessary to achieve their goals. One participant who was highly skeptical about the coaching process in the beginning said, "I 'drank the Kool-Aid' and found out I liked it. Coaching has been a very beneficial learning experience."

In NASA we have found that coaching is more effective when it is not implemented as a standalone activity hidden behind closed doors, but actually becomes a way of communicating that is shared by all. Coaching is fully leveraged when it is an integrated part of the larger learning system.

Our key learning/Recommendation:
Coaching is more effective when it aligns with the culture and becomes a way of communicating that is shared by all. Coaching is fully leveraged when it is an integrated part of the larger learning system and organizational culture.

Questions and exercises for further reflection and to integrate practice and theory:

1. What is the business case for coaching in NASA?

2. What coaching forms were implemented? What are the benefits/outcomes?

3. How has the company succeeded in aligning the coaching programme with its culture?

4. What could the organisation do to further enhance coaching as a way of communication and as an integrated part of their learning and organisational culture?

5. What is your key learning from this case study?

www.frank-bresser-consulting.com

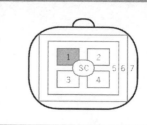

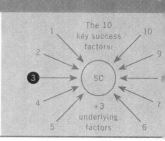

3.2. Organisation coaching forms

This category of coaching forms represents a particularly new discipline within the field of coaching and is still in its very infancy. The coaching industry and companies are right at the beginning of exploring and understanding this area.

Therefore, we can only introduce this new discipline and cover these coaching forms quite briefly and generally, rather than setting them out in great depth or giving sophisticated answers.

However, these forms are expected to gain more and more importance in the future. This section, only being a small part for now, may thus develop significantly and increase in size within the next years.

So what is this group of organisation coaching forms all about? – This new discipline is concerned with **the question of modern dynamic appropriateness of the organisational system as such, its structures, processes and operations.** Like people, also organisational entities show behaviours and have a kind of configuration and way of being. What is applicable to people in organisations, may therefore also be applicable to the organisational system as such (and/or to parts of it).

The organisation coaching forms are thus the discipline of putting organisational structures, processes and operations on the basis of modern, dynamic appropriateness. This new basis can be seen as more eclectic, proactive, pluralistic, dynamic, inclusive, differentiating and integrating than all previous and existing approaches to appropriateness and designing companies.

The organisation coaching forms invite you to identify and review existing assumptions around organisational design, have an open mind and seek optimal appropriateness in this area. What does really fit best where and how? How to bring organisation, people and technology & tools requirements

together in an optimal win-win way through organisational design? How to best integrate external and internal requirements through organisational structures etc.?

Consciously or unconsciously, most of the current organisational design is still largely based on conventional, traditional paradigms and dogmas. There is also still enormous rigidity, thinking within fixed boxes (rather than getting out of the box), thinking in terms of right and wrong (rather than in continuums), and assuming there is an absolute, final truth about the right design.

It may well be that you find the previous practice or the traditional approach is still the most suitable way – then definitely keep it! Dynamic appropriateness is first of all about real choice, rather than fostering a certain approach to organisational design.

Then, secondly, in this discipline you may find useful best practice recommendations for designing an organisation in order to best meet the contemporary challenges in business today.

Thirdly, you may also understand by an organisation coaching form only a specific option, a certain way of designing organisational structures (e.g. flat organisations, flexible processes). Be aware that this is then only part of the whole coaching story.

These three levels may complement each other very well.

In today's times, we need more than ever creativity, innovation and sophistication in designing effective, efficient and sustainable organisations. The organisation coaching forms acknowledge and build on the existing disciplines around organisational design, and put them on the footing of modern, dynamic appropriateness.

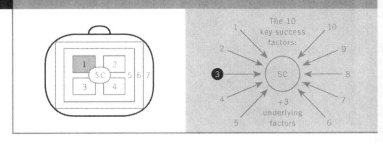

Here is an **overview of all main organisation coaching forms:**

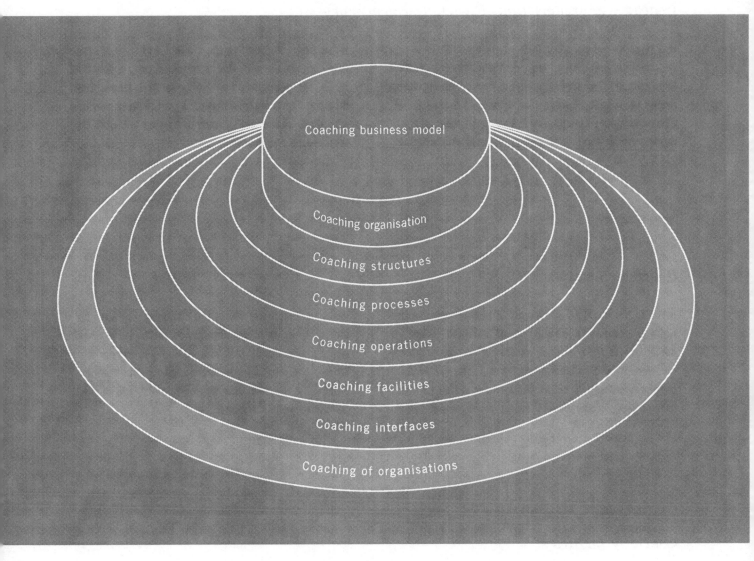

Figure: The various forms and levels of coaching regarding the organisational system

We will very briefly look at each of these possible sub-disciplines of coaching.

For clarification once again, it is your choice what is finally your definition of coaching and whether you want to use the term coaching in these areas (or dismiss it). The point here is to acknowledge that these coaching forms have already started to exist in some way and they do make sense to some organisations in some way. So for now, give it a chance: feel invited to consider seeing whole businesses and organisational systems and structures from a coaching perspective.

We will focus on asking more generic questions to open the discipline, rather than giving sophisticated answers.

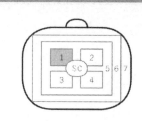

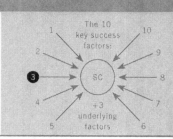

Coaching of organisations (Coaching consultancy)

is a professional coaching form where a professional coach or 'coaching consultant' supports the whole organisation (or a part of it) to achieve higher dynamic appropriateness overall or in specific areas. The difference to traditional, classic company consultancy is that it is based on the modern understanding of appropriateness which highly influences and modifies the content and style of consulting. It is comparable with the professional people coaching forms. For example, as an individual in 1:1 coaching, here the whole organisation (or a part of it) is provided with time, space and support to develop and work on their issues and goals.

Coaching interfaces

refers to the question of dynamic appropriateness in the way your company's links to outside stakeholders are designed – is there a coaching level of communication, involvement and collaboration? Consider, for example, sophisticated supply chain management systems (links to suppliers), customer relationship management systems (links to customers) where the customer may even be directly involved in developing new products, or corporate social responsibility programmes (links to the community). What is the most appropriate design for your company? What value may dynamic appropriateness add in the context of your interfaces?

Coaching facilities

is where your company facilities and offices are characterized by dynamic appropriateness: Are the geographical locations, their equipment and allocated tasks adequate? Are they flexible enough to adjust to changing market requirements? Are the workplaces ergonomically designed and appropriate for the people working in them? Are all needed technical communication devices available? Are the supply and delivery of goods, services and information suitably organised? What may dynamic appropriateness mean in the design of your facilities?

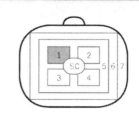

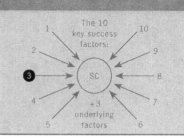

Coaching operations

is about ingraining dynamic appropriateness in your organisational operations. What could this discipline add to conventional questions of operations design and management? For example, it is concerned with going still deeper into issues like: How flexible or fixed should your production lines and service offerings be? What is the human element around your operations and how does this need to be reflected? What level of employee involvement is appropriate? How lean or bureaucratic should the operations be? What is the ideal balance of push and pull, of standardization and individual tailoring to best meet your people and customer needs? How intelligent, adaptive and adjustable is your system of operations?

Flexible working cells, mass customization, lean systems and fixed versus flexible line flows may be possible starting points for further discussions in this context. Get out of the box and rethink your operations from a more dynamic coaching perspective!

Coaching processes

is about the characteristic of dynamic appropriateness of your various processes. Beyond operational processes (see above), there are other important processes like decision-making processes and communication processes in the firm. Do these also properly include the coaching dimension? What difference may dynamically appropriate processes actually make when compared to classic process design? This question may lead you to explore more:

How intelligent, adaptable and adjustable are your processes? What mix of top down, bottom up and/or shared group decision-making is most suitable? What is the human factor in all this and how is this best reflected? How rigid and flexible should the processes be? What is the optimal balance of process reengineering and process improvement? To what extent does empowerment and employee involvement make sense? Think beyond the current status quo and dare to consider and explore new ways and to think innovation!

Coaching structures

refers to the question of dynamic appropriateness of your organisational structures. What value may it add in this context? Think out of the box and review in greater depth issues like:

How flat is ideally your organisation, what kind of hierarchy is most appropriate in your firm? How many layers do you need, and/or would a matrix structure be suitable? What is the human factor in all this and how does this need to be reflected? To what extent should your organisational structure be project-, product- and/or geographic-based? What is the balance between centralisation and decentralisation for your firm? Are there cross-functional teams? How flexible do your structures need to be? What role may the idea of 2.0 organisations, of virtual organisations, of loosely connected network organisations play in your firm? How intelligent, adaptive and adjustable are your structures? – Are these truly dynamically appropriate?

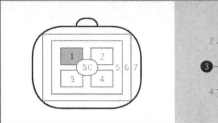

Coaching organisation

is about dynamic appropriateness as a characteristic of the whole organisational system (or parts of it). Think beyond conventional approaches and rethink organisations from a dynamic coaching perspective by digging deeper e.g. around the following questions:

What kind of system is most adequate? What are the most suitable structures, processes and operations and what does their proper integration mean? What is the most appropriate mission statement and strategy for a firm? What is the human element in all this and how does this need to be reflected? How authoritative, bureaucratic, mechanistic or organic, dynamic and flexible should the system be? What components and assets does the system need? What is the ideal size? What are the most adequate core competencies and competitive priorities? How temporary and permanent,

how flexible and specialized should the workforce be and have what other characteristics? What are the most suitable performance measurement, appraisal and evaluation and control systems for your company? How intelligent, adaptable and adjustable is your system?

Generally speaking, as a best practice recommendation given today's business challenges, there is classically a tendency to refrain from all too rigid systems of the past and adopt more flexible organisational structures, processes and operations. Likewise, there is a trend for more empowerment and flatter hierarchies. All this may help better respond to the volatility of the market and the diverse, changing needs of customers – and is thus in greater alignment with the spirit of dynamic appropriateness.

Coaching business model

is one step before organisational existence, where people come together to found a new company and base their decisions from scratch on the coaching principles. This may put the whole business on the fundament of dynamic appropriateness. Coaching thus may become the 'DNA' of the firm right from its birth. This may require new or more sophisticated answers to further questions like:

What is really a most suitable organisational purpose and mission statement? What is the most suitable legal form

for the organisation? What kind of owner structure is best needed (one or more owners, employee shares, etc.)? How can we/you best ensure that, at any time, the whole firm actually represents and embodies ...

- the process and practice of dynamic appropriateness
- the proper integration of business, people and technology & tools requirements
- the proper integration of external and internal requirements now and in the future?

www.frank-bresser-consulting.com

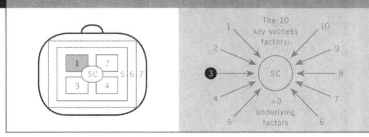

Relationship to the people coaching forms

While we clearly distinguish between people and organisation coaching forms at this stage, it is also evident that there is a high level of overlap and interconnection between the two. First of all, it is important to highlight that organisations actually are people: It is people who found, design, lead, manage, constitute, work for and dissolve organisations. But also, vice versa, organisational systems and their structures and processes may have enormous impact on people's behaviours and attitudes.

So people's mindset and the organisational system/structures are highly interdependent and mutually conditioning. As people may shape structure, also structure may shape people. It is an interactive, two-way process.

Where you want to develop a strong coaching mindset among your people, but don't accompany and support this with

suitable changes at the organisational structure level as well, your coaching initiative may quickly wither and become an empty shell and lip service only. So in order to implement coaching in companies properly, not only the people, but also the organisational structures and processes need to support and be in alignment with the coaching principles.

Vice versa, if you only change the organisational structure, but neglect the people side, change may also not happen either, as the structure may then not get accepted and be ignored or reversed. So both elements need to be taken into account in an integrated way.

We have now looked at all people and organisation coaching forms. We come to the third and last group, which also represents a rather new discipline within the field of coaching.

www.frank-bresser-consulting.com

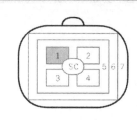

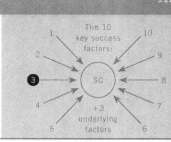

3.3. Technology & tools coaching forms

In order to achieve their organisational purpose, companies and their people make use of numerous tools and kinds of technology. (For example, this book, all frameworks included in it, and all presented coaching forms are tools.) In this context, the question of dynamic appropriateness is equally valid, raising issues like:

- What tools/technologies fit best where and how?
- To what extent can you revert to already existing tools/technologies or need to develop new ones?
- How appropriate is each tool/technology in each case?
- What degree of flexibility and adjustability of your tools/technologies is required?
- How effective and efficient are the technologies/tools actually?
- What is the human element in these, and how does this need to be reflected?
- How user-friendly are your tools/technologies?
- To what extent should it be possible for users to configure the tool/technology individually around their specific needs?

- What qualification and integrity do the users need, and what control mechanisms may be required?
- What are the limits of tools/technology, so that they truly add value and continue to serve the organisation and its people in a sustainable manner?

Coaching forms in this context are about the characteristic of dynamic appropriateness of your technologies and tools in use.

This includes two dimensions which complement each other: firstly the appropriateness of the technology or tool as such, and secondly the appropriateness of its use. This is an important aspect to be highlighted: The best tool may cause poor or even counterproductive results, if it is used in an inappropriate way.

Now, here is a short overview of the main technology & tools coaching forms:

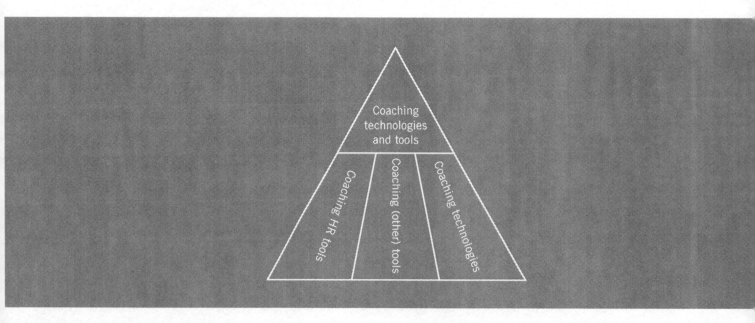

www.frank-bresser-consulting.com

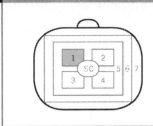
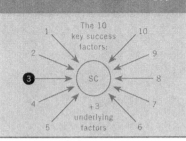

As all these forms represent a rather new discipline within coaching, we only outline and introduce these areas for your further consideration, rather than presenting detailed models and answers. However, they are expected to gain further importance in the future.

Coaching HR tools

is about ingraining dynamic appropriateness in the tools deployed in the field of human resources (e.g. all people coaching forms as set out above; psychometric tests; MBTI; 360 degree feedback; skills training; etc.).

Among other things, the proper use of these tools requires a realistic assessment of their validity and reliability. For example, where tools are aimed to give people self-awareness by giving a certain output (e.g. test results or profile results on the basis of a test, MBTI or feedback),

there needs to be an understanding that these results are not absolute, but can only be a basis for debate and self-reflection. They can be, but not necessarily are, the truth. So putting any tool and its results into proper perspective is important.

So what added value may dynamic appropriateness mean and create for the design and use of your HR tools? Think beyond classic conventions and assumptions – get out of the box!

Coaching (other) tools

is about designing and using a tool in a way that it is most appropriate for its purpose. Often, coaching tools are labelled with the prefix 'coaching', because they are more sophisticated, flexible, adaptable or customized than other more standardized, off-the-shelf solutions. However, the latter also have their role to play and can be most appropriate depending on each case.

Please note that the term 'tool' here may apply to specific as well as general tools/areas. Terms like 'coaching evaluation', 'coaching consulting' or 'coaching research' for

example may emphasize that these areas are understood and done in a (more) coaching way.

So put all kinds of tools on the basis of dynamic appropriateness. This new basis can be seen as more eclectic, proactive, pluralistic, dynamic, inclusive, differentiating, sophisticated and integrating than all previous approaches. So always ask yourself:

What kind of tool really fits best where and how?

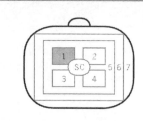 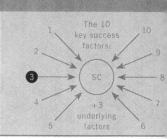

Coaching technologies

is about ingraining modern, dynamic appropriateness in the design and use of technology in your firm. Technologies represent an increasing, fundamental enabler and component of organisations today. IT, telecommunications, instruments, machines and devices may facilitate instant communication throughout a company worldwide, may streamline and adapt most complex processes and operations, and may open up new knowledge and network resources and ways of learning. At the same time, technologies also have their downsides and risks: Over-dependence on technology, ignoring the human factor, too complicated or expensive technology, all need to be avoided.

So what makes coaching technology different from classic technology? – Classic technology may be dynamically appropriate, this is not the point. It is rather about finding the optimal kind and use of technology that fits best in your context for your specific purposes. It means really putting technology on the basis of modern, dynamic appropriateness.

Often coaching technology is the label applied to those technologies that are particularly sophisticated, adaptable and intelligent (e.g. a programme, laptop or information portal that is especially user-friendly and can be fully customized to the individual needs of the user). This may especially be the case where there is a strong interactive and/ or human-like element (e.g. a voice asking questions and navigating the user through an issue; robots operating like human beings). Meanwhile, you also increasingly find coaching software in business that may coach a person to some degree and thus starts to replace real professional coaches.

In particular the new developments of the internet and mobile applications and the new social media provide unprecedented opportunities for possible coaching technologies.

Summary and closing note (Key success factor 3)

We have now looked at all three groups of coaching forms (regarding people, organisation and technology & tools) and the various coaching forms within each of them. This explanation was designed to give you a clear picture of the choices available to you when implementing or improving coaching in your organisation. It helps you choose the appropriate level of organisational penetration of coaching for your company. You may use one, more or all of the coaching forms.

Please note, that each single coaching form is able to build coaching capacity in your firm in some way or other. The various coaching forms only show different, possible entry points of coaching (dynamic appropriateness) into your company.

Equally, the groups of coaching show different sides of the same coin. Naturally there is a great overlap between the three dimensions, and each one will have immediate, direct impact on the other two in some way.

Here is the overview of all existing coaching forms and groups you may choose from (see next page):

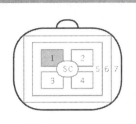

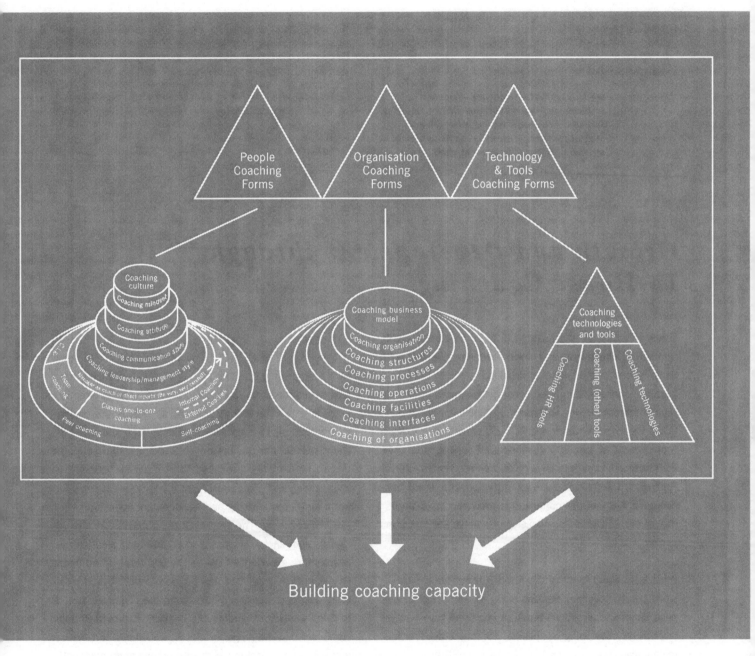

Building coaching capacity

Remember that coaching can be infectious within an organisation, i.e. it may spread beyond the layer and, also the group where it was initially implemented. For example, a company that is implementing a massive one-to-one coaching programme may find after some time that some degree of a coaching culture and more coaching structures have evolved in the organisation as a result of it. Thus in implementing and managing your coaching programme, you may also want to consider influencing the direction and control of this spread of coaching.

Geographical focus: *Ukraine, Europe*

CASE STUDY 8	BAKER TILLY UKRAINE

Company: *Baker Tilly Ukraine LLP*

(an independent Ukrainian professional services company offering audit and accounting services, as well as business valuation and advisory services since 1999; an independent member of Baker Tilly International)

www.bakertillyukraine.com

Author: *Irina Zinchenko*

Function: *Director of Marketing and PR, based in Kiev*

Growth and Development through In-House Coaching

Baker Tilly Ukraine was founded in 1999 as a small audit firm with 5 employees, and seven years later the firm was listed as one of the largest professional services firms in Ukraine, providing audit and consulting services for numerous businesses in key sectors of Ukraine's economy. Since 2006 the firm has continued its rapid growth, and today the firm consists of over 200 qualified staff serving more than 400 business clients in Ukraine as well as clients in Russia, Belarus, UK & Cyprus. Even going through the recent financial crisis the firm has continued to grow and maintain its role as one of Ukraine's premier professional services companies.

What has helped to make this rapid, successful and constant growth possible? Besides being driven by a clear business vision and ambitious business goals, we have focused strongly on developing our people. To do this the firm has mainly used internal resources and strengthened its own learning and development capacities.

How this idea of using internal resources for most effective staff development works out in practice, is illustrated in the following:

1. Knowledge sharing

As a fast growing business, the firm quickly realized that new employees with very good professional skills needed to know in depth the various practical aspects of the company's operations to maintain the existing high standards in client service. For this reason, in 2005, the firm created the first in-house program called "Sort it out for yourself? Help your colleagues!" This wasn't just a one-time training course, but a long-term learning and development opportunity in the spirit of coaching. The program's key purpose was sharing useful experiences, lessons learned and best practice between more experienced specialists and newly-hired employees. A critical aspect of this program was to touch upon every aspect of our firm's life – from the corporate culture to deep analytical studies. As needed, it provided and combined mini-trainings, seminars, workshops and focused mentoring and coaching work with groups and individuals.

Svetlana Vorobieva, professional auditor said about the program: "I joined the firm two years ago and was happy to start taking that program. It was an extremely useful learning opportunity. Now I can say that it helped me to avoid some

Geographical focus: *Ukraine, Europe*

BAKER TILLY UKRAINE CASE STUDY: *Growth and Development through In-House Coaching*

typical mistakes in my everyday work at the beginning. Every time I faced some difficulties working on an audit project I knew what to do. I could always rely on my mature colleagues, and now I am happy to help my younger colleagues".

2. Development of theme-specific coaching courses

For example, in 2005 Baker Tilly Ukraine provided audit services in connection with the first IPO (Initial Public Stock Offering) of an Ukrainian company, requiring audited financial statements prepared under IFRS (= International Financial Reporting Standards). Based on the experience gained working on this IPO, the partners and top managers of our firm designed and delivered a special in-house coaching course specifically covering all aspects of IFRS. About 20 specialists attended the course. As a result the firm has developed a core group of knowledgeable and pragmatic specialists to implement additional IPO projects. Today, Baker Tilly Ukraine is recognized as one of the leading Ukrainian audit firms with extensive IPO experience.

More recently, in May 2008 we designed and implemented an Induction Course on the basis of our firm's business needs and our experience gained from the "Sort It Out Yourself? Help your colleagues!" program. Its aim was not only to train new employees, but also to improve employees' professional skills and, most importantly, to encourage communication within the firm's team. The Induction Course is a five-day coaching program consisting of three main units that focus on the interrelated aspects of general information, professional best practice, and corporate communications (communication standards, team-building). After one year of enthusiastic and co-operative work by many people – ranging from top managers to entry-level accountants – the Induction Course, delivered annually, has become a well-structured and advanced in-house coaching program.

3. Establishing an Educational Center and Coaching Unit

The experience of delivering the Induction Course for our own staff led us to create a separate Center. Its services would be available to Baker Tilly Ukraine's staff as well as to its clients and counterparts. This resource could be mutually beneficial to both the firm as well as its clients.

The Baker Tilly Ukraine Coaching Unit will improve the confidence of the client and, in turn, the firm will understand better the client's needs and problems. Combining up-to-date solutions as well as examples from educational institutions and elsewhere, Baker Tilly Ukraine has succeeded in developing a scheme that allows the firm to propose unique coaching solutions to each of its clients that will be consistent with their business requirements.

Conclusion

Baker Tilly Ukraine recognizes the value of coaching as an important means of improving both client services and professional development of its staff. In addition, as recent experience in particular shows, it also helps the firm work more efficiently.

It is well known that – because of the financial crisis – some companies in Ukraine had to decrease their budgets for training and professional development. In spite of the financial crisis, Baker Tilly Ukraine has chosen to augment its internal coaching and professional development activities. This decision has allowed Baker Tilly Ukraine to reduce costs for external educational programs and, instead, channel these funds to enrich internal Learning & Development practices, as well as to share professional knowledge and experience with its clients.

Geographical focus: *Ukraine, Europe*

BAKER TILLY UKRAINE CASE STUDY: *Growth and Development through In-House Coaching*

Baker Tilly Ukraine's internal coaching approaches have given the firm an opportunity to use its own experience, knowledge and resources in order to develop new lines of business.

Our key learning/Recommendation:
Always think of ways to use your internal resources more effectively in order to improve both client services and the professional development of your staff through in-house coaching programs.

Questions and exercises for further reflection and to integrate practice and theory:

1. What is the business case for coaching in the company?

2. What kind of coaching forms were implemented? What are the outcomes?

3. What coaching dimensions (people/organisation/technology & tools) do these coaching forms represent?

4. What are the advantages of such in-house (versus external) coaching programmes? What are the risks?

5. What is your key learning from this case study?

www.frank-bresser-consulting.com

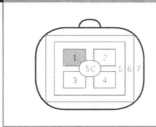 

INVOLVE THE TOP

Two major aspects come into play in this context:

4.1. Get the support of top management

One critical success factor for the implementation and improvement of a coaching programme is public affirmation from the top. This is to ensure the necessary organisational support and resources for the coaching initiative as well as strategic consistency throughout the organisation. It enhances the credibility of the whole coaching programme, simply makes things much easier, and is a good foundation for enlarging the coaching programme further in the future as and when required.

The importance of getting support from the top increases, the ...
... more massive the coaching programme is/becomes.
... the more the coaching initiative affects business strategy.
... the higher the envisaged level of penetration of coaching is.

However, localised, autonomous coaching programmes may not always require explicit endorsement. Top management may also give implicit or indirect consent to coaching measures at first. This is classically the case, where the board provides the HR or L&D department with a general budget to take measures as appropriate. Then, within the latitude and responsibility exercised by the HR or L&D department, the latter makes use of coaching. Here, the top may not have expressed a real commitment to coaching specifically, and yet coaching happens in the organisation and is indirectly affirmed by the top.

Exactly this situation is still common in a number of organisations today. Typically such coaching initiatives without the explicit support of the top remain limited, i.e. they are not that widespread in the organisation, or are not sustainable.

When the HR/L&D/OD department wants to use coaching beyond the limits of this weak, implicit support by the top, they will inevitably need to seek their explicit consent. At that point, they may realize they should have started to raise awareness of coaching at Board level much earlier. So do not wait, start with it immediately in your company.

Ways of enhancing the support of the top

Possible ways of building top management support are ...

- position yourself as a strategic business partner of the top helping it build capability to achieve business success

- develop a high-quality, organisation-specific coaching plan exactly meeting the company needs

- lobby for coaching up to the board level (e.g. raise awareness of coaching; communicate its benefits; find one – or more – advocates of coaching within the boardroom itself, sometimes an HR or L&D representative is already a board member; ideally you also find a strong advocate outside HR/L&D)

- integrate coaching in HR/L&D/OD measures for the top management (e.g. top executive coaching; inviting an outstanding key figure from the coaching field to make a short, high impact presentation to the board)

- continuously demonstrate the real benefits and outcomes of the company's existing coaching programmes to the top

- create a strong success story, which acts as a role model, argument and business case for coaching,

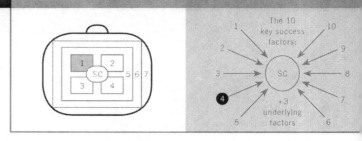

- use coaching pro-actively and with self-confidence within the responsibility of the HR/L&D/OD function and take the same approach with the board: don't hide yourself, but be bold and act as a strong partner to the board. You are the one(s) who can and should recommend making coaching an explicit top management issue, as and when appropriate.

- sell coaching in appropriate language (e.g. in your communication adjust your focus and language to top management requirements; evaluate and demonstrate tangible – financial and other relevant – business benefits of coaching; establish clear links between coaching initiatives and the current top management strategy and objectives; show that you have the business objectives in mind)

Take into consideration that the level of support by the top may sometimes be subject to high volatility, depending on the concrete situation of your company and current priorities and policies of the board (e.g. change of CEO; sudden situation of crisis). Top management enthusiasm for or aversion to coaching may sometimes go as quickly as it came. On the one hand, adjust your coaching programme to these circumstances. On the other hand, build in resilience and make sure there is enough continuity to allow the coaching initiative to thrive.

The degree to which you may get support from the top, also depends on the overall acceptance and standing of HR/L&D/OD in your company. Where, for example, people development is generally neglected and hardly taken seriously by the board, you are unlikely to get strong support for coaching specifically. However, where the top considers HR/L&D as crucial for business success and as a key driver to gain and maintain competitive advantage, gaining support will be easier.

As a final note, getting the support of the middle and lower levels in the organisation is also very important. However, the support from the top is particularly vital for the sustainable success of coaching programmes.

4.2. Begin with the implementation at the top

It is highly recommended to start the implementation of coaching from the top – with the top managers making effective use of coaching forms themselves and thereby becoming role models and a living demonstration of coaching for the whole organisation.

Such a top-down approach gives your coaching measures much greater credibility and authority in the firm right from the beginning and increases their appeal, making it likely that others will copy.

This significantly helps create an overall positive learning atmosphere in the whole organisation, ideal to help coaching thrive. This is increasingly important...
… the more massive the coaching programme is/becomes.
… the higher the envisaged level of penetration of coaching is.
… the more the coaching initiative affects the whole organisation.

Where the commitment is insufficient to involve the top directly, you may also – under certain circumstances – consider starting implementation at the middle and/or lower level first.

However, this may only work well, if the coaching programme ...
… is rather limited in its scope and size
… means a low level of penetration of coaching
… has at least the general (implicit) support by the top.

Therefore, your job as an HR, L&D or OD manager in the field of coaching is sometimes this: doing the right groundwork at the lower levels first to give the top the right arguments to pick up coaching for themselves and then support it on a broader scale. Having gained their explicit commitment in that way, you can then start to implement coaching at the top level as well and involve them directly (= bottom-up approach). Implementing coaching from the bottom-up is not impossible, but is likely to be slower and more limited in scope, until you can achieve the top level commitment.

Geographical focus: *Austria, Croatia, Slovakia*

CASE STUDY 9	WÜSTENROT, AUSTRIA

Company: *Wüstenrot Group Austria*

(The core businesses are savings, mortgages and insurance.)

www.wuestenrot.at

Author: *Andreas Wieland*

Function: *Manager of the organizational and personal development department (based in Salzburg)*

Certificate Coaching Program drives cultural change at Wüstenrot

Coaching background at Wüstenrot

Until four years ago, coaching at Wüstenrot was still very individual and informal. Some employees with good relationships with the HR staff received coaching in a very unstructured way. In particular, new sales reps had three obligatory one-to-one meetings with a trainer to reflect on their sales progress. In some critical cases the HR department arranged for an external coach. The skills of the coaches were very varied. We had no quality standards and no explicit coaching process.

Change drivers

The inconsistent practice, the idea to offer a high quality qualification program for successful managers and trainers and the personal energy of opinion leaders to improve their coaching competence were the main reasons for the change initiative in 2007.

Change strategy

How did we design the change process?

In 2006 we hosted a coaching conference with participants from Wüstenrot and a panel of famous experts (business

leaders, HR managers, professional coaches). The participants were corporate opinion-leaders with the personal goal of improving their leadership and/or coaching competence. First, the experts gave a short presentation about their own coaching experiences and how they benefited from it. Then the participants had the opportunity to discuss different coaching aspects with the panel in small work groups. The intimate nature of the groups provided the participants with new insights and motivation to improve their coaching competence.

The result was that 30 conference participants requested our foundation coaching program, newly developed by Wüstenrot in that period. This program contained 120 hours of training, ten hours of literature study and twelve hours with peer groups. It focussed on enabling managers to improve their effectiveness and communication behaviours by using coaching tools, rather than on training them as professional coaches. (We were aware of and took into account that many theories stated managers couldn't be coaches due to risks of role conflicts and role confusion.) Our underlying objective was to build up a strong coaching network at Wüstenrot.

In addition, we designed and offered an advanced level course with 54 hours of training, ten hours of personal

Geographical focus: *Austria, Croatia, Slovakia*

WÜSTENROT CASE STUDY: *Certificate Coaching Program drives cultural change at Wüstenrot*

coaching and ten hours of case reflection, designed for 12 participants. At the end of this course, we organized an external exam by the Austrian Coaching Council including a live coaching session and a discussion on two completed coaching processes. This course allowed participants to become certified internal coaches. It was soon very clear that you could only pass the exam if you had coaching cases. Therefore the participants had to market coaching and themselves in their work environment. These activities were supported by an internal coaching guide, a coaching centre on the intranet and articles in the company journal.

Participation in the whole coaching program was exclusive, so we had extremely successful managers and trainers on board. This was instrumental in attracting top candidates, when we offered the third round in 2009: Three top executives were among the 17 participants.

Where are we today? – Our results

Many managers had the opportunity to obtain high level coaching tools and get a clear view of the effectiveness of coaching. This enabled them to improve their leadership qualities, particularly in the area of delegation and developing their employees on the job. In addition, they recommended new coaching clients to the personal development department.

In the last three years we've had more than 100 coaching cases at Wüstenrot with a consistent coaching procedure. Twelve colleagues passed the course exam and now work as professional coaches. New coaching contracts are established weekly. The community of coaches organize peer groups and supervision.

Currently, the third group is underway and we already have people interested in the fourth course starting at the end of

2010. We find that the demand in the sales area is higher than in the administrative departments. There is a broad range of topics for coaching:

- Professional role behaviour
- Personal barriers at work
- Career planning
- Work life balance
- Customer-orientation

Embedding coaching more in our organization

In the future it will be necessary to strengthen the structural roots of our coaching approach. Three aspects are essential:

- The development plans for new employees and colleagues in a new job should include the option of receiving coaching. New employees have a lot of challenges and can benefit from working with a qualified coach. This experience may also lead to a higher acceptance of coaching in our company.

- The qualification as a coach must be an ongoing process. New coaching methods and tools should be taught and two annual reviews must be the standard. Otherwise our high quality approach will deteriorate. International cultural aspects should be considered with regard to the Croatian and Slovakian participants, so that the coaching concept gets customized to these nations.

- The number of executive coaching cases is an indicator of how successful coaching is as part of the company's culture. How do we get the executives interested? Coaching is a very intimate matter. Therefore a lot of personal and cultural barriers exist. Top executives prefer to learn individually, in a very confidential atmosphere and in a flexible

Geographical focus: *Austria, Croatia, Slovakia*

WÜSTENROT CASE STUDY: *Certificate Coaching Program drives cultural change at Wüstenrot*

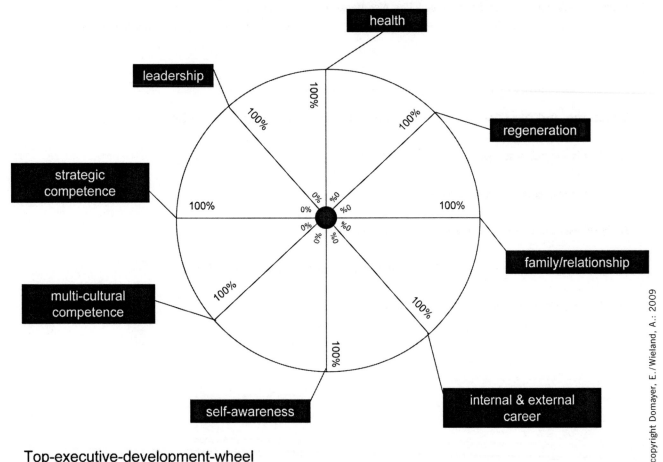

copyright Domayer, E./Wieland, A.: 2009

Top-executive-development-wheel

setting. One way we meet these needs is by using our top-executive-development-wheel for self assessment, which easily builds the bridge to coaching.

Each item of the wheel contains specific questions to get a self assessment of one's strengths and weaknesses. To give an example, the questions on self-awareness are:

• I take periodical time-outs to reflect on my company.

• I discuss my reflection results with my close colleagues and subordinates.

• I ask for feedback on my personal behaviour and performance, and change as needed.

• I can handle my emotions. I maintain composure.

We ask our executives to discuss their results with their life partner to get honest feedback. The fact that we published the top-executive-development-wheel in an independent

Geographical focus: *Austria, Croatia, Slovakia*

WÜSTENROT CASE STUDY: *Certificate Coaching Program drives cultural change at Wüstenrot*

magazine gave our approach further credibility. Also because of this, coaching will continue to be top-of-mind for our executives.

Our key learning/Recommendation:
Think of coaching as part of your long-term strategic plans!

Questions and exercises for further reflection and to integrate practice and theory:

1. What is the business case for coaching at Wüstenrot?

2. What coaching forms were implemented?

3. How does the company ensure high quality in coaching?

4. In what ways has the programme fostered the support from and involvement of the top?

5. What is your key learning from this case study?

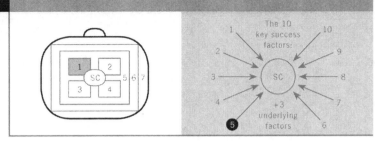

PROMOTE COACHING AS A POSITIVE DEVELOPMENTAL TOOL

This success factor includes two major aspects:

5.1. Coaching for excellence

Coaching is about high performance and excellence, about optimal dynamic appropriateness and it's important to make sure people understand that. Whatever level of performance people are currently at, coaching is potentially able to add value – to weak as well as to peak performers. For example, it may empower all kinds of people by facilitating self-directed learning, personal growth and significant performance improvement in the workplace.

When you encounter opinions saying that coaching is just remedial, only a tool for weak performers or people with personal problems, a form of therapy and not a business tool, it is your responsibility to position coaching more accurately and positively. Educate people on coaching and identify the underlying beliefs and attitudes in your company that you may need to address. We've found that exactly these kinds of views are often still present or sometimes even predominant in a number of organisations today.

Ask this question: what is the current, prevalent view on coaching in your company today? What kind of reservations may need to be overcome to make coaching thrive? Be honest with yourself as well: what is your own view and attitude on coaching?

By credibly and genuinely using coaching as a positive, developmental business tool for high performance and dynamic appropriateness, you can make the best use of it and leverage its full potential for your firm. You then have the best chance to disprove and overcome any opposing views and reservations about coaching that may exist in your company.

Such a 'coaching for excellence' approach enables you to produce optimal commitment and readiness for coaching in your organisation and therefore achieve quality results. This approach encourages people to perceive and experience coaching as a positive incentive provided by their company.

In contrast, defining coaching as remedial by nature is rather misleading and will deter people from making (more beneficial) use of coaching. It will immediately limit the potential of coaching, and confirm existing false reservations. This, in turn, may at worst lead to situations where employees are afraid of coaching, feel ashamed when they use it, and/or feel highly manipulated. Once coaching gets a negative image and reputation in a company, it is very difficult to change it.

5.2. Branding and marketing

The aim is for your promotion of coaching in your company to build a truly positive reputation for your coaching programme from the very beginning.

In this context, a good coaching concept is not enough, you also need to be pro-active and bold in your communications and offering. While doing this, use accurate language avoiding exaggeration (e.g. be careful about using superlatives), and do not fall into a selling mode that may alienate people. The point is: if you have something really valuable and attractive to offer, don't hide it – show it.

To achieve this, consider developing a quality in-house coaching brochure or intranet site and coaching logo specifically designed for your company coaching programme. Offer interesting, accessible presentations and open door events. Let your branding and marketing be a living demonstration of your own positive coaching approach.

Geographical focus: *Uganda*

CASE STUDY 10	MTN UGANDA

Company: *MTN Uganda*

(leading telecommunications company in Uganda – providing payphone, fixed lines, fax/data, internet and mobile services)

www.mtn.co.ug

Author: *Solomy Luyombo*

Function: *Human Resources, based in Kampala*

Coaching for Performance – the Case for MTN Uganda

Ever since its inception, MTN Uganda has consistently and steadily grown and consequently undergone significant transformations over the years to become the leading brand in the telecom industry in Uganda. The company's strategy to achieve and sustain its top position in the telecommunication industry is centred on integrating the Leadership and Talent Management (LTM) program in its strategic objectives. Through this program, MTN Uganda has demonstrated its commitment to continuously improve its leadership and has equipped its managers with the necessary soft skills to effectively lead and produce results. Coaching and mentoring have been adopted as pivotal initiatives in the implementation of the LTM program in MTN Uganda.

Drivers of the coaching initiative

Owing to the strong competitive environment within the telecommunications industry in Uganda, MTN Uganda had to develop employee value propositions that did not necessarily relate to pay but would enhance staff performance and retention. Employee coaching was identified as one of those initiatives that would enable managers/supervisors to appreciate their staff challenges and begin not only to drive for results, but also provide their people with support to better understand their roles and deliver on expectations.

In particular, we found that the middle level positions were filled by technical experts requiring better soft skills for leadership. Some managers lacked leadership exposure, while others were applying the boss/subordinate management style which was frustrating and demotivating young and enthusiastic employees. There was a need to get these managers to consider their direct reports as partners with whom to work together to achieve strategic and departmental objectives. As a result, we designed and implemented the Coaching for Performance Program to bridge this gap.

It is worth mentioning here, that our senior managers – Heads of departments in MTN Uganda – were not included in the target group of this Coaching for Performance Program. For these, we have developed a different approach: They complete a 360 feedback assessment with their peers, subordinates and clients (if they work together closely) and may have an external expert coach contracted to discuss the results, provide feedback and formulate/address further areas of improvement.

Designing and implementing the "Coaching for Performance" Program

We first conducted an organizational analysis to identify, among other things, the possible factors that could impede

Geographical focus: *Uganda*

MTN UGANDA CASE STUDY: *Coaching for Performance – the Case for MTN Uganda*

the successful implementation of such a program. All people participating in the program were involved in the analysis. The results were taken into account in the design:

* Founders syndrome ("I have been here longer than you")
* Superiority complex
* Heavy workloads that would not allow for managers to create time for coaching
* Lack of support by top management to have coaching adopted as a culture.
* Big numbers of direct reports
* Difficult managers that cannot coach effectively
* Procrastination

Then we had a pilot coach training for the first 25 managers provided by a local consulting firm that we partnered with. The training aims were to enable the managers to adopt a coaching leadership style towards their people on the one hand, and to coach individuals in a 1:1 setting on the other hand. In order to experience and assess the various roles that coaching may play in improving staff performance, each trainee was asked to coach two employees – one whose performance did not meet the performance expectations, and one whose performance met the required standards and should definitely be maintained.

Supervised coaching sessions took place to evaluate the level of coaching skills acquired by the managers: An external expert coach joined a coaching session and observed how the coach (i.e. MTN manager) conducted it. At its end, the expert coach gave the manager feedback on the skills requiring improvement and the areas where he or she was doing well.

Our managers followed up on this feedback and further developed their coaching skills – especially active listening, exploration, questioning and closing. The progress was tracked by manager review sessions.

Program Outcomes

MTN Uganda has greatly benefited from the Coaching for Performance Program in various ways:

It has improved the level of professionalism amongst managers. The blending of both the technical and soft skills has enabled them to better take on any business challenge during the execution of their duties. The power distance that existed between the managers and their respective direct reports has been substantially reduced. The supervisor – supervisee relationship has improved.

For example, program participant Ms. Fiona Abamako Ucanda (Customer Management & Training Manager) said the following: "This Coaching Program has helped me gain the skills to take a step back and make my subordinate more focused, motivated and confident. I learnt that the greater reward is not about having the right answers all the time but about helping the employee find the right answer. Most importantly, the Program has changed my perception of coaching as a negative form of managing perception to a positive, assertive and creative form of development of self and others."

The 1:1 coach element – focusing on skills transfer – has also greatly facilitated the Leadership and Talent Management strategy: Coached employees are now clearly better prepared and equipped to take on senior positions that may fall vacant. Career planning and business continuity have been made easier.

One of the coachees said: "I have always looked forward to my coaching sessions. Through coaching I have been helped to understand and fit into the MTN culture. Having moved from a parastatal to a private sector work environment, my coach has shared a lot that has helped me to appreciate the telecommunications industry and how it operates. I have

www.frank-bresser-consulting.com

Geographical focus: *Uganda*

MTN UGANDA CASE STUDY: *Coaching for Performance – the Case for MTN Uganda*

greatly improved in areas that I was struggling with, such as time management. I can confidently say that without support from my coach, I would still be grappling in the dark. Thanks to MTN Uganda for introducing the Coaching for Performance program"

Here is another comment – from Joy Gureme (Training Supervisor): "Coaching is a wonderful initiative. When you first assume a new position, you are very enthusiastic, you have grand goals and you believe you can achieve anything. Soon reality hits – you cannot do everything. You may not even know how to do many things. With coaching you're not just thrust into the position and left to flounder, or work things out on your own; you are guided, supported until you are comfortable and confident in your new role. Mistakes are not disastrous, rather they are used as positive learning experiences."

Overall, the Coaching for Performance program has made quantum contributions to the company performance and to sustaining its position as a leading telecommunications company in Uganda.

Our key learning/Recommendation:
Coaching is one of the greatest initiatives that provide visible results and enhance employee development and retention, which are still big challenges for organisations today.

Questions and exercises for further reflection and to integrate practice and theory:

1. What is the business case for coaching in the company?

2. What coaching forms were implemented? What are the outcomes?

3. How has MTN positioned coaching in terms of developmental/remedial?

4. What kind of reservations towards coaching had to be overcome on the way?

5. What is your key learning from this case study?

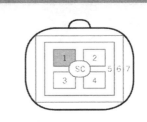
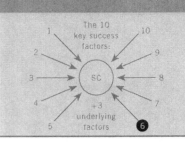

CREATE AN OPTIMAL WIN-WIN VALUE FOR ALL STAKEHOLDERS

Coaching is about integrating the requirements of people, organisation, and technology & tools – both external and internal – in an optimal win-win way. It is in the nature of coaching that the interests of all stakeholders are adequately appreciated, acknowledged and balanced appropriately. Coaching fosters creative solutions that reconcile and integrate the various interests.

While every stakeholder has the right that his or her interests are part of the equation and are taken into account, the various kinds of interests, of course, cannot always all be satisfied. Higher priority interests may take precedence. So creating an optimal win-win value for all stakeholders is about balance of interests – not about unconditionally trying to suit everybody and meet everybody's needs and wishes in each situation.

Well-implemented coaching will provide enormous benefits for the individual, the team, the organisation as well as potentially the wider society. Additionally, these benefits can reinforce and nurture each other. This is a key strength of coaching – every stakeholder may benefit from coaching, not at the others' expense, but in support of one another.

6.1. Benefits of coaching

The main benefits of coaching – both short and long term – can be identified at an individual, team, organisational and social level:

Benefits at the individual level
- Improved performance and excellence
- Higher motivation/commitment
- More effective management of change processes
- Faster mastery of new roles/tasks
- More accurate use of technologies & tools
- Better leadership skills
- Improved communication and relationships
- Greater clarity in goals, strategy and process
- Increased self-awareness and self-reflection
- Personal growth and development
- Greater agility and versatility
- Work life balance
- Optimal sustainability in all these areas
- etc.

Benefits at the team level
- Improved team performance and efficiency
- Higher motivation/team spirit
- More effective management of change processes
- Better communication/team work/relationships
- Greater clarity in goal, strategy and process
- Creation of synergies
- Effective conflict management
- Team building, growth and development
- Greater agility and versatility
- Optimal sustainability in all these areas
- etc.

Benefits at the organisational level
- Improved organisational performance and excellence
- Improved organisational capability
- Higher profitability/return on investment/productivity/sales
- Better agility and ability of the organisation to adjust to changing circumstances
- Buy-in to organisational values and behaviours
- More effective organisational structures, processes and operations
- More accurate use of technologies & tools
- Effective communication
- Higher creativity/innovation

www.frank-bresser-consulting.com

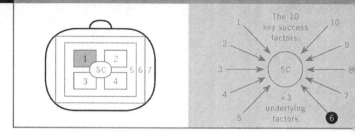

- Better staff motivation and retention
- Less absenteeism
- Employer attractiveness for current and future employees, in particular for talent
- Open and productive organisational culture and climate
- Developing the learning organisation
- Sustainable form of learning and development
- Optimal sustainability in all these areas
- etc.

Benefits at the social level
- More successful company (with the associated benefits for society like more secure jobs, higher tax incomes, etc.)
- Positive role model for other organisations
- Creates a working atmosphere that promotes the achievement of high performance and excellence in an ethical, legal way

- The positive atmosphere in the company can spread to its social environment.
- Increasing company contributions to the wider community/ protection of the environment (more value-adding products, corporate social responsibility and sustainability initiatives)
- etc.

The social benefits, in turn, may lead to an additional increase in the acceptance of the organisation and its products/ services in the external environment, further raise its sales and employer attractiveness and thus directly influence the overall organisational performance in a positive way as well. The social benefits therefore can gain great importance and are more than just a by-product of coaching programmes.

Ideally, in your coaching initiative, all levels of benefits reinforce each other and finally feed into and nurture improved organisational performance and excellence overall:

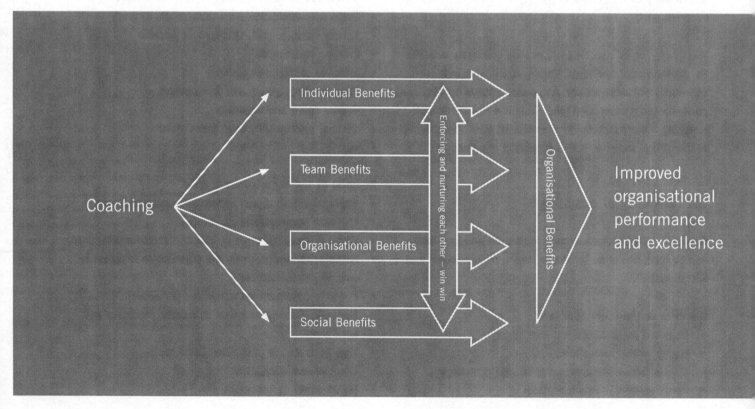

www.frank-bresser-consulting.com

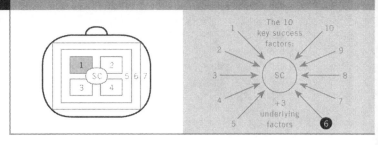

When coaching is implemented well, there is in principle no fixed, limited 'cake' of coaching benefits that could only be divided among the various stakeholders. Quite the contrary, the benefits are in principle "infinite" and have no upper limits.

While planning or improving your coaching initiative, it is important that you develop a clear idea of what kind of key benefits you want to get out of coaching and how coaching is actually going to work for your company.

You may define your goals and objectives regarding your envisaged benefits as broad or deep as meets your company's needs. Depending on what kind of benefits you actually strive for, different coaching forms will be preferable according to their respective focus and entry point in the company. However, all coaching forms will have indirect influence at various levels in some way. For example, while 1:1 leadership coaching is first of all focussing on the leadership skills of the individual, it will then – directly or indirectly – have an impact on the team spirit and performance, thereby also on organisational performance, and potentially even on the wider community.

Here is an overview of the various people coaching forms and their main entry points:

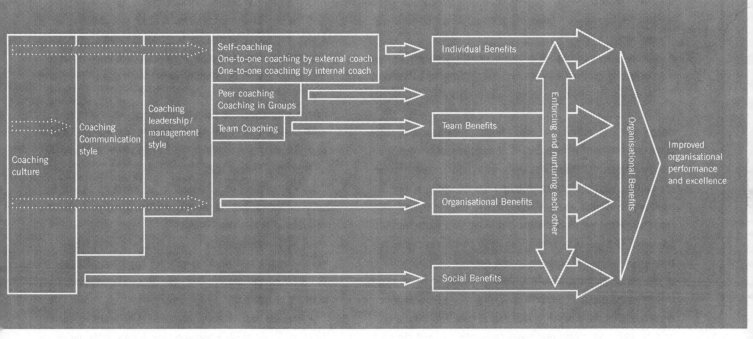

In today's rapidly changing business environment, the effective use of coaching (in its various forms) is increasingly becoming a potential source of competitive advantage and key success factor for companies.

For any business case it is important that the benefits of the coaching initiative outweigh its costs (e.g. invested resources like budget, time, energy, staff).

6.2. Pitfalls and guidelines

In practice, there are many pitfalls organisations may fall into, which prevent the creation of an optimal win-win value for all stakeholders. Classic examples are:

- Overlooking and missing an existing stakeholder and his or her interests (e.g. ignoring the coachees'

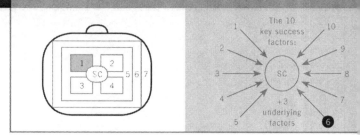

line managers as possible stakeholders of the coaching programme)

- Imposing coaching on people, not considering the human factor properly
- Lack of clear provision on what happens if the goals of the coachee start to differ from the goals of the organisation (e.g. the coachee starts to consider leaving the organisation during the coaching process, though this was not intended by the company)
- Lack of or insufficient confidentiality provisions
- Hidden agendas not made transparent to people concerned
- Ignoring major conflicts of roles (e.g. of internal part time coaches, in particular the manager as coach of his or her direct report)
- Not taking people's concerns and resistance to coaching seriously
- Inconsistency of coaching measures with company strategy
- Confusing optimal win-win and an acceptable balance of interests with trying to always suit everybody

Coaching is only a tool, and, like any tool, people and organisations may use it in a more or less appropriate way. Inadequate implementation of coaching may lead to poor, if not counterproductive results. In extreme cases (for example, where 1:1 coaching is abused as an instrument and used to intentionally manipulate the employee without making this transparent in any way), the use of coaching can even be unacceptably contrary to its nature and purpose. In this extreme case the violation of the coaching principles is evident, however, in some cases, this is less obvious. It is worth critiquing your own and your organisation's daily practice and use of coaching regularly, and checking your own and your organisation's attitude on a continuous basis.

There are many things to consider in order to use coaching properly and create the much desired win-win situations and benefits. The following guidelines may serve you as useful orientation:

1. Identify the various stakeholders of your (planned or already running) coaching programme.
2. Identify the key benefits (and costs) for each stakeholder.
3. Develop or improve the coaching concept in such a way that each stakeholder may win without doing this at the expense of another.
4. Where a trade-off/compromise is necessary, acknowledge all stakeholders' interests, take them into account and find the optimal balance of interests.
5. Get the buy-in and commitment of all stakeholders for a highly collaborative approach. Make sure all stakeholders understand that the better they work with each other in coaching, the more benefits each single one of them will get out of it.
6. Check your coaching plan on a regular basis with regard to potential conflicts of interests (among any of the stakeholders) and redesign your programme accordingly, so that they cannot occur.
7. Where a certain potential conflict of interests cannot be fully excluded, have a clear provision/agreement on how to proceed if this does occur.
8. Have a general provision in your coaching plan, which reinforces the collaborative win-win approach and provides for cooperation in the case of an unpredicted conflict of interests.
9. See and use resistance or complaints as learning opportunities. They provide you with invaluable information on why and where you need to further improve or better communicate your coaching programme.
10. Regularly review the coaching initiative to create an optimal win-win value for all stakeholders.

www.frank-bresser-consulting.com

Geographical focus: *Africa*

CASE STUDY 11	X-BANK, AFRICA

Company: *X-Bank*

(company name changed/made anonymous)
(Financial services, based in Southern Africa)

Author: *Anonymous, HR, based in Southern Africa*

Team coaching at work

For about five years, our bank has an internal coaching & mentoring framework in place to support our business and people. It is a well developed offering that meanwhile also includes team coaching at the executive team (exco) level.

Our model allows coaching requests also from individual business unit heads, and one day there was a particular request coming in from a country head in Africa, i.e. the Managing Director (MD) of the country: Less than satisfactory business results and a prevailing poor performance atmosphere led to a deeper needs analysis (conducted as a series of coaching conversations) and a proposal to introduce team coaching at the business exco level.

The objectives and key issues to work on in the team coaching intervention were leadership and how to bring the team together to improve the performance and country numbers, while forging a strong team for sustainability to meet and exceed the targets for Africa.

The team coaching process

The whole intervention was built on a positive strength perspective and acknowledged different learning styles as being key to developing strong relationships, creating connections and supporting a shift towards a coaching leadership style.

The process ran over 3 to 4 months with an initial 2 days and a further 3 days delivered 1 day per month to allow for progress checks and reflection on what was working well and what needed further improvement. As business landscapes change rapidly, the current reality was always the first check.

The coaching was facilitated by an experienced team coach who could work in the moment with the messiness of the current reality and coach the team towards a meaningful and purposeful team contribution and accountability for individual performance.

An important element of the intervention was the sharing of individual stories, which allowed the participants to get more personal access to each other as human beings. This proved to be really powerful in creating new understanding, as we found that delegates had worked together for many years, yet sometimes still knew very little about their colleagues.

Also, it was recognized by the MD that the shifts in behaviour supported by the coaching intervention would also impact the wider community and families. So these were also engaged in the latter stages of the coaching process to unpack the changes further.

We also took proper care in choosing the right place for coaching, which is important. The venues actually chosen for the different components reflected a steady move up the

www.frank-bresser-consulting.com

Geographical focus: *Africa*

X-BANK CASE STUDY: *Team coaching at work*

mountainous terrain in the country, which proved to be a wonderfully inspiring metaphor for the leadership journey.

The outcomes

While it is difficult to assign direct ROI, the results of the country while on this journey speak volumes. There has been a threefold improvement in the bottom line, which the country MD attributes primarily to the coaching intervention.

For example, a positive culture shift took place in the operating space, where giving feedback on loans had been considered counter culture. This limiting assumption was unbundled and shown not to be reality, so that loans could now be granted on the basis of sound business practice.

Because of this positive experience, a much broader initiative at our bank has resulted from this: several countries will be invited to take advantage of similar (but uniquely their) team interventions.

Talent identification and succession planning support by the use of coaching & mentoring have also been put in place, explicitly also addressing female executives in tough business roles.

The above experience of team coaching was a coaching journey for the participants, also having additional effects/ benefits beyond the ones already mentioned. One feedback received was: "I am a different human being in the world, not just in the organization."

Another one was: "Corporates can be more benevolent in using some of their wealth more responsibly. If we want to see a different world, leaders will need to lead us differently. This is where we should start from."

Our key learning/Recommendation:
Human beings are resourceful, so honour their experience and they will flourish when played to their strengths. Coaching helps achieve exactly this.

Questions and exercises for further reflection and to integrate practice and theory:

1. What is the business case for coaching in the company?

2. Identify the various beneficiaries of the team coaching intervention? What are their respective benefits?

3. What distinguishes team coaching from individual one-to-one coaching?

4. What is your key learning from this case study?

www.frank-bresser-consulting.com

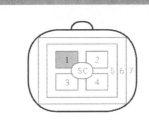 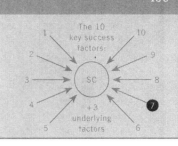

<table>
<tr><td>**KEY SUCCESS
FACTOR 7**</td></tr>
</table>

ACHIEVE FULL CONSISTENCY OF COACHING WITH BUSINESS STRATEGY

This factor includes two aspects – firstly how to position coaching strategically, secondly how to ensure consistency between strategy and coaching measures. Achieving the alignment of coaching measures with the corporate, business and functional strategies of an organisation is vital, in order that they tie in with the other business activities and support the overall organisational strategy to add value and sustain.

7.1. Strategic use and positioning of coaching

For any coaching form to be successful, it needs to be clearly linked to the company's strategy. However, in some organisations, you still come across coaching programmes that simply ...

- contradict and work against existing corporate, business and/or functional strategy.

- do not contradict current strategies, but also do not support them – they run in parallel without really impacting business success in any way.

- could be easily linked to strategy, but negligently are not and, as a result, lose momentum, acceptance and impact.
All these scenarios are not satisfactory.

Coaching only starts to become value adding and sustainable, where it visibly serves business strategy and success. This link can be achieved in various ways, depending on the positioning of coaching and the desired impact on business performance:

1. An ad hoc way to support strategy

At a very low level, coaching is only used ad hoc and in a rather fragmented way, when and where needed, for emerging issues here and there in an organisation without systematic planning or an integrated approach. Coaching at this level is not an explicit part of corporate or HR/L&D strategy.

As long as there is a business case for each coaching intervention in advance, confirming that it makes sense and fits within corporate, business and functional strategy, each single intervention may well serve business strategy and success. However, the impact is certainly limited as there is no strategic plan for coaching and the business benefits will be more difficult to justify, due to the general doubts about the success of ad hoc coaching (e.g. see key success factor 2: have a systematic approach).

2. A low key, standard part of HR or L&D strategy

This is also quite a low level of strategic use of coaching: in this case the organisation has integrated the use of coaching as a standard personal development tool into their HR or L&D portfolio. However they do it because industry research and practice have shown it is generally useful for improving people's performance. The firm doesn't specifically link coaching to business strategy and thus only makes a very general use of it. The thinking is: "This kind of tool is generally good for people's performance and for pursuing strategies, so we use it in our firm. As long as we don't see a specific problem or contradiction in our case, we assume this works for us and helps achieve the company strategy." Many organisations have this approach today.

While this approach may work and have a positive impact on business success to a certain degree, it remains rather general and off-the-shelf. The question is: "To what extent does this approach actually produce benefits for your firm and support achieving your strategy?" Recall key success factor 1: Have an organisation-specific understanding of

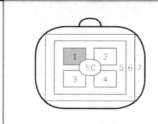
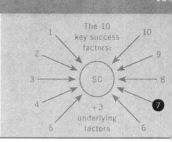

coaching. Be very careful about one-size-fits-all or standard solutions in coaching. If you really want to use coaching effectively and leverage its full potential, tailor it as specifically as possible around your organisational needs and strategy.

3. An integrated part of HR/L&D strategy

At a more advanced level, companies deploy coaching as a direct means or tool to achieve strategic objectives. They establish strong links between coaching interventions and corporate, business and/or functional strategy.

Thus the strategies directly inform and shape the design of a coaching programme. Coaching is adjusted to the strategic requirements of the firm and becomes a specific expression of its strategy. In this way, high consistency is achieved. All links between coaching activities and strategy are also clearly communicated in the organisation.

This approach is increasingly emerging and developing in organisations these days. The great advantages are obvious: Coaching fits the needs more accurately, produces greater benefits and can be better communicated to your people. It thus becomes much easier to get the support and buy-in of top management and the people participating in the coaching programme, as they can all understand and engage with it more quickly.

At this level, the HR/L&D functions act as strategic business partners helping the top achieve business success by coaching. While being strongly linked and integrated in HR/L&D strategy, this level of coaching is still seen as a tool to implement and accomplish a given, formulated strategy only.

4. A key part of functional, business and/or corporate strategy

Where coaching has high strategic importance for the company, it may also be explicitly included and reflected in the strategy itself. Coaching may thus play a role not only in strategy implementation, but also in strategy formulation.

Take for example a business, where the top management sees the development and maintenance of a strong coaching culture as a key success factor for their whole business and as a precondition for survival and sustainable growth. The board therefore may include coaching as an fundamental part of their corporate strategy. The same may also happen at the business unit or functional level in organisations and inform the way a single business/functional strategy is defined.

Given the hierarchy of strategies: where the corporate and/or business strategy contains coaching, HR/L&D clearly needs to represent this coaching element in their strategy formulation.

The HR/OD/L&D manager or director has a role to play as a strategic business partner in influencing the Board to make coaching part of strategy, as and when appropriate. For this you need evidence or a strong business case that it has great strategic relevance in developing capability for the whole business.

For example, as strong strategic business partner, it is your responsibility to work with the top management to ensure that the organisations' resources have the learning needed to meet strategic goals. This may involve challenging existing strategies in a constructive way to come up with new, innovative ideas and approaches that may help the organisation gain a competitive advantage now and/or in the future. Coaching as a highly flexible tool, designed to support this more innovative approach, may be a suitable strategic driver and response to this and thus be included as part of strategy.

So coaching here is seen not only as a tool to implement a given, formulated strategy, but also as an ingredient of strategy itself. It may inform and shape strategy or become a substantial, explicit part of the functional, business or cor-

www.frank-bresser-consulting.com

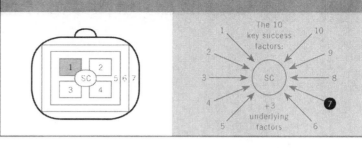

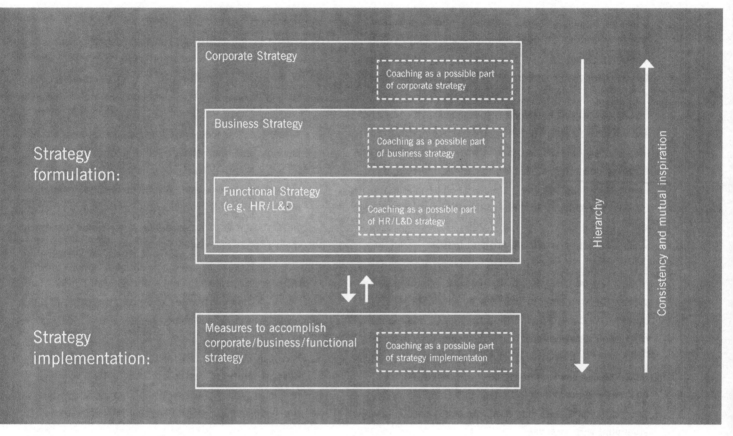

Figure: Coaching as part of strategy formulation and strategy implementation

porate strategy. In particular cases, coaching may even become part of the mission statement of a company.

Whether it is desirable and makes business sense for a company to use coaching at this highly strategic level cannot be answered in general, but is specific to each case. It depends on the specific organisational needs and the circumstances of each case.

As general rules of thumb and a helpful checklist, it can be said that making coaching an explicit part of your corporate strategy becomes more relevant, ...

- the more strategic importance coaching actually has or gains

- the more you find the use of coaching becomes a critical success factor for your business

- the greater the importance and spread of coaching in your organisation (for example, a company-wide coaching culture or coaching leadership style programme)

- the more common it is in your firm to formulate corporate strategies not only in financial, but also in non-financial terms (e.g. corporate culture, people development)

- the higher the overall acceptance and importance of HR/L&D/OD in general in your company is (i.e. the more it is seen as a real strategic partner) and of coaching in particular.

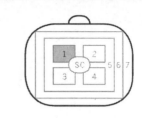
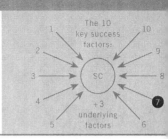

When a company commits to the strategic integration of coaching, it requires great knowledge and maturity in the use of coaching. As most organisations are not there (yet), for now they rightly use coaching as a tactical tool first.

Having said this, it is important to highlight that some organisations have already started to use coaching at this strategic level successfully. In fact, this is where a great part of the future of coaching is expected to lie. The more organisations understand coaching, the better they will be able to use it as part of their strategy to thrive and gain a competitive edge.

7.2. Creating optimal consistency

In deciding on how you use and position coaching strategically, the challenge is to ensure optimal consistency between coaching activities and functional, business and corporate strategies in detail. Also, coaching initiatives need to tie in with other existing business activities and programmes. The clearer you have identified the exact links between coaching initiatives and company strategy, the better you ensure your coaching programme is in full alignment with strategy.

Be aware that strategy formulation is a **dynamic** process: Strategies may change or need to be changed rather quickly in today's business (e.g. because of a new CEO or a major change in business environment). Accordingly, coaching strategies and measures need to be regularly reviewed and, as appropriate, adjusted to remain suitable on a continuous basis.

There is a **hierarchy** between strategies (1. corporate, 2. business 3. functional strategy) and between any strategy and the measures taken to accomplish it, allowing for a certain degree of latitude in interpreting and implementing strategy. On the basis of this, consider the following **general guidelines** for strategy alignment:

1. Any coaching measure should support all three kinds of strategies (corporate, business and functional).

If it doesn't, it will most likely be rejected by the organisation (or parts of it) in some way or other.

2. Where coaching becomes part of a strategy make sure this strategy remains fully consistent up and down the hierarchy.

3. Where coaching measures/strategies are inconsistent with business activities/strategies on the same level, there is no automatic priority of one over the other. Accordingly, there is now choice and latitude in the implementation of those strategies. This may be within your remit or a wider debate in the organisation or for senior management to intervene and decide.

In particular be attentive to (and avoid/remove) the **10 classic types of inconsistencies of implementation** that may be encountered in organisations:

1. **Pushing coaching too far in the organisation beyond strategic limits** e.g. striving for a very high level of organisational penetration of coaching, while the strategy only permits coaching in specific cases.

2. **Keeping coaching very limited despite an explicit broader coaching strategy** e.g. the board wants to create a real coaching culture in the whole organisation, but HR/L&D doesn't get the full message and limits itself to using coaching only marginally, if at all.

3. **Taking an unsuitable coaching measure to achieve strategic goals because of a lack of understanding of the coaching forms** e.g. the strategic focus is clearly on developing a coaching leadership style as an integrated part of leaders' daily work, but this is confused by HR/L&D with just building a pool of internal coaches or with implementing the manager as coach of direct reports.

4. **Missing the specific focus of a strategy** e.g. the strategy clearly says the support of high potentials

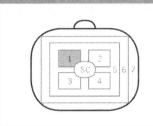 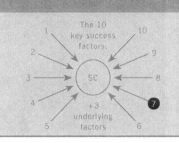

should be the main focus of HR measures, but only one-to-one coaching for senior executives is planned.

5. **Implementing coaching for its own sake** e.g. an HR/L&D manager is such a fan of coaching, that he or she loses the view of the actual business requirements, and builds up a coaching programme without any link to what is actually needed.

6. **Inconsistency of coaching programmes with other HR/L&D measures, concepts or strategies** e.g. HR starts to implement a coaching leadership style programme, but ignores the fact that the term "coaching leadership style" is already used in a rather different way in the concept of "situational leadership" in the company. They don't integrate the two concepts, nor do they provide clear explanations about the different use. The two programmes run in parallel, but are inconsistent with each other.

7. **Inconsistency with other coaching measures in the company** e.g. this is particularly often the case where coaching is used in a very fragmented way without a systematic, integrated approach. Then you may find inconsistencies among the various coaching approaches taken, e.g. contradicting coaching definitions that remain unexplained.

8. **Inconsistency within the same coaching initiative/ concept** e.g. in a coaching programme, you define coaching in a certain way, but in application you do not stick to this definition and use coaching very differently.

9. **Potential for more consistency**
There are cases where you do not necessarily have inconsistency, but there is in fact room for more optimal consistency: For example, there is a massive coaching leadership style programme in the company, but the performance measurement system in place only includes individual financial parameters – rather than also parameters like people and team development and performance.

Or line managers are trained and regularly deployed as professional internal part time coaches, but the reward system only recognises their line management activities. In both examples above, there is a choice to keep everything as it is, to change the coaching programme and/ or to change the performance measurement or reward system in place. Optimal consistency would imply changing something to make the whole even more consistent.

10. **Only seeming inconsistencies**
Sometimes, there are at first glance inconsistencies that turn out not to be the case, when you have a closer look at them. The seeming inconsistency is only the result of a lack of clarity and/or of communication.

In order to remove inconsistencies, it may sometimes be necessary to develop a new coaching plan from scratch. Or, you may only need to slightly change a bit or add a detail to your coaching plan, and everything is fully aligned again. Or you may discover a new aspect or way of seeing it, so that the coaching programme, re-designed from that different perspective, actually is supportive of and fully consistent with the company strategy.

Inconsistency is sometimes caused by the overemphasis of coaching. In fact, where people see coaching as some kind of panacea and give it priority over other activities that are equally or even more important, people will naturally resist. Knowing the limits of coaching and giving coaching appropriate space and significance is the answer.

For example, instead of presenting a coaching leadership style as any kind of panacea, the following formulation and proper positioning of it may ensure high consistency and receptiveness in the following: 'We want to introduce a coaching leadership style programme which is a pilot designed to see how we can further complement our existing leadership skills portfolio in the company to build our capability to achieve the company strategy of …'

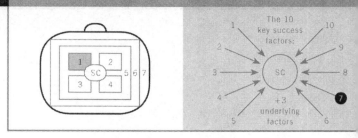

Whenever there is a lack of alignment, there are always in principle three possible ways of achieving consistency: Either adjusting the coaching plan to fit strategy, or adjusting the strategy to fit coaching, or doing both.

Given the hierarchy of strategies, it is likely that you will need to adjust your coaching concept to the current strategy – or even fully give up your coaching plan in the case of insurmountable inconsistency. For strategies to work, everybody needs to adhere to and support them. Therefore, it is vital to respect the requirement of consistency at any time.

So whatever coaching measures you finally take, make sure that you strongly link them to your company strategies and that they complement all other business activities. Equally important: do not forget to communicate this properly in your firm.

Geographical focus: *Serbia*

CASE STUDY 12	UNIQA, SERBIA

Company: *UNIQUA*
(Insurance Company)
www.uniqa.rs

Author: *Ljiljana Zdravković*

Function: *Team Leader for education and professional development of employees, based in Belgrade*

Coaching at UNIQA (Serbia)

UNIQA Group entered the Serbian market in 2006 by a local insurance company. In a traditional environment with a fairly long absence of the insurance industry on the market, the implementation of UNIQA standards and values required a specific approach. UNIQA Group established a new organizational structure in which the basic organizational units became specialized teams for specific parts of the process. With the restructured sales network, the construction of the UNIQA Team of the new generation began. What is more, the number of employees increased significantly during the first year. This clearly indicated the need to identify and form a pool of key people within the company – and to enhance their knowledge and skills in order to embrace change and achieve the company goals.

A support concept was developed covering the following areas:
* Sales education for the company sales force, based mainly on product knowledge
* Academy UNIQA, a broad, educational, specifically tailored program for all levels of management providing higher standards in communication, management tools and implementation techniques
* Coaching in collaboration with an external consulting company and experienced coach, supporting several team leaders and directors in enhancing their professional effectiveness and on-the-job performance through the development of new, more efficient team skills.

The UNIQA management team defined a particular need to design the coaching program in a way that it would create synergies with the UNIQA Academy program – and thereby facilitate and accelerate a fast transfer of the acquired leadership knowledge by key managers through coaching sessions. This would help the managers and their teams to support and effect the needed change and rapid development of UNIQA in Serbia.

Our coaching approach mainly included two coaching models: appreciative inquiry and observational coaching. In the context of the first model, the coach used assessment techniques around personality style, job profile, self-awareness, leadership and managerial competences. The second model was achieved on the basis of the following three phases:

1. Observation and data collection (involving also active self-monitoring by the coachee)
2. Analysis (identifying and clarifying pertinent coaching issues)
3. Formulation and realization of strategies/action plans to achieve the identified goals/desired outcomes

(While most coaching interventions were based on an observation model, the coach could also use other techniques like brainstorming and problem solution generation.)

The main purpose of the coaching programme was to bring about improvements in the following areas for our managers:

Geographical focus: *Serbia*

UNIQA CASE STUDY: *Coaching at UNIQA (Serbia)*

- Social skills through the recognition and removal of personal limiting factors
- Balance between demands and possibilities
- Leadership abilities, managing and working with a team
- Taking a more active role in the positive change of the organisation culture
- Motivation to participate more actively in the further development of the company
- UNIQA unique management style

In the coaching sessions, the managers had the opportunity to learn in particular the following skills: how to bring together their personal objectives and the company's strategic goals; methods and techniques for more flexible behaviours in everyday situations; practical guidelines for using tools for the improvement of daily activities; ways to achieve company goals through a team approach.

The biggest benefit of this cognitive process was unlocking the potential for higher dedication to resolving a problem/task and for optimized cooperation within the team. Team members clearly noticed differences in the communication of certain problems or tasks by their managers in the daily work – thus producing better synergies and more creativity in achieving the goals of the group. The commitment was also positively influenced by this more productive atmosphere in the team.

Such new behaviours of managers involved in the coaching program were recognized and well received by their teams. They created and role-modelled the new desired models of behaviour within the group. Coaching techniques were applied at different levels within the teams. Leadership not only meant engaging the individual, but also impacting and handling group dynamics.

In accordance with the rapid changes in the market, today's management of a company has to create conditions in which the organisation can quickly integrate the newly acquired knowledge and adjust the existing knowledge and processes to the clients' needs. Over more than a decade of emphasis on services rather than on products, social skills have increasingly come into focus. Coaching helps develop these and allows managers to overcome and improve traditional ways of doing things as needed.

Our key learning/Recommendation:
Have in mind that the success of managerial positions depends on a well-balanced relationship between expert knowledge and social skills – and even more on the willingness and openness of managers to lifelong learning. Coaching is an approach that clearly supports all of this.

Questions and exercises for further reflection and to integrate practice and theory:

1. What is the business case for coaching in the company?
2. How do they define coaching for their purposes? What kind of coaching approach(es) do they use?
3. What is the strategic positioning of coaching?
4. What are the coaching outcomes?
5. What is your key learning from this case study?

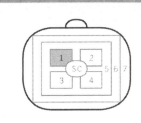
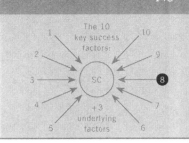

<table>
<tr><td>

**KEY SUCCESS
FACTOR 8**

</td><td>

ENSURE COMPLETE TRANSPARENCY OF THE WHOLE COACHING CONCEPT

</td></tr>
</table>

Comprehensive information about a coaching programme to all stakeholders is crucial to enable the various parties to use coaching effectively and to contribute in a positive way to the overall success of the programme. Where everybody has a pre-cise idea of, and clear expectations about, the procedures and steps in place and the rationale behind these, coaching initiatives become trustworthy, well-understood and attractive to people.

In order that complete transparency is ensured, the coaching concept and its governing rules must be worked out very clearly and must be adequately and continuously communi-cated in a professional and succinct way throughout the orga-nisation. Coaching should not be kept secret in any way by the HR/L&D management, but made fully open and inviting. Any hidden agendas or hidden contracts (e.g. secret evaluation or reporting) are to be avoided.

In this way coaching programmes not only become more trust-worthy and operable, but also enable the stakeholders to give well-informed feedback and make appropriate suggestions to help improve and further develop the coaching concept on a continuous basis. Transparency also gives ownership to the people involved, fosters their high-quality dialogue, and makes coaching a highly collaborative, common effort.

As the manager or director responsible for coaching in your organisation, you definitely need all relevant information con-cerning the coaching programme. However, other stakeholders may not – and there is no sense in overloading people with dispensable information. It is therefore your task to organise the relevant information, but also to customize it to the dif-ferent stakeholders according to their requirements.

8.1. Conceptual transparency

This involves providing general information on the conceptual and operational aspects of the coaching initiative, answering questions like:

- Why this programme?/What is this programme for?
- What coaching forms/initiatives are part of the programme?
- How do these distinguish from other tools/disciplines in the company?
- How does this coaching programme work precisely?
- What is the role of the various stakeholders within the programme?
- Who is the initiator and responsible for the coaching programme?

This information needs to be available to all stakeholders, so that they all can see the whole picture and work together on implementation.

Beyond transparency of the coaching concept as such, care must be taken about what kind of further information you actually disclose to each of the stakeholders. Sensitive, confidential areas may be affected. The following general rules of thumb may give some initial guidance here:

1. Only provide people with the information they actually need and is relevant for them in terms of the coaching programme, not with all the information you have or they ask for.

2. Confidential information about the company (e.g. confi-dential internal data, fee structures), yourself (e.g. per-sonal strategies or plans) or others (e.g. coachee: confi-dential contents of a one-to-one coaching session) must remain fully confidential (unless otherwise agreed by all people protected by the existing confidentiality agreement).

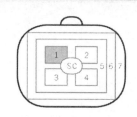

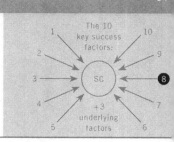

3. Your coaching concept and work around it needs to be fully transparent – not your or anyone else's inviolable private sphere.

4. Don't disclose information to people, you don't trust (yet). Of course, the better you know someone, the more insight you will be ready to give. Take for example an applicant whom you see for the first time – you may not even want to disclose any information on your coaching concept to this person, if you don't find you can trust him or her.

5. Give selected coaching providers adequate access to the required information about/in your company to enable them to provide the contracted services.

6. Ensure all selected coaching providers are clear and transparent in their own approach as well – and that they also accept the above limits (e.g. respect of people's private sphere).

7. Make the scope and limits of transparency itself transparent to the stakeholders.success.

8.2. Driver transparency

Transparency includes making the rationale and business case of a coaching programme transparent.

Seen from a purely **professional perspective**, coaching programmes are (and should) normally be driven by, based on and take place within the limits of:

- your given task/job responsibility
- the organisational needs
- the company strategy
- the appropriateness of coaching in each case
- best practice in coaching

You may also have **personal drivers** that may motivate you to promote coaching or not, and influence your decisions whether and how to implement and improve coaching. In order to be professional, it is important that you are aware of your personal drivers and agendas and deal with them properly. So there is not just a requirement for transparency of your coaching plan to the various stakeholders, but also a question of transparency of your personal drivers towards yourself.

Answering the following questions may help you raise your awareness of these drivers:

- Can you think of any personal agendas or issues you have that could overlap with your professional engagement in coaching?
- What exactly are your personal drivers, if any, with regard to coaching?
- To what extent do your personal drivers actually support you in implementing and improving coaching professionally? To what extent do they not?
- To the extent that they don't: How could you turn the destructive elements into positive ones?
- If this is not possible, to what degree are you able to at least manage them in a way that they don't actually become a burden or get destructive?
- What kind of support may be useful to seek to ensure professionalism at all times?

Most personal drivers are not per se good or bad. But it depends on the context, whether they actually support or hinder the professional use of coaching. So you need to acknowledge this and deal with the opportunities and risks of any personal driver you may have.

For example, great personal passion for coaching will motivate and empower a person in a most positive way and make them very present and engaged. But where a person gets too enthusiastic about and too focussed on coaching, this can also cause blindness, impatience, an overemphasis on coaching and thus a lack of professionalism.

On the other hand, an indifferent view on coaching – e.g. you were given the task to implement, but never asked for

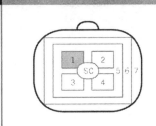
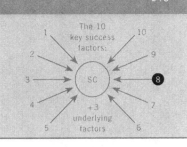

it – may at first hinder you in becoming a real champion and role model of coaching, but it may also be a great strength where a very rational, unemotional perspective on coaching is required.

Generally speaking, where drivers become too extreme, they hinder the effective use of coaching. The following is a check-list of possible indicators of a counterproductive effect of personal drivers and agendas. When you find one or more of these indicators are true for you, do a self-check to manage your drivers in order to ensure a professional, effective use of coaching in your firm at any time.

Be particularly alert when you ...

- confuse coaching with therapy
- use coaching in a manipulative way
- see coaching as a panacea or ideology
- lose the ability to make necessary compromises
- implement coaching for its own sake/as an end itself (not as a means)
- cannot let go of a coaching plan and still stick to it, though there is no chance to make it happen in your company
- take coaching measures that work against the organisation you are working for
- daydream and idealise rather than linking coaching to concrete business reality
- use coaching in a way that is only about being nice to each other
- think coaching is the only right way
- abuse coaching as a personal means to achieve a specific change that is not actually needed by the organisation, but is desired by you
- put yourself over others
- use coaching in a past-oriented way
- become too much of a moralizer
- stigmatise/have apathy against any approaches other than coaching
- think too much in terms of black and white/right and wrong

- push away relevant facts and thoughts
- are in extreme emotional states
- behave in an unprofessional way without having an explanation for it

(What is said on the personal drivers above, may in principle equally apply to the various other stakeholders involved in coaching initiatives.)

Geographical focus: *Portugal*

CASE STUDY 13	PEPSICO, PORTUGAL

Company: PepsiCo Portugal
(PepsiCo is a global consumer products company focused on convenient foods and beverages)

www.pepsico.pt

Main Author: *Sandra Silva, Head of Human Resources (based in Lisbon)*

Co-author: *Ana Oliveira Pinto, Executive Coach*

Effective leadership development by combining 360° feedback and one-to-one coaching

PepsiCo's Leadership Development System

PepsiCo has a strong commitment to making leaders out of its employees. The company has a robust leadership model that identifies talent, develops readiness and prepares the individual for the required movement. In this model, the employee takes primary ownership for his learning and self development. The company provides the tools and resources.

One possible leadership development tool to apply within the whole portfolio of different interventions at PepsiCo Portugal is one-to-one coaching.

The reasons for considering coaching are diverse: Firstly, a leader's success is strongly related to his or her way of thinking, feeling, behaving and acting – coaching is able to address each of these. Secondly, leaders today need high interpersonal skills in their role, especially at upper levels. As coaching not only focuses on behaviour, but also on attitudes and beliefs, it is more effective than traditional training methods. Thirdly, it is no secret that it can be quite lonely at the upper levels – and there is an increasingly perceived business need for managers to have a trusted coach with whom it is possible to speak safely, openly and honestly about the issues one is facing.

A concrete example of 1:1 coaching

In order to support and prepare an upper-level manager for a role with higher levels of responsibility and to broaden his profile in the short/medium term, PepsiCo decided to sponsor a one-to-one coaching assignment for the manager with an external executive coach.

Design of the coaching intervention

The coaching process included eight two-hour face-to-face sessions for the upper-level manager over a period of around a year. Also, it contained a multi-source feedback, involving an initial perceptions' assessment, followed by a reassessment one year later.

The multiple raters were chosen by the manager, and the feedback was gathered through semi-structured, one hour face-to-face interviews. In total, 14 people were interviewed: the manager's direct report (the local general manager), the top general manager of the larger business unit, local and regional peers, staff, and family (spouse). An evidence-based approach was followed. The key was to get specific and accurate data.

We built trust with these 14 by assuring unconditional confidentiality, explaining the rationale and design of the

www.frank-bresser-consulting.com

Geographical focus: *Portugal*

PEPSICO CASE STUDY: *Effective leadership development by combining 360° feedback and one-to-one coaching*

process, and addressing their questions and concerns. In order to ensure optimal feedback source credibility, we also asked the participants to what degree they thought they were actually familiar with the upper-level manager and able to provide a perspective on the manager's behaviour, role and performance.

Additionally, the coach attended several key business meetings and thus observed the manager's style and pattern of communication and interaction and its impact on people at work. The resulting feedback from the coach also got integrated in the coaching process.

This multiple source assessment provided the manager with a wide and rich range of feedback and enabled the identification of behavioural strengths and weaknesses, along with recommended changes. The feedback allowed the manager to check, test and challenge his own thinking and perceptions, reflect on what the results mean to him and think about how he may need to change.

Supported by coaching, the manager could pinpoint specific leadership behaviours which needed improvement/change/reinforcement, and took action in a couple of areas simultaneously.

By taking a holistic approach, mirroring and asking questions, the coach also helped the manager to think more systemically, relate the feedback to his own way of thinking, feeling and behaving, better understand the different perspectives, see the link between his values/beliefs/behaviours and his performance outcomes, explore and assess coping strategies, and be authentic.

As an observation, it was also the manager's openness to share private thoughts and perceptions, that enabled him to really question his attitudes and behaviours, see situations

and issues from different angles and develop and integrate new approaches at work.

Two sessions were held in a three-person setting – including the coach, the manager and the manager's manager. The purpose of these meetings was to evaluate the progress made and facilitate the dialogue between manager and supervisor.

Results

Positive changes were identified, in particular shifts in the manager's attitude. It was perceived, especially by peers, that the manager evolved into a more collaborative and self-aware way of thinking and taking action, of discussing and resolving difficult issues and of achieving results.

The manager's readiness to learn and change increased and he asked more open questions encouraging people to share their opinion and listened more attentively.

Additionally, he developed a stronger attitude of going forward and higher skills in managing emotions. To give an example, he was better able to address growing pains and admit mistakes.

Challenges

The higher one goes up the corporate ladder, the harder it is to get honest and useful feedback. The practice of seeking feedback, stepping back and reflecting may be a challenge at first, but, if perceived as important and continuously applied, becomes a valued habit.

Giving up old, trusted ways of doing things can be very hard, thus implying the possibility of setbacks. Defence may often

Geographical focus: *Portugal*

PEPSICO CASE STUDY: *Effective leadership development by combining 360° feedback and one-to-one coaching*

be a natural reaction to avoid difficult change. So the costs of change also always need to be identified and addressed properly.

A commitment for ongoing reflection by the manager is very important to continue self-improvement and consolidate the change. Encouraging the manager to schedule time for reflection in his diary and installing a buddy coaching system are two useful, additional ways of ensuring sustainable results from coaching.

Our key learning/Recommendation:
360° feedback is always a challenging process. Combined with a one-to-one coaching program and being done through semi-directed interviews at the beginning and at the end of the program, it is a powerful enabler of leadership development.

Questions and exercises for further reflection and to integrate practice and theory:

1. What is the business case for coaching in the company?

2. What coaching approach was chosen?

3. What are the outcomes?

4. What are the advantages of combining 360° feedback and one-to-one coaching?

5. What does optimal transparency mean in this context? Why is it so important in this case?

6. What is your key learning from this case study?

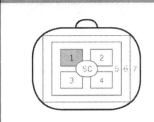

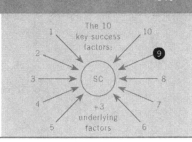

KEY SUCCESS FACTOR 9

EVALUATE EFFECTIVELY AND CAREFULLY

Adequate evaluation is essential to track the outcomes achieved by coaching and to continuously improve the coaching programme. By demonstrating the benefits of coaching interventions, you will raise their credibility and acceptance in the organisation. This key success factor may be a very challenging one, but is very important.

There are two main aspects to keep in mind when it comes to evaluating coaching:

On the one hand, it is important that the data on the coaching programme is as valid and reliable as possible. This call for effective evaluation can be understood in the spirit of: you get what you measure, and you can only manage what you measure. Evaluation, after all, is an enabler and a continuous source of learning for everybody involved in the coaching initiative. Of course, it is also a basis for the tougher business decisions concerning the coaching programme, in particular when the results are not satisfying (e.g. budget cuts, replacing some coaching providers by

others, giving up a whole programme or parts of it, redesigning the whole coaching initiative).

On the other hand, as coaching is largely about people, their behaviours and attitudes, there is a need for care in evaluating that respects people's privacy, fosters buy-in and commitment and supports the overall coaching processes and outcomes, rather than hinder them. Also, coaching may have direct as well as indirect benefits, short as well as long term, at the individual, team, business unit, organisational and/or social level. So special care must be taken in finding evaluation approaches and methods that adequately address the whole complexity of the impact of coaching.

Hence evaluate effectively and carefully. Also, consider both quantitative and qualitative evaluation. A clear vision of how coaching will work for your organisation and a well thought-through coaching plan are essential to evaluate progress against. Only on the basis of this, can you develop an appropriate coaching evaluation plan.

9.1. The nature of the evaluation of coaching

If the core of coaching is dynamic appropriateness – how to evaluate dynamic appropriateness? The crucial point is that this actually depends on each specific context. You cannot evaluate dynamic appropriateness as such, universally, but need to put it into **proper context**.

It is like evaluating sports. While you may well measure the impact of a specific kind of sports on a specific type of person with a specific aim and specific way of taking exercises, it may be extremely difficult, if not impossible, to evaluate sports in a fully abstract way. The same is true for coaching.

So the one simple, easy answer for all evaluation of coaching doesn't exist. Evaluation may take very different forms depending on the kind of coaching programme and the context in which it takes place. Once you specify the purpose and goal of the coaching, its concrete forms and levels used and so on, it becomes measurable.

Therefore, develop a clear coaching concept and a coaching evaluation plan before you start taking any coaching measures. What to consider, which decisions to make and what choices are available to you in this context, is set out in this section.

What is more, as coaching, like all HR and L&D tools, is largely about people and may have a rather complex, direct as well as indirect impact on business performance at various levels – short as well as long term, the attempt to 100% scientifically prove causal relationships between coaching measures taken and final outcomes may be illusory. Evaluation of coaching is more around identifying **high probabilities of causality** – at best, of course, as near to 100% as possible.

Take for example a company where coaching is implemented in a sales force team, subsequently this specific team suddenly achieves higher sales figures (contrary to all other sales forces in the company). There have been no other changes and all the sales team see the reason for the rise of the sales as due to the coaching measures taken. In this case, there may be a nearly 100% probability that coaching actually led to the increase in sales. However, this is not 100% evidence of causality, as – however improbable this may seem – there may be unrecognised, other contributing factors for the increase in sales. Such as a sudden increase in demand in the area of this team, due to many minor external events.

Evaluation on the basis of probabilities is actually common in other areas of business – take for example marketing and advertising in the media. You may well measure how sales increase after an advertising campaign, and sometimes you may even ask consumers whether they saw and liked the advert and bought the product because of it. But still, there will never be 100% scientific evidence, as all kinds of reasons for the increase in buying behaviour may exist. However this evidence is generally considered adequate to support the use of advertising.

When building your business case for coaching as well as in evaluating the results, it is relevant to recognise that 100% certainty on causality doesn't exist, but only probabilities of causality. For example, while you may well assess the return on investment of a coaching programme and whether it is positive (or not) to justify the investment, make sure that you communicate the results properly and do not fall into the pitfall of exaggerating their reliability and exactness.

It is very important to make your chosen evaluation methods fully transparent at any time and to explain the degree of reliability in the evaluation results. In this way, all stakeholders using the results will get a fair understanding of the outcomes and can make well-informed decisions.

9.2. The current practice of coaching evaluation

There are some examples of firms today that really have thought through their coaching initiatives and evaluation. However, in business, the overall current practice of coaching evaluation is still rather poor. This is mainly due to the following reasons:

1. **Coaching is often implemented and improved only in an ad hoc way.** A great number of companies using coaching still haven't worked out what they really want to achieve by coaching and how this is going to work. They may have coaching simply because it is trendy or they have heard it is good – without investing any systematic,

detailed thoughts in its concrete implementation and evaluation. In these cases, a low level of qualitative evaluation by the client (or just having "a good gut feeling") may sometimes already be seen as sufficient evaluation.

2. **There is a general lack of coaching implementation and improvement literacy.** This is true for many decision-makers in companies, but also true for great parts of the coaching industry itself. As a result, many companies prefer to keep their hands off when it comes to working out a professional comprehensive coaching and evaluation

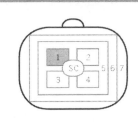

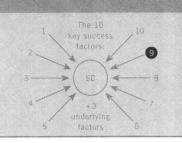

plan. However, by identifying properly qualified external (or internal) support, this problem could be solved.

3. **Resources available for coaching may be very limited.** Where resources (e.g. in terms of budget, time, personnel) are scarce for implementing and improving coaching, firms may be tempted to abandon evaluation. In particular cost-cutting pressures on HR/L&D may influence this. However, renouncing evaluation may turn out to be the wrong decision, as only by evaluating coaching effectively can you get evidence of the benefits (and costs) of coaching and thereby have legitimacy to ask for more resources as appropriate.

4. **Coaching may be seen as having negligible importance.** This is typically true where coaching plays only a minor, subordinate, supporting role without any truly strategic relevance. In particular where the HR/L&D function remains at an operational level and is far from being a strategic business partner at Board level, this is often the case.

5. **There is interest in, but a lack of readiness to pay for coaching evaluation.** Companies may sometimes ask for evaluation of coaching interventions from coaching providers, but at the same time not be ready to pay for it. Neither are they able to carry out proper evaluation themselves. In this case there is an interest in and need for good evaluation, but the benefits are not perceived as overriding the costs. However, given the investment made in coaching, this practice may turn out to mean saving costs at the wrong end.

6. **The benefits of evaluation in the starting phase of coaching are often underestimated.** Effective evaluation of coaching only makes sense, if the expected benefits of evaluation outweigh the costs. When starting a small coaching programme or pilot, the assumption is often that the investment in evaluation should also be small. However, there may be a catch in the reasoning: Especially in the start-up phase, more detailed evaluation is needed, as this is the test and pilot for the acceptance and impact of coaching in the firm and may highly shape and determine the further use of coaching in the organisation.

7. **Evaluation is sometimes abandoned in order to foster the evolving coaching process.** HR/L&D may sometimes be reluctant to evaluate coaching thoroughly, because they fear this may significantly impair and harm the actual coaching process and implementation. Instead of control, they trust in the coaching process and in the people involved. Now, while care is indeed required in evaluating, there is no real contradiction between careful and effective evaluation. If done properly, both rather work together and support each other. So yes, do respect for example people's privacy and any agreed confidentiality provisions, but this doesn't mean you should renounce evaluation overall.

In summary, there is a much stronger business case for the proper evaluation of coaching, than the current, still quite poor practice of coaching evaluation in business may suggest. Businesses are well advised to reconsider their stance on coaching evaluation, its feasibility and value – and to plan for it.

9.3. Effective evaluation

Good evaluation is no coincidence – it is a result of clear and thorough planning, and of choosing the most appropriate evaluation methods for your context.

A clear coaching concept/plan

Only when you know precisely what you want to achieve through coaching for your company and how exactly that process is

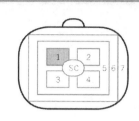

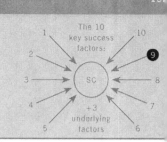

going to work, are you able to identify the right levers and approaches for effective evaluation. In contrast, where organisations are unclear or only make ad hoc use of coaching, evaluation can only be done in a rather sporadic, fragmented way.

So what is actually happening in and through a coaching programme? What are the core processes and outcomes

of any coaching initiative? The figure below gives a useful outline of the core value-adding process.

Be prepared that it may stretch your thinking and be quite challenging at first. So it may take some time to settle. (Also please note: The elements of the core value-adding process will be explained in full detail in Framework 2 & 3 in this book.)

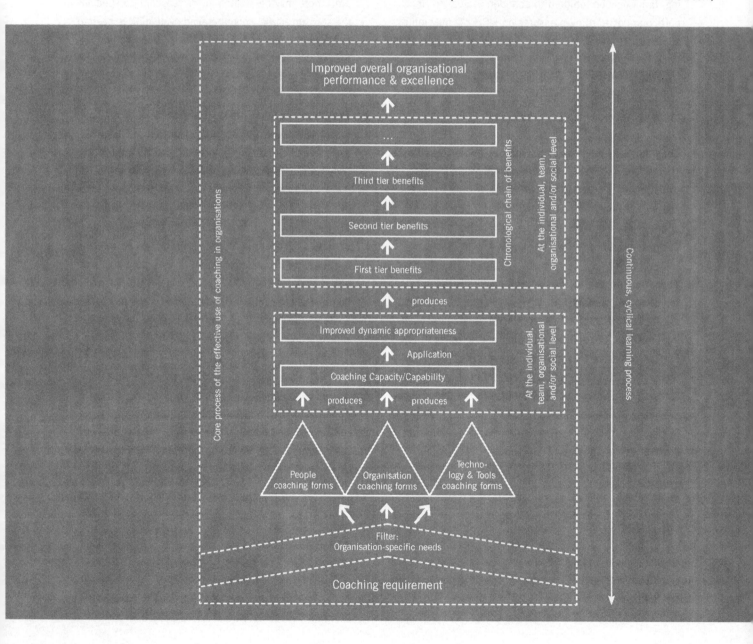

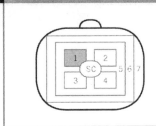
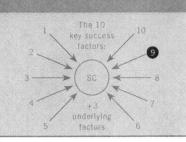

Starting from the coaching requirement (whatever you may understand by it at the beginning), you filter what are your company-specific coaching needs and, on the basis of this, define coaching specifically and choose and implement the most suitable coaching forms in your organisation. This produces coaching capacity/capability in your firm at an individual, team, organisational and/or social level and, in its application, leads to improved dynamic appropriateness. This in turn produces and triggers a whole chain of following benefits (first, second, third , ... tier benefits) at various levels and leads to overall improved organisational performance and excellence. (See again the overview of potential benefits of coaching in key success factor 6). Of course, building up coaching capacity can also be seen as a first tier benefit itself.

For example, a company needs and therefore implements a 1:1 leadership coaching programme. By building a suitable, qualified 1:1 coach pool, professional coaching capacity is made available to company leaders. The actual use of the coaches enhances the leaders' individual coaching capacity in the area of leadership (indirectly also their team's and the firm's coaching capacity). Leadership becomes more appropriate in the workplace and more effective (first tier benefit). The team performance improves accordingly (second tier benefit). Also the company culture overall may become more versatile (third tier benefit). As a final result, overall organisational performance and excellence may improve, becoming visible through higher profitability, higher staff motivation and retention.

So from a coaching perspective, there are mainly **three subsequent types of benefits** in any coaching initiative: The first one is about building coaching capacity/capability, the second about improved dynamic appropriateness through its application, and the third about the actual concrete benefits throughout the company as a result of the first two.

Make sure you think through the above core process (i.e. all steps from the initial idea of coaching to the final improvement of overall organisational performance and excellence in your firm) not only for your whole coaching programme, but also for each part of it and each single coaching intervention/measure:

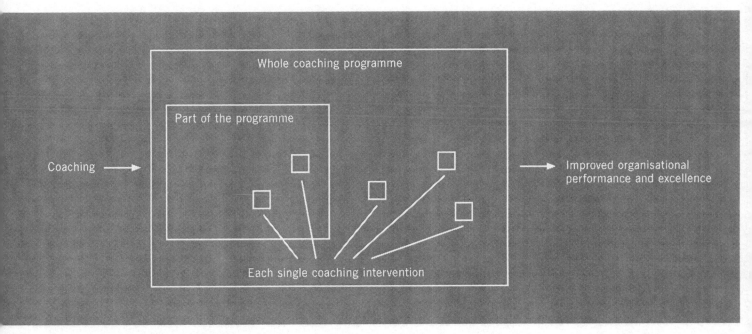

www.frank-bresser-consulting.com

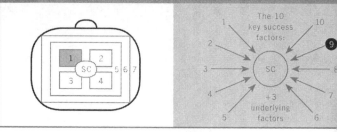

A clear coaching goal and plan is essential, however, coaching is an evolving learning process, and you may need to review and adjust your plan on a continuous basis. In particular where you are still in the testing phase of coaching, there will still be some evolution in formulating your coaching plan, as you learn from the test. What is more, you may have different coaching plans for different phases of the implementation process. Finally, it can also be appropriate to plan a general programme for now and develop specific goals case by case for each concrete coaching intervention later on.

Around the above core process, you also need to design the many primary and support activities to make everything actually happen – see Framework 2.

Regarding the coaching outcomes, planning and tracking **the benefits of coaching** is just one part of the whole story. Developing an appropriate coaching plan also implies consideration of **the limits, possible costs, risks and failure scenarios** of a coaching programme, and how you may avoid these or best deal with them, where they occur. Thereby you are able to weigh up the costs and benefits of a coaching programme and assess the business sense of your planned/current coaching initiative.

This is important, as in the coaching industry you can sometimes observe a taboo around failures or drawbacks of coaching. Also, positive thinking is quite widespread in the coaching industry, which is helpful, as long as it doesn't make people blind for reality and the existing, real risks of coaching. So make sure you see and evaluate coaching properly in an honest and un-biased way.

A professional coaching plan should contain guidance on all these aspects, covering the opportunities and benefits as well as the costs and risks of coaching. It thus gives you a clear picture not only of how coaching is meant to work for your organisation – but also of how you can know when you are not on track any more (and how you need to behave in these cases). Also, it enables you to make a realistic estimate of the expected return on investment of your coaching programme – be it in financial or non-financial terms – as well as of the potential loss that may occur in a worst case scenario.

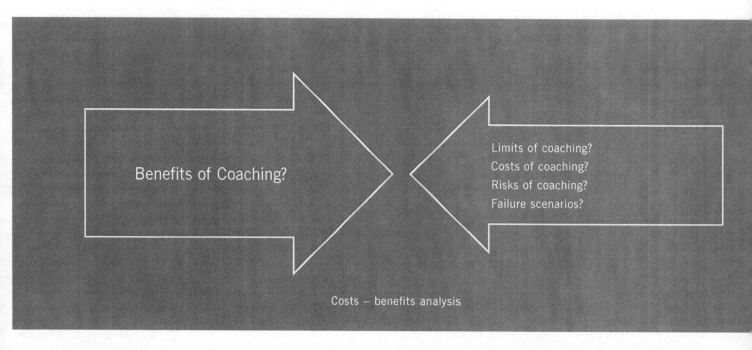

Benefits of Coaching?

Limits of coaching?
Costs of coaching?
Risks of coaching?
Failure scenarios?

Costs – benefits analysis

www.frank-bresser-consulting.com

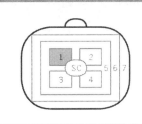 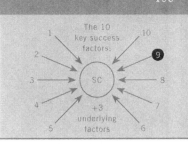

Take an evaluation perspective right from the beginning

By having evaluation in mind right from the start, you can significantly enhance the overall quality of your coaching plan. This is because you have to think through the whole coaching initiative from beginning to end and do not permit yourself to settle with vague statements on the envisaged programme outcomes and processes. Weak objectives, that sound ok at first glance, may instantly be identified and removed.

For example, the responsible manager may be content to just say that 'a 1:1 coaching programme is designed to increase the coachees' charisma'. By considering the evaluation requirements upfront, the manager would now ask for suitable measurement criteria and think through the programme more thoroughly. He or she would identify the business-related purpose more clearly, e.g. 'The purpose of the 1:1 coaching assignment is to improve the coachees' leadership skills (covering in particular the aspect of charisma) in order to enhance the individual and team performance.' Success indicators may include higher acceptance of the coachees as leaders in their teams, improved collaboration and communication and achievement of the individual's business goals (e.g. sales numbers). This provides a number of suitable, measurable parameters for effective evaluation. Additionally the manager would also enhance the overall accuracy and quality of the whole programme.

Another example is when a company implements a coaching culture initiative with only a blurred vision on what it wants to achieve by it. Having evaluation in mind right from the outset prompts the responsible manager to specify what kind of a coaching culture is actually needed for what particular purpose – and how each part of the coaching culture programme is meant to contribute to this. The intention could be to develop a highly collaborative corporate culture in the firm in order to raise sales and staff retention. This allows various measurement parameters to be identified. All this not only fosters effective evaluation, but also enhances the programme's momentum and accuracy. The business purpose and envisaged processes become clearer and can be communicated better.

So taking an evaluation perspective not only helps measure the results of a given coaching programme effectively, but also is a substantial enabler for formulating high-quality coaching plans.

Develop a detailed coaching evaluation plan

On the basis of a well-designed, overall coaching concept, develop a comprehensive coaching evaluation plan covering the aspects why, for whom, what, how, when and at what cost to evaluate.

Key driver of evaluation (why evaluation)

The main reason why you are evaluating your coaching programme will inform and shape the 'what' and 'how' of your evaluation. Reasons why may include:

- Evaluation is a required key instrument to achieve best results through coaching: By reviewing the process and tracking the impact of coaching, you know what really works and what needs further improvement.

- There is a particular need to demonstrate and give evidence of the benefits of coaching, as there are reservations in the firm around its effectiveness and business case. Good evaluation will help raise the acceptance of and support for coaching among people in the company.

- Coaching (or a specific element of it) is still in the early testing phase, and evaluation is a vital requirement to get to know more about coaching as such, before you consider using it in the workplace on any wider scale.

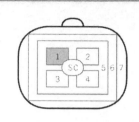

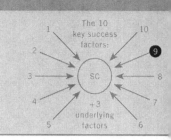

- It is a general standard business requirement to evaluate all business activities. As coaching is one of these, evaluation has to be done here as well. There is no difference to any other business activity.

Evaluating for whom

Who is meant to actually receive and use the evaluation results? Different people may have different expectations and requirements when it comes to evaluation. Also, different users of the evaluation results may require from you different ways of communicating and presenting the results.

Possible receivers of evaluation results are:
- the top management
- the manager/director(s) responsible for coaching in the organisation (i.e. yourself)
- the HR/L&D/OD function (overall)
- people involved in the coaching programme (e.g. coachees, coached team, coaches, trainers, line managers, consultancies)
- all other people concerned or interested in the department/business unit/firm
- the public, e.g. a company presentation on the ROI of coaching on a conference

Evaluating what

In terms of areas of evaluation, you may consider evaluating and assessing:
- the coaching concept/plan/programme as such
- the actual process of designing, implementing and improving the coaching programme
- the whole coaching initiative, part(s) of it or each/a single coaching intervention
- the usefulness of the chosen evaluation approach itself
- the degree to which the various stakeholders involved in the coaching initiative have fulfilled their roles properly (external/internal coaches, trainers, consultants, coaching

champion, HR/L&D/OD function, top management, coachees, line managers, etc.)
- the personal, subjective experience of the coaching measure/initiative
- the level of people's commitment for the coaching programme
- the **outcomes** of the coaching programme (quantitative and qualitative, direct and indirect, short and long term, intermediary and final, at the individual, team, firm and social level): the actually achieved benefits, the costs occurred and the ROI.

Regarding the **outcomes**, you may again differentiate between the following sub-areas for possible measurement and evaluation (which are in particular true for the people coaching forms):

- The immediate costs caused by organising the coaching programme, also including any lost productivity (e.g. by the coachees not doing their normal work during the coaching sessions)

- Theoretical learning/ways of thinking and being/insights gained by people from coaching measures (as well as possibly disadvantageous effects)

- People's ability to demonstrate during the coaching intervention or in a separate testing situation that they can apply and put the learning into practice

- The actual practice, transfer and integration of the learning at work

- The actual impact of this on the people (individually and in teams) in terms of personal growth and performance improvement (qualitative and quantitative aspects)

- The actual impact on customers, suppliers, social environment, etc.

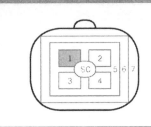

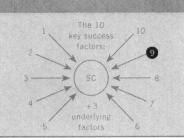

- The actual impact of this on business overall in terms of state, development and performance (qualitative and quantitative aspects)

In all areas, both **quantitative as well as qualitative parameters** may complement each other very well:

1. Quantitative evaluation

The strength of quantitative evaluation (i.e. on the basis of numerical, mostly financial parameters) is that it may make things more tangible, easy to grasp, business-compatible and comparable. But it has weaknesses as well: It may tell only part of the story, distract from other things that may be even more important, and suggest precision and comprehensiveness where these are not really there.

The main financial quantitative criteria for a possible coaching evaluation are classically:

- Costs occurred/Investments made (fees for external coaches, trainers, consultants; absence from the workplace during the coaching; budget for coaching infrastructure: e.g. coaching managers/champions, internal coaches/trainers/ consultants, intranet, brochures, facilities)

- Change in turnover/sales numbers

- Change in productivity and identified cost savings

- Change in profitability

- Savings generated through the coaching/Avoided costs that would have occurred without coaching (e.g. saving additional wages and penalty costs by averting a project prolongation)

- Change in staff retention rate and the related normal costs/savings in recruiting and familiarizing new, suitable employees with the same quality

- Change in employee absenteeism and the related cost savings

- Comparison of coaching costs with alternative methods to reach the same results (e.g. seminars/training programmes)

On the basis of the above quantitative data, you may then establish the **Return on Investment (ROI)**.

There are different ways of understanding and defining the ROI. The following are two possible, tenable ways of calculating it:

ROI = Gain from the Coaching Investment divided by the Costs of the Coaching Investment

(e.g. Gain: 80,000 Euros; Costs: 30,000 Euros; ROI = 80,000 / 30,000 = 2,67)

ROI (in percentage) = Gain from the Coaching Investment divided by the Costs of the Coaching Investment times 100 (e.g. ROI = 80,000 / 30,000 x 100 = 267%)

Whatever quantitative approach for coaching evaluation you choose, take into account that there is always a **qualitative, subjective element**. As stated above, the causality of the outcomes from any investment can never be 100% scientifically proven, so there always remains some element of uncertainty and qualitative assessment.

This qualitative element may in particular come into play in the following two areas:

a. *Qualitative assessment of the causality between coaching measures and the change in quantitative parameters*

Whatever quantitative parameters you may measure to identify the outcomes of coaching, the big question is to what extent the coaching initiative is actually causal for this. You can do a lot to improve the precision of your assessment:

www.frank-bresser-consulting.com

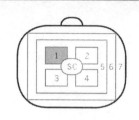

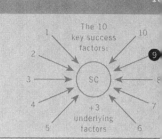

- Identify and track the process and the chain of steps from the coaching measure to the final outcome as exactly as possible in order to actively show the existence and character of the relationship between coaching and the quantitative parameter.

- Identify and add any other possible causes (exclude or assess multi-causality).

- Chart the quantitative measure and the coaching programme over time to identify any patterns – the commonalities and parallels on the one hand and the differences on the other hand (see also the figure). On this basis, identify any likely relationships and correlations and draw conclusions for the question of causality.

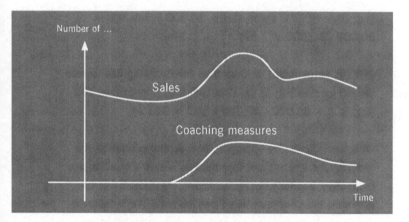

- Ask the participants or stakeholders for their assessment of the causality and how sure they are about their own assessment (e.g. project managers being supported by a coaching programme on average say that the contribution of the coaching measures to the success and profitability of their project was roughly about 20%, and that they were on average 70% sure about the rough accuracy of their own assessment)

- Use coaching in a clear setting (or even some kind of a 'laboratory') where overlapping reasons can largely be excluded (or at least are very well known)

- Have comparison groups to show the difference caused by coaching (one sales team is going through a coaching programme, the others, which are very similar, not)

- Measure the exact status quo before the coaching programme, so that you have a clear benchmark to measure against

- Implement coaching in self-contained units (e.g. team/unit) where the outcomes of the whole unit are already or can easily be evaluated

- Make a well-prepared pilot first, where you investigate the relationship methodically

- Make use of existing research findings on the causalities between coaching and quantitative parameters

On the basis of the above, you may now make a more realistic assessment of the causality between your coaching initiative and the actual change of the quantitative parameter, and adjust your calculations accordingly. You may…

- exclude areas where coaching hasn't really had a significant effect

- assess the contribution of coaching to an outcome and adjust the figures accordingly (e.g. a turnover increase of 1 million Yen and the assessed percentage attributable to coaching is 40%, so the adjusted outcome is: 40% of 1 million = 400,000 Yen)

- keep the numbers as they are, where you may fairly assume a 100% causality (e.g. a project head was very obviously enabled by 1:1 coaching to stand high pressure and make sure the project could meet the deadline and deliver the product to the client in time. Without coaching, the project would clearly have failed to deliver as contracted and the company would have penalty costs.)

www.frank-bresser-consulting.com

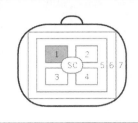 

For significant robustness you can also **assess the reliability of the assessments** of the coaching outcomes. This 'assessment of the assessment' is about how sure you or others are about the assessed causality between the coaching initiative and the identified outcomes.

One useful way of doing this is to give/ask for **a percentage of how sure** you (others) are about the assessed contribution of a coaching programme to quantitative outcomes.

By including both qualitative assessments in a formula, we derive the following equation:

(Measured change of a quantitative parameter within a period)

x **(assessed percentage of causality by coaching)**

x **(assessed percentage of sureness of the previous assessment)**

= **attributable impact of coaching on this quantitative parameter**

Example: There is a sales increase of 90,000 Euros within a time period. The contribution of the coaching programme to this rise is assessed at 30%. The reliability of this assessment is assessed at 80% (quite sure).

Benefit of the coaching: 90,000 Euros x 30% x 80% = 21,600 Euro

As shown, quantitative evaluation may thus imply significant elements of qualitative, subjective assessment. This is important to know – not just for your own coaching evaluation, but also for understanding any published results of coaching evaluation by others. Some publish only a quantitative result (e.g. ROI of xyz %) without mentioning and specifying the qualitative elements included in it. Thereby – consciously or not – objectivity and exactness may be suggested, which are actually not given.

Do ensure you make your evaluation approach transparent to the users of results. In this way, they can put the data into proper perspective and assess their true validity and reliability.

b Qualitative assessment as part of a quantitative parameter

Qualitative assessment may play another very important role in quantitative evaluation. While the previous section was mainly about assessing the causality between a given quantitative parameter and a coaching programme, this aspect precedes it – it is about the qualitative, subjective, personal assessment element within a quantitative parameter.

For sure, you may also use quantitative parameters like sales that are purely quantitative, i.e. clear figures without ambiguity that don't require any subjective, qualitative assessment. In these cases, you only measure and identify the number. However, other quantitative parameters may be less clear/objective and contain a qualitative assessment.

Example 1: Thirty managers joined a comprehensive programme on coaching communication style. They have demonstrably acquired skills in that area, are applying these in their daily work and find their communication has become more effective.

Let's say you want to use a quantitative parameter like cost savings due to the coaching programme and find there are no obvious hard figures on this available. In this case numerical data can be derived, based on qualitative assessment.

One approach could be to ask the 30 managers to assess how much time per day on average they think they save (/lose) by their more effective communication. Let us assume, they on average say 20 minutes. Drawing on this, you could then establish the following equation:

20 minutes at average hourly rate is, say, 40 Euros x 30 managers = 1200 Euro cost savings per day

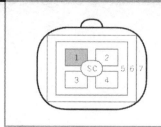
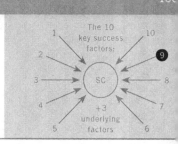

So the number you derive is based on an indicator that is not a figure (quantitative), but the subjective opinion of your people (qualitative).

For the sake of completeness, you may apply here the same accuracy assessment as shown in causality above: Ask the managers how sure they are about their own assessment, and adjust the above equation accordingly. Say people are 50% sure on average, the most likely cost savings would then only be about 600 Euro per day (= 1200 Euro x 50%). Also be aware that the above costs are only theoretically saved, as the managers will work full day anyway. However, you may justify the calculation if you assume the managers will use the additional time in a way that creates value and is at least worth their wages.

Example 2: You have a new 1:1 leadership coaching programme that has led to a higher level of desired skills and attitudes among the participants. You find that these benefits could also have been achieved by seminars and training, as already done in the past. You compare the costs of both approaches and on this basis identify the value gained from the coaching programme. If the coaching programme cost say 50,000 dollar, but training with the supposed same results normally cost 100,000 dollars, then the gain from coaching would be worth 100,000 dollars. (The cost saving is then 50,000.) Again, you come up with figures, but be aware: It was a qualitative assessment (at least partly) to say at what point the results of the two approaches – coaching and training – would be comparable and exactly the same. You do not just read off an objective hard number, but clearly (also) refer to your own personal assessment and opinion to create the figure.

So quantitative evaluation usually contains a qualitative, subjective element. This makes it even more important to make your quantitative evaluation approach and methods transparent.

2. Qualitative evaluation

The classic strength of **qualitative evaluation** is that it shows more of the whole picture and complexity of people's behaviours and attitudes, the triggered processes and the wider impact of coaching. It may capture and illuminate less tangible things that happen and which cannot be expressed by numbers. Its weakness is that the results are less tangible and more difficult to understand and interpret consistently and comparably.

The main qualitative criteria for a possible coaching evaluation are:

- Level of acquisition of coaching skills, behaviours and attitudes

- Change in leadership/management/communication skills

- Personal growth, level of fulfilment in the workplace and work-life balance

- Change in the level of motivation/buy in/commitment/ engagement/satisfaction at the workplace

- Change in ability to change/cope with transition/move into new roles and positions

- Change in the level of creativity and innovation

- Change of level and speed of knowledge transfer to practice

- Change in level of self-reflection and resulting improvement in inter-personal relationships

- Change in career development

- Any (other) benefits taken out of the programme

- Any further remarks/observations/comments (covered in particular by open questions)

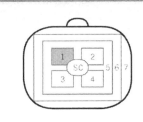
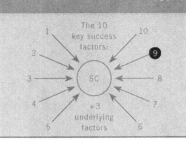

- Change in corporate culture and climate

- Change in employer attractiveness

- Change in the level of customer satisfaction

- Change in brand reputation

- Quality of the experience of the coaching programme

- Assessment of the coaching programme and its various parts and elements

- Assessment of the contributions of the various people involved in the coaching initiative

- Achievement of any non-quantitative goals agreed upon in the coaching contract

These outcomes and benefits also need to be integrated in your **assessment** of whether and to what extent the coaching programme is worth its investment.

For example, on the cost side, you have a 200,000 dollar investment. On the benefit side, you have significantly improved leadership and communication skills of your staff, a more collaborative culture, higher customer satisfaction and employer attractiveness. In the light of your organisation-specific needs, you can then conduct a cost benefit analysis.

You may also call this a **Qualitative Return on Investment (QROI)**. It is an equation with only the cost side being expressed in financial terms, but which is a very helpful tool for analysis and decision-making nevertheless.

Depending on the purpose of your coaching programme, you may also give it a more specific name like Social Return on Investment or Motivation Return on Investment.

The QROI concept may be applied to the whole programme, to parts of it or to a single 1:1 or team coaching assignment only. (Please do distinguish it from the approach commonly called Return on Expectations (ROE) where you just measure to what extent your initial qualitative goals have been achieved.)

As already mentioned above, quantitative evaluation always contains a qualitative element. Now, it is important to know that the opposite is also true: **qualitative evaluation also works a lot with numbers and quantities**. This may occur in many ways – here are some examples:

- Quantifying the qualitative responses received (e.g. '87% of the respondents said that their participation in the coaching programme enhanced their leadership skills')

- Asking for responses on a numerical scale (e.g. 'On a scale of 1 to 10, what is your level of commitment?'; 'we have found out that on a scale of 1 to 10, commitment rose by two points from 5 to 7 because of the coaching programme'; 'our index in customer satisfaction changed from 7 to 9')

- Measuring or testing qualitative outcomes by giving marks in terms of percentages or points out of a maximum number (e.g. 'from 100 possible points, the participants of the coach training on average got 76 points in the final live testing'; 'through my 1:1 coaching, I have reached 70% of my goals')

- Weighting qualitative issues by allocating percentages/points (e.g. 'the weighting underlying our final evaluation was as follows: Key coaching skills counted 50%, establishing the relationship with the coachee 25% and contracting: 25%.)

This quantification aims to make the intangible more tangible, comparable and thus manageable. Here again, it is particularly important to make the subjective, personal, qualitative assessment behind the numbers transparent.

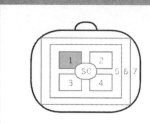

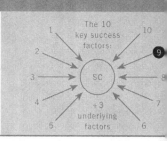

As a conclusion: it will rarely happen that you will find a purely qualitative or purely quantitative evaluation approach in the context of coaching. The boundaries between the two types of evaluation are much less straight-forward, than one may think at first glance.

3. Integrating both approaches

Generally speaking, using both – quantitative as well as qualitative evaluation – in a complementary manner produces the most comprehensive, reliable and valid results. It gives you the whole picture – the numbers as well as what is happening between the lines.

Actually, you can integrate both types of evaluation within the same tool. One well-known and commonly used approach to combine financial and non-financial evaluation parameters is the **balanced scorecard**. When applied to coaching, it is also sometimes called **coaching scorecard**.

Typically the fields of evaluation in a balanced scorecard include 1. Financial results, 2. People, 3. Customers, 4. Process improvement. Feel free to define and create your own company-specific headings of the fields of evaluation, as needed. It is the general idea behind the scorecard that is most important. The fields are usually weighted to indicate impact/importance.

So identify the most essential – quantitative as well as qualitative – goals and evaluation criteria for your coaching initiative within the fields and give them proper weightings. This helps you work towards your objectives and get a more holistic picture of the impact of your coaching programme. Regarding a coaching culture initiative, you may for example choose to focus on sales, staff motivation, team spirit, customer satisfaction and level of knowledge transfer. Maybe you already use the balanced scorecard in other business areas and may easily transfer it to the coaching context.

You can use the scorecard model not only at the level of the whole programme, but also for each part of it and even for a single coaching intervention, as appropriate. You can, for example, ask the coach and the coachee to fill out their own coaching scorecard at the beginning of the coaching sessions as a useful goal setting and evaluation tool.

4. Different focus of evaluation depending on the coaching form

There is a key distinction to make when evaluating coaching: Differentiate between the professional coaching forms on the one hand, that require a professional coach, and the coaching forms on the other hand that are aimed at ingraining coaching principles in the firm.

Regarding the latter forms, you need to evaluate to what extent coaching is actually becoming part of organisational life as envisaged in your company, and what contribution the interventions (e.g. training) have actually made to this development.

As to the professional coaching forms, the focus is a different one: Here the emphasis of evaluation needs to be on whether and to what extent coaching as a service has actually helped coachees and coached teams (and the organisation) to achieve their specific goals. It is normally not the primary purpose of professional coaching forms to also help the coachees ingrain coaching into their daily work overall. Coaching services provide a coaching space to be used by coachees to formulate and reach set objectives – be these linked to coaching or not.

The exact goals of professional one-to-one and team coaching interventions are often set only in the contracting phase of each coaching assignment case-by-case. So you do not know upfront what goals are actually pursued by coachees. For sure, you may limit the scope of coaching and standardize coaching in some way or other, so that you have a rough idea beforehand. But what is actually happening in coach-

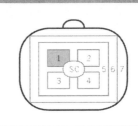
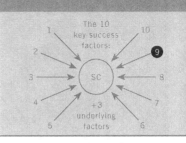

ing, will become concrete only in the contracting phase at the earliest. Also, you have the important issue of confidentiality to be respected (see also 9.4. on careful evaluation below).

Evaluation needs to address all this and, for example, evaluate what goals have been set and pursued. Also, you need to delegate some element of evaluation to the coach and the coachee – and acknowledge that your evaluation is dependent on and can only build on theirs. For good evaluation to happen, good contracting at the beginning and setting a clear benchmark to measure against is key.

Evaluation in professional coaching normally covers the 3 key aspects of relationship coach – coachee (or coach – coached team), the quality of the process and the results. However, be careful about who to make accountable for the results. While it is true that under the same conditions a great coach will most probably facilitate better results than a poorly skilled one, it is important to see that …

- it is above all the coachee who is accountable for his or her own behaviours and action

- the success of the coachee also depends on the matching of coachee and coach (which is outside the influence of the coach), but where the matching is poor, success is likely to be limited

- you are (also) responsible for ensuring the coachee is well-informed and equipped to make proper use of coaching

- the success or failure in reaching set goals can be due to external factors that neither coach nor coachee have influence over

So by having a thorough look at the relationship and the process, you may find what is and has been the coach's real contribution (and what not).

Additionally, professional 1:1 coaching can provide a **unique opportunity for organisational learning** – when the professional coaches share their insights into your company and the emerging themes for organisational learning. This needs to be done in an anonymous and aggregated way in order to respect confidentiality requirements.

5. What (kind of parameters) to actually evaluate?

The following sequence of steps may help you find the best approach for your firm:

1. Consider the aspect of evaluation right from the beginning.

2. Thoroughly think through your coaching plan/concept. Get full clarity on what you want to achieve by coaching and how coaching is meant to work for your firm to achieve these desired outcomes. (Also think about: What may you lose by coaching?)

3. Formulate the steps of the process in an as precise and measurable way as possible.

4. Think about what areas/parameters definitely need to be evaluated. Which are the most important ones? What mix of quantitative and qualitative elements do you need?

5. Prioritise areas by a) very important b) important c) useful d) negligible to be evaluated.

6. Assess how easy or difficult is it to evaluate/measure each of the points on your list under the headings 'very important', 'important' and 'useful'?

7. Consider additional, new ways to make evaluation as easy as possible (by finding smarter methods of evaluation or by re-defining and re-formulating the areas to measure).

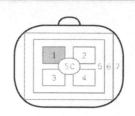

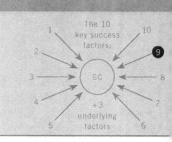

8. Identify the costs and benefits of evaluation of the various points on your list and mark the ones where the benefits significantly outweigh the costs. (Delete areas, where the costs outweigh the benefits.)

9. Revisit the overall coaching plan/concept and consider re-designing it to enhance fit with evaluation requirements. Update and adjust your evaluation considerations accordingly.

10. On the basis of the above, choose the areas and parameters that you are actually going to evaluate and measure.

11. Ensure proper evaluation of these in practice.

12. Evaluate and review your choices regularly and adjust them as and when required.

How to evaluate

The 'what of evaluation' set out above already considers the 'how of evaluation'. Here we add further aspects.

Classic coaching evaluation methods used to generate information are:

- Questionnaires/Surveys
  - hard or digital form;
  - anonymous or not;
  - covering perception/personal estimate/assessment (self or others)/experience/learning/practical transfer/impact/results/skills level/attitude/mindset/culture;
  - asking for quantitative/qualitative responses;
  - various forms: smile sheets/detailed, individualized questionnaires/issue-related survey (e.g. engagement survey; employee satisfaction survey)/etc.;
  - asking for particularly successful areas/areas that need to be improved

- Interviews

- Testing
  (e.g. coaching live testing at the end of a coach training; coach and other accreditation/certification)

- 360 or 180 degree feedback

- Psychometric tools

- Evaluation meetings
  (e.g. round table meeting to assess the progress made and level of achievement towards the goals agreed upon at the beginning of a coaching assignment)

- Management audits

- Using existing and generating new statistics
  (e.g. profit, turnover, productivity, ROI, staff retention rate, level of absenteeism, quantified index of customer satisfaction/staff motivation/leadership skills)

Depending on the nature of your coaching programme, your evaluation methods may need to be more or less sophisticated. Also the emphasis may be on different evaluation methods.

In **professional 1:1 coaching**, confidential questionnaires and evaluation meetings classically play a central role. Contracting and setting a clear benchmark at the beginning are also key requirements in this context to identify what to measure against. This implies formulating the current state, the desired state and finally the actually achieved state in a qualitative and/or quantitative way.

Also, due to confidentiality in professional coaching forms, you may need to differentiate between public and private goals. Only the achievement of the public goals may be evaluated in a public forum, for example in a round table evaluation meeting.

www.frank-bresser-consulting.com

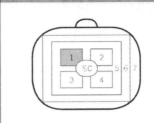

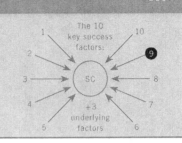

Depending on the coaching contract and the design of your coaching programme, one, more or all of the following people may be involved in the evaluation of a specific 1:1 coaching assignment:
• Coachee
• Coach
• HR/L&D/OD manager/director (you)
• Coachee's line manager
• Coachee's colleagues
Each person has subjective, personal views to take into account when interpreting the responses and assessing the validity and reliability of your final results.

Regarding **coaching leadership programmes**, it is self-assessment, feedback tools and wider surveys that are typically used. Clarity on the definition of coaching leadership style for your firm specifically and how it becomes visible and measurable in people's behaviours, attitudes and performance is needed to develop a questionnaire or other kind of measurement tool around these parameters.

When it comes to **building a coaching culture**, exactly knowing what kind of coaching culture you want to achieve for what purpose and how this is going to work, is even more important. In terms of evaluation methods, you may, among other things, consider using (or developing) tools to make changes in mindset and values in the firm visible. These can for example be surveys which ...

• explicitly ask people about their individual attitudes, beliefs and values
• ask people about how they perceive their team's or the firm's culture
• ask questions in order to draw indirect conclusions on people's mindset and culture from the responses
• identify the change in predominant behaviours, dynamics and characteristics in and of your firm that may be interpreted as expressions of a certain cultural mindset
• find out the predominant stories that go round the organisation that may characterize the inner state and value

system of a firm (stories may sometimes tell more about a company's culture than thousands of formal questionnaires)

Any change in culture includes consideration of organisational structures, technologies and tools. Therefore, when designing and evaluating coaching culture initiatives, do not just focus on the people dimension, but also on the organisation structures & controls and technology & tools dimensions.

In using any of the above evaluation methods, seek to ensure they are truly **unbiased** and don't anticipate the answer. For example the way you ask may influence the way people will actually respond. Similarly the overall context, in which evaluation takes place may influence responses. (Please also see the detailed sections on careful evaluation further below.)

In designing your evaluation, consider whether to ask **specific** questions for specific information or **general** questions to elicit what is important to the respondent. **Closed** questions deliver specific responses, whereas **open** questions allow for further self-reflection and exploration by the respondent, and thus may produce a more differentiated and comprehensive picture. Open questions may also draw out additional, unexpected information/feedback and be a suitable means to foster people's ownership and create momentum for the future.

Very basic open questions commonly used in the context of evaluation are:

• What have you particularly liked about the coaching programme?

• What needs to be improved in the coaching initiative?

• What have you got out of the programme? (Benefits)

• Have there been any disadvantages of the programme for you – and if so, which? (Costs)

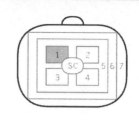 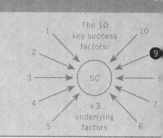

- What are your plans around coaching for the future?

- As a next step, what more do you need from us to sustain momentum and get the most out of the coaching?

- Any further remarks/comments?

When choosing any of the above evaluation methods, consider whether and to what extent it is better to use **existing standard evaluation tools** or **evaluation tools specifically developed** for your coaching programme (by yourself or others).

In practice, the limits between the two are not that straightforward. High quality standard tools normally do have a flexible element and thus can be adjusted to and tailored around your specific needs. Vice versa, when developing a new unique tool for your coaching initiative, it is advisable to also refer to and integrate well-proven elements of existing, standard tools.

Having said this, the classic advantages of standardized tools (and standardization in general) are:
- Easy use and implementation
- Uniformity and comparability of the evaluation approach and results
- Experience and knowledge about its strengths and weaknesses in practice

The advantages of specifically developed tools for your firm (and of flexibility in general), in turn, are:
- Optimal fit and tailoring around your company-specific evaluation needs
- Adjustability as and when required
- Ability for your company to take full ownership of evaluation as desired (more independence from external providers)

Of course, your choices will also depend on what evaluation methods you are already applying in your firm in other areas

and how effective and well-received these have proved to be. Also, you may be able to use the results of evaluation in other areas in your company for your coaching evaluation. So before implementing any new measurement procedures, check first whether you can easily get the desired information simply by using (or slightly refining) existing evaluation systems.

Besides **formal evaluation** as set out above, also be aware of and leverage the full value and benefits of **informal evaluation**. You may evaluate your coaching programme for example by ...

- talking to people involved in the coaching programme

- attending selected (or all) events and parts of the coaching initiative

- observing people's behaviours and attitudes at the workplace and whether these are changing in some way

- being attentive to stories and gossip on the coaching programme and coaching 'in the floors'/'on the streets'

- keeping all your senses open, embracing your head and heart, as well as your gut feeling

- being open and receptive to people's comments, concerns, feedback and critique

This last point is particularly vital: Any coaching measure should take place in the atmosphere of **open dialogue**. This allows for steady informal evaluation, optimal co-creation, high commitment and best results from coaching programmes. Accordingly, this aspect of informal evaluation and open dialogue should also be internalized by all coaches, trainers and consultants involved in the implementation and delivery of the coaching programme.

As a final note on the how of evaluation, consider your **methods of presenting the evaluation results** to the various

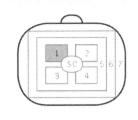
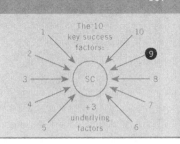

users. Different users may need different information and communication styles or channels. For example, reporting the results to the top management will be different to reporting the results to the participants of coach training. Evaluation results need to be formulated in the language of each user target group, and be tailored around their respective information needs. They may be presented in written (e.g. detailed report, one summary sheet, company coaching newsletter), oral form (confidential 1:1 conversation, presentation before a group) or in a mix of both forms (e.g. visual powerpoint presentation).

When to evaluate

An essential question in any coaching plan is how often and when exactly to evaluate. Depending on the nature of your coaching programme, you will have to consider different points in time and time frames for evaluation. Generally speaking, it is recommended to …

- start the evaluation process before (or latest at the beginning of) your coaching initiative to set a clear **benchmark** and be able to compare the situation before and after the coaching programme (**pre and post** evaluation)

- evaluate **at regular intervals** in order to track the process and identify the intermediary outcomes (this may in particular be required in the case of more complex, evolving coaching initiatives like building a strong coaching culture in a company)

- choose a long-enough time frame for evaluation in order to capture also the medium and long term outcomes of the coaching programme, as well as the sustainability of the shorter term ones. Thereby you avoid two main pitfall scenarios in particular:

  1. You measure only the immediate outcomes of the coaching programme and may find these are extremely positive. However, once the programme is over, it may

well happen that the benefits lose momentum, decrease and largely disappear (some kind of a honeymoon effect).

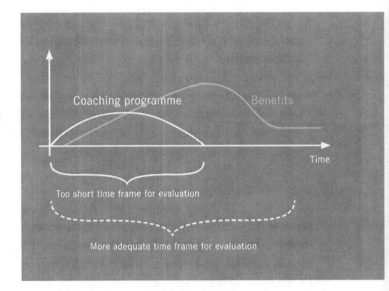

2. Like above, you only measure the immediate outcomes, but this time, you find the results are, in the contrary, very poor. Now, it may happen that a coaching programme takes some time to produce the desired benefits, so not measuring the longer term benefits may also lead to rash, inappropriate conclusions.

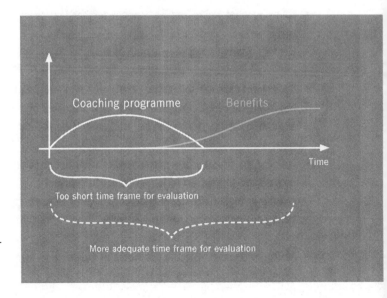

www.frank-bresser-consulting.com

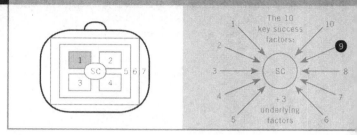

• Beyond formal evaluation which may require a clear time schedule, use **continuous, informal evaluation**.

• See the right timing of coaching evaluation as a permanent learning process that requires constant review and evaluation itself.

• Fully internalize the aspect of continuous evaluation which may best reflect and address the evolving nature of any coaching initiative, and allow for further development and adjustments during the coaching interventions.

Evaluating at what costs

Consider the value-add of your evaluation plan specifically – to what extent the evaluation is worth its investment. It may be nice and desirable to have a perfect, complete evaluation system in place, but as soon as its costs outweigh its benefits, there is actually no case any more for doing it that extensively, and you need to redesign it and reduce it to a reasonable size and shape.

The **classic business case for/benefits of** coaching evaluation are:

• Knowing what works and what needs further improvement

• Better understanding of coaching as such

• Opportunity for self-reflection, -motivation and learning for the evaluation participants as well as for the users of the evaluation results (these can be, but needn't be the same)

• Helping the firm achieve better results from the coaching programme (higher effectiveness and efficiency of coaching; higher (Q)ROI of coaching; savings of costs by taking out or refining inapt measures)

• Ability to demonstrate the outcomes of coaching to top management in order to get the needed resources

The **classic costs/disadvantages** of coaching evaluation are:

• Financial costs of evaluation (e.g. payment for external evaluation tools)

• Time investment of those participating in evaluation, those who process it, and those who are given the results for use.

• Risk of overstraining and/or boring people, taking away the momentum from coaching

• Possible concerns of people about how the coaching evaluation results are used in the firm

Set priorities and focus on what is most relevant for your company. The clearer you are on your coaching purpose and plan, the more precisely and cost-effectively you can design your coaching evaluation plan. You need to be clear on the key parameters that are really important in your case.

Another way of reducing costs of evaluation is to use the existing evaluation systems and results from other areas in your firm. Also consider developing company-specific coaching evaluation tools yourself instead of paying any licence fees to externals. After all, whatever formal evaluation methods you apply, informal evaluation methods (e.g. of open dialogue) are normally for free.

If there are no special circumstances, as a very general rule of thumb, it is recommended to invest about 10% of your overall coaching budget in the evaluation of the coaching programme. However, the less you know about and the less certain you are on the process and outcomes of coaching, the more budget you may want to invest to track these and get to know more about the impact. In particular, this may be the case in the starting and/or a testing phase of coaching.

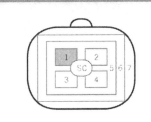

9.4. Careful evaluation

Effective evaluation is just one aspect of appropriate coaching evaluation. The other, no less important aspect, is to ensure careful evaluation.

All coaching forms (especially the people coaching forms) may concern and affect people, their behaviours and attitudes. The professional coaching forms in particular aim to create a space for confidential self-reflection and to work very closely at the human level. Therefore, there is a clear need for careful methods of evaluating these that respect people's privacy, foster buy-in and commitment, produce valid results and support the overall coaching process and outcomes.

Human beings are complex, living organisms with their own privacy, and with a clear sense of what is going on around them. This informs their perceptions and response to the evaluation systems in place around them. So there are three aspects to be particularly aware of when designing your evaluation plan:

1. Protection of people's privacy

2. Sophisticated evaluation methods that embrace human complexity

3. Consideration of the impact of evaluation on people's behaviours and attitudes

In order to **take the human side of coaching into account** and achieve best results, make sure evaluation ...

- is made fully transparent (in terms of all evaluation methods used)

- is positioned and used as a support and learning opportunity for further self-reflection and improvement (e.g. filling out a survey as an opportunity for self-reflection and -evaluation and as a reminder to keep on track; using evaluation results as a source for learning; having 'round tables' of evaluation to learn from and support each other; using qualitative questions in evaluation tools to allow people to explore further)

- is designed in a way that it is appealing and motivating for people to participate (e.g. evaluation shouldn't be too extensive and time-consuming, but quick and straightforward. People should be able to understand what the evaluation is for and what they can get out of it themselves)

- takes into account that people have different styles and ways of learning

- fosters quality and appropriateness of the use of coaching

- respects confidentiality provisions and agreements

- doesn't ask for information that affects people's privacy

- only measures the effectiveness of coaching and/or people's performance using coaching, but not the individual person as such

- abides by legal requirements (e.g. to ask your company work council for their approval of specific evaluation methods first)

- doesn't come across as too mechanical (e.g. by asking too formal/standardized questions)

- is meeting organisation-specific needs and requirements, so that people immediately understand the link to the company

www.frank-bresser-consulting.com

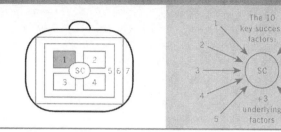

- is not used as a way of imposing coaching through the back-door (e.g. saying officially that coaching is a purely voluntary additional source of personal development without any assessment element, but the evaluation actually makes it obligatory, where, for example, the use of coaching and its outcomes become a precondition for further promotion/employment.)

- doesn't give coaching more significance than it actually has

- doesn't degenerate into a compulsory and boring exercise, where people just pretend or display coaching behaviours, because evaluation asks them to do this

- covers all important parameters (e.g. when you only measure whether coachees enjoyed the coaching process, one day you may find you only have entertainers in your coach pool rather than professional coaches who are able to challenge the coachee as and when appropriate)

- doesn't go beyond what was agreed upon at the beginning

- adequately takes into account the strengths and weaknesses of each evaluation method used (e.g. high subjectivity of 'happy-sheet' surveys)

- is done in a way that the evaluation results, be they positive or negative, are always communicated in a constructive way (e.g. seeing feedback as a learning opportunity not something to be afraid of; offering people a coaching session with a professional coach to review evaluation results)

- is properly understood and used as a tool only, rather than as an irrevocable truth – there must always be room for interpretation and discussion of the results

- includes the evaluation of the evaluation methods themselves, so they can be critically reviewed and improved on a continuous basis

- is thus a living demonstration of dynamic appropriateness and coaching principles

By taking all these points into account, evaluation becomes a very helpful enabler and an integrated part of the implementation and improvement process. It may significantly enhance the quality and benefits of your coaching initiative and will provide you with as valid and reliable data on your coaching programme as possible.

Precisely what carefulness in evaluation actually means in practice, may differ depending on your organisation-specific needs, the concrete design of your coaching programme and your people's preferred behaviours and attitudes.

In order to illustrate this, let us have a more detailed look at the three aspects of confidentiality, commitment and volunteering (/compulsion) and how evaluation methods may respect and work around these in practice. This focuses on the people coaching forms (for your orientation, here is again an overview of the existing forms):

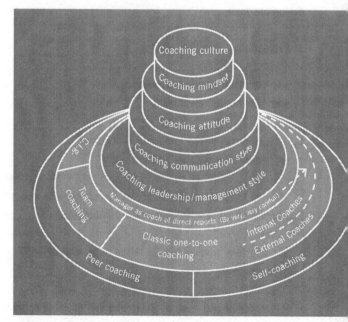

Figure: Overview of the people coaching forms

www.frank-bresser-consulting.com

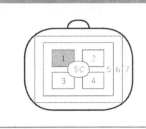

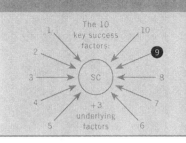

Impact of confidentiality on evaluation

When implementing any **professional coaching form** (one-to-one coaching, team coaching, coaching in groups, or manager as coach of direct report: all marked in grey in the above figure), a clear confidentiality provision or agreement is – for good reasons – needed upfront before starting with the coaching intervention. This requirement is a reflection of the nature of such a coaching form, because a core element of the service is to provide a safe space for self-reflection. Therefore, in the spirit of careful evaluation, any method of evaluation needs to respect this confidential space.

The same principle applies to the more informal and less professional coaching forms of self-coaching and peer coaching.

However, you don't have this confidentiality issue in those coaching forms that focus on integrating the coaching principles into the everyday life at the workplace (i.e. **coaching leadership/management style, coaching communication style, coaching attitude, coaching mindset, coaching culture**). This is because the nature of these is not to guarantee an additional, specific confidential space, but just to use the coaching principles within the confidentiality limits that are already in place in the organisation.

Therefore, evaluation in these coaching forms only needs to respect the normal confidentiality and privacy in the workplace you always have, not any specific professional coach confidentiality.

Let us now take a closer look at confidentiality in the professional coaching forms. In fact, there is to some extent latitude in deciding how far this confidentiality should actually go in a coaching programme and how evaluation may work around this. Let us first illustrate the available models and their impact on evaluation in classic one-to-one coaching as the most well-known and commonly used coaching form:

1. **Complete confidentiality**
   You may decide coachees shall have complete confidentiality, including even the information that they are being coached. This may make sense, for example, for top managers who wouldn't otherwise make use of coaching. One way of managing this is to install an anonymous budget stamp paying system: The coaching target group receives a monthly or yearly set of budget stamps with which they can pay for the services of a coach without the need to inform HR. In these cases, your choice of evaluation methods is rather limited – coachee and coach may fill out anonymous questionnaires in paper form or online and/or make regular reviews and internal evaluation for themselves. Also, you could consider having the evaluation carried out by an external provider who could then serve as an additional 'firewall' of confidentiality from the coachee's perspective.

2. **HR confidentiality**
   Confidentiality may also mean: you as HR manager are part of the confidential space. In that case, you support the process (e.g. by finding a good match coach – coachee) and may evaluate more directly. For example, you can have personalized questionnaires or make an evaluation interview afterwards as appropriate. But you still need to keep the information on the coachee confidential outside HR. So asking the line manager for feedback or applying a specific 360 degree feedback tool among the coachees' colleagues to evaluate a one-to-one coaching intervention may not be suitable. How far this confidentiality outside HR actually goes, may vary depending on each coaching contract.

3. **Small 'round table' confidentiality**
   Another approach commonly used in organisations is that coachee, coach and an HR manager as organisational representative (= small round table model) shall together agree the contract and the business goals of a coaching intervention upfront. Then the coaching process itself is confidential (at least as far as coachee-spe-

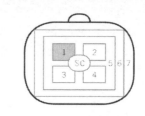

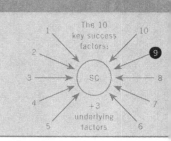

cific information is concerned). After the coaching intervention, the round table comes together and evaluates the outcomes (i.e. to what degree the agreed goals have been achieved). They may also evaluate the coaching process, but without revealing any confidential information about the coachee. For example, the coachee may be asked to assess the coach's performance and way of working, or the whole coaching concept, or to make suggestions to further improve the concept and process.

So the HR manager is directly and explicitly involved in the contracting and evaluation stage of the coaching intervention. But everything in between is confidential. There is a clear distinction between public goals and issues that can be evaluated and private goals and issues that cannot. Coach and HR manager do not disclose any coachee-specific information to third parties.

4. **Possible, additional provisions regarding the small round table confidentiality**

Where a coaching assignment takes place over a longer time period, interim review points are often agreed to give some formalized feedback (e.g. survey form) to the HR/L&D manager on the progress, so that the latter knows whether they are on track or not.

This is also an opportunity to signal the need to re-contract if the coaching has taken a different path than originally planned.

In general, any reporting should ideally be done by coach and coachee in mutual coordination. This means that whenever the coach is asked to assess or report anything to HR/L&D or the line manager, he or she should normally confirm with the coachee beforehand.

5. **Large round table confidentiality (including the coachee's line manager)**

Another approach is to extend the small round table model by the inclusion of the coachee's line manager (= large round table model). In these cases, the line manager will support the use of coaching by his or her

report (e.g. help with smooth scheduling of coaching sessions), give valuable feedback and be involved in contracting and evaluating the success of the coaching intervention. Coach, HR/L&D manager and line manager do not disclose any coachee-specific information to third parties without the consent of the coachee.

Where the manager is involved, this may naturally inform – deliberately or not – his or her assessment of the coachee's potential and performance. So there is some inherent assessment element here which should be openly dealt with and made transparent.

6. **Round table confidentiality with official use of evaluation results for the coachee's assessment (e.g. for promotion/employment)**

Under certain circumstances – in particular where there is urgency – it may even be possible to use evaluation results as a base for assessment in the workplace and link the outcomes of the coaching directly to promotion/employment.

For example, where there are great time pressures to get someone into a new role with greater responsibilities (e.g. new role as a manager of a very large project starting soon) and it is not clear yet whether this person will be able to develop the skills needed, one-to-one coaching may be used to develop the required skills rapidly. If successful, he or she will get the new role, however, if not, the line manager has the option to appoint or recruit someone else for the role.

This early 'alarm' system is also in the interest of the coachee: He or she can honestly and realistically identify and assess where he or she stands, and avoids the stress of a role that doesn't suit.

Time constraints and risk management do not allow for the individual to actually lead the project and see whether it works.

(Under normal circumstances, you may also consider using coaching in a purely developmental way and only make the participant accountable for his or her actual behaviour and performance in the workplace.)

www.frank-bresser-consulting.com

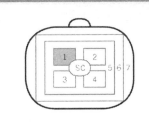

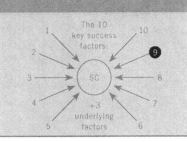

7. Other possible reporting obligations by coach and coachee may be agreed upon, e.g. for the case that ...

- they find the chemistry between them doesn't work and there is no desire to continue the process
- the coaching process reveals illegal or highly unethical behaviours of coachee or coach
- the coaching topic is clearly outside the agreed coaching scope (e.g. the coachee starts to seriously talk with the coach about leaving the company, though this was clearly excluded at the beginning)
- there is a major breech of contractual agreements (e.g. coachee or coach missing sessions regularly without good reason)

8. Coachee is open about the coaching to get peer, team and/or organisational support and feedback

In this case the coachee may get valuable support and feedback on his or her progress from the colleagues in the workplace. The coach/coachee can now also use a coaching specific 360 degree feedback tool for effective evaluation. As a positive side effect, the coachee may serve as a role model and living demonstration of coaching and help create a learning atmosphere in the organisation. The coachee's privacy within the coaching process still needs to be respected in the evaluation.

9. Public live coaching before an audience for demonstration purposes only

In these cases, there is no space of confidentiality (or at best the expressed intent of all audience members not to tell others about it). The purpose of this kind of coaching setting is to demonstrate how coaching works, not really to protect the coachee. Therefore, it is important to make this absolutely clear and transparent to the volunteer coachee, who may still choose to be coached on a real issue. The coach has the responsibility to lead the coaching session with propriety and protect the coachee's privacy as appropriate.

(Distinguish public coaching demonstrations from those also having an audience, but taking place in a protected setting, e.g. as part of a coach recruitment process before a selection panel bound by a confidentiality agreement to evaluate the performance of the coach.)

10. Coaching and evaluation by the HR/L&D manager

This is included only for the sake of completeness: It may happen, especially at the beginning of the use of coaching in a company, that HR/L&D managers want to 'coach' people in their organisation themselves instead of having professional (external or internal) coaches. Please note that this is not professional 1:1 coaching then, but at best a coaching conversation or peer coaching. In this situation, there can also be a strong confidential space between the HR manager and the other person, but this is due to the special status of the HR function then, not due to professional coach confidentiality. Evaluation in these cases normally doesn't take place or only very informally.

So depending on how confidentiality is defined and agreed upon in each case, effective and careful evaluation will need to observe different limits. Whatever confidentiality and evaluation model you choose, make it transparent right from the beginning, so that people know exactly what to expect.

Overall, we can say that the more confidentiality is guaranteed, the fewer evaluation options are available. Depending on each case, you may choose to give one or the other higher priority or both equal priority.

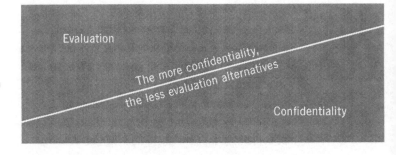

www.frank-bresser-consulting.com

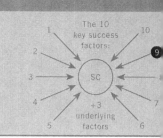

In all professional coaching forms you have a core space of confidentiality for the coachee only. It is the coachee's decision how much they are willing to share (e.g. share a story with close colleagues or in a company coaching newsletter). For evaluation purposes, it is only possible to ask a question like: 'Is there anything else you want to share?'/'Other remarks you want to make?' You may never demand such information.

These rules of care in evaluation are for **external as well as internal coaches alike, bearing in mind that with internal coaches** there is an increased risk of breech of confidentiality, which demands particular care in evaluation.

Also in **team coaching**, the above rules for confidentiality in evaluation apply, but there is an additional dimension to confidentiality here that requires special attention: The team includes a number of people who all hear what the others say, but are not professional coaches themselves. They are not bound by a professional code of ethics and it is important to avoid any temptation to spread confidential information about the coaching process and other team members. It is therefore essential to also clarify the question of participant confidentiality.

This requires an explicit agreement/provision regarding the exact degree to which team members shall be bound by confidentiality. Depending on each case, it may for example be agreed that...

a. no information about the coaching process and about other participants gained in the coaching sessions may be disclosed to others (unless all people concerned by the information agree to this disclosure)

b. only certain kinds of information may be disclosed to others (e.g. people may talk about what happened in team coaching in an abstract way, but may not mention names or describe things that obviously are associated with a specific person)

c. there is no general confidentiality obligation for the participants except where participants explicitly announce that something they say should be kept confidential

Evaluation of team coaching also has to respect the participant confidentiality and may not use any shared information by participants in breech of their confidentiality agreement. For example, if a participant, in violation of the confidentiality provision, reveals disadvantageous information about another team member – evaluation has to ignore this information.

Finally, where the manager of the team is a participant him or herself in team coaching, he or she may use – consciously or unconsciously – the experience and information gained in the coaching sessions as a basis for assessment of the people's potential and performance. So there is some inherent assessment element here which should be openly dealt with and made transparent.

Concerning **coaching in groups**, the need to have a clear participant confidentiality agreement is even more obvious, as participants are coached individually on their own issues. As every participant attends and is an active part of an extended one-to-one coaching session, they need to be properly educated in confidentiality and agree to a rigorous participant confidentiality provision upfront.

With regard to the **manager as coach of his or her direct report**, we have identified the risks associated with this specific one-to-one coaching form: There is a great risk of conflict of roles and the very problematic issue that the coaching process cannot really be confidential, as it is the manager him or herself who is coaching. This is why this coaching form may only be used under very exceptional circumstances – and requires, but also allows, very thorough and detailed monitoring and evaluation by HR/L&D.

Relationship between people's commitment and evaluation

While effective and careful evaluation may significantly help raise people's commitment, poorly handled evaluation may

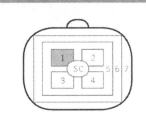
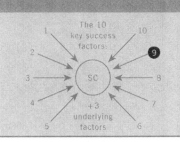

decrease it. It is particularly important that your evaluation methods …

- get the individuals' buy-in and commitment
- are appealing and straight-forward
- have a human touch without losing business focus
- are made fully transparent
- stick to what has been said and agreed upon
- provide useful results in a constructive way that best fosters learning
- not only measure the final outcomes of coaching, but also evaluate the process towards these – in particular also the existing degree of people's commitment (and the ways to improve the coaching measures in order to enhance their buy-in)

In this context, you may need to consider what is people's attitude to evaluation overall in your company or to your specific evaluation methods. For example, where there is high trust that evaluation is done in a professional way and with integrity in your organisation, people will be more likely to welcome your evaluation methods and be ready for it. If there is distrust, a much more careful and maybe limited evaluation approach may be necessary. Also, where people don't like – for whatever reasons – a certain evaluation tool, better avoid it, if possible, and replace it by others.

In particular the top management commitment to support and/or get involved in coaching will also highly shape evaluation. For example, if the top is rather hypercritical about coaching, and so there are strong requirements to give high evidence of the benefits of coaching, evaluation may need to be much more rigorous, than if the top was already fully committed to it.

The level of rigidity of evaluation, in turn, may influence the readiness of people to make use of coaching. For example, people with a sensitive issue may feel uncomfortable with a large round table approach involving their line manager in the contracting and evaluation phase of 1:1 coaching – and so may be prevented from making use of coaching. However,

others may find that such rigorous, more far-reaching evaluation motivates them, fosters their learning and makes the coaching programme especially credible for them.

Similarly, a very thorough evaluation of a coaching leadership style training programme may be experienced as highly motivating for some (potential) training participants, but also as highly disturbing and as too mechanical by others.

Typically, you will need to prioritise whose commitment is critical.

In order to encourage everyone's buy-in and commitment, emphasise **continuous evaluation through open dialogue**. This contains in particular:

- Informing and educating on coaching
- Involving the people (including the top and all others concerned)
- Listening to people
- Asking questions
- Asking for feedback
- Giving people ownership
- Allowing people to develop a coaching attitude from the inside out
- Seeing the implementation and improvement of coaching as an evolving process based on dialogue
- Taking resistance and concerns seriously
- Learning continuously
- Taking action from the feedback received (i.e. adjust, change and develop your coaching plan further, where it needs improvement; communicate your plan in a better way, where the plan is good, but people simply don't understand it properly.)
- Always making clear the limits of people's involvement and influence, and who is responsible for any decisions (e.g. the top/you/the people)

Careful evaluation with regard to commitment also requires working around the different levels of **possible drivers** for people to get involved in coaching measures:

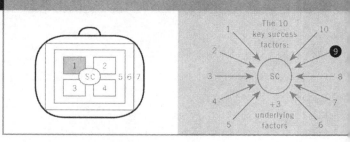

1. Professional drivers

fulfilling your given task/job role; improving individual, team, organisational performance; meeting business requirements; appropriate use of coaching for optimal business success

2. Personal drivers

personal interest in and identification with coaching; seeking also private benefits from coaching, e.g. better social skills, self-management, work-life balance; joy in coaching initiatives; personal ambition to climb up the career ladder and be promoted with the help of coaching

3. Contractual driver

using or adopting coaching, because it is part of the contractual, legal obligations deriving from the employment contract

4. Fear of unemployment/demotion – driver

using or adopting coaching in order not to lose one's job or position

Generally speaking, it is fair to say that the higher people's drivers are in the above list, the better for their professional commitment for and use of coaching. Ideally, the focus is on the professional drivers. These are additionally highly supported by constructive personal drivers.

Therefore, your coaching plan and evaluation should above all emphasize and seek to build and support the first two drivers – and only utilise the third and fourth drivers where needed.

Also, accordingly, proper evaluation should not only measure the outcomes of coaching initiatives, but find out as well ...
- what is the various stakeholders' level of commitment for coaching
- what are their professional and personal drivers
- what can be done to enhance further their commitment/ build up their professional and personal drivers

It is exactly this kind of evaluation process that makes people more aware of their drivers/commitment, and enables them to address and enhance these.

Please note, that people's commitment may not always be high right at the beginning. It may develop during the coaching programme. So as long as there is a minimum commitment to participate in a coaching measure, this may be fine. However, depending on your context and requirements, you may demand a higher level of commitment as a precondition of participation in a coaching programme in your firm.

The aspect of commitment is in principle equally important for all people coaching forms. However, there is one important distinction to make: Classically, the coachees' commitment in the professional coaching forms first of all only means commitment to be coached by a professional coach on the basis of the coaching principles. In contrast, in the coaching forms that aim to ingrain coaching at the workplace, the participants' commitment means commitment to integrate the coaching principles into their own daily work.

Impact of volunteering/ compulsion on evaluation

First, it is important to **demystify the notion of 'volunteering'** in coaching in business and put it into proper perspective.

Actually, to a great extent, it is a myth and inappropriate to think willingness would always have to be ensured in coaching measures. While it is true that the higher the commitment, the better for the success of your coaching programme, this cannot generally be stated as true for the voluntary notion. There is also, accordingly, no direct correlation between commitment and volunteering. Depending on each case, both, a voluntary as well as a compulsory approach, may potentially increase or decrease people's commitment for coaching and support the success of a coaching initiative.

www.frank-bresser-consulting.com

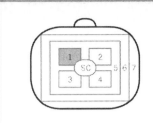 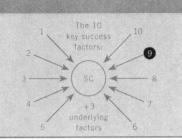

Coaching, as a business tool, takes place in the business context which can be very tough and is characterized by high business pressures. Coaching is concerned with meeting business requirements, otherwise it wouldn't be used. In all companies there are organisational constraints and business pressures. Coaching should not be naively misunderstood as a way of creating a free world beyond any organisational constraints where everybody may just do what he or she wants, neither is it about 'just being nice to each other'.

So where coaching is identified as a strong business requirement, it should have a binding quality in some way within the organisation. Where it has central significance for your firm's success, it is even your job to ensure some form of compliance.

It is essential to give people choice and latitude so they can deal with coaching in a professional, constructive way. They may need education and induction upfront to be able to make well-informed decisions. Where, for example, people could use coaching to cope with certain current challenges, but they don't know the tool yet and so are not able to make an informed, voluntary decision about whether to make use of coaching, a compulsory educational coaching training and one-to-one coaching may be appropriate and to everyone's benefit.

Finally, depending on each case, compulsory coaching may also make the use of coaching much easier and motivating for people. For example, coachees don't need to justify to their line manager why they take time off for the coaching sessions. It thus enhances its legitimacy in the whole firm. Also some people may prefer (or even only attend) compulsory measures, because they are more extrinsically motivated, because they appreciate clear direction, because they have very little time at work and therefore focus mainly or only on compulsory activities, because they feel overwhelmed by choice, or other reasons.

Thus, compulsory coaching, when used appropriately, is in no way a contradiction to coaching and its principles, but

may even be a requirement of these. Voluntary coaching may be appropriate in most cases, but it is far from being absolute. Depending on the specific requirements in each case, **coaching may thus be voluntary or compulsory**.

When the individual is not ready for coaching, this needs to be accepted. There is no sense in physically forcing a person to attend, if he or she definitely doesn't want to. At the same time, it is also clear that any person who refuses a compulsory coaching intervention without good reason will need to take the consequences.

What is the best choice of and balance between voluntary and compulsory elements in a coaching programme? As general rules of thumb, **voluntary** participation in a coaching measure may be appropriate, where coaching …

- is seen and used as one possible tool among many available to achieve certain desired outcomes/required skills

- has minor importance in the firm/is facing low receptiveness within the organisation, so that it would be impossible to offer it on a compulsory basis

- requires a high degree of commitment by the participants

- is already well known, accepted and used, so that it doesn't require a compulsory approach/rule

- is positioned as a development source rather than as an assessment tool or strategic business requirement

- is in the testing or piloting phase

- is implemented in a work environment, where voluntary activities count and are appreciated

Compulsory participation in a coaching intervention may be appropriate, where coaching …

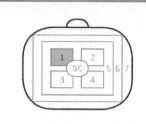

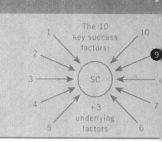

- is a top priority issue in the firm

- is an explicit part of company strategy

- is seen as the only or best way to achieve a specific, desired outcome

- is new to people and therefore requires a compulsory induction phase of educating and familiarizing people with it so that they have a real chance to consider and use it properly

- is facing high receptiveness within the organisation and acknowledged as a business requirement

- needs compulsoriness not to go under (for example, if coaching is not compulsory, people may not get the time off from daily obligations to make use of one-to-one coaching)

- may also be enforced in the organisation as compulsory (otherwise compulsion would only be an empty shell)

Whatever approach you take, make it fully transparent to all stakeholders, so there is shared understanding of the reasons for the choice of compulsory or voluntary elements.

Careful **evaluation** in this context implies the following:

Where coaching is compulsory, continuous evaluation of open dialogue becomes even more important. It makes sure there is sufficient space for discussion about the interventions (before, during and after them) and people can express their concerns and thoughts on coaching.

Remain aware of people's attitude to the voluntary or compulsory nature of the coaching programme – and what impact this has on their behaviour and commitment.

Make sure your evaluation system is fully consistent with the coaching plan and set rules accordingly. For example, where

coaching is fully voluntary, it would be inappropriate to link non-participation to sanctions. But if participation is compulsory, you also then need to monitor and evaluate participation.

It is important to highlight that **the choice between voluntary and compulsory comes into play in various forms at various points** with an impact on how careful evaluation may need to work around this: In a coaching initiative, you may need to decide whether and to what extent …

1. people have to participate in a coaching initiative (implies monitoring of participation)

2. once they participate, they have to continue it for a certain time (monitoring of continuous participation)

3. once they participate, they have to do it in a certain, prescribed way (monitoring of adherence to a prescribed process)

4. once they participate, they have to participate in an assessment or other kind of evaluation of coaching (monitoring of participation in assessment/evaluation)

5. they have to accept the evaluated outcomes of the coaching intervention as a basis for decisions affecting their further career (use of evaluation results as a base for assessment in the workplace)

Let us have a closer look at each of these points in turn, and see what options are available:

1. People's choice with regard to the participation in a coaching programme (monitoring and evaluation of participation)

Depending on the requirements of each case, you may decide in one of the following ways:

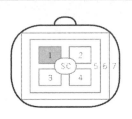

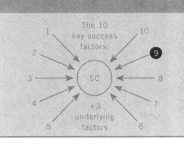

- People manage their own development and request access to coaching (e.g. need to contact HR manager to ask for a coach; ask L&D manager if it is possible to go to an external coaching training which is not available in-house)

- Coaching for an individual may be suggested by HR/L&D or the line manager, but the individual decides (HR manager suggests employee or team to consider having a professional coach)

- People may choose from a range of tools offered to them, e.g. the company makes a whole range of personal development options available to employees. Sometimes these are all voluntary, sometimes the employee may have to take one of these, but is free to choose which one.

- Coaching is explicitly recommended, but not required as a must.

- Coaching is a standard measure people normally attend. However, people may individually renounce participation without any consequences or need for justification.

- Coaching is offered as a standard tool and people are expected to participate, unless they can give a plausible reason not to use it (i.e. in principle compulsory, but there remains a possibility of justified non-participation)

- A coaching measure is a precondition to get a task with greater responsibility/be promoted/get employed (e.g. one-to-one coaching to quickly develop the skills needed for a new position in a case of urgency; coaching leadership style training to get a higher leadership position, where this was identified as an inevitable need and requirement for this position; professional coach training to become an internal coach) (i.e. compulsory if the person wants the new position, otherwise not)

- A coaching measure is a precondition for a low performer to keep his position/job (compulsory, if the person wants to keep the job, otherwise not)

- Coaching is used as a standard element of larger programmes (e.g. as a standard follow-up tool to review the results of a 360 degree feedback; as a standard part in a training programme to allow for optimal learning transfer from the training) (i.e. it is a required element, once people have decided to participate in the wider programme)

- Participation in a coaching measure is a business requirement and thus compulsory. Non-participation can only be justified by specific reasons (e.g. illness)

In all options where coaching is compulsory, it is also legitimate and consistent to monitor participation and link non-participation to possible sanctions.

2. People's choice with regard to the continuation of a coaching programme once started (monitoring of continuous participation)

This point refers to the question of what time period a participant is bound by, once he or she has started a coaching measure. There are three options available:

- There is no time period obligation, but coaching is just used once/on demand as and when needed (e.g. on the spot coaching or only one coaching session to review feedback results; continuation and agreement of coaching hour by hour only)

- The final duration of the coaching measure may be handled in a flexible way depending on how the process evolves (e.g. a set of maximum 10 coaching hours is agreed upon, but if the purpose of the coaching assignment is achieved before, the remaining hours may expire. Vice versa, if the 10 hours turn out not to be sufficient, it may still be possible to ask for more hours.)

- The participant needs to stick to a coaching measure for a certain time (e.g. 10 hours or a 6-month coaching

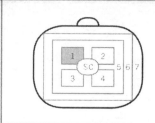

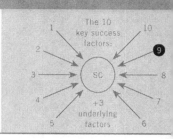

assignment; 12 month professional coach or coaching leadership style training)

3. People's choice to use the coaching programme in a specific prescribed way or not (monitoring of accordance to a more or less prescribed process)

You may give the participants a range of latitude in deciding how they want to use a coaching programme. The process of a coaching intervention may be ...

- very flexible and include significant choice (e.g. employees may get only a budget and the obligation to seek a suitable external coach once a year to work on a topic of their choice: here designing the whole coaching process itself is the responsibility of the employee)

- medium flexible (e.g. free choice between modules during a longer coaching style training; free choice in fixing the venue and dates of one-to-one coaching sessions; free choice of the coach by having three chemistry meetings with different coaches at the beginning)

- fixed (e.g. a one-day coaching leadership training with a fixed agenda; a clearly structured, fixed 10 hours coaching process with a pre-allocated coach).

Accordingly, the evaluation focus may vary enormously: In a fixed design, very specific, straight-forward evaluation may be possible, whereas in a flexible design, evaluation methods may be less fixed, and/or more flexible and sophisticated.

4. People's choice with regard to the participation in an assessment or other kind of evaluation of coaching (monitoring of participation in assessment/evaluation)

Depending on the requirements of each case, you may provide in your coaching plan that participation in evaluation is ...

- voluntary (e.g. by offering a voluntary, anonymous online questionnaire; participants of a coach or coaching leadership style training are given free choice to be tested or go for accreditation at the end of the training; free choice to involve colleagues and ask for their feedback on one's progress)

- partly voluntary and partly compulsory (an evaluation questionnaire may contain obligatory as well as optional questions; some standard evaluation methods may be compulsory, other ones take place on a voluntary basis only)

- obligatory (e.g. all participants of a coaching skills training need to fill out a questionnaire/go through a testing; round table evaluation at the end of 1:1 coaching is compulsory)

5. People's choice with regard to the use of any coaching evaluation results as a basis for decisions affecting their further career (use of evaluation results as a base for assessment at the workplace)

In this regard, the main options available are:

- Evaluation is fully confidential and only has the purpose of evaluation of the coaching programme in general and/or serve the participant as a useful source for feedback and further learning

- Evaluation is in principle confidential, but each participant can freely decide (at the beginning or at the end of a coaching initiative) whether results of evaluation shall become part of his or her official profile/track record

- The results (fully or partly) automatically become part of the participant's official profile/track record (i.e. there is no choice).

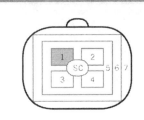

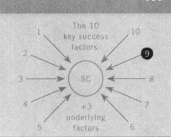

- It may be the purpose of a coaching initiative to use its results as a basis for making a specific decision on the participant's position/promotion/employment. Accordingly, if this was agreed upon by all people involved upfront, the results can be used immediately in this way. (This approach may particularly make sense in the case of urgency. However, under normal circumstances, you may also consider using coaching in a purely developmental way and only make the participant accountable for his or her actual behaviour and performance in the workplace.)

- When taking a compulsory round table approach in 1:1 coaching (i.e. involving also the coachee's line manager) or where the manager of a team is participating in the team coaching process him or herself, there is an inherent assessment element, which needs to be made transparent and dealt with properly.

So make sure you always have an appropriate mix and balance of voluntary and compulsory elements for your coaching programme.

Careful evaluation is highly important and an enabler of effective evaluation.

www.frank-bresser-consulting.com

CASE STUDY 14	RAMADA HOTEL, COSTA RICA

Company: *Ramada Plaza Herradura Hotel* *(four-star hotel, golf resort and conference center)* *www.ramadaherradura.com*	**Main Author:** *Gustavo J. Segura, General Manager* **Co-author:** *Francisco Villalta, Professional Certfied Coach*

Coaching for team collaboration and strategy alignment

Background

Ramada Plaza Herradura is a hotel of 230 rooms, three restaurants and a convention center which is the most spacious and modern in Costa Rica, with over 30,000 square feet of meeting space for conferences and conventions. It was built in the late seventies and in its late history has carried the Sheraton flag, since 2005 the Ramada Plaza flag, with several periods of time without an international brand. It is known in the local market as "the Hotel Herradura", one of the pioneers of the Costa Rican tourism industry. There have been four Latin American presidential summits, NASA conferences, hundreds of weddings, and all kinds of conferences and conventions of the most diverse nature. Also, its location near the international airport and the business centers of the capital makes it an attractive and important hotel proposition in Costa Rica Central Valley.

As the need for hotels in Costa Rica has increased, development towards new and more diverse offerings of modern hotels to target emerging markets is taking place today. The service – understood as the ability to fulfill the promise of consistent quality – is an imperative to achieve our goals in the medium and long term.

Initial situation

In early 2007, Ramada Plaza Herradura had a management team that was typical of the Costa Rican hotel industry. Our human capital was mostly empirical, i.e. based on vast experience gained from long permanence in previous jobs and the time of employment at our hotel, but only with limited formal university education.

At that time, the management team acted more as a group than as a team. There was not a clear strategy and direction to follow. Instead you could encounter uncoordinated actions, passive-aggressive communication, poor interpersonal relationships, departmental "islands" working against each other and also ethically "questionable" leaders. All this ended in an unsatisfactory organisational climate and poor business results.

The arrival of a new General Manager in 2007, with a high academic profile, started a process of management by values and of substantial professionalization of the management team.

The objective since then has been to form a management team that, although still heterogeneous (in training, experience, age, skills, leadership styles, etc.), would surpass

Geographical focus: *Costa Rica*

RAMADA HOTEL CASE STUDY: *Coaching for team collaboration and strategy alignment*

the status quo and become self-challenging, forward looking and committed to work with a shared vision.

During this process there have been gradual substitutions of executives who no longer fitted within the new philosophy of the organisation. So the challenge of building a team also meant bringing together both the established executives and those who had just joined.

Coaching request and intervention

With the support of an external coach, a coaching process was designed comprising one-to-one sessions (with each executive) and teamwork coaching.

The first phase mainly focused on developing skills of two team leaders in order to improve their effectiveness, leadership and contributions to the team and the organisation as a whole. It included nearly 20 individual coaching sessions.

The second coaching phase's primary aim was to create alignment and implement procedures and competencies to coordinate actions and execute our business strategy. This was a program of about a year, which supported the team to act in a consistent manner around a set of shared key goals, build its own capacity to manage and coordinate actions, and create a favorable environment and good working relationships within the team.

The coaching sessions addressed, among other things, visualization and planning, the development of conversational skills, conflict resolution techniques, effective knowledge transfer and other skills. The sessions were complemented by and combined with specific training and consulting as well as interventions to create key goals. Also teambuilding activities were undertaken.

Results and learning

The process made the weaknesses of some of the group members visible and led to changes in the team composition. Those unable to align with the new management philosophy are meanwhile not part of the executive team of the Ramada Plaza Herradura any more. In turn, new managers with a high level of formal education, value alignment and professionalism have been added to the executive committee.

With this scope and practice, the desired results have been achieved: The management learned to work together as a real team and developed conversational communication that made the coordination of actions around key goals – be it of the hotel, each area or each executive – more effective.

One of the greatest contributions of the coaching process lay in the articulation, development and actual achievement of organizational and individual goals: Each member learned to internalize, help develop and contribute to the team-shared vision and set individual goals on its basis. In this way, the contributions of all executives could intertwine and work well with each other to reach the team and organizational goals. This became a cascade effect within the organization – and is in principle what alignment is all about.

The growth in trust among the team members is another outcome worth highlighting. Today, despite the heterogeneity that characterizes them, they have become a real team, where each member is understood, viewpoints are discussed, valuable judgments are identified, everyone supports each other and business success is seen as a joint effort on the basis of a shared vision.

The organisation has improved its business results (including customer satisfaction and economic indicators) and can

www.frank-bresser-consulting.com

Geographical focus: *Costa Rica*

RAMADA HOTEL CASE STUDY: *Coaching for team collaboration and strategy alignment*

today present a high-performing team of individuals at the top management level, capable of improving the work relationships and environment by using a coaching perspective as a key tool for achievement.

Certainly, implementing the coaching program was key to moving the organization forward. Tangible, objective results have been achieved (e.g. time savings, staff turnover reduction, energy and resources savings). Moreover, a new mind-set, skill-set and tool-set have been installed in the management team in order to achieve sustained results.

In summary, the coaching process led to the following lessons and results:

1. Renewal (regarding both its members and abilities)

2. Alignment (under one management team that knows where it wants to go and how to get there)

3. Connectivity (by listening, respect for differences, acceptance, mutual trust and commitment for optimal interaction/team dynamics)

Our key learning/Recommendation:
Make the best use of the power of coaching for achieving management team alignment and full synchrony with your business strategy.

Questions and exercises for further reflection and to integrate practice and theory:

1. What is the business case for coaching in the company?

2. What coaching forms were implemented? What are the outcomes?

3. How has the company evaluated the coaching programme?

4. What are the quantitative and qualitative parameters they refer to?

5. What is your key learning from this case study?

www.frank-bresser-consulting.com

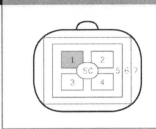
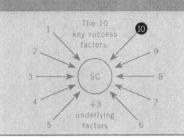

KEY SUCCESS FACTOR 10

ENSURE HIGH INTEGRITY AND QUALITY AT ALL LEVELS

However excellent coaching as a tool as such may be, it can only actually produce benefits and unfold its potential, if it is properly implemented and used. This, in turn, requires high quality and integrity at all levels of your coaching programme. The best tool in the world doesn't add value, if it is applied and used in an inappropriate way. A slight lack of integrity and quality in a coaching initiative may lead to a significant loss of trust, consistency or functionality and bring about the failure of a whole coaching programme.

However, high quality and integrity in coaching may mean different things to different people, organisations and coaching initiatives. This is because both, quality and integrity, are largely **perceptual, a matter of perspective and subjective**.

For example, the same coach (e.g. a highly non-directive coach who specialises in offering space for pure self-reflection) may represent excellent quality in one coaching initiative, but very poor quality in another, where a more directive coach is needed. Likewise, the involvement of a coachee's line manager in the contracting and evaluation phase of coaching, for example, may be permissible and very desirable in some cases, but also be seen as threatening the integrity of a coaching intervention in other situations.

What is high integrity and quality, depends on what the purpose of your coaching programme is, your company-specific requirements, and whether and to what extent everything and everybody involved fit these specifications in theory and practice.

So there is not the one and only objective way of understanding integrity and quality in coaching. It is more about **finding most appropriate standards and requirements for your specific context**.

Accordingly, integrity and quality above all mean **being fit for purpose.**

This means that you can build on the quality and integrity standards for coaching you may find in the coaching industry, to develop your own company-specific ones. While doing this, do not let yourself be intimidated by people or providers claiming to have the one and only 'holy grail' of quality or integrity. Appropriateness for your purpose is the most important criterion for high quality and integrity.

It is important to highlight that high quality for your purpose can, but may not always require for example highly qualified coaches or coaching trainers. Your people do need relevant qualifications for their respective roles. But even as they shouldn't be **underqualified**, they also needn't be **overqualified**. Too many qualifications may sometimes be a burden in fulfilling a role, causing people to over-complicate matters, which can mean a decrease in quality.

Similarly, high integrity can, but doesn't necessarily require your people to be 'exceptionally ethical'. Indeed, your people definitely need proper ethics to fulfil their roles – and here the requirements may in fact be particularly rigorous for professional coaches. But it is mainly about how they actually live values and ethics in their daily work, rather than the ethics they espouse.

Coaches are human beings and therefore flawed. Also, life is complex and requires a continuous search for the best ways of dealing with conflicts of interests and balancing values. There is often no easy solution, and this whole complexity needs to be acknowledged. In this context different cultures may have fundamentally different ethics and values, and so there may be a need for a flexible cultural fit and adjustments.

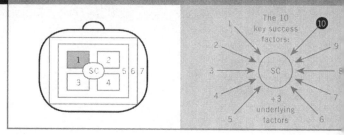

Tolerance and appreciation of others' ethics and values is needed, without this there is a danger of ignoring parts of reality, hindering constructive reflection, open dialogue and learning, and thus – consciously or not – of fostering a non-ethical environment. So just as a **lack of ethics** may impede the coaching success, also **too specific ethics** may sometimes turn out to be limiting, inappropriate and even unethical in a coaching initiative. Therefore, you need sound, adequate ethics that really do have a true fit for purpose in your coaching programme.

It is worth mentioning, that the price a provider charges may have little to do with their qualifications and ethics.

Clarity on the quality and integrity needed to make your coaching initiative work will allow you to be a living demonstration and role model of what you want to see in your firm. The level you choose will depend on the circumstances of each case and probably also on the budget available.

Only go for integrity and quality that are realistic and feasible. Where you define too high standards for your coaching programme, these may quickly become an empty shell: They may paralyse people, who feel overwhelmed, or get ignored by people not taking them seriously. On the other hand, however, the effect of not setting high enough standards is to undermine the whole programme's credibility and functionality, under-challenge people involved in the delivery, and deter people from participating in coaching measures.

When you find you really cannot realistically achieve the required high quality and integrity to run a coaching programme properly, simply don't run it. Instead think about how you may redesign it to make it feasible. **It is better to do less, confident in the standards, than run a big programme of questionable quality.** Recognizing and accepting objective limits of feasibility is important and raises your own integrity and quality.

While you are still in the process of developing high quality and integrity for your coaching programme, stick with it and make the current status transparent. This acknowledgment of the ongoing process demonstrates and enhances the programme's credibility.

As business is highly dynamic, the quality and integrity requirements may change and evolve over time. There is therefore a continuous improvement process in identifying and meeting these.

The key steps or elements of a suitable coaching plan should be the following:
1. Identify and define your company-specific integrity and quality standards for coaching
2. Get and/or develop suitable people to meet the requirements properly, monitor integrity and quality effectively and carefully (see key success factor 9)
3. Intervene and act promptly where the standards are not fulfilled and ensured

Thoroughly think through how you can deal in a constructive way with any failures and mistakes that occur, so that you allow for optimal learning and thereby higher quality and integrity in the long term. It is particularly important to create a **learning atmosphere** where people are encouraged and feel comfortable to talk openly about their setbacks, problems and concerns regarding coaching.

Pay particular attention to ensuring high quality and integrity **at all levels**. This means not only considering **professional coaches, coaching trainers and consultants** (external or internal), but all people involved and all aspects of your coaching initiative:

It all starts with **you** as the developer and manager of the coaching programme, your qualifications and integrity for this task are important. Does the **coaching plan** have the required integrity and quality? Do you **implement** it appropriately? If for example, a coaching initiative creates situations with insurmountable conflicts of roles for people, it is not the coaches and trainers that can be blamed for this, but

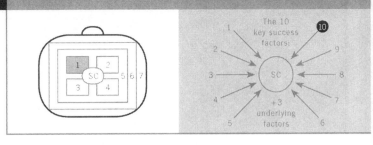

the designer/manager of the initiative. Are the **coachees and the participants of coaching training** adequately prepared and educated for their role/participation? What do you need to do to ensure they are? When a **coachee's line manager** gets involved in the contracting and evaluation phase of a coaching assignment, what integrity and quality requirements are applicable to him or her? What kind of information and education does the **top management** need to make well informed, qualified decisions about the coaching programme? And so on.

The coaching programme is a full package. Each element of it, as well as the package as a whole, needs to meet a certain level of quality and integrity in order to make the initiative a success.

As quality and integrity are subjective and a matter of perspective, it is important to clearly identify and communicate these in a coaching initiative. Only by saying very clearly what is actually expected of the various stakeholders in terms of quality and integrity, will they know what to do, to operate to these standards. It is a frequent pitfall to assume people would have the same quality specifications, ethics and values

as oneself. For this reason, **formulate the governing rules and expectations as succinctly as possible**. The rules regarding quality and integrity may be set unilaterally (e.g. by you), in co-creation (workshop to develop standards involving your people) and/or as a result of a mutual agreement (e.g. 1:1 coaching contract).

When developing your standards, it is useful to distinguish between quality and integrity requirements that **are general and in principle applicable to everyone**, those that are **role-specific** (e.g. coach profile) and finally and most importantly your **own programme-specific** ones, i.e. those derived from the application of the first two types in your specific context.

As a final remark, before we address integrity and quality in more detail, it is worth highlighting that the two are highly related to each other. Quality always embraces integrity in some way (e.g. respecting the rules put in place and meeting legal/ethical requirements as a quality characteristic), and integrity also refers to quality (e.g. knowing one's limits of quality/qualification; offering services or taking on tasks only in the areas where one is properly qualified).

10.1. High integrity of your coaching initiative

This requires the development of suitable integrity standards for your coaching programme as well as a process to ensure compliance.

Suitable integrity standards

Depending on your context, you may define integrity for your coaching programme in different ways and focus on different aspects. We will first illuminate general and role-specific integrity elements, before giving guidance for developing your own, programme-specific integrity requirements on the basis of these:

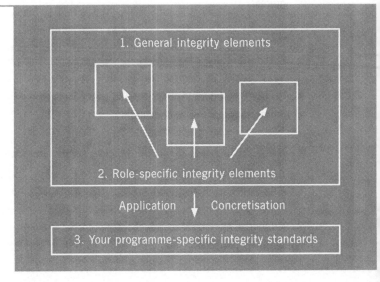

www.frank-bresser-consulting.com

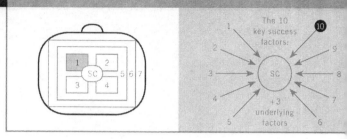

1. *General integrity elements:*

(These are in principle applicable to everyone in coaching)

• Respectful behaviour towards others

• Making appropriate use of coaching/Striving for highest appropriateness

• Aiming for legitimate goals by legitimate means only

• Abiding by the rules set and agreed upon

• Not allowing any personal agenda to impede the professional fulfilment of one's given role/task

• Being sensitive to one's personal and professional limits

• Not seeing coaching as a 'panacea' or as 'the only right way'

• Being attentive to existing and emerging conflicts of roles/interests and dealing with these appropriately

• Acknowledging and working towards a fair balance of interests

• Aiming to be integrated, consistent and credible (good alignment of one's behaviours)

• Pluralistic mindset (respect for and acknowledgement of other approaches and attitudes)

• Sensitivity to issues of culture, religion, gender and race

• Compliance with any statutory/legal requirements

To summarize the above in one short sentence:
Being professional.

2. *Role-specific integrity elements*

For each specific role in a coaching initiative, additional aspects of integrity may need to be highlighted, which complement or reinforce the above. We will have a particular look at the role of coaching champions (you) in an organisation, professional coaches, trainers, consultants, coachees/coached teams, trainees, coachees' line managers and the top management.

Manager/director responsible for the implementation/improvement of coaching in your company (= you)

• Making appropriate use of coaching

• Being aware of your professional limits regarding coaching qualification and of any personal agendas and drivers when it comes to coaching

• Being transparent and giving adequate information on coaching overall and your coaching programme

• Not having any hidden agendas (e.g. a secret deal with a coach to manipulate the coachee in a certain way)

• Respecting confidentiality/privacy (e.g. not asking the coach for information that he or she mustn't disclose according to the coaching contract)

• Sticking to what you have promised/agreed upon

• Avoiding conflicts of interests/roles in your coaching programme (e.g. not implementing the "manager as coach of direct reports" – see key success factor 3 – on a too broad scale), developing protocols on how to behave if these occur (e.g. where a coachee is starting to seriously consider leaving the company in a coaching process, you determine that coach and coachee are obliged to inform the HR manager to discuss further steps) and openly addressing these where they actually do occur (e.g. where

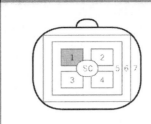
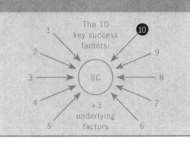

an internal part time coach becomes the line manager of the coachee, you discuss it openly and may replace the coach by another).

- Intervening immediately where integrity rules/contracts are broken (e.g. removing a coach who has clearly violated the principle of confidentiality or has treated a coachee with high disrespect).

- Treating external coaching service providers in an appropriate way, in particular not giving untrue or misleading information (e.g. claiming unrealistically big deals in the future to manipulate price, or using a tender to get companies to submit proposals for a coaching programme, but the actual intention is not to contract a provider, but to use the information to put together an internal programme)

- Doing honest, unbiased and careful coaching evaluation

- Continuously monitoring your own integrity, e.g. by self-reflection, feedback by others and continuous further development

- Possible reference to a general professional code of ethics for HR/L&D/OD managers

Professional coaches (external and internal):

- Giving accurate information on coaching overall and on one's own specific coaching approach and qualifications

- Doing proper contracting before the start of any coaching process (addressing the issues of confidentiality, evaluation methods and ways to terminate a coaching process)

- Abiding by the rules put in place, especially by coaching contracts agreed upon

- Respecting confidentiality/privacy as a particularly important element in professional coaching

- Ensuring optimal win-win for the coachee/coached team and the organisation

- Being transparent in one's methods and tools deployed

- Avoiding any conflicts of roles/interests and openly addressing and resolving these where they occur

- Not engaging in any hidden agendas

- Being particularly sensitive to one's own personal agenda/limits not interfering with and hindering the coaching process

- No importunate selling

- Referring the coachee/coached team/company to other coaches and/or disciplines where the coach comes to his or her personal or professional limits

- Monitoring the integrity of one's own work, e.g. through self-reflection, coachee/team/company feedback, continuing professional development, keeping up-to-date with any statutory or legal requirements, supervision/coach the coach/consultative support

- Keeping records of coaching sessions in accordance with contractual, statutory, legal requirements

- Being respectful of existing, different coaching approaches and contributions by others

- Not bringing the organisation, the coachee/coached team or the coaching profession into disrepute in any way

- Possible reference to a professional code of ethics for coaches (including the possibility of a formal complaint procedure in the case of a breech of these)

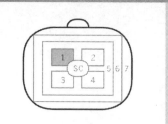

Extra point of particular importance for internal coaches:

- Being especially aware of the risks of breeches of confidentiality and possible conflicts of roles/interests in the context of internal professional coaching within organisations, and how to deal with these properly where they occur.

Extra points of particular importance for team coaches:

- Setting clear rules in the group upfront, in particular regarding confidentiality, and ensuring a safe and respectful learning environment for all participants

- Understanding and dealing with team dynamics properly

Coaching trainers

- Respectful treatment of all training participants

- Setting clear rules for the training right at the beginning (also regarding confidentiality)

- Ensuring a safe learning environment, including respectful behaviour among the participants

- Not letting one's own personal issues interfere with the professional delivery of the training

- Acknowledging one's own limits of qualification and communicating these as appropriate

- Accepting people's privacy

- Keeping confidential information confidential

- No importunate selling

- Ensuring optimal win-win for the participants and the organisation

- Possible reference to a professional code of ethics for trainers

Coaching programme consultants

- Respecting full confidentiality of all received company data and information

- Giving realistic, true information on the possibilities of coaching and one's qualifications in the field

- Truly aiming to add optimal value to the firm and not trying to make a client company dependent on one's services

- Being open and transparent

- Respecting the organisation and all its people at all times

- No importunate selling

- Possible reference to a professional code of ethics for consultants

Coachee/coached team

- Making appropriate use of coaching

- Not abusing company-paid coaching to the disadvantage of the organisation, e.g. using paid 1:1 coaching to find a job in the main competitor firm

- Respecting confidentiality/privacy towards others where applicable (in particular in team coaching and coaching in groups)

- Abiding by the rules put in place and contracts agreed upon (i.e. coming to the sessions in time or cancelling them upfront)

- Showing respect towards everyone involved/participating in the coaching programme (e.g. coaches, trainers, consultants, HR/OD/L&D managers, trainees, coachees)

www.frank-bresser-consulting.com

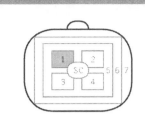
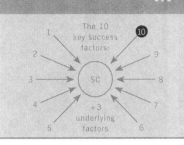

Coaching trainees

- Respecting the trainer(s) and the other trainees

- Abiding by the rules put in place

- Trying to learn and add value, not being disruptive

- Keeping confidential information confidential

Line managers involved in the contracting/evaluation phase of a 1:1 coaching assignment

- Showing respect towards coaching and all involved

- Respecting confidentiality/privacy of coaching

- Trying to learn and add value, not being disruptive

- Sticking to all rules agreed upon

- Possible reference to a professional code of ethics for managers/leaders

Top management

- Having respect for coaching and all involved

- Abiding by what has been agreed upon

- Respecting confidentiality/privacy of coaching

- Not abusing coaching against its purpose (e.g. telling a coach to manipulate an 'uncomfortable' employee in a certain way)

- Striving for optimal appropriateness

- Possible reference to a professional code of ethics for managers/leaders

3. *Programme-specific integrity requirements*

So far, we have covered integrity in a rather **abstract** way, i.e. we have had a look at the general and the role-specific integrity elements. The tricky point about these is that they still **leave a lot of space and latitude for interpretation**. In fact, this is where the subjective element of integrity fully comes through: Depending on your perspective, you may draw very different conclusions from the above.

For example, what is respect? Some may see giving honest, direct feedback – be it positive or negative in content – as a highly respectful behaviour, others may perceive it as impertinent and insulting. **The application of the same abstract value may lead to very different practices in reality.**

To give other examples, there is much talk about confidentiality and coachee commitment in professional coaching, but what are the exact limits? Some may see any report from coach and coachee as a contradiction to confidentiality, many others may not. Some may argue the use of coaching as an assessment tool would violate the ethics of coaching, others may not. Some may reject any involvement of the coachee's line manager in the coaching process because of ethical concerns, others may not. Some (in particular external coaches) may see external coaching as the only coaching form with true integrity, (many) others may see this very differently. Some may see compulsion in coaching as a breech of the coaching code of ethics, others may not at all.

And the list can be continued: Some may see giving advice in a 1:1 or team coaching session as a violation of coaching principles, others may not. Some may question the integrity and legitimacy of coaching being provided to people doing a "questionable" job (in terms of integrity and legitimacy of goals/means), others may have a very different standpoint on this. Some see in advertising copy on coaching already untrue, misleading information, others don't. Some may have a different approach to copyright of coaching material, or to giving presents to get a deal, than others (highly

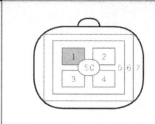
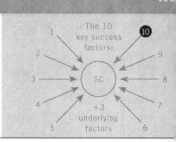

depending on the culture and legal systems in place in each country).

Actually, this list could be continued forever. The point is: Precisely what is most appropriate and what has most integrity, depends on the specific perspective and context. All of the above views may have their role to play and may be tenable under certain circumstances in some way.

So what? – We simply have to acknowledge that too **abstract and vague** formulations of ethics may quickly become an **empty shell and end in saying nothing**, because they can be interpreted in many ways.

It may be no coincidence that the first thing all coaching associations have is a code of ethics. Of course, this may also emphasize the importance of such a code. But at the same time, we need to realize that it is typically formulated in such a general way that no one really runs a risk when subscribing to it. There is so much room for interpretation and at the same time there are such poor means of enforcement. It seems that formal complaint procedures offered by coaching associations have had limited impact so far. So while it sounds good when coaches say they are bound by a professional code of ethics, it may often remain open to question what substance and credibility are actually behind this.

This is also why **existing codes of ethics in the field of coaching are questioned**. In fact, there is controversy about these within the coaching industry itself. The **main criticisms** to consider are:

- Many existing codes of ethics are formulated in such a way that they only apply to professional 1:1 coaches (or even only to external, not internal 1:1 coaches). Professional team coaching for example is often fully ignored. The same is true for other relevant groups in coaching (e.g. HR/OD/L&D managers, coaching trainers) where a coaching-specific code of ethics would also make sense.

- Many codes of ethics are too general to provide real guidance.

- Many codes of ethics are too flexible and can be interpreted at will. In this way, they cannot be enforced and don't add real value.

- Codes of ethics often only provide values (possibly also some dos and don'ts), but not really approaches and strategies to deal with tricky situations (e.g. conflicts of roles/interests). The coach is still left without guidance on the dilemmas of his or her work in their daily practice.

- Some codes of ethics reflect a certain culture and/or miss sufficient cultural flexibility, but claim to be universal.

- Codes of ethics, which seem to be neutral and independent at first glance, may quickly turn out to reflect the fingerprint and interests of special lobby groups (e.g. external coach providers/life coaches). As organisational internal coaches and HR/OD/L&D representatives are often under-represented in most coaching associations, you may sometimes find insufficient understanding of business reality. As a result, not many codes of ethics are tailored around and fully applicable to business.

For all the above reasons, **do not over-rely** on existing codes of ethics in the coaching industry or the above lists of general and role-specific integrity elements. Do refer to them, they are useful – but they can only be a starting point for you to define **your own programme-specific integrity requirements**.

In order to produce appropriate and well-accepted integrity standards for your coaching initiative, you need two steps: Firstly, get fully familiarized with the more general, abstract integrity elements. Secondly, **state very precisely what their proper application means specifically for your coaching programme**.

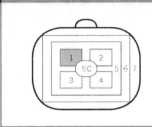
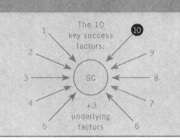

This means developing tailor-made, executable integrity standards: Make the general as specific and operational as possible for your coaching initiative. Set clear rules and guidelines. Formulate precisely what behaviours you expect from the various stakeholders of your coaching initiative. The less room for arbitrary interpretation, the more succinct the responsibilities for all involved. You thereby make your coaching programme transparent and predictable in a most positive sense, and people can really understand what is asked for and stick to this. As a result, any infringements of integrity can easily be identified, tracked and removed.

While this undertaking may require some effort and time from your side, the investment is most likely to pay off tremendously. In considering and formulating the practical rules, guidelines and calls for action, think about ...

- Respect: What does respectful behaviour mean for your coaching initiative and each person involved?

- Confidentiality: What level of confidentiality is most appropriate for your coaching programme?

- Conflicts of roles/interests: What kind of conflicts may occur, and how to actually behave when these occur?

- Being attentive to one's personal and professional limits: What kind of limits? How do they become visible? How to deal with them, and what to do, when they are reached?

- Cultural sensitivity: What does it exactly mean for your specific context? What culture(s) do you have in your branch, organisation and/or country/region/continent? What does this mean for the integrity standards in your coaching initiative?

- Etc.

While developing most appropriate answers to this kind of questions, you may find useful the following guidelines:

- Link the answers as closely as possible to the specific goals, nature, needs and context of your coaching initiative/company/people

- Keep the rules and guidelines straight-forward, practical, clear and well-grounded

- Involve the various stakeholders of your coaching programme and co-create answers (the more perspectives you can integrate upfront, the better)

- Foster mutual agreements/contracts on integrity issues to increase people's buy-in, reinforce integrity and further reduce any ambiguities

- Work towards optimal cultural fit and receptiveness of your definition/rules of integrity

- Argue on the basis of well-grounded appropriateness for the purpose of your coaching initiative, rather than with abstract ethical or moral considerations

- Act only as a facilitator of best practice ethics for your coaching programme (not as an objective moral authority)

- Remain open for feedback and dialogue at all times

Have in mind, that your integrity needs and requirements may change over time. Therefore review your integrity standards and their practice on a continuous basis.

Optimal integrity compliance

The more precisely you have specified integrity in clear rules and guidelines (exactly setting out the behaviours expected and determining the consequences that may result from not abiding by these), the easier it becomes for you to monitor and ensure people's compliance with the integrity standards – and to intervene promptly and effectively, where any infringements may occur.

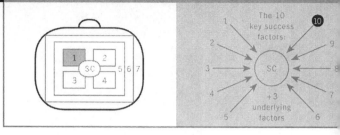

It is about setting and/or agreeing on a clear frame and well defined limits that give proper orientation and guidance right from the beginning. Once you have formulated your programme-specific integrity requirements, it is very important to communicate these (and their rationale) well and consistently to all people concerned.

Ensuring high integrity in a coaching initiative includes the following areas:

Recruiting and selecting people with optimal integrity for the purposes of your coaching programme

Find out what your prospective coaches (or other kind of applicants) understand by integrity in the context of coaching and how flexible they are about their understanding.

Explore how they ensure their own integrity: For example, do external coaches make use of supervision/coach the coach? Are they bound by a professional code of ethics – and is a complaint procedure available? Do they know their limits and are they able to talk about and deal with conflicts, problems, risks and failures in coaching properly? Are they accredited, and does this say anything about their integrity? Do they have high self-awareness and responsibility?

As a particular recommendation, it may be very useful to confront people with questions around specific (fictitious or real) situations of conflicts of interests/roles, and see how they behave or whether they give satisfactory responses/reactions.

Whether you use application forms, interviews, integrity tests/tools, assessment centres, live testing and/or other means, establishing the whole picture and overall impression of a person's integrity for the purposes of your coaching initiative is critical.

Assessing integrity is a tricky, difficult task, not least because people may try to hide where they don't have integrity, or may simply not be aware of it. Unfortunately, experience shows that even well-known coaches with the greatest formal qualifications, accreditations and codes of ethics may suddenly turn out to lack some basics of integrity (e.g. clear breeches of confidentiality agreements; insults towards a coachee/the company; invoicing too much). There is no sense in being naïve here. People in the coaching industry are not better people than others. They are and remain human beings like anyone else with the same basic challenges and problems.

So seek multiple sources of information on this topic and **nothing substitutes the real experience of people**. This is particularly relevant with regard to coaches and coaching trainers who work with people directly. Therefore elements like interviews, live demonstrations or assessment centres are indispensable. Also probationary periods are advisable to allow for a more reliable assessment of a person's integrity.

On the basis of all the above, you may then assess to what extent the integrity of a person is congruent or at least compatible with your integrity standards – and/or to what degree the integrity needed may still be developed by the person in the near future.

Of course, while selecting people, you must be professional and have integrity yourself. Assess people's integrity on the basis of your integrity profile requirements, not on arbitrary, biased or even inadmissible criteria. Don't let your personal agenda interfere with the professional selection process. Always be aware that you may only assess the professional fit of a person for your programme purposes. Remain open for dialogue and feedback, and see recruitment and selection as a two-way communication and learning process.

Building, enhancing and maintaining the required integrity

Develop optimal integrity where it is still (or again) missing, and ensure high integrity on a permanent basis. For this to happen, it is important to ...

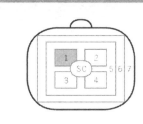

- familiarize people entering the coaching programme with the integrity rules and guidelines right at the beginning, in detail

- provide people with continuous further education and training on integrity issues (e.g. regarding confidentiality, contracting, conflicts of roles, consequences of non-compliance with agreements)

- openly address all relevant issues and possible/current problems around integrity

- have an atmosphere of open dialogue and no-blame

- communicate and update the current integrity standards continuously

- allow for optimal learning and a certain error tolerance (within boundaries; in particular at the beginning)

- provide people with additional support to address and work on integrity (e.g. supervision, peer support, coach the coach, learning networks, exchange meetings, an independent contact point or hotline by phone and/ or email giving the opportunity to raise concerns and insecurities around integrity)

- engage people in developing commitment to the rules and guidelines put in place from the inside out (and to recognize that this authentic integrity may need some time to grow)

- invite and involve people to give open feedback and to help develop the integrity standards further

- role model yourself the kind of integrity you want to see in your coaching programme

Once a certain level of integrity is established in a coaching programme, it may still change and be highly volatile. This may be due to various influences (e.g. change of the economic, social and political climate and business situation, change in management style, pressures/stress, individual situations). The same person may show very high integrity in one year and suddenly a severe lack of it in the next year. For this reason you need permanent monitoring and maintenance of integrity.

Monitoring integrity compliance effectively and carefully, and intervening immediately in a case of infringement of integrity rules

In order to make sure that your integrity rules and guidelines don't become a toothless tiger, proper monitoring and enforcement are necessary. This also implies encouraging all people to immediately give notification of any infringements of integrity (and for example not to wait until evaluation questionnaires covering this aspect are sent out to them).

In this spirit, it is advisable for optimal prevention and intervention to provide a safe, independent contact point/hotline for people observing or being affected by breaches of integrity. You may also offer and put formal complaint procedures in place (e.g. for your managers using your company coach pool). This clearly signals right from the beginning: You take integrity seriously and want the best protection for your people against any infringements.

Where you identify a violation of agreements or other rules put in place, act immediately and address the issue in a straight-forward, open way. First listen to all people concerned and clarify the situation. Consider the next steps thoroughly. Then take proper action in a way that enforces the integrity rules, supports optimal learning and makes people responsible for their behaviours. Where the breech is significant, you may consider removing a person from his or her role. (In extreme cases, e.g. of criminal behaviour, also contact the police or other relevant authority immediately in accordance with your company's policy on gross misconduct.)

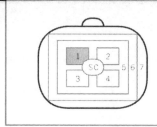
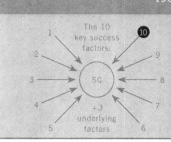

With reference to key success factor 9: Evaluate effectively and carefully, the monitoring and enforcement of integrity need to take place within limits. For example, too closely monitoring may not only impede the success of your coaching programme, but also violate people's privacy and the contracting terms.

When deciding on the consequences of a breech of integrity and the actions required, distinguish between different types of drivers. People may break the rules of integrity …

• unintentionally, because they simply don't know them. In this case action must be taken on your own communication!

• intentionally, but in principle with 'good' intent: They see the current rules in force as inappropriate and feel the need to deviate from them. Here, make clear that any such deviation needs to be agreed in advance and that you may consider further action, but that you are open to any concerns and feedback and are happy to review your coaching plan and integrity standards accordingly. Check whether and to what extent the concerns of the person are justified.

• negligently (neither really intentionally nor unintentionally): They just don't care and/or are not attentive enough, which is very unprofessional. This might also be a more general alarm signal. So in such a case, this infringement should not only be addressed with the individual, but also critically review the level of commitment and professionalism in your coaching programme overall.

• knowingly, but 'only' because they felt forced by circumstances: In this case, make very clear that their behaviour is not acceptable, and consider further appropriate action. At the same time, consider providing people with adequate support, e.g. by showing ways of dealing better with the circumstances and encouraging the person to get support in such cases much earlier in the future.

Also very thoroughly explore what has actually led to this situation (e.g. market pressures; system/organisational pressures; insurmountable conflicts of roles/interests; pressures exercised by another person; individual circumstances) and how these conditions can be avoided or improved for the future.

• intentionally, and with 'bad' intention: Malicious behaviour to knowingly do harm to others is in no way acceptable and must lead to full consequences for the person. Also review and optimize your integrity standards, your recruitment and selection process as well as your whole coaching programme to better avoid such cases in the future. But remember to maintain respect for the person – and, as appropriate and reasonable, take measures and offer guidance and support to facilitate the person's path back to integrity.

Having said this, don't focus too much on the people who have violated the rules. Equally provide support for the people who have integrity and are now disappointed and/or suffer from those incidents. Any violation of integrity rules damages the coaching programme, the organisation and its people in some way or other. It may even, in extreme cases, lead to the failure of whole coaching initiatives.

In handling violations it is important to take all possible measures to reduce the possible damage, re-establish trust, compensate any damage actually occurred and recover full integrity. Take responsibility yourself and apologize to people as appropriate. Provide support, take appropriate action, learn, and keep people up to date on the progress to rebuild optimal integrity.

Reviewing, updating and adjusting your integrity standards on a continuous basis

As the internal and external business environments change, so your integrity requirements may have to evolve over time.

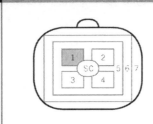
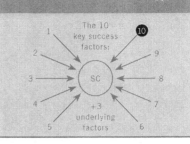

Integrity of organisational structures and technology & tools

Ensure integrity not only with regard to people, but also to organisational structures, processes and operations as well as to technologies and tools deployed.

If you employ people of high integrity, but the organisational system lacks integrity, this will put pressure on them pushing them to compromise their integrity. As HR/OD/L&D manager, you may have limited power to manage this and effect change, but the point is to be aware of such pressures for compromise and take it into account in the design of your coaching programme.

Take a company, where the drive to deliver the quarterly figures is so intense that everything else is neglected, and all structures and processes have been designed around this one-sided focus. When this is really getting out of balance, people may start to disregard the official company integrity standards. It is then a problem of the whole system. People are responsible for their behaviour and some will respond differently from others, but the fact is that many people will feel pressured by the current system into behaviours that represent a breech of the firm's own integrity standards. Figures may be manipulated. Laws and regulations may be disobeyed. Any sense of a proper balance of interests may get lost, generating a systemic lack of integrity.

While building a coaching culture may work to re-establish the proper balance and integrity, you need to be attentive to these dynamics with any kind of coaching programme.

It is important to ensure that the coaching structures and processes are fully consistent and in conformity with your own integrity standards and the existing regulations and laws. For example the criteria in the coach selection process, or any risk of conflict of interest in a coaching initiative.

Also consider the integrity of your technologies & tools deployed: For example, the coaching evaluation tools may include inadmissible questions on personal issues thereby violating privacy and/or data protection laws. No tool may – implicitly or explicitly – include any discriminating elements or assumptions. You must ensure that any tool/approach in coaching is used only by those qualified to do so.

Similarly, in terms of technologies, your IT systems and data recording need to meet the requirements of data protection regulation and be sufficiently secure against any abuse and access by unauthorized people. Your company intranet providing coaching resources needs to be in alignment with copyright legislation and its discussion forums may not have any offensive or discriminating content.

Integrity of your coaching initiative embraces the integrity of all people involved, of all organisational structures and processes set up and of all technologies & tools used.

10.2. High quality of your coaching initiative

This requires the development of suitable quality standards for your coaching initiative as well as a process for proper quality assurance and control.

Suitable quality standards (and profiles)

Depending on your context, you may define quality for your coaching programme in different ways and focus on different aspects. Similarly to integrity above, we will first look at ge-

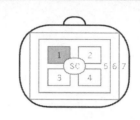
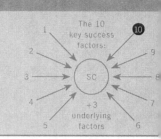

neral and role-specific quality elements, before giving guidance for developing your own, programme-specific quality requirements on the basis of these:

1. General quality elements

These are in principle applicable to everyone in a coaching initiative:

- Clarity on the purpose and overall design of the coaching programme

- Clarity on one's role

- Proper qualities and qualifications for one's role (= fit for purpose)

- Integrity (see above)

- Actual delivery and fulfilment of one's role in practice

- Required qualifications according to legislation/regulation (e.g. laws on who may work as a professional coach)

2. Role-specific quality elements

For each specific role in a coaching initiative, additional aspects of quality may need to be highlighted complementing or reinforcing the above. Again, like with integrity, we will have a particular look at the role of coaching champions (you) in an organisation, professional coaches, trainers, consultants, coachees/coached teams, trainees, coachees' line managers and the top management.

Manager/director responsible for the implementation/ improvement of coaching in your company (= you)

- Proper understanding of coaching and business

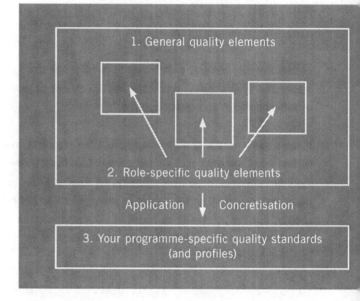

1. General quality elements

2. Role-specific quality elements

Application ↓ Concretisation

3. Your programme-specific quality standards (and profiles)

- Coaching implementation and improvement intelligence (in theory and practice)

- Learning attitude, continuous further development

Professional coaches (external and internal):
(Select from this list as appropriate)

- Clarity on the overall purpose, design and process of the coaching programme

- Understanding of coaching and business

- A well developed, integrated coaching concept/approach that is congruent with the personality, behaviour and skills of the coach

- Being able to explain for whom one's coaching approach/ style fits best and how

- Proven coaching talent

- Proper coach training and education as needed

www.frank-bresser-consulting.com

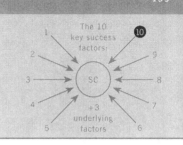

- Coach testing/certification/accreditation

- Coaching experience (what kind and level of experience is required for the purpose of your coaching programme?)

- Suitable coaching mindset/attitude

- Fundamental coaching skills: Having presence, building relationships, active listening, asking questions, giving and receiving learning feedback

- Key skills/knowledge around contracting and respecting integrity/ethics in coaching

- Additional skills and tools around coaching (if and as required)(e.g. a coaching process; psychometric tools like MBTI, 360 degree feedback tool)

- Offering the exact type of coaching required

- Able to use a mix of coaching methodologies and tools, or representing a specific coaching school of thought/coaching approach? (depending on what is needed)

- Expertise and background in the context of the assignment (e.g. leading own business, sales expertise, etc) – as a must have, nice to have or not to have (this depends on the coaching approach and coaching programme purpose)

- Sufficient psychological knowledge to know their boundaries, particularly where the need may stray into counselling or therapy

- Cultural fit/compatibility/receptiveness in the coaching target group and the company overall (e.g. values, style, language, status, level of results orientation)

- Geographical fit (to avoid cost and time of travel)

- Proper individual fit of the coach with the coachee

(including chemistry, and competency to deal with their specific issues)

- Understanding of the overall company context

- Flexibility

- Continuous professional development, learning attitude

- Making use of supervision/coach the coach (as a must have or nice to have)

- Being a member of a coaching association (as a must have or nice to have)

- Contributions to the coaching industry (publications, speeches, etc.) and reputation in business overall (as a must have or nice to have)

(see also key success factor 3: building coach pools)

Extra point of particular importance for internal coaches:

- Being educated/trained in the particular risks of breeches of confidentiality and possible conflicts of roles/interests in the context of internal professional coaching within organisations, and how to deal with these properly where they occur

Extra points of particular importance for team coaches:

- Having a concept for setting clear rules in the group upfront, in particular regarding confidentiality

- Ability to ensure a safe and respectful learning environment for all participants

- Knowledge of and dealing with team dynamics properly

- General social skills

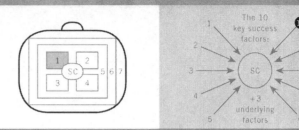

Understanding well the subjective element of quality

The above lists of coach quality criteria clearly show that quality is a matter of perspective and context-dependent, rather than fixed and objective.

By understanding this key point, you ensure optimal choice and avoid being too dogmatic about promoting one certain coaching approach or other. Practically all approaches have a role to play dependent on what is required by a company and its people.

There are various **coaching schools of thought** each having its specific benefits, purpose and style. For example, you find (in arbitrary order) the systemic, GROW, cognitive, behavioural, solution-focused, integrative, appreciative, Gestalt, NLP, transactional analysis, transpersonal, eclectic and ontological coaching approaches – and many others.

It is possible that you may focus on one or more of these, when you find they particularly add value for your firm and specifically meet your needs. But equally, the purpose and nature of a coaching programme may require that you and your coaches/coaching trainers are flexible and open to all kinds of approaches.

Similarly, it would be inappropriate to say that only **non-directive coaching** (or vice versa only **directive coaching**) could be of high-quality, or that a high-quality coach always has to have **expertise and experience** in the field he or she is coaching in (or vice versa). Actually, all of these options are tenable and may be excellent quality depending on your needs.

Similarly, what **proper coach training/education** is, will depend on each individual and your company needs. While training may be an important element to develop a person into a high-quality coach, it is still just part of the story. It is – besides talent and experience – only one main factor. So an individual may have years of training and still be a

poor coach, whereas another individual may just have a few days of training and already be a great coach in what he or she does.

The essence of quality is the ability to coach which is fit for purpose. What precise mix of talent, training and experience has led to this ability is only a secondary question.

Training cannot be seen in an isolated way: What the coach brings to the training and what followed after the training is equally important. For example, it is impossible to build a coaching attitude or mindset within two days, but if someone already has a coaching mindset when entering a coach training, two days may be enough to make the person more aware of this and enable him or her to make better, more conscious use of it in coaching.

Coach training programmes vary tremendously in terms of duration (ranging from 1 or 2 days to about 2 years or more), content (e.g. different schools of thoughts and approaches) and style (e.g. trainer personalities; degree of structure; teaching versus facilitating; directive versus non-directive). Their purpose and focus differs.

So you can match your coaching programme's purpose and focus to that of the training the coach has completed for some indication of suitable quality.

After this detailed explanation on the subjective element of quality, we now continue with the lists of role-specific quality elements.

Coaching trainers

- Clarity on the overall purpose and design of the coaching programme

- Well-worked out coaching training concept/approach that is congruent with the personality, behaviour and skills of the trainer

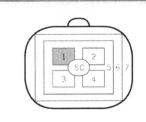
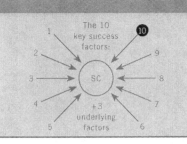

- Being able to explain where and for whom one's training content/style fits best when and how

- Talent, skills, qualifications and experience in the delivery of coaching training (plus any acquired coaching trainer certifications/accreditations, if needed, as a must have or nice to have)

- Proper qualifications regarding specific training topics (depending on your company needs)

- Social and communication skills and the ability to deal with team dynamics properly

- Clarity on how to ensure a safe and respectful learning environment for all participants

- Adequate coaching trainer mindset/personality

- Being a role model of the training content

- Offering the exact type of coaching training required (e.g. coaching skills in general/coaching leadership style/coaching communication style/coaching culture; focussing on specific coaching schools of thought or models; teaching versus facilitating style; appropriate duration; integration of specific elements and tools; proper alignment with the whole coaching initiative and company strategy)

- Cultural fit/compatibility/acceptability/receptiveness in the training target group and the company overall (e.g. mindset, style, language, status, reputation)

- Geographical fit (to avoid travel costs and save time)

- Continuous professional development, learning attitude, reflection

- Being a member of a training (and coaching) association (as a must have or nice to have)

- Contributions to the coaching training industry (publications, speeches, etc.) and reputation in business overall (must have or nice to have)

Coaching programme consultants

- Understanding of coaching and business

- Coaching implementation and improvement intelligence

- Having a well-worked out, competent coaching-programme consulting concept/approach

- Being able to explain where and how one's consulting services best fit

- Having talent, skills, qualifications and experience in coaching programme consulting as needed for your purposes (Please note: As this is a particularly new discipline within the young field of coaching, it is inappropriate to expect great experience in this area. Major coaching programme consulting certifications/ accreditations do not exist yet, but may still develop and emerge in the future.)

- Offering the exact type of coaching-programme consulting services required (e.g. development/optimization/implementation of a coaching programme – as a whole or specific, selected parts of it only; one-off/on-demand/regular/ continuous; local/regional/global; face-to-face/online; proper alignment with the company strategy)

- Proper cultural fit/compatibility/acceptability/receptiveness in the company (e.g. mindset, style, language, status, reputation)

- Adequate coaching consultant mindset/personality

- Continuous professional development, learning attitude, reflection

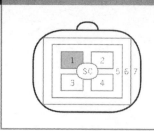

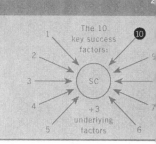

- Being a member of a coaching/consulting association (as a must have or nice to have)

- Contributions to the coaching consulting industry (publications, speeches, etc.) and reputation in business overall (as a must have or nice to have)

Coachee/coached team

- Clarity on the overall purpose and design of the 1:1 coaching programme, and on the exact process of making use of it

- Clarity on one's role (as a coachee/coached team) and on the associated possibilities and duties

- Any qualification requirements needed to be entitled to make use of coaching/Being part of the target group

Coaching trainees

- Clarity on the overall purpose and design of the coaching training programme and on the specific coaching training and the rules put in place around it

- Any qualifications requirements for participation (e.g. only for people having passed training X already/managers accepted only after a rigorous application and selection process/everyone who is interested)

Line managers involved in the contracting/evaluation phase of a 1:1 coaching assignment

- Clarity on the overall purpose and design of the 1:1 coaching programme, and on the exact process of getting involved as a coachee's line manager

- Clarity on the associated possibilities and duties of one's role

Top management

- Clarity on what is coaching

- Clarity on the purpose and design (and outcomes) of the coaching programme already run or planned for the future

3. Programme-specific quality requirements

So far, we have covered quality in a rather **abstract** way, i.e. we have had a look at the general and the role-specific quality elements. The tricky point about these (like with integrity above) is that **their application in different company contexts may lead to totally different definitions and standards of quality**. Depending on your perspective, you may draw very different conclusions from the above. The same coach may be excellent quality in one coaching initiative and bottom quality in another. This is where the subjective element of quality comes through.

So what? We need to acknowledge that – like with the codes of ethics in integrity above – **the above generally formulated quality standards/requirements may end in saying nothing**, if you do not apply and specify these properly for your explicit purposes.

This raises the question of what value and substance any standardized **coach accreditation** and/or **coach training accreditation** provided by coaching associations (or others like universities or chambers of commerce) can have. In fact, such schemes are far from being undisputed – also within the coaching industry itself. Let us look at criticisms of and arguments for accreditation.

The **main criticisms** to consider and have in mind are:

- Accreditation is usually on general coaching competencies, so it still remains with the company to assess the coach

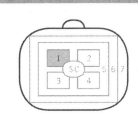

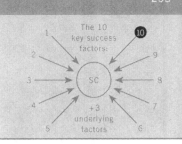

(or coaching trainer) for their specific purposes, be they accredited or not.

- Accreditation may sometimes be based on quite superficial and formal criteria that don't really assess and reflect the true quality of a coach (or coaching trainer).

- Accreditation sometimes suggests objectivity and thus ignores and negates the highly perceptual, subjective nature of quality.

- Some accreditation criteria are questionable and/or may give the wrong incentives for coaches and coaching trainers: For example, having the criterion of a certain number of coaching sessions delivered may not necessarily be a suitable indicator of quality. A highly professional coach who refuses coaching assignments (e.g. for integrity reasons), openly refers clients to other more specialized coaches, and works very effectively and quickly with the coachees, is then at a disadvantage. In contrast, the coach taking any client at any cost, protracting coaching processes and persuading companies to have coaching that is actually not needed, will clock up the hours much quicker.

- Coaches with the greatest accreditations sometimes turn out to be highly unprofessional and very poorly performing. Due to these practical, negative experiences made with accredited coaches, there are severe doubts about the reliability of accreditation.

- In some cases, associations that give accreditation don't let anyone fail – or are highly hesitant to do so. Such a practice may greatly undermine the substance and credibility of accreditation.

- Sometimes, individuals who seek accreditation are not convinced of the accreditation scheme itself, but do it for their branding/marketing only.

- Where the accreditation panel is less qualified than applicants, the latter may reject going for accreditation. For this reason, among others, you also find a number of top quality coaches in the market without any accreditation.

- Some accreditations are given "forever" and needn't be renewed or updated. So accreditation remains, but there are no further checks on quality, which may decrease.

- The payable fee for going through accreditation is sometimes disproportionate to its actual value (and quality). This may be particularly the case for coaches from poorer regions of the world, if the fee is the same globally, i.e. not adjusted to regional levels of income.

- Sometimes, accreditation schemes purport to be universal and neutral/independent, but in reality actually lack cultural flexibility and/or highly reflect the interests of specific groups. In addition, not many quality standards and accreditation schemes are tailored around and fully applicable to the business context specifically.

For the above reasons, some coaching associations also explicitly and deliberately don't offer any coach or coaching trainer accreditation at all. They prefer to promote quality in coaching in other ways (e.g. through CPD, dialogue, education and information).

So while it sounds good when coaches/coaching trainers say they are accredited, it is worth finding out what substance and credibility are actually behind the accreditation scheme.

The **arguments for accreditation** are as follows:

- If accreditation is made transparent, it is definitely a very useful part of professional quality assurance by coaches/coaching trainers: These go through a process where they are measured against a set of criteria, receive feedback and are assessed by an independent body.

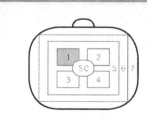

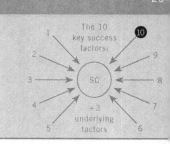

- Mostly, going through the accreditation process provides a tremendous learning opportunity for the applicants as well as the accrediting panel. For example, the coach/coaching trainer may get greater clarity on their coaching approach by formulating, communicating, defending and discussing it with the accreditation panel.

- Accreditation may at least ensure a minimum of quality, so it should help exclude the poor coaches who may otherwise do harm to people and organisations.

- Accreditation embraces and can properly take into account the subjective element of quality (for example, coaches only get accreditation, when they can give sufficient evidence that they have fully worked out their own coaching concept and are able to demonstrate for what purpose this approach works best).

- You can find differentiated accreditation schemes in the coaching industry that explicitly acknowledge different quality requirements for different contexts of coaching (e.g. choice to go through a basic or a specific 'executive coach' accreditation process). Or they offer different levels of accreditation for the same context (e.g. first level, advanced and master accreditation).

- The leading accreditation schemes require revalidation every few years to sustain the standards of the individual's accreditation.

- Where the accreditation process is professionally done by qualified, reputable people on the basis of reasonable and transparent accreditation criteria, accreditation has substance and credibility and adds great value for companies and individuals who seek suitable providers.

- Any criticism of existing accreditation processes must be taken seriously, but should only lead to their optimization, rather than to their removal.

Therefore, accreditation of coaches/coaching trainers can be a true demonstration of high professionalism and quality. So when people say they are accredited, first check that they are not confusing a qualification from a training/education establishment with an independent accreditation and then have a closer look at the scheme and make up your own mind in each case.

So, for the above reasons, do not over-rely on existing accreditations in the coaching industry, but equally do not settle for the above given lists of general and role-specific integrity elements. Do refer to them, they are valuable and useful – but they can only be a starting point for you to define **your own programme-specific quality requirements**.

In order to produce most appropriate and well-accepted quality standards for your coaching initiative, you need two steps: Firstly, get fully familiarized with the above more general, abstract quality elements. Secondly, **state very precisely what their proper application means for the specific context of your coaching programme**.

The clearer you define quality for your coaching initiative (e.g. coach quality profiles setting out your specific quality requirements) and thus know what you want, the easier the recruitment, selection and further development of your people will automatically become.

If done well, you may also consider taking this one step further and develop **your own company-specific coach (and/or coaching trainer) accreditation scheme**.

This may imply the following advantages for your firm: Your organisation has full ownership of the scheme and demonstrates credibility in and commitment for coaching. It can also enhance your employer attractiveness overall. You can fully tailor the scheme around your company-specific needs and thus change and adjust it as needed.

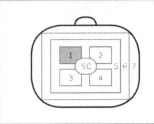
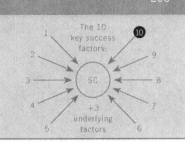

Developing and launching such a scheme requires a rather high level of coaching implementation and improvement intelligence. Therefore, beginners should definitely stay away from such an undertaking – or, as an alternative, seek proper external support.

Your own accreditation scheme may apply to internal and/or to external coaches. In practice today, it is quite often used for internal part-time coaches in a firm having successfully completed a firm's internal coach training.

You may also consider giving official company accreditation to external coaches – for example directly after being selected (i.e. after the successful passing of the recruitment and selection process) or only after proving and having demonstrated their suitability as a coach for a longer time in the firm and/or after a separate accreditation process.

This allows you to install internal accreditation possibly as a precondition for anyone working as a coach in your firm. Or you can implement it as an optional offer for further development of your advanced coaches who want to get to the next level; they can go through this accreditation process and demonstrate, and have certified, their higher level of coaching skills.

You may also establish an internal accreditation scheme containing more than one level or area (Level 1: Accredited Company-Coach/Level 2: Accredited Company-Master-Coach; Areas: Accredited Executive Coach/Accredited Coaching Trainer/Accredited Coaching Consultant).

We hear some comment about the lack of transparency in the coaching market and the associated difficulties in identifying high-quality coaches and coaching trainers. But when having a closer look, this is mostly simply because companies are **not yet sufficiently clear themselves on what they want to achieve by coaching and what exactly to look for**. Thus, with no clear orientation and goal, it is no surprise that some HR/OD/L&D mana-

gers get confused given the enormous diversity and fragmentation of the coaching industry.

While undertaking a specific review of quality standards for your coaching programme may require some effort and time from your side, the investment is most likely to pay off tremendously. It's a good idea to involve your people and co-create answers. Get external support if and where required.

Also have in mind that your quality needs and requirements may change over time. Therefore review your quality standards and their practice on a continuous basis.

Optimal quality assurance

The more precisely you have specified what quality actually means for your coaching programme, the easier it becomes for you to monitor and ensure proper quality – and to also intervene effectively, where a lack of quality occurs.

Quality management and control in a coaching initiative contains in particular the following areas:

Recruiting and selecting people with an optimal fit for your purposes (= quality)

Communicate your quality requirements (e.g. your coach quality profile) clearly, so that coaches who are not suitable for the role are deterred from applying right from the beginning. This will save you as well as potential applicants a lot of time and effort and also enhance the overall credibility of your coaching initiative.

Beyond checking the compliance with more formal qualification criteria (e.g. on the basis of applications forms), do make sure the candidates are able to really **put into practice what is on paper**. Experience shows that formal qualifications alone are not reliable indicators of high competence and fit. Even people with formal qualifications may

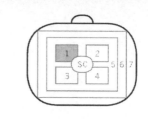 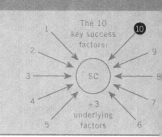

turn out to lack basic quality (e.g. contradicting their own coaching approach in their practice).

To get at the actual practice of a coach, elements like more extensive interviews, live testing (e.g. a live coaching session with a coachee having a fictitious or real issue to be coached on) or assessment centres are indispensable. While the face-to-face experience is generally preferable, another tenable alternative is by phone. Also probationary periods are advisable to allow for a more reliable quality assessment.

In this context, be careful about **recording** e.g. a live coaching session (on tape and/or in particular on video) for selection purposes. While this may be helpful to allow a selection panel to discuss the quality of a coach, it also raises issues of confidentiality, copyright and data protection. Experience also shows that coaches may sometimes feel highly uncomfortable with this and underperform significantly, though they could do much better in reality.

Coach assessment centres, which by their nature are always face-to-face, may help assess applicants from different perspectives and provide a consistent benchmark against which to compare all coaches. Also, they may be useful for standardizing coaching fees and coaching procedures in the company and save time and costs (when compared with meeting each coach one-by-one).

At the same time, assessment centres are time and cost-intensive (for the company as well as for the applicants) and thus need to be justified by a corresponding demand for a number of qualified coaches. If they are not, it is inappropriate to have them.

Recently, coach assessment centres have fallen into some disrepute among coaches, as some assessment centres have required from them significant time and energy investment, and finally only resulted in the selection of very few coaches, and even those coaches selected rarely got any coaching assignments. Also the companies themselves were disap-

pointed by the low value finally derived from them. So make sure you consider this and only undertake assessment centres when you can prove the cost-benefit.

When recruiting and selecting coaches and coaching trainers, one can't expect to get perfect **fit and coverage** for every possible case. Prioritise and make sure there is good coverage of the "must have" areas.

Coaching is – despite its strong development within the last decades – still a rather young discipline and the quality in the coaching industry is still evolving. Some coaching programme designs with great potential and value (e.g. in the area of coaching culture initiatives), are not yet implementable, because companies can't find sufficient suitable, qualified people in the market. So you may say, the breadth of **quality in the coaching market is still lagging behind** in a number of areas. However, particularly in 1:1 coaching, providers already offer great experience and substance of quality in many regions of the world.

The pressure on coaches to sell themselves well is significant. Companies are demanding a lot, often wrongly assuming that top quality is required and available. This leads to a point where some coaches and training and other providers feel tempted to find ways to formulate their expertise in a very appealing way to raise their profile. This requires careful reading, listening and further questions from your side, to uncover the substance behind the statements.

For example, take the term "CEO-" or "Top executive coach". What does this actually mean? There is a great difference between coaching CEOs of big, global firms or only of very small companies employing less than 10 people. Also, is this a service the coach offers, or does it mean the person is already working in this area – and if the latter, for how many years?

If using the number of coaching sessions delivered by a coach to indicate quality, you will need to uncover the detail

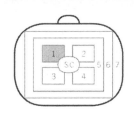
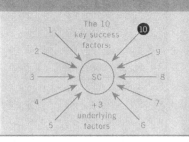

behind the number. Is this only pure professional coaching sessions, or does it include other kinds of coaching conversations (e.g. counselling, development talks, management experience, therapeutic sessions)? What is the average number of coaching sessions per coachee, and what does this say about the coach's approach and the quality of his or her work? How does the coach win assignments and what does this say about the coaching quality?

So information given and language used may tell one story. Questioning, further exploring and interpreting these may lead to a very different one. Once again, be very careful about relying only on what is on paper.

Equally, don't get blinded by the **number of tools** (and their sometimes appealing, impressive names) that coaches say they use and/or have been trained to use. A great tool doesn't necessarily make a great coach, while a coach just listening and asking questions may be absolutely excellent. So have a closer look in each case. Do the tools make sense and is the coach able to apply them properly?

Likewise, **coach certifications** may sound very impressive at first glance. But what is actually behind these also requires further investigation, as everybody may invent and provide a "coach certificate" for their training/education.

Also it is advisable to ask the person how they experienced the training and what they actually got out of it. After all, as already mentioned above, training is – besides talent and experience – only one important element that makes a good coach. So be aware it only tells part of the story.

As a conclusion, be careful not to rashly accept any information given, but ask questions, get more details and aim to complete your picture of the applicant.

What areas high-quality training in coaching should **typically cover:**

We first need to acknowledge that training may vary enormously. However, as a minimum core, coaching training, in the context of the people coaching forms, should contain the following elements in some way or other:

• Coaching understanding
• Building rapport/Social skills
• Active listening
• Asking effective questions
• Giving and receiving learning feedback
• Continuous further development
• Choice and integration for optimal fit
(• Other elements…)

Beyond this, in particular depending on the specific coaching form, the training may need to include further elements.

In order to develop a **coaching leadership/management style**, the above basic training agenda may be adequate or it can be extended as needed.

However, **professional 1:1 coach training** will require further elements as a core minimum which are:

• Ethics in coaching
• Professional contracting
• The coaching process
• Evaluation of coaching
• Relevant coaching models and approaches
• Continuous professional development
• Choice and integration for optimal fit

For **internal part-time coaches**, there should be yet another element, i.e. an additional emphasis on:
• Possible conflicts of roles/interests for internal part-time coaches specifically and how to avoid and deal with them

Training agendas to implement other coaching forms may again look different. In particular, training in coaching culture initiatives may be significantly different.

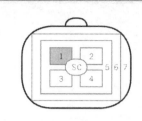
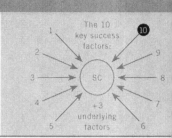

Using the above as a rough orientation and benchmark may help you to assess the quality of the training that a coach or other provider presents as a qualification (or service). Also, it may serve you as a very basic guideline to design internal coach or other training within your company.

Generally speaking, it is also always useful to ask what your candidates themselves understand by quality in their area and how they ensure it in their daily work. This in particular requires an ability to explain where their approach and way of working fit best when and how, and how all this may best link to your coaching programme. How they role model their skills in the recruitment process will give you a good indicator of the coach in practice – their ability to understand the company context, their listening and questioning skills, and so on.

Whether you finally use application forms, interviews, integrity tests/tools, assessment centres, live testing and/or whatever else, the **whole picture and overall impression** of a person's quality for the purposes of your coaching initiative is critical.

On the basis of all the above, you may then assess to what extent the quality of a coach is compatible with your quality standards – and/or to what degree the quality needed may still be developed by the person in the near future.

Where you have an **official, company-specific accreditation scheme** that gives selected coaches automatically the title of an accredited company coach, be particularly aware of the significance of your decision, as the company brand name is involved.

Similarly, where your coaching concept provides that people – after having successfully completed an **internal coach training** – not only get certified, but also automatically join the official coach pool, be particularly careful about the pass criteria. Also, identify upfront who should be entitled to participate in an internal coach training, and what areas the internal training should cover (see above).

Overall, when selecting coaches, keep an eye on not getting lost in detail or even the irrelevant. Make sure you **check the essentials** very thoroughly (i.e. listening, asking questions and giving and receiving learning feedback). Sometimes there is too much of a tendency among HR/L&D/OD managers to focus on rather marginal things, only because they feel more safe when they can grab hold of something.

As another general recommendation building on the above, **have self-confidence and assertiveness in making your own choices and trust also your senses and intuition**. While it is important to be able to account for and defend your choices of coaches in terms of measurable and/or at least tangible criteria, this shouldn't lead to the specious point where you choose low-quality coaches because you emphasize too rigidly purely formal qualifications under the illusion that you are "on the safe side".

Also keep in mind that being selected is only the first step for the coach. After an induction and familiarisation phase, the coach, when becoming active in the company, will undergo permanent further assessment and evaluation, in order to continue to prove his or her suitability. This is the more important element of assessing quality, as only in practice will you actually find out how credibly and effectively a coach really works.

Of course, while selecting people, **make sure your own choices are themselves of high quality**. Unfortunately, very often HR/L&D/OD managers are not properly qualified to select coaches, but seek to do it themselves nevertheless. In these cases, consider getting proper internal and/or external support. Depending on the size of your coaching initiative and the practice and responsibilities in your company, you may choose to have the coaches selected by ...

- yourself only
- yourself plus a double-check by another colleague
- a selection panel
- a proper, external service provider

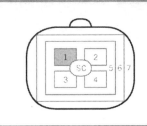

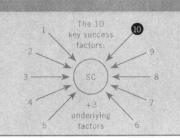

- a combination of any of the above (e.g. a panel including an external coaching consultant; pre-selection by yourself plus a final selection round for the remaining coaches by a panel)

Take care that, where you involve an external service provider, this company is truly independent and doesn't just get their network of coaches into your coach pool.

Finally, always see recruitment and selection as a two-way communication and learning process. Remain open for dialogue and feedback and optimize your processes on a continuous basis. Actually, you can learn a lot about coaching during the process.

Building, enhancing and maintaining the required fit for purpose (quality)

Develop optimal quality where it is still (or again) missing, and ensure high quality on a permanent basis. For this to happen, it is important to …

- provide coaches (and all others involved in the delivery of the coaching programme like coaching trainers or yourself) with proper training/education as needed before they start any coaching activity. This particularly applies to the preparation of internal part-time coaches for their coaching assignments.

- have an adequate familiarization and induction phase for all involved

- provide people with continuous further training, education and information (e.g. coaching newsletter, briefing, coach teleconferences, intranet, coaching literature made available)

- communicate and update your coaching business case and coaching quality requirements on a regular basis

- provide people with opportunities for further development (e.g. offering different levels of accreditation; organising coaching days/events; supervision, peer support, coach the coach, learning networks; installing a contact point or hotline by phone and/or email giving the opportunity to discuss and raise questions of quality)

- require from coaches, coaching trainers and others evidence of their continuous professional development and activities for quality assurance

- keep your coaching programme fresh

- invite and involve people to give open feedback and to help develop the quality standards further

- openly address all relevant issues and possible/current problems around quality; have an atmosphere of open dialogue and no-blame; allow for optimal learning and a certain error tolerance (within boundaries)

- evaluate effectively and carefully

- role model yourself the kind of quality you want to see in your coaching programme.

Once a certain level of quality is established in a coaching programme, it may again change over time. This may be true overall – or for a specific person or part in a coaching initiative. So you need permanent monitoring and maintenance of quality.

Monitoring quality compliance effectively and carefully, and intervening immediately in case of low quality

In order to make sure that your quality standards don't become an empty shell or a toothless tiger, proper monitoring, evaluation and enforcement are necessary.

www.frank-bresser-consulting.com

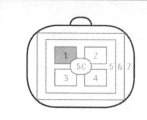
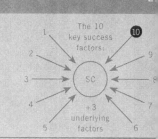

This may also imply encouraging all people to immediately give notification of any significant decrease of quality – and for example not to wait until evaluation questionnaires covering this aspect will be sent out to them at a later date.

In this spirit, it may be advisable (for optimal prevention and intervention) to provide a contact point/hotline for people observing, or themselves being affected by, elements of low quality in your coaching programme. You may also offer and put formal complaint procedures in place. This signals right from the beginning that you take high quality seriously.

Where you encounter low quality, take action immediately – and address the issue in a straight-forward, open way. Clarify the situation, consider steps thoroughly and take proper action (also see above: Building, enhancing and maintaining the required fit for purpose). Use an approach that enforces the quality standards, supports optimal learning and makes people accountable for their behaviours. In grave cases, you may also consider redesigning the coaching programme (or parts of it) from scratch or removing a person from his or her role.

With reference to key success factor 9 (see above: Evaluate effectively and carefully), keep in mind that also the monitoring and enforcement of quality standards need to take place within clear limits. For example, too close monitoring may violate people's privacy and be illegal, but also lead to low quality itself and impede the success of your coaching programme.

When deciding on the consequences of non-observance of quality standards and your actions required, distinguish between a lack of ability on the one hand and a lack of willingness/commitment on the other hand.

Ways to address a lack of ability are:
• Providing further support, training, education, information to develop/reactivate the ability
• Redesigning the coaching programme in a way that the abilities that are there do fulfil the quality requirements

• Replacing or deleting a programme element/person where the needed quality cannot be met by taking reasonable measures as appropriate

Ways to address a lack of willingness/commitment are:
• Better communication of the purpose and benefits of your coaching programme
• Involving your people
• Open dialogue
• Making the coaching programme more appealing and fresher
• Redesigning the coaching programme in a way that it better fosters motivation
• Checking and ensuring optimal win-win
• Replacing or deleting a programme element/person where the needed commitment and quality cannot be met by reasonable measures

Whatever the reason for the low quality, thoroughly explore and identify the impact it has already had on the programme, the people involved and your organisation – and take appropriate measures to reduce the possible damage, re-establish trust, compensate any damage actually occurred and recover high quality. Take responsibility yourself and apologize to people for areas that are within your responsibility. Provide support, take the appropriate measures, learn, and keep people up to date on the progress to rebuild optimal quality.

Reviewing, updating and adjusting your quality standards and profiles on a continuous basis

As the internal and external business environment change, also your quality requirements may evolve over time.

Quality of organisational structures and technology & tools

Ensure high quality not only regarding people, but also the organisational structures, processes and operations as well as technologies and tools deployed.

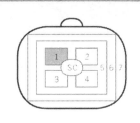

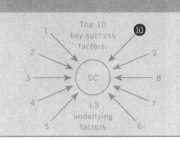

The coaching initiative itself also creates organisational structures and processes in some way or other. If these are badly designed – e.g. your coaching programme contradicts business strategy, systematically fosters insurmountable conflicts of roles or provides a low quality recruitment and selection process – and thus are not fit for purpose themselves, the best quality of people will be wasted, unless you also change the system, structures and processes in place.

Similarly, consider the quality of your technologies & tools deployed: For example, is there a true fit for purpose of your chosen coaching forms, your coaching models and techniques and your ways of coaching evaluation? Likewise, do your IT systems perform and deliver what they are actually meant to do? Are the chosen communication technologies truly appropriate for what and how they are used?

So quality of your coaching initiative embraces the quality of all people involved, of all organisational structures and processes set up and of all technologies & tools used.

CASE STUDY 15	BBC, UNITED KINGDOM (UK)

Company: BBC (British Broadcasting Corporation)

(Largest broadcasting corporation in the world)

www.bbc.co.uk

Author: Liz Macann
Function: Head of Executive, Leadership and Management Coaching
(based in London)

Creating an in-house coaching service at the BBC

The beginnings

In the late 90's some of our very top executive tier were receiving coaching from an assortment of expensive, external coaches whose selection, standards, ethics and success criteria were not scrutinised or monitored. Our aim was to provide evaluated Executive Coaching to all leaders and managers at a standard equal to or better than that which was available from external providers – and at a lower cost.

At this stage in the development of the coaching profession, there was little written about what and how to do it. So we simply coached ourselves through what we wanted to achieve and how we could achieve it.

We established, that there was sufficient interest from the staff to have this strange new process called coaching, by piloting short coaching programmes from which we learned that we needed …

* coaches to believe in the process and have thorough skills training – enthusiasm is not enough
* a shared understanding of the coaching objectives by the line manager/client/coach
* structure around the coaching offering
* quality control

As the demand for coaching slowly grew, we knew that we needed to expand our existing small number of trained coaches, especially when it was decided to incorporate coaching as an integral part of the corporate Leadership Programme, which caused the demand to rocket.

Having failed to find externally the level of training we wanted our developing network to have, we created our own course and devised a selection procedure to ensure that anyone who we invested in already had a high level of the competencies we required.

Selection and composition of the coach pool

We wanted coaches to come from all over the business, not just the people professions, so we posted flyers in strategic places and were astonished at the level and spread of interest in something which most people knew little about. Applications came from programme makers, engineers, techies, professional services – all categories of staff are now represented in our mix.

We currently have 90 coaches, all volunteers from the ranks of established and senior leaders and managers, who fit their coaching activities into already demanding diaries and who receive no reward for this work other than the sense of fulfilment that it gives them.

Geographical focus: *United Kingdom (UK)*

BBC CASE STUDY: *Creating an in-house coaching service at the BBC*

Over time the details of the infrastructure have evolved. But because we began with nothing to copy and simply started with the end in mind, what we created in those early days remains largely the same.

Selection process

The selection process begins with a purpose built application form asking only for information which relates to someone's suitability to train as a coach. Other corporate considerations are disregarded. The shortlisted applicants are then interviewed against the 5 main competencies we regard as important for our coaches to possess, and those achieving the required standard are then offered a place on the Coach Foundation Course.

Coach training

Twice a year 12 senior managers/leaders are trained as coaches by two senior coaches and an external tutor, the course being divided into three modules over a four months period:

Coach Foundation Course

Module 1
pre reading
3 days skills training, input, practice, observation and feedback
6 weeks field work supported by coach mentor

Module 2
pre reading
3 days psychological underpinnings, practice, observation and feedback
6 weeks field work supported by coach mentor

Module 3
pre reading
2 days of final observed assessment plus tools and techniques

The Coach Foundation Course is accredited by the European Mentoring and Coaching Council at intermediate level.

Trainees who are deemed to meet the standard necessary to be a BBC Coach are then required to coach a minimum of three clients at any one time and enter into continuous professional development by attending:

* one to one supervision quarterly
* regular shared learning sessions
* a number of master classes, workshops and refresher sessions

Coaches who wish to pursue external accreditation through the ICF will be supported by development within our network, and a growing number of our coaches go on to take advanced or specialised coach training external to the BBC. This is not a requirement and the BBC does not fund it, but it is increasingly something which our more experienced coaches want to do for personal development.

The Portfolio

We have grown from offering short informal coaching sessions to having a portfolio of four different offerings. All programmes begin and end with a 3 way meeting between coach, client and line manager.

1. The Executive Coaching Programme – for established and senior leaders and managers with objectives agreed with line managers. The duration of the programme

www.frank-bresser-consulting.com

Geographical focus: *United Kingdom (UK)*

BBC CASE STUDY: *Creating an in-house coaching service at the BBC*

depends on the level of the executive, but is typically 10 hours over a period of 6 months.

2. The Leadership Coaching Programme – for anyone attending the corporate leadership programme with goals derived from the clients' training objectives

3. The First One Hundred Days – for established and senior leaders and managers transitioning into a new role or entering the corporation from another organisation

4. Coaching Skills for Managers – as the value of coaching is increasingly recognised, many mangers who do not wish to be a coach want the basic coaching skills to enhance their management style. This is a three day, two module course which teaches them the basic coaching skills of active listening, open questioning and the GROW model. This short course is being credited with helping the organisation shift towards a coaching culture. Still a long way to go!

What's next?

It has been an amazing learning journey during which we have had to have enormous self belief and resilience in the face of internal challenge, external competition and massive restructuring of the whole organisation. We have continuously developed the network, its coaches, its structure and the coaching it provides to respond to this. By partnering constantly evolving business needs, we will continue to support the change programme, strategic initiatives and help to embed the coaching culture as the preferred management style within the corporation.

Meaningful evaluation of coaching is notoriously difficult, but our four studies and ongoing individual coach evaluation have shown that the coaching provision is a much valued intervention which has benefited both the individual and the business.

In those early days the BBC buzz words were: 'Just do it', 'make it happen'. And we did.

Our key learning/Recommendation:
Insist on first rate training of coaches, before they ever reach a client, and on continuous coach-specific professional development from the day they graduate onwards – plus best procedural practice.

Questions and exercises for further reflection and to integrate practice and theory:

1. What is the business case for coaching in the company?

2. What coaching forms were implemented? What are the outcomes?

3. How does the company ensure the quality of its coaching programmes?

4. What is company-specific about their way of defining quality?

5. What is your key learning from this case study?

www.frank-bresser-consulting.com

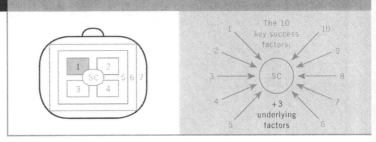

OVERVIEW OF THE 10 KEY SUCCESS FACTORS

As a summary, here is an overview of all 10 key success factors for the implementation and improvement of coaching in organisations:

1. **Develop an organisation-specific understanding of coaching.**
2. **Adopt a systematic approach.**
3. **Choose an adequate level of organisational penetration of coaching.**
4. **Involve the top.**
5. **Promote coaching as a positive developmental tool.**
6. **Create an optimal win-win value for all stakeholders.**
7. **Achieve full consistency of coaching with business strategy.**
8. **Ensure complete transparency of the whole coaching concept.**
9. **Evaluate effectively and carefully.**
10. **Ensure high integrity and quality at all levels.**

These may serve you as a central thread and starting point to plan, design and implement new coaching programmes or you may use them as a measure and means to review and optimize existing coaching initiatives. Either way, you will find them an invaluable tool to support achieving outstanding results through coaching.

For further reflection and to integrate practice and theory, we invite you to take any of the case studies included in this book and apply the above set of 10 key success factors. What role does each success factor play in each case study? What has been done particularly well, and where do you see potential for further development and optimization?

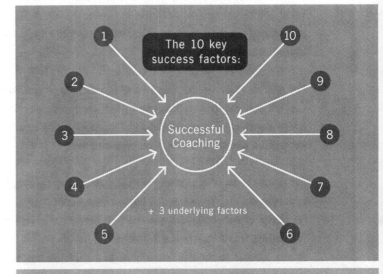

THE 3 UNDERLYING FACTORS

While applying the 10 key success factors, you also need to consider the influence of these three underlying factors:

1. **Impact and importance of culture**
2. **Continuous Learning Process**
3. **Coaching implementation and improvement intelligence**

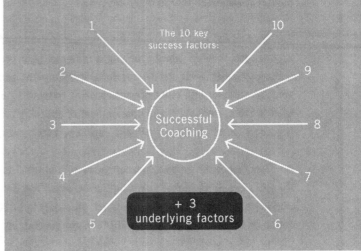

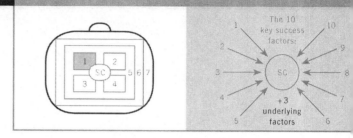

<table>
<tr><td>UNDERLYING
FACTOR 1</td><td># IMPACT AND IMPORTANCE OF CULTURE</td></tr>
</table>

In previous sections of this book we have acknowledged that any coaching programme contains a cultural dimension and requires some kind of culture management/change.

One of your key tasks as HR/OD/L&D manager, responsible for coaching in your organisation, is to take into account the existing culture in your company and design and implement your coaching plan accordingly. In fact, you also need to develop and/or strengthen a positive culture and environment around any coaching form in your firm in order to ensure its acceptance and successful use.

You may also take the perspective that all coaching programmes (i.e. not only the explicit coaching culture initiatives) are – in some way or other – ambassadors of some kind of a coaching culture and thus coaching culture initiatives.

For guidance on how to effect culture change and develop a coaching culture, please revisit key success factor 3 (3.1.8. on coaching cultures). Also see the high performance coaching culture framework below (framework 3 in this book). It is also tenable to see the whole book as a guide on how to build a coaching culture in organisations.

The specific focus of the following sections is to examine whether and to what extent coaching is universal (and/or culture-specific), what are the key cultural dimensions and kinds of cultures with relevance for coaching initiatives, and what is the current state and development of coaching in the world overall, in each continent, region and country.

An extra box at the end will set out the results of the Frank Bresser Consulting Global Coaching Survey which has won worldwide acclaim and covered research on coaching in 162 countries (accounting for almost 100% world population).

The impact of culture on your coaching programme

The most suitable coaching programme design for you will depend on and be tailored around your organisation-specific needs, your people's receptiveness and what is already there in your company. Culture is an element of all these three areas.

As culture is an inner state, it can only evolve from within, i.e. from where it is. It cannot simply be switched or ordered as one may change clothes. So it is important to build on and work with the existing culture in your company and encourage and foster development towards a desired state.

When having a look at the 10 key success factors above, you will find that culture can significantly shape the way each of them may be interpreted and applied in practice:

Developing an organisation-specific understanding of coaching (Key Success Factor 1) needs to address corporate culture-specific aspects. Cultures with a high affiliation to systematic thinking and planning may find it easier to adopt a systematic approach (KSF 2) than other cultures having a more spontaneous and ad hoc approach. Some cultures favour certain coaching forms or deeper levels of organisational penetration by coaching (KSF 3) than others (e.g. because they already embrace certain coaching culture elements).

Different cultures may also imply very different approaches to top down/bottom up implementation of coaching and the resulting involvement of the top (KSF 4): Think for example of cultures where top management thinking is they already know everything. In some cultures, by their nature, the idea of coaching as a positive developmental tool (KSF 5) may be much more accessible to people than in others (e.g. because

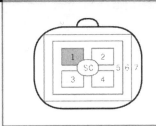 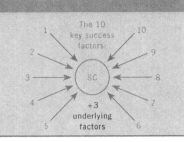

asking for support is very widespread in general and seen as a strength, rather than a weakness). Also, while the idea of win-win (KSF 6) may be already embraced in some cultures, it is something quite new for others (e.g. compare more collaborative and competitive cultures).

Think of achieving full consistency of coaching with business strategy (KSF 7): This may be much easier to strive for in those cultures where strategic thinking is more inherent and the human asset is highly valued and seen as potentially strategic (as well as HR/OD/L&D seen as a possible strategic business partner). Some cultures appreciate and foster transparency of measures and initiatives (KSF 8), whereas others may tend to keep things more in secret.

Effective and careful monitoring and evaluation (KSF 9) may also be interpreted and assessed very differently by different cultures, e.g. regarding the value and focus of evaluation and its limits. Finally defining high integrity and quality in coaching (KSF 10), is highly subjective and perceptual and thus must also depend on the cultural priorities and value systems in a company and its environment.

So when implementing and optimizing coaching initiatives, the cultural dimension is ubiquitous. It is underlying any use of coaching in organisations.

Please note that there are **various types and levels of cultures**, not just national and corporate ones, to take into consideration.

Geographically, you may have differences in continental, regional, national and local cultures. From an organisational perspective, companies may vary in their overall corporate culture, but also there may be many sub-cultures within the same organisation at the firm, business unit or team level. You may encounter very different professional cultures in a firm (e.g. compare engineering, IT, creative and banker cultures). Your workforce may represent very different generational, social or religious background cultures. In addition,

each employee may represent a different, individual cultural orientation and way of being.

In particular, we need to acknowledge that in today's world of globalization, each organisation/individual is subject to an increasingly diverse mix of different cultural influences.

Embracing all cultures

The essence of coaching (see the core of the coaching pyramid model set out in the book introduction) is about dynamic appropriateness concerned with what fits best where and how, with more choice, a more eclectic, dynamic and pluralistic perspective, more balance and integration. Coaching works towards dynamic appropriateness and achieving best practice in potentially any area and context.

Coaching at its heart explicitly doesn't foster a specific culture per se, but first of all acknowledges and values each of them. No culture can claim to be the "only right" one, but cultures may at best be dynamically appropriate for their specific purposes and contexts.

Coaching fosters **mutual learning and cultural respect and diversity**. It provides an umbrella and common base for all existing cultures and reconciles and integrates these in an optimal win-win way. In fact, coaching has a cosmopolitan dimension – and it represents a **way of thinking that invites any existing culture to challenge itself, widen its scope and think beyond its current boundaries**.

So no culture can rest on its laurels complacently and claim to exclusively have reached any 'holy grail' of dynamic appropriateness. Striving for dynamic appropriateness is an ongoing, evolving process that lasts forever for every person, organisation and culture.

In particular in today's times of increased globalisation, a faster changing business environment, a more pluralistic

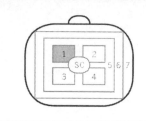
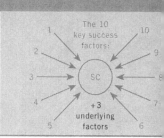

and diverse society, of rising questioning and break-up of traditional values and systems, of increasing complexity in all aspects of our work and life, coaching is increasingly becoming a **universal principle with high validity**.

The essence of coaching is about best fit in whatever culture and context and is thus highly flexible. It is universally applicable and in principle able to adjust to all cultures of the world.

Varying cultural openness to coaching

While the very core of coaching may well be universally applicable, this doesn't necessarily mean that the coaching approach is also immediately welcome, understood, adopted and integrated in all cultures equally.

Coaching, by embracing all cultures and acting as a uniting umbrella over these, is **a culture proposition in its own right**: It fosters a more inclusive culture of diversity and integration that strives for best practice. Indeed, it represents a way of thinking that challenges any existing culture to widen its scope and move beyond its current boundaries.

Not every culture will be ready to buy in to these ideas, some are more compatible with and open to best fit thinking and dynamic appropriateness than others.

Different cultures may also have different access points to coaching. The challenge is to find the **most suitable opening in each culture for coaching** to be accepted and thrive.

For some cultures, a coaching approach may even be viewed with serious concern, raising fears like fear of change, fear of loss of power, fear of loss of control, fear of feeling overstrained, fear of failure or other fears caused by misconceptions around coaching (e.g. "coaching is only about being nice to each other"; coaching is about laissez-faire"; "coaching always takes a lot of time"; "coaching is only for poor

performers"; "coaching is just for softies"; "coaching is therapy for people with personal problems").

Targeted information and education, involving people, communicating the coaching benefits (and maybe the business requirement to adopt coaching), tailoring your coaching initiative, as well as choosing an appropriate pace and style and suitable degree of coaching may help remove or overcome those fears. Awareness of readiness will tell you if the organisation or people are not yet in the right frame of mind for coaching, in this case coaching cannot be forced on them, but accept the situation, continue your efforts and work with those who are ready.

So, depending on the cultural preferences and levels of ability and readiness for coaching, coaching can be more or less easily accepted and adopted and may take very different forms in different cultures.

Culture-specific

While the core of coaching may be universally applicable, how it is applied will always be culture-specific. The cultural context needs to be taken into account when designing any coaching initiative.

Where this is not sufficiently done, coaching cannot reach its full potential and is most likely to lead to friction and justified resistance among people. Coaching is about what fits best where and how. So blindly transferring and applying a coaching methodology from one context to another tends to contradict the essence of coaching.

While coaching is a global phenomenon today, there is still a striking lack of culture-specific coaching approaches and styles across the globe. Instead, it is often the US coaching approach and style that is dominant in many regions of the world without being really questioned in terms of cultural compatibility and fit.

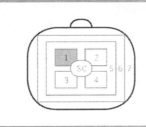 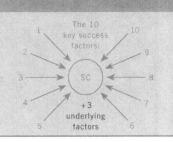

While it is important to acknowledge and appreciate the US style and its innovations and approaches, make sure you are aware of the possible cultural limits, historical roots and underlying assumptions of US coaching models. The same is also true for other coaching approaches coming from any other region of the world. To what degree are these truly applicable to different contexts and in particular to yours?

Where US coaching models dominate out of context, it implies the following risks:

- The true potential of coaching for the local culture is not leveraged.
- Coaching is seen as a US or Western tool only.
- Ownership to develop culture-specific coaching concepts is rarely encouraged or taken.
- The essence of coaching is ignored.
- Coaching models with no or a bad fit may lead to friction, resistance and unsatisfactory results.
- The whole story of coaching may mistakenly be reduced to very culture-specific applications of it.
- Coaching may be brought into disrepute overall.

Therefore, make a clear differentiation between the universally applicable core of coaching and the actual, culture-specific applications. With the relevant cultural understanding you can have confidence in taking appropriate ownership and developing a coaching approach and programme for your particular cultural context.

The question of what kind of coaching understanding and coaching forms fit best in each part of the world, is only just beginning to be answered.

Besides Northern America, parts of Europe and Australia are taking real ownership and have adjusted coaching to their own cultures. Also Latin America, parts of Asia as well as South Africa have recently begun to embark on this journey and define coaching more autonomously for their context.

As food for thought, we invite you to consider the following:

That one-to-one coaching is today the most well-known coaching form may be attributed to the US influence, which is based on a highly individualistic cultural orientation and the assumption that every individual has the power to determine his or her own destiny. Now imagine that China – having a much more collective-oriented culture – had first invented modern coaching as a business tool. Would team coaching or coaching cultures have been more popular? Or a totally different coaching form?

Equally, that the origins of coaching in the US are largely rooted in the area of life coaching may help explain the focus on external coaches for such a long time.

Drivers in a national or regional culture may influence why and in what form coaching is adopted. While it may be useful to identify these drivers, it is equally important not to reduce coaching to these.

For example, some argue that Northern America and Europe have mainly developed one-to-one coaching as a response to their specific challenges as highly industrialised regions: Issues of anonymity, stress, alienation, the break-up of social systems, search for meaning etc. were particularly widespread and pressing here – and thus led to the development of coaching. There may be some truth in this statement.

However, even if coaching started in theses regions as a remedial tool, it spread to developmental learning very quickly, which is an indicator of the dynamic appropriateness for potentially all contexts. Also, the above doesn't impact on the possibility for any other region or culture of the world to use coaching for other reasons.

Summary observations on **the culture-specific or universal nature of coaching** in the business context:

1. While today's global business landscape is changing rapidly and tremendously, there has been strong influence on global business by the US, in particular in terms of

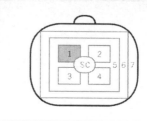
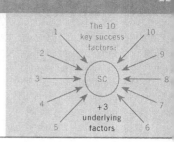

schools of management, leadership and related tools like coaching. Therefore it is not surprising that the US coaching style is (still) predominant in a number of regions across the globe and that coaching in its current practice often seems quite "Western" at first glance. However, coaching is far from being US or Western specific per se.

2. Coaching cannot be fully explained by one culture only, but combines and brings together elements from various cultures (e.g. integrating contrasts: ying and yang from Asia, performance and goal-directedness from the US). It also contains common elements that may be found in practically all cultures in some way or other (e.g. awareness, responsibility).

3. While the heart of coaching is universally applicable, its application is always culture-specific.

4. Coaching is inclusive, embracing all cultures, and aimed at building best practice in organisations that respect, embrace and leverage the strengths of existing cultures.

5. The question of what specific coaching form and method of implementation to choose, is dependent on the respective culture (e.g. favouring individual 1:1 coaching in individualistically oriented cultures; defining coaching as a specific consulting form to achieve cultural acceptance and compatibility in more authoritarian and less emotional cultures).

6. Relevant cultural dimensions you may encounter that influence the way coaching is actually defined and used in organisations, are for example:
   - Rational/Emotional
   - Direct/Indirect
   - Authoritarian/Empowering
   - Emphasis on the individual/group
   - Diverse/Homogeneous
   - Integrating, harmony, consensus-oriented/Confronting, polarizing, controversy-oriented
   - Power & choice/Destiny & pre-determination
   - Transparency/Secrecy

- Relationship-based/Knowledge-based
- Structured/Unstructured
- Strict/Flexible
- Short/Long term
- Active/Passive
- Focus on achievement/process
- Open/Closed
- Status, titles & age/Meritocracy
- Attitude on time
- Hierarchy/Collaboration
- Reflective/Intuitive
- Introverted/Extroverted
- Materialistic/non-materialistic
- Systematic, planning/Ad hoc, spontaneity

7. The universally applicable core of coaching is itself a product of and an expression of culture. Everything has a cultural dimension in some way or other. Accordingly, the very heart of coaching is culture-specific in its own way – and it is a culture proposition in its own right, as already set out above.

In this context, we want to take the opportunity to explicitly **acknowledge our own culture in writing this book**. While this publication is a global business guide for the successful use of coaching in organisations, it would be presumptuous to claim it would be totally culture-free. We sought a global, culture-free, meta perspective in writing this book and are confident that this publication has actually achieved a high level of universal applicability. Yet – consciously or unconsciously – our cultures will have impacted and shaped our writing in one way or other. So we encourage you to identify the culture-specific characteristics and contents of this book. Change the frameworks if and as needed to make them fit your culture better, whilst being aware of how your culture is influencing your thinking.

Extra Box 2 on the next pages will give you an overview of the current state and development of coaching in the world overall, in each continent, region and country.

www.frank-bresser-consulting.com

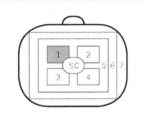

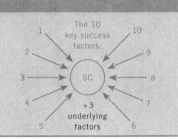

The state of coaching across the globe: Results of the Frank Bresser Consulting Global Coaching Survey 2008/2009

The Global Coaching Survey 2008/2009, conducted by Frank Bresser Consulting, for the first time examined the current state and development of coaching in the world overall, in each continent, region and country (covering 162 countries).

The results have an influence on current international debates on coaching and have won worldwide acclaim. They were included in the list of top achievements of the coaching industry within the year 2009 by the renowned magazine "Coaching at Work". Media across the globe have reported on it in detail.

Please note: This Extra Box only gives an executive summary of the project results. **In order to get the detailed report (pdf file, 170 pages), which complements this book, please download it for free at:**

www.frank-bresser-consulting.com/
globalcoachingsurvey.html

The full report also provides, among many other things, specific information on the typical coaching characteristics and the coaching market in each of the 162 countries. On the website you will also find special editions for each continent as free downloads.

As HR/OD/L&D manager responsible for coaching in your organisation, you may benefit from reading the research findings in various ways:

- The results help you identify region-, country- and culture-specific aspects that are important to consider when implementing/improving coaching in a company (e.g. preferred coaching styles and forms, possible pitfalls, development stage of/resources in the local coaching markets)

- You will discover what is international and national best practice – and what is not. For example, there is an overall balance of directive and non-directive coaching approaches in the world. So if there is a global best practice in this regard, it is to consider the value of both styles rather than to focus on only one upfront.

- By getting an overview of the very different, possible ways of defining and using coaching across the globe, you widen your understanding of coaching and its possibilities.

- The results provide you with an excellent knowledge base to raise the issue of coaching at top levels and discuss it more in the firm.

- There is a lot of speculative and wrong information on the situation of coaching in the world going around. This research actually examined the situation of coaching in 162 countries and gathered information and expert opinions from across the globe. So the report is a useful reference point and benchmark by which you may compare and check what others say.

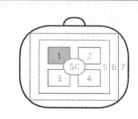

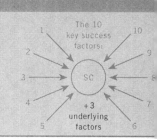

Extra-Box 2: *The state of coaching across the globe: Results of the Frank Bresser Consulting Global Coaching Survey 2008/2009*

- By getting a clearer picture of the situation of coaching across the globe and becoming more culturally aware of your own local, national and regional characteristics of coaching, you may raise your awareness of what is most appropriate for your specific, cultural context and develop higher respect for and understanding of the existing diversity of approaches.

- You will be better equipped to actively participate in international debates on coaching, and develop greater confidence in defining coaching more autonomously for your context.

EXECUTIVE SUMMARY

This summary gives an overview of the situation of coaching across the globe by presenting the key results of the Frank Bresser Consulting Global Coaching Survey 2008/2009. The project covered 162 countries and, for the first time, systematically examined the situation and development of coaching in the world overall, in each continent, region and country. The first part sets out the research purpose and design. Then a summary of the most important results regarding the world overall and each continent (in alphabetical order) follows.

The Project

Purpose

The Global Coaching Survey 2008/2009 examined the current state and development of coaching in the world overall, in each continent, region and country. Frank Bresser Consulting conducted research in 162 countries (which account for almost 100% world population).

Research design

The research topic and the general lack of statistics on coaching (and of valid quantitative samples across the globe) supported a qualitative – rather than quantitative – approach: The research team identified qualified organisations and people, who have a good overview of coaching in their country and the resources to gather further relevant information as needed, as the main sources of data.

Participant selection and data generation

Identifying participants:
First, we identified the existing national and international coaching associations around the world, as it is their remit to gather relevant information on their local coaching markets. The second step was to identify a leading one in each country and invite these to respond to our questionnaire. Where we couldn't identify a coaching association in a country, we searched for a suitable, leading coaching-related association (e.g. Human Resources), coaching provider, con-

Extra-Box 2: *The state of coaching across the globe: Results of the Frank Bresser Consulting Global Coaching Survey 2008/2009*

sultancy, coaching expert or coaching-related university faculty with credibility in providing relevant information.

Questionnaire design:

The questionnaire included open and closed questions. Partly, questions were similar to each other to allow for cross-checking within the answers given by a participant. The questions generally allowed for interpretation by the participants in order to embrace maximum diversity of coaching practices and approaches, rather than putting participants in a pre-set box that might not fit. We were eager to listen and learn, not prescribe or promote a certain way of doing th ings.

Accordingly, we deliberately kept the questions broad and did not define terms precisely or assume a specific understanding of coaching. How questions were interpreted and answered provided insights into the understanding, practice and development of coaching in each country.

Participant responses:

It was the responsibility of each participating organisation to decide on the most appropriate approach/resources to gather the required information. This ranged from local surveys and board-meetings to market researches/analyses to the use of existing statistics. In fact, this survey actually triggered many local research initiatives on coaching across the globe. However, it is important to highlight that in many cases responses are rough estimates. Coaching is a young discipline, and exact figures are rarely available (e.g. as most countries have no requirement to register as a coach, it is difficult to identify their number of coaches). So whilst the survey can provide a good first idea of coaching around the world, in each continent, region and country, it is far from being absolutely accurate. Where the results open up controversial discussions, this is welcome and in the spirit of the survey.

Validation and comparability:

After receiving participants´ information, we reviewed this data and checked it for internal and external consistency, relevance, clarity and validity. As appropriate, we made further enquiries of participants to gather further information and clarification. This stage of dialogue and discussion was a very valuable part of the whole process producing further highly interesting insights and giving much more background information. Another final review and editing stage followed, and only then did we take the answers as accepted country information. Only at this stage, did we work towards making sense of the data and align them for optimal consistency and comparability (inductive approach). The point is: in order to avoid comparing apples with oranges, you first need to know what kind of fruits there are and be able to recognize them.

Setting the foundation:

The Global Coaching Survey will be conducted regularly from now on and is definitely an ongoing project. The Global Coaching Survey 2008/2009 has now set the right foundation. In the next run, we will be able to build on and compare with these findings.

In this first run of the survey, there is a focus on professional one-to-one business coaching. This was deliberately chosen as it is the most visible and well-known coaching form so far in the corporate world and thus was a valid starting point. However, it is only the starting point. Next time, there will be much more coverage of other coaching forms (e.g. coaching leadership style, coaching culture, team coaching).

Additionally researched countries

It was our initial ambition to find suitable participants in every country, and we actually identified qualified partici-

www.frank-bresser-consulting.com

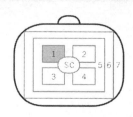

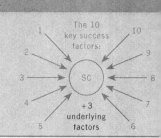

Extra-Box 2: *The state of coaching across the globe: Results of the*
Frank Bresser Consulting Global Coaching Survey 2008/2009

pants in most countries (covering 88 % of the world population). All countries with a visible coaching industry have participated. However, research was very difficult in a number of countries where coaching wasn't yet developed. Here, we were successful in a great number of cases, but not all. With regard to these latter cases, where the following possible research activities found nothing tangible, we decided to stop and share our own findings on the basis of these activities instead:

• Extensive online research on coaching in the country

• Conversations with people in the country

• Conversations with participants from neighbour countries

• Researching memberships of people/organisations from the country in international coaching associations (or related associations)

• Contacting local institutions for further information, e.g. Chambers of Commerce, international representations in countries, UNDP (United Nations Development Programme, the UN's global development network)

• Making use of other networks

We acknowledge that it remains possible that there are coaching providers and communities in these countries we haven't yet discovered. This may be especially true, where organisations/people don't have internet access, are very locally organized and/or are operating and presenting themselves in a rarely known language.
However, we have assumed that if there was a strong, growing coaching industry in the country, we would have been able to discover it in the given time. As a result we can only give a very rough estimate/impression of the lack of coaching in these countries.
It remains our aim to get participants from all countries in future runs of the survey. In fact, the survey is work in progress, and we are happy to include anyone knowledgeable about coaching in these countries in the future.

Further remarks

It is the first time that coaching associations from all over the world were identified, contacted and successfully brought together in a big project like this. The list of participating organisations and people alone is worth reading. Remarkably, just two of all participants mentioned the financial crisis in their answers – and this only marginally. Therefore, when the answers were generated (2008 and early 2009), the financial crisis hadn't already hit the coaching market in a significant way. This makes the Global Coaching Survey 2008/2009 particularly important and valuable: It is not just the snapshot of very exceptional circumstances. It reflects and documents the state and (longer term) development of coaching right up to the point before any potential volatility in the coaching market due to the global crisis occurred.

The Results

We will first look at the situation of coaching in the world overall and then go into detail for each continent (in alphabetical order).

www.frank-bresser-consulting.com

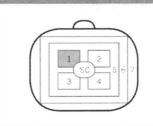
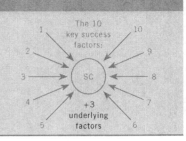

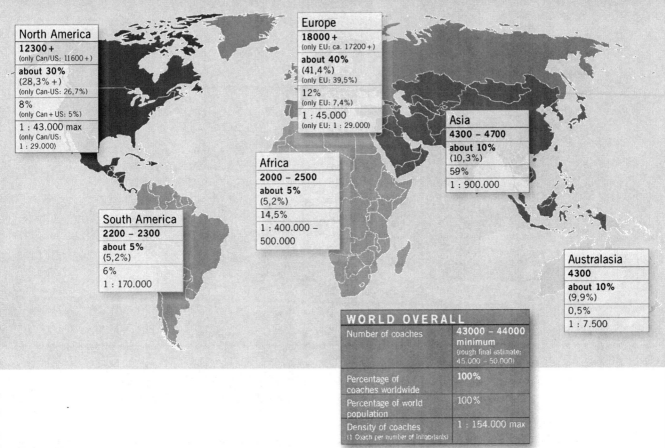

North America
12300 +
(only Can/US: 11600 +)
about 30%
(28,3% +)
(only Can-US: 26,7%)
8%
(only Can + US: 5%)
1 : 43.000 max
(only Can/US: 1 : 29.000)

Europe
18000 +
(only EU: ca. 17200 +)
about 40%
(41,4%)
(only EU: 39,5%)
12%
(only EU: 7,4%)
1 : 45.000
(only EU: 1 : 29.000)

Asia
4300 – 4700
about 10%
(10,3%)
59%
1 : 900.000

Africa
2000 – 2500
about 5%
(5,2%)
14,5%
1 : 400.000 – 500.000

South America
2200 – 2300
about 5%
(5,2%)
6%
1 : 170.000

Australasia
4300
about 10%
(9,9%)
0,5%
1 : 7.500

WORLD OVERALL	
Number of coaches	43000 – 44000 minimum (rough final estimate: 45.000 – 50.000)
Percentage of coaches worldwide	100%
Percentage of world population	100%
Density of coaches (1 Coach per number of inhabitants)	1 : 154.000 max

World overall

There are about 43,000-44,000 business coaches minimum operating in the world.

Coaching is definitely a global phenomenon; the top 10 countries with the highest numbers of coaches include an Asian, an African and a South American country (Japan, South Africa, Brazil). However, there remain extreme differences in the development and size of coaching markets depending on each continent and country.

Europe, North America and Australia – representing just 20% of the world population – comprise 80% of all business coaches of the world. More than two thirds of all coaches are based in the European Union, USA and Canada which represent just 13% of the world population.

Specifically: The 7 countries with the highest numbers of coaches (US, UK, Germany, Australia, Japan, Canada, South Africa) comprise only 10% of the world population, but about 73% of all coaches.

www.frank-bresser-consulting.com

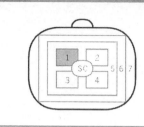

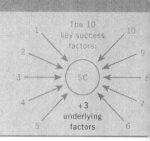

Extra-Box 2: *The state of coaching across the globe: Results of the Frank Bresser Consulting Global Coaching Survey 2008/2009*

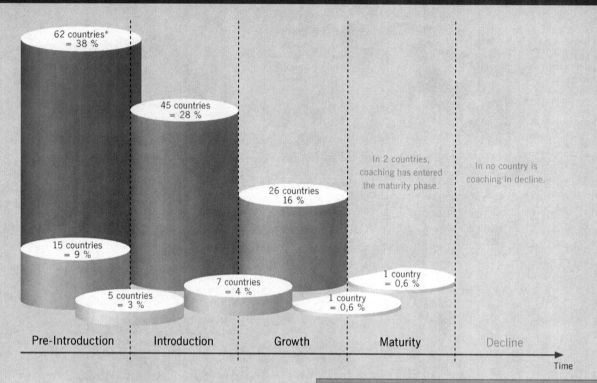

Figure: Product-life-cycle stage of coaching in the 162 countries (number and percentage of countries in each stage)

* = countries that are in the pre-introduction phase and possibly early introduction

Coaching is on the rise across the globe and there are singular, highly developed and dynamic "centres" of coaching. But comprehensive area-wide coverage of coaching is far from a reality. This is true for all continents. This can be further illustrated by the following findings:

- Coaching is already widely accepted and used as a business tool in 28 countries (of these 14 are European). However, in 114 countries (about 70 % of all countries), it is not. In another 20 countries, this is undecided.

- In 33 countries, coaching is in the growth phase (7 of these in early stages of growth). In a further 50 countries coaching has entered the introduction phase (5 of these being in between pre-introduction and introduction). In the remaining 77 countries (nearly 50 %), business coaching hasn't yet visibly developed. In two countries (Norway and the Netherlands), coaching has already entered the maturity phase.

- In 27 countries from all continents, business coaching is well advanced towards becoming a profession (15 from Europe). However, in 125 countries, i.e. in nearly four fifths of all countries, it is not. In 10 countries, this is undecided.

- National and international coaching associations exist in Northern America, Europe, and Australasia. There are

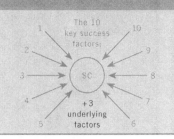

Extra-Box 2: *The state of coaching across the globe: Results of the Frank Bresser Consulting Global Coaching Survey 2008/2009*

also some in South America, but few in Asia and even less in Africa. In nearly half of the 162 countries, there is no single member of any national or international coaching body in the country.

- The concept of coaching cultures is quite well known in 19 countries. In a further 29 countries there is slight knowledge and use of it. However, in 111 countries, the concept is hardly or not known at all.

- There is an overall balance of directive and non-directive coaching approaches in the world. The predominant coaching style is directive in 28 countries, non-directive in 24 countries. In 110 countries, this is undecided.

- The use of coach supervision is widely spread in 23 countries (around 15 % of all countries).

Generally speaking, there is no dominant picture of coaching yet and diversity prevails. There is not the African, Asian, Australasian, European, North American or South American approach. But you need to look into each continent to find out more.

Africa

There are about 2,000-2,500 business coaches operating in Africa.

South Africa – with about 5 % of the African population – has around 1600 business coaches comprising about 70 % of the total. Approximately 12% of African coaches (260) are based in Egypt, Kenya and Morocco, so the other 44 African countries have the remaining 18% of business coaches on the continent.

The density of coaches in Africa is 1 coach per 400,000-500,000 inhabitants (without South Africa it would be 1 coach per 1-2.3 million inhabitants).

In Africa, coaching is still in its infancy. The following findings illustrate this further:

- Only in Morocco is coaching already widely accepted and used as a business tool. In three other countries (South Africa, Egypt, Libya,) this is undecided.

- In two countries (Morocco and South Africa) coaching is already in the growth phase, and in another 9 countries it is in the introduction phase. In the remaining 36 countries, however, business coaching hasn't yet visibly developed.

- In Morocco and South Africa, one-to-one business coaching is already well advanced towards becoming a profession. In all other 46 countries, it is not. No country is undecided.

- National coaching associations have successfully developed in Morocco and South Africa. Emerging coaching communities may also be found in Uganda and Nigeria. However, the overall situation with regard to professional coaching bodies in Africa (national or international ones) is very poor.

- The coaching culture concept is almost unknown in Africa. Only in South Africa, and here above all in the context of multinational companies rather than in local companies, is it mentioned.

- There are few local coaching initiatives in Africa yet (only in Morocco, South Africa and partly in Uganda, Nigeria

www.frank-bresser-consulting.com

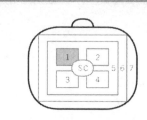

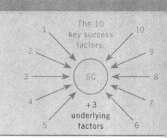

Extra-Box 2: *The state of coaching across the globe: Results of the Frank Bresser Consulting Global Coaching Survey 2008/2009*

and Egypt) which define and develop coaching specifically for their country or region. Coaching is more driven and determined by multinational clients and international coaching, if it exists at all. You rarely find specifically African coaching approaches on the continent at this early stage. General issues are the need for better education of clients and the challenge to overcome existing cultural barriers.

- Geographically speaking there are huge gaps: coaching features in Northern Africa and in South Africa plus Botswana and in Kenya and Uganda in the East and Nigeria and Gabon in the West, but the rest of the continent is still undiscovered in terms of coaching.

- The use of coach supervision is widely spread in 4 countries. Remarkably, these have a rather "small" coaching industry (10-60 business coaches). In contrast, in South Africa with about 1600 coaches, supervision is not widely used.

- There is a strong directive dimension to coaching in Africa. In 6 countries a directive coaching approach prevails and a non-directive approach predominates in no single country. Also, where it is undecided, it is mainly because there is simply no coaching industry yet. In nearly all countries, it is an issue that clients expect to get advice and direction from (potential) coaches.

Asia

There are about 4,300-4,700 business coaches operating in Asia.

Japan und South Korea – with about 4 % of the Asian population – have around 2,500 business coaches comprising about 55% of all Asian coaches. Another 10% of coaches are based in the region of Singapore, Malaysia and the Philippines.

The density of coaches is 1 coach per 900,000 inhabitants in Asia (without Japan it would be 1 coach per 1.4 – 1.6 million inhabitants).

In general, Eastern and South-eastern Asia may be regarded as the two largest and most dynamic coaching regions. There are major coaching activities in only a few other countries (e.g. United Arab Emirates, Israel, India). Apart from these, however, coaching is still in its infancy (if at all) in Asia.

The following findings illustrate this further:

- In Japan, Malaysia, Singapore and South Korea, coaching is widely accepted and used as a business tool. In 32 countries (about 75%), it is not. In another six countries this is undecided (India, United Arab Emirates, Israel, Philippines, Lebanon, Bahrain).

- In Japan and South Korea, one-to-one business coaching is well advanced towards a profession. In 37 countries, it is not. Only in 3 countries, this is undecided. There is a tendency in Asia to see and develop coaching more as a service rather than as a profession.

- In 5 countries (Japan, Singapore, South Korea, United Arab Emirates and the Philippines) coaching is in the growth phase, in another 17 countries it is in the introduction phase. In the remaining 20 countries, however, business coaching hasn't yet visibly developed – no coaching industry could be identified.

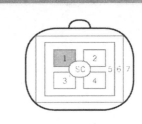

Extra-Box 2: *The state of coaching across the globe: Results of the Frank Bresser Consulting Global Coaching Survey 2008/2009*

- There is no prevailing coaching style in Asia. However, there is a slight slant towards directive coaching: 13 countries claim directive as the dominant style (in Bangladesh and Pakistan coaching is highly directive), whereas 6 countries claim non-directive coaching as the predominant style. In 23 countries, this is undecided. So there is not the Asian approach. Depending on each country, there are many different local characteristics and preferences in the way coaching is understood and delivered.

- In three countries (Japan, Philippines, Malaysia), the coaching culture concept is already well known and used. In another five countries (China, India, Israel, Saudi-Arabia, United Arab Emirates) this is partially the case.

- International coaching associations are quite active in Asia and contribute to the development of coaching there. At the same time, a number of local coaching initiatives have already emerged in Asia and have started to define and develop coaching specifically for the respective region or country. National or regional coaching bodies partly exist or are starting to emerge and be formalized. Also a first international (i.e. Asia Pacific) coaching association in the region has been set up. So coaching is clearly on the rise and in the process of becoming more mature in Asia in terms of quality and infrastructure.

- However, coaching is still mainly driven and determined by multinational clients or international coaching. As a result, you rarely find specific Asian coaching forms and approaches. So while local initiatives increasingly take place in Asia, these still remain rather limited.

Australasia

There are about 4,300 business coaches operating in Australasia, of which around 4,000 are based in Australia and 300 in New Zealand (in Papua New Guinea, the estimate is up to 10).

Australasia is the continent with the highest density of coaches (1 coach per 7,500 inhabitants). Although it only represents 0.5 % of the world population, about 10% of all business coaches across the globe are based here.

There is a clear divide between Australia and New Zealand on the one hand, where coaching is in the growth phase, widely accepted and used as a business tool and well advanced towards becoming a profession and Papua New Guinea on the other hand, where it is still in the pre-introduction phase.

Australia has the highest density of coaches in the world (1 : 5,300); New Zealand has the fifth highest (1 : 14,300). Accreditation, codes of ethics and professional coaching bodies are highly developed in Australia in particular.

A directive and straight-forward style of coaching is generally preferred and common practice in both countries.

Supervision is not currently widespread in Australasia, however it is increasingly gaining momentum in Australia and New Zealand.

In New Zealand, the coaching culture concept is well known and widely used, in Australia this is also the case, but less strongly.

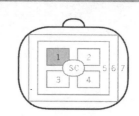
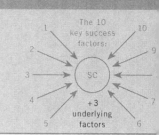

Extra-Box 2: *The state of coaching across the globe: Results of the Frank Bresser Consulting Global Coaching Survey 2008/2009*

Europe

There are about 18,000 business coaches operating in Europe. It is therefore the continent with the highest number of coaches.

However, this is not evenly distributed; UK and Germany (nearly 20% of the European population) comprise around 70% of all business coaches on the continent. In contrast, only about 5% of all coaches are based in the area of the former communist countries (40% of the population).

The density of coaches in Europe is 1 coach per 45,000 inhabitants (without Germany and UK it would be 1:120,000). The density in the European Union is 1:29,000 (which is the same as the density of coaches in USA plus Canada.

The nature of coaching in Europe is generally characterized by a great diversity of coaching styles, practices and development degrees; probably due to the existing multiplicity of cultures and countries on the continent. Another significant element of coaching in Europe is the high degree of internationalisation and continuous convergence in the field.

Generally speaking, there is a West-East and a slight North-South divide in the development of coaching. The Anglo region, the Founder Countries of the European Community and Scandinavia, have well developed coaching industries. This is less true for the Mediterranean region, and even less the case for the former communist area. Within each of these regions, however, the practice and development of coaching may differ enormously.

Coaching may be far advanced in Europe, but there also remains a lot to be done. This is illustrated further by the following findings:

- In 14 countries (all Western/Northern Europe), coaching is widely accepted and used as a business tool. However, in 22 countries it is not. In 5 countries this question is undecided.

- In 15 countries (mainly Western/Northern Europe), professional one-to-one coaching is far advanced towards becoming a profession. However, in 21 countries it is not. In 5 cases this is undecided.

- In 16 countries, business coaching is already in the growth phase, in another 15 countries it is in the introduction phase. In 2 countries, coaching has already entered the maturity phase. However, in 8 countries, coaching is still in the pre-introduction phase.

- Plenty of national as well as international coaching associations exist across Europe. In some countries there are even several (e.g. Germany: about 20 major ones). So the infrastructure in terms of coaching bodies is well advanced in Europe. However this is less the case in Eastern and Southern Europe.

- There is a slight slant towards non-directive coaching in Europe. While in 4 countries a directive coaching approach prevails (Greece, Ireland, Latvia, Portugal), non-directive coaching predominates in 12 countries. However, in most countries (25), this is undecided.

- The use of coach supervision is widely spread in one fourth of the European countries (10), in 17 it is not. In 14 this is undecided.

- The concept of coaching cultures is quite well known and widely used in 10 countries; in another 10 countries

www.frank-bresser-consulting.com

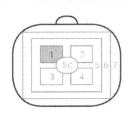

Extra-Box 2: *The state of coaching across the globe: Results of the Frank Bresser Consulting Global Coaching Survey 2008/2009*

coaching cultures are known. In 21 countries, however, the coaching culture concept is hardly or not known at all.

North America

There are at least 12,300 business coaches operating in North America.

USA and Canada comprise around 11,600 business coaches, Mexico another 600. So in all Central America and the Caribbean, there are only 100 to 150 business coaches.

USA, accommodating about 10,000 business coaches (minimum), is the country with the highest number of coaches in the world in terms of absolute coach figures. Canada is the 6th (with at least 1,600 coaches).

The density of coaches on the whole continent is 1 coach per 43,000 inhabitants. In Northern America (USA and Canada) it is 1:29,000 (which is the same as the European Union).

There is an extreme North-South divide in the development of coaching within North America. USA and Canada have highly advanced coaching industries, whereas the whole of Central America is in the pre-introduction phase, and in the Caribbean few coaches are operating. Coaching in Mexico is located somewhere in between the two poles.

The following findings illustrate this further:

- In USA, Canada, Mexico and Puerto Rico (which is a country associated with the USA) coaching is widely accepted and used as a business tool. In all the other 12 countries, it is not. No country reports undecided.

- In Canada, USA and Mexico, coaching is in the growth phase. In 10 countries (including also all Central America) it is still in the pre-introduction phase (no coaching industry could be identified). In three other countries (Puerto Rico, Dominican Republic and partly in Jamaica) coaching has entered the introduction phase.

- In USA, Canada and Puerto Rico coaching is well advanced towards becoming a profession. In all others, it is clearly not, not even in Mexico.

- There are well-developed professional coaching associations in USA and Canada, but coaching bodies are absent in Central America and the Caribbean. Mexico is in between: coaching associations are already emerging, but these haven't yet been able to establish professional standards successfully in the market and take coaching as a profession to the next level in the country.

- The coaching culture concept is well known and used in USA. This is partly true in Canada and Puerto Rico. However, in Mexico, the concept is only slightly used. In the remaining 11 countries, it is not known (at all).

- There is no prevailing coaching style in North America, the whole range from directive to non-directive coaching can be found. Interestingly, coaching in USA and Mexico is mostly non-directive, whereas it is undecided in Canada. Depending on each country, there may be many different local characteristics and preferences in the way coaching is understood and delivered.

- A typical coaching feature in both USA and Canada is a high emphasis on the (self-directed) role of the individual. Additionally a lot of remote coaching (usually by telephone)

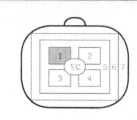

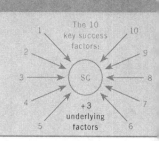

Extra-Box 2: *The state of coaching across the globe: Results of the*
Frank Bresser Consulting Global Coaching Survey 2008/2009

as opposed to face-to-face coaching is taking place in the north.

- In Central America, while 1:1 coaching is indeed in its infancy, in Honduras and Costa Rica coaching is emerging as a tool of group facilitation (group coaching) in multinational organisations.

- The use of coach supervision is widely spread only in USA, not for example in Canada and Mexico.

South America

There are about 2,200-2,300 business coaches operating in South America.

Comparing this with other regions of the world, the number is quite low, in particular given the overall high development of coaching on the continent.

The density of coaches in South America is 1 coach per 170,000 inhabitants. Interestingly, while Brazil is the country with the highest number of business coaches at 1,000, due to its large population its density of coaches is lower (1:195,000) than the continent average. The highest density of coaches on the continent is in Columbia at 1 coach per 88,000 inhabitants.

South America is generally quite advanced in the development of coaching which is illustrated by the following findings:

- In Argentina, Colombia and Peru, coaching is already widely accepted and used as a business tool. In another 6 countries, this is undecided. In 3 (comparatively small) countries coaching is not much used.

- In 5 of the 12 countries – Argentina, Brazil, Colombia, Peru and Chile – coaching is in the growth phase. In another 5 it is in the introduction phase. In 2 countries, business coaching hasn't yet visibly developed.

- In Argentina, Chile and Peru, coaching is well advanced towards a profession. In 7 countries it is not. In two this is undecided.

- A characteristic of coaching in South America is the high number of countries having a national coaching association (e.g. Argentina, Brazil, Chile, Peru). This suggests that coaching bodies are actively shaping the development and understanding of coaching in a more local way. International coaching associations are also present on the continent.

- The South American coaching approach doesn't exist. Depending on each country, there are many different local characteristics and preferences in the way coaching is understood and delivered. Coaching is not predominantly directive on the continent; on the contrary, there is a slight slant towards non-directive coaching.

- Despite coaching being already quite advanced in a number of countries, the number of business coaches is low when compared with developed coaching markets on other continents.

- There are sometimes cultural reservations about coaching (e.g. conservative style, authoritarian attitude, resistance, expectation of a directive coach) that need to be overcome (e.g. in Uruguay, Ecuador, Brazil, Chile).

- Venezuela is the only country in South America where coach supervision is widely spread. This is mainly due

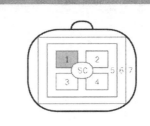

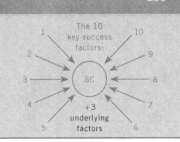

Extra-Box 2: *The state of coaching across the globe: Results of the Frank Bresser Consulting Global Coaching Survey 2008/2009*

to the fact that key providers of coach training in the country strongly promote it. Apart from this, supervision doesn't play a major role in South America.

- The coaching culture concept is well known and widely used in Argentina. This is slightly true in Brazil, Uruguay, Venezuela, Colombia and Chile, but in the remaining 6 countries, the concept is not known.

Closing Note

There is still a lot of research on coaching in the world to be done. This survey will hopefully serve as an invitation and starting point for others to undertake further research in the field.

Geographical focus: *Iran, Middle East*

CASE STUDY 16	ATIEH ROSHAN CONSULTING
Company: *Atieh Roshan Consulting* *(HR Consultancy)* *www.atiehroshan.com*	**Author:** *Pari Namazie* **Function:** *Managing Director, based in Tehran*

Coaching in Iran

Although coaching is a very new concept in Iran and hardly used, we make use of it in our organisation, Atieh Roshan Consulting (meaning a bright future). We are an HR consultancy based in Iran, and have a team of nine staff people – six consultants and three administrative and support employees. Since introducing our performance appraisal system in 2006, one of the outputs and development tools we decided to use was coaching.

The performance management system in Atieh Roshan consists of an annual appraisal, mid year review, peer appraisal (180 feedback) and performance log. During the annual appraisal, the achievement of the objectives of the past appraisal period is reviewed and assessed: Firstly, we discuss together whether and to what extent the appraisee has managed to meet the objectives (or not). Secondly, we set new objectives for the forthcoming 12 month period and identify and examine development areas. Objectives are SMART, but more importantly must be positively stretching.

Following our appraisals, we found that some were not developing the way we anticipated. Although we thought our performance system was complete, we were not getting the results we expected. Some staff people seemed to need more guidance and feedback. When we explained development areas and critical issues, they did not accept these and did not understand what was expected. As a result we identified a great need for a large part of our staff to receive

more feedback to develop. For this to happen, we suggested using coaching as a tool for development. This was welcomed, especially because coaching meant face to face individual meetings between coach and coachee.

The objective of coaching from the perspective of the coachee was:
1) To understand the organisational expectations and one's role/ability in reaching these objectives
2) A supportive environment to discuss personal and professional growth
3) To be closer to the manager

The objective of coaching from the perspective of the coach was to:
1) Provide objective feedback
2) Provide a space for personal and professional development
3) Help the coachee reach set objectives and goals within a specific timeframe

Coaching sessions are set up usually every month or two months, depending on the work load. An agenda is prepared in advance based on the appraisal objectives and development needs. The agenda starts with a review of the period before, the work the coachee has done, what challenges, stories, insights the coachee wishes to share. Some observations made by the coach follow.

Geographical focus: *Iran, Middle East*

ATIEH ROSHAN CONSULTING CASE STUDY: *Coaching in Iran*

The development area is then dealt with in appropriate detail. For example one of the areas might be "giving constructive feedback". The coach may share information/knowledge/theories and best practice on giving feedback. Examples – both personal and professional – may be discussed. It is examined how the coachee may use this in his/her work. Finally an action plan for the next meeting is agreed upon. This action plan may include specific outputs that need to be addressed and examined before the next coaching session.

The outcomes of the coaching initiative have been very positive, however time consuming. Not only have we seen better performance results from coachees, but it has also allowed our staff to feel closer to management. Interestingly the positive relationship and time invested in coaching has produced a stronger organisational culture and additional credibility that the organisation cares for its staff and their development.

In Iran, the staff generally distrusts management. Coaching, if done correctly and as a complement to a professional, transparent HR system, can transform that distrust into engagement, commitment and higher performance. Having said that, it is imperative that the coach is credible, has the right skills (active listening, giving constructive feedback, remains objective), and spends time building trust and allowing the coachee to feel they are getting something worthwhile out of the experience. At the same time, it is imperative not to engage on a personal or emotional level with the coachee. The relationship must remain objective and the coach must remain detached.

The knowledge and credibility of the coach and building trust are two very important dimensions of coaching in the Iranian culture.

Our key learning/Recommendation:
Coaching can improve performance and add value to the organisation and the individual.

Questions and exercises for further reflection and to integrate practice and theory:

1. What is the business case for coaching in the company?
2. What kind of coaching form/approach was implemented? What are the outcomes?
3. What is the role of culture in this case study?
4. How has the cultural dimension been addressed by the company?
5. What is your key learning from this case study?

Questions and exercises for the folowing case study 17 (Calouste Gulbenkian):

1. What is the business case for coaching in this organisation?
2. What is the mix of coaching forms and approaches they have used? What are the outcomes?
3. What cultural aspects (e.g. national, corporate, individual) come through in this case study (and in what way)?
4. How has the company dealt with/addressed these aspects?
5. What is your key learning from this case study?

Geographical focus: *Portugal*

CASE STUDY 17	CALOUSTE GULBENKIAN, PORTUGAL

Company: *Calouste Gulbenkian Foundation*

(a Portuguese private institution of public service promoting the fields of arts, charity, education and science)

www.gulbenkian.pt

Author: *Ana Rijo da Silva*

Function: *Head of Human Resources Department (based in Lisbon)*

Coaching for Self-Awareness and Leadership

Background

The Calouste Gulbenkian Foundation (CGF) is a private institution in Portugal, which is active in the fields of arts, charity, education and science. Created in 1956, the Foundation pursues its aims in Portugal and abroad through a wide range of activities and also through grants supporting projects and programmes.

The Central Services Department (CSD) provides technical and logistical support for the activities that are organised at the Foundation's head office. In 2008, the Foundation arranged a coaching programme specifically designed for the 8 line managers of the CSD. They have demanding, complex leadership roles: It is them who solve the problems, make things happen on time and get things done.

The coaching programme was aimed at enhancing their self-awareness and self-knowledge as leaders, particularly with regard to a more systemic perspective of their leadership role within both the CSD and the CGF. It was designed in partnership with an external executive coach and consultant.

Programme Objectives

The aims of the coaching programme were to enable the participants to ...

- develop greater understanding of their leadership strengths and challenges

- maintain greater self-confidence and balance in the midst of pressure and uncertainty

- see and understand situations from a more systemic point of view by putting themselves in the position of others

- be more aware of CGF dynamics and more skilled in working with those dynamics

- increase their levels of engagement, trust and accountability

- improve the levels of interaction and partnership within the line management team

Rationale

Coaching provides a structured approach that powerfully supports the developmental transformation of leaders by encouraging them to reflect on the effectiveness of their actions and behaviours. In this way it can produce both higher levels of performance and healthier relationships. The coaching initiative was focussed on developing the participants' awareness of their own leadership role and

www.frank-bresser-consulting.com

Geographical focus: *Portugal*

CALOUSTE GULBENKIAN CASE STUDY: *Coaching for Self-Awareness and Leadership*

patterns of behaviour, rather than on developing particular skills. It was therefore, above all, an opportunity for line managers to expand their awareness of their own capacities.

Challenges

As it was the first time that this kind of approach has been adopted at CGF, it was clear that a lot could be at stake.

The decision in itself suggested a change in the approach to leadership development – from a formal classroom setting to a holistic developmental process. It was vital that the programme could be perceived as being worthwhile, applicable to the CGF reality, and both adequate and significant in terms of dealing with the challenges that each line manager was facing.

It also required an investment in time, a personal commitment and a sense of ownership on the part of the participants. As a result, establishing trust between participants and coach was vital, together with a sense of responsibility among the participants. The aim was to make it possible for the participants to safely explore difficult issues without fear of office politics, and also to reflect on their own blind spots (such as attitude issues) from a non-judgmental perspective and without the risk of disclosure. It was therefore necessary to create an atmosphere of sincerity, courage and engagement.

Beyond the reflection level, it was also important to actually effect changes in the accepted ways of doing things and of achieving performance and leadership goals. Clearly, the aim was to create an environment in which each line manager could take action in a sensitive, thoughtful and effective way.

Programme Design

The initiative contained eight two-hour sessions for each participant on a one-to-one basis plus a one-day team coaching session.

The 1:1 sessions were held every four weeks over about eight months. A self-assessment questionnaire (using the Success Insights DISC assessment) was the starting point for each line manager's reflection on their views of the world, particularly their way of thinking about the problems/issues at hand.

A development plan was then drawn up by each participant. It was based on their specific goals and identified their individual problems, issues and expectations.

The team coaching session was held after the second one-to-one session. It enabled the 8 line managers to reflect on themselves as a team in mainly two ways: Firstly, were they actually a team, or did they simply suppose they ought to be a team? Secondly, what was their role as leaders? What was their vision, their purpose? What were their goals? An action plan was drawn up to identify shared goals and was subsequently presented to the CSD top management team.

As the programme was being carried out, we realised that it would also be relevant to reflect on their competencies profile and responsibility portfolio, with the involvement of the CSD top management team (and the Human Resources department). This was achieved by interviewing the 8 line managers as well as the CSD top management team, i.e. one director and two deputy directors. These interviews (semi-directive, using the Behavioural Event Interviewing technique) fostered a deeper discussion on the activities and responsibilities of the job and what skills were demonstrated and/or needed. The Success Insights Competencies Portfolio was used as a reference.

This step was important in order to create an alignment of perspectives and points of view about the role of the line manager, the boundaries of their responsibility and autonomy, and the required skills.

Geographical focus: *Portugal*

CALOUSTE GULBENKIAN CASE STUDY: *Coaching for Self-Awareness and Leadership*

Findings/Outcomes

The 1:1 coaching sessions gave the participants a greater understanding of their leadership experiences, and what was behind their thinking and action. They structured their experiences in terms of a coherent worldview and patterns of behaviour and explored the profound effect on their leadership approach (with its subsequent effect on the system). This, in turn, led to a fundamentally important step forward towards a more integrated and comprehensive approach to their role as leaders.

Further results were improved effectiveness and greater clarity on their sphere of influence. Instead of worrying about issues over which they did not have real control, they focussed on finding out what they could do and taking action. Being prepared for challenges, looking at things in a new way, and being willing to face up to hard issues are the factors which make the difference.

They also explored a different view on the tensions related to their job and now feel greater balance both within themselves and in relation to others. They now approach tensions from a more sober-minded and less personal perspective – and have increased their understanding and ability to intervene in ways that do not isolate or backfire on them.

In the team coaching session, the dialogue with the other managers helped identify and explore common (and different) perceptions and views of their leadership roles and how they handle it – especially in terms of managing upwards and downwards. The participants found they had mutual interests, affinities and views, got closer to each other and were able to build a more appealing and productive relationship. In fact, they moved from relative isolation to a more collective approach – recognising and gathering support from each other.

The programme benefitted from the close co-operation between the coach and the CGF Human Resources department. Critical issues regarding the working context of the line managers were taken into consideration right from the beginning.

Learning Points

The beginning of any coaching relationship can be awkward. The participant often feels both apprehensive and excited, as though expected to perform in a particular way, often wondering what the coach expects from him/her. Once the participant accepts that real learning and growth can emerge from looking into oneself and finding one's own answers to challenges, a much broader perspective and greater set of resources with which to work become available. Getting there is a challenge and was one for CGF. Building a relationship of trust between the participant and the coach was decisive in making this work.

Another learning point is that 1:1 coaching of managers at the same level can become even more powerful and be greatly complemented by team coaching, which gives the participants the opportunity to exchange views and experiences and compare actions, assumptions and results.

What could have been done differently? The fact that the programme was not delivered in accordance with the agreed timeframe was perceived as being counter-productive to the dynamics of learning and change (the programme lasted for a year with a couple of interruptions). In addition, the participants felt that the team coaching dimension could have gone further.

Our key learning/Recommendation:
In order to best foster the learning and development of managers at the same level, consider implementing individual as well as team coaching.

You find the questions and exercises for further reflection on the page before this case study.

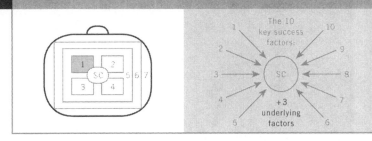

UNDERLYING FACTOR 2

CONTINUOUS LEARNING PROCESS

The implementation and improvement of coaching in organisations requires constant review and optimization and is an evolving, ongoing learning process.

Only by having a genuine learning attitude are you able to fill the 10 key success factors with real lifeblood and create the needed dynamics in their application to achieve great results through coaching.

The optimal use of coaching in companies is thus an iterative, cyclical learning process. This in turn requires continuous integration of theory and practice of coaching for your purposes.

On the one hand, learn and acquire coaching literacy and plan carefully (better start small and good quality, than big and unplanned). On the other hand, have the courage to make a start, go into action, make things happen, gain actual experience – and learn from it. Only by doing and trying things out, are you able to get real feedback and find out what really works.

Learning takes place in loops, and setbacks are a natural part of this process. However well prepared you may be in planning a coaching initiative, you cannot really avoid that you will also make some "mistakes", that you will find areas which you can optimize and that you will encounter and reach limits. This is all part of the process. Without the courage to face possible failures, there is no way to make experiences, learn and develop further.

Very generally speaking, learning in coaching may be deep or broad: Deep learning means getting better in the same coaching discipline and area you are already in (e.g. you

have a 1 : 1 coaching programme and optimize it further over time, while the business conditions remain the same). Broad learning means extending the scope of your coaching capacity (e.g. you learn to develop a totally new kind of coaching programme for your firm because of significant changes in the external/internal business environment).

Several learning resources are available to you...

- Continuous professional development (e.g. this book, seminars, training, coaching for yourself, magazines, internet resources)
- Your reflection, planning and actual experience of implementing and improving coaching in your firm (e.g. reviewing evaluation outcomes, feedback by people, personal experience)
- Learning through guidance and support by a proper coaching consultancy specializing in the effective use of coaching in organisations
- Knowledge sharing/Exchange of ideas and experiences with others (e.g. HR/OD/L&D managers from other organisations, coaching conferences, other coaching networks)
- Encouraging open discussions on coaching within your firm
- Membership and involvement in coaching associations and/or other related bodies

It is through the long-term commitment to continuous learning that coaching implementation and improvement intelligence may develop. This is true for the whole coaching initiative. So make sure not only you, but everyone involved in your coaching programme buys in to the requirement of ongoing learning.

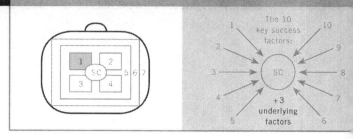

UNDERLYING FACTOR 3

IMPLEMENTATION AND IMPROVEMENT INTELLIGENCE

Through continuous further development, you will enhance the use of coaching in your company. It is all about building the ability to initiate and execute the truly transformative processes towards higher dynamic appropriateness, i.e. to make change and transformation towards optimal fit happen.

The ability to practise and make this kind of transformation a reality on a continuous basis is what we call "coaching capability", "coaching capacity" or "coaching implementation and improvement intelligence".

This is something you cannot just get by taking a quick crash course. It needs to grow over time on the basis of talent, continuous professional development, experience and a genuine commitment to continuous learning in the field of coaching. The position, reputation and power of HR/L&D/OD within a company and the associated financial and staff resources available also directly affect the possibilities regarding developing coaching capability and practice in an organisation.

Building this ability is a life-long learning process – striving for excellence is a goal to work hard for day-by-day. Continue to work on your successful integration of theory and practice around coaching in organisations.

Of course, the application of the 10 key success factors will vary significantly depending on your level of coaching implementation and improvement intelligence. The higher your coaching capability is, the easier, more appropriately and intuitively you will use them.

The success of coaching programmes is far from just being a matter of applying pre-cast frameworks. Any concept, any knowledge about coaching is only as valuable as their user is able to apply them in a dynamically appropriate way (i.e. in a coaching way).

The 10 key success factors themselves are to be used in a coaching way as much as possible – with intelligence and vigilance for optimal fit in each case. Appropriate **co-creation** is a key principle to be considered at all times in this context. Be a role model of what you want to see in your firm and support the development of proper coaching implementation and improvement intelligence in your company as needed.

www.frank-bresser-consulting.com

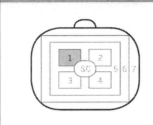

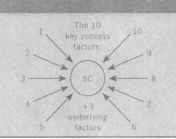

Summary:

COACHING SUCCESS FACTORS FRAMEWORK (FRAMEWORK 1)

We have covered the complete Framework 1 as well as all recurrent key issues also encountered in other frameworks of the book in detail. This first management tool is in principle the most general and high-level one of the core frameworks. Here is once again an overview of the 10 key success factors and their 3 underlying factors:

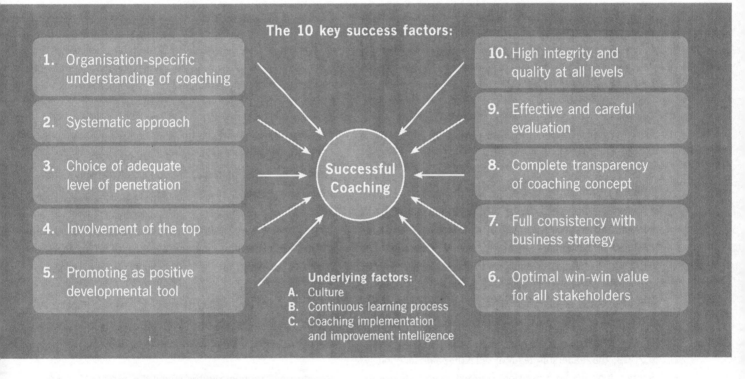

The 10 key success factors:

1. Organisation-specific understanding of coaching
2. Systematic approach
3. Choice of adequate level of penetration
4. Involvement of the top
5. Promoting as positive developmental tool

Successful Coaching

10. High integrity and quality at all levels
9. Effective and careful evaluation
8. Complete transparency of coaching concept
7. Full consistency with business strategy
6. Optimal win-win value for all stakeholders

Underlying factors:
A. Culture
B. Continuous learning process
C. Coaching implementation and improvement intelligence

As already mentioned, there are two ways of making use of this management tool: On the one hand, it may serve you as a central thread and starting point to plan, design and implement new coaching programmes. On the other hand, you may use it as a measure and means to review and optimize existing coaching initiatives. Either way, you will find it an invaluable tool to support achieving outstanding results through coaching.

For further reflection and to integrate practice and theory, we invite you to apply the above framework to the next case study and/or to any of the other case studies included in this book. What role does each success factor and underlying factor play in each case study? What has been done particularly well, and where do you see potential for further development and optimization?

Framework 2 (the coaching value chain framework), which follows after the next case study, will introduce another approach and perspective on how to successfully implement and optimize coaching in organisations. Imagine looking at the above coaching success factors framework through a magnifying glass or microscope with increased precision and exploring more precisely what is going on within it. This is what Framework 2 is about.

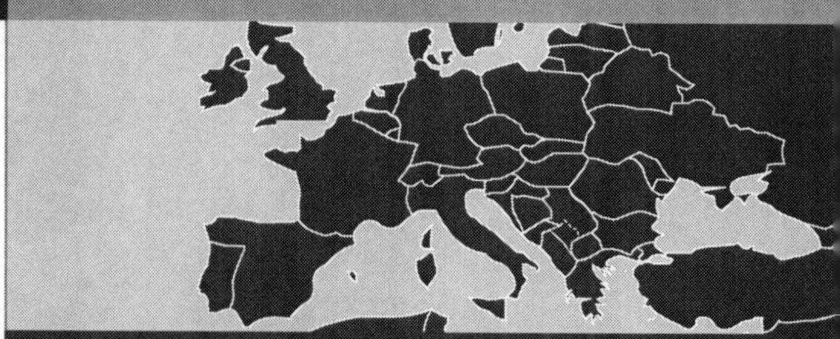

Geographical focus: *Europe*

| CASE STUDY 18 | T-MOBILE INTERNATIONAL, EUROPE |

Company: *T-Mobile International*

(Mobile Communications)

www.t-mobile.net

Author: *Russell Whitworth*

Function: *Head of Project Management Excellence*

Coaching Drives Skills Development in T-Mobile

The Challenge: Developing and Improving our Project Management Skills

T-Mobile's competitive advantage also depends on the skills of our project managers. Being able to launch market-leading products and services such as iPhone, T-Mobile G1 and web'n' walk, and achieving the Company's vision of "Connected Life and Work" (a full user experience to share your life with your community with superior user experience and simplicity – on all your screens) requires our technical project managers to be at the peak of their game. How best to develop these skills?

In 2008, the leadership team of our European Technology function took the bold decision to invest in an in-house Project Management Accreditation scheme. Comparable with external industry schemes such as IPMA, APM, Prince2, etc., T-Mobile's scheme defines five levels of project management skills: from Level E (Project Administrator) to Level A (Project Director). The priority area for skills improvement has been on the two levels most in demand for our challenging technical projects: Levels C and B, containing our community of Senior Project Managers and Programme Managers.

For these two levels, we have defined a 9-month accreditation process comprising four components (including coaching):

Training: Three two-day training modules, run by an external training partner. These concentrate on project management skills, and in particular on "soft skills" of team management, stakeholder management, etc.

Work Experience: Throughout the accreditation period, candidates are expected to manage a project at an appropriate level to apply and exercise their project management skills.

Check-Up: Project managers are assessed periodically, to check that their project management skills are being applied correctly, to the satisfaction of senior stakeholders.

Coaching: Continuously throughout the accreditation period, candidates work with a peer coach. The aim of the coaching relationship is to empower and support the candidate in exercising their developing skills.

Implementing a Coaching Scheme

With support from leading coaching experts in 2007, we successfully introduced our project management community to the use of coaching techniques in managing their project teams. Now the challenge was to identify and train peer coaches to support our accreditation participants. We took a simple and pragmatic approach:

Geographical focus: *Europe*

T-MOBILE INTERNATIONAL CASE STUDY: *Coaching Drives Skills Development in T-Mobile*

THE ACCREDITATION SCHEME

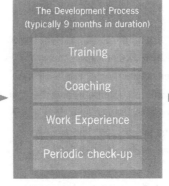

- In the first instance, participants are asked to nominate their own coaches. This encourages a true peer-coaching relationship, and empowers the participants to take control right from the start. If they cannot find a suitable coach, then we will help.
- Coaches – who may lack formal coaching training or awareness – are provided with a short introductory pack of information that explains the basics: the coaching framework in the context of the accreditation scheme, how to be an effective non-directive coach, establishing a contract, confidentiality rules, etc.
- Coaches are encouraged but not forced to attend a short (four-hour) training workshop in which the GROW model is introduced and practised. They are also provided with access to further resources including reading materials and more in-depth coaching training if required.

Throughout the coaching relationship, the participant – not the coach – takes responsibility for its success. They are expected to schedule sessions, to set the agenda, and to develop their skills.

Coaches are asked to provide feedback to the accreditation panel, which might appear to be a violation of confidentiality. We avoid any conflict by clearly delimiting the nature of the feedback and making participants fully aware of the confidentiality rules (i.e. it forms part of the "contract"). Our guidelines instruct the coaches to report only on the following:

- Did the candidate participate fully and willingly in the coaching scheme?
- Did the candidate work with the coach towards accreditation?
- Did the candidate set their own targets, agree actions, and carry out those actions in the pursuit of self-development?

The coach should not be assessing the candidate's capability as a project manager!

Learning and Next Steps

To date, five candidates have successfully achieved accreditation, 32 are part way through the process, and a further 30 will start in early 2010. Over 40 project management coaches have been nominated and briefed. So far, the indi-

Geographical focus: *Europe*

T-MOBILE INTERNATIONAL CASE STUDY: *Coaching Drives Skills Development in T-Mobile*

cations are strongly positive. Candidates unanimously state that the coaching element is extremely important, and many have described it as the most valuable part of the scheme.

One of the scheme's first successful participants, Neal Harper, was recently awarded his Level B Accreditation by our CTO. Of the coaching element, Neal says: "A coach is a bit like an 'agony aunt' – someone you can confide in and they can help you explore options to resolve the problem. It is essential that the coach is someone you respect and trust to ensure conversations are open and productive."

Dr. Mike Corrigall, VP of Demand and Project Management, is a keen advocate: "Coaching is the key that unlocks the potential of our project managers."

Clearly incorporating coaching into our development scheme for project managers was the right decision, and we will continue to use this approach.

As an improvement, we recognise that the coaches themselves need more support. A training seminar is not enough. In 2010 we will explore the options for giving our coaches more opportunity for practising and developing their own skills, to share their experiences, and a more formal support mechanism to enable them to adopt best practice in their coaching sessions.

Our key learning/Recommendation:
When designing a staff development plan, include coaching as a key activity to maximise effectiveness.

Questions and exercises for further reflection and to integrate practice and theory:

1. What is the business case for coaching in the company?

2. What coaching form(s) have they implemented? What are the outcomes?

3. Apply each of the 10 key success factors of framework 1 to this case study.
   Are some factors more relevant than others?

4. Apply each of the 3 underlying factors of framework 1 to this case study.

5. The company is planning to explore more options for providing their coaches with stronger support in the future. What are your suggestions for this added support?

6. What is your key learning from this case study?

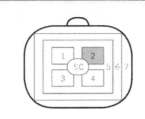

PART II

THE COACHING VALUE CHAIN FRAMEWORK

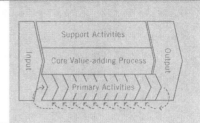

FRAMEWORK 2

This second management tool brings another approach to and perspective on how to use coaching in organisations effectively.

It provides you with a step-by-step guide to achieve best practice in coaching and sets out the chronological steps towards the successful implementation and improvement of coaching programmes.

In this way, it will enable you to fully think through the whole coaching initiative and gain greater clarity on the process and how coaching adds value.

The key idea of the coaching value chain is that for an organisation to improve performance (output) by using coaching (input), it needs to initiate and realize the core value-adding process of coaching by accomplishing both the primary activities and the support activities of implementation.

According to extensive research and experience, managers responsible for the implementation and improvement of coaching in their companies are well advised to think through the coaching value chain for their context and establish a clear picture of its operation.

Here is an overview of the coaching value chain in full detail (see the next two pages). We will have a closer look at each of its elements.

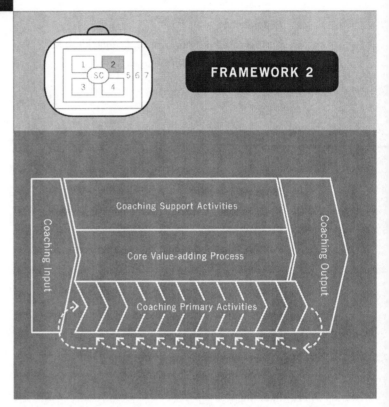

Framework 2: Coaching value chain framework (simplified version)

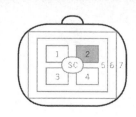
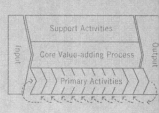

The Input

1. Coaching
2. Further inputs: time, budget, energy, know-how, external input, other resources

The Output

1. Individual, team, organisational and social benefits (level perspective)
2. First, second, third, ... tier benefits (chronological perspective)
3. Finally: Improved overall organisational performance and excellence

From input to output: The Core Value-adding Process

1. Filtering
2. Implementing/Optimizing suitable coaching forms
3. Building coaching capacity
4. Achieving higher dynamic appropriateness (better fit)
5. Realisation of the output (chain of benefits)

The Primary Activities

1. Put coaching on the radar screen
2. Acquire coaching literacy
3. Make a needs analysis
4. Identify potential areas of application
5. Develop the coaching concept
6. Ensure the availability of required resources
7. Prepare carefully
8. Introduce coaching/the coaching programme properly
9. Enlarge the coaching initiative step-by-step
10. Manage and maintain the programme
11. Evaluate effectively and carefully
12. Develop the concept and measures further

The Support Activities

1. Company-specific implementation/improvement
2. Systematic and careful planning
3. Keeping a realistic view
4. Promoting coaching as positive, developmental tool
5. Involving the top
6. Alignment with business strategy and ensuring optimal win-win
7. Communication and transparency
8. People involvement and co-creation
9. Ensuring high integrity and quality
10. Considering the cultural dimension
11. Continuous learning & development of intelligence
12. Making relevant 'make-or-buy' decisions

The coaching value chain is very comprehensive (in particular the core value-adding process and the primary activity of developing a coaching concept) and may stretch your thinking and be quite challenging at first. This framework may thus take some time to settle.

Like with Framework 1, there are two main ways of making use of this management tool: On the one hand, it may serve you as a central thread and starting point to plan, design and implement new coaching programmes. On the other hand, you may use it as a measure and means to review and optimize existing coaching initiatives.

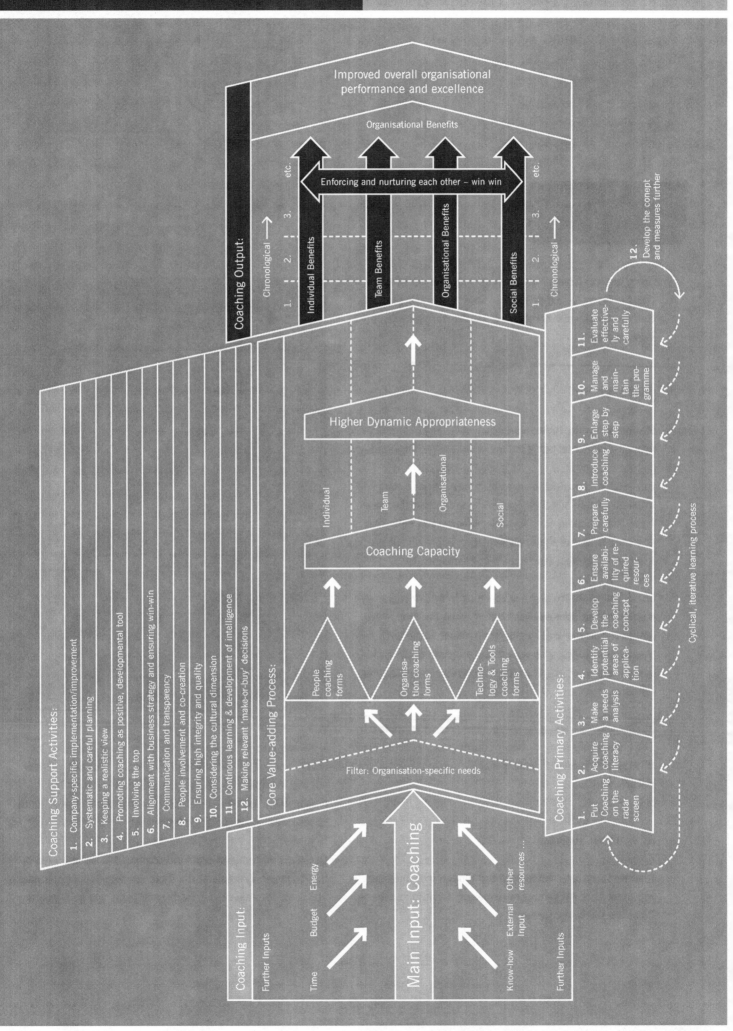

www.frank-bresser-consulting.com

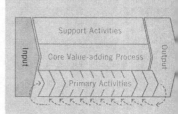

1. THE INPUT

There are two types of inputs going into the coaching value chain – firstly, coaching itself as main input and secondly further inputs while considering, implementing and optimizing coaching:

1. Coaching

By definition, the main input of any coaching programme is coaching, which is being implemented and/or improved.

But what is coaching? It may mean very different things to different people and organisations – and in fact the development of a company-specific understanding and definition of coaching is part of the implementation/improvement process itself (see Key Success Factor 1 in Framework 1).

The essence and core of any coaching form is modern, dynamic appropriateness – optimal fit: what fits best where and how (see the coaching pyramid model in the book introduction). So you may regard this principle of dynamic appropriateness/best fit as the core input of any coaching initiative.

At another level, you may take a more pragmatic approach: The input of coaching is simply coaching as you come across it. Whatever form and content that is, this is the initial input you work with.

2. Further inputs

In order to actually implement and improve coaching, you will need to invest various resources on a continuous basis, these are the secondary inputs.

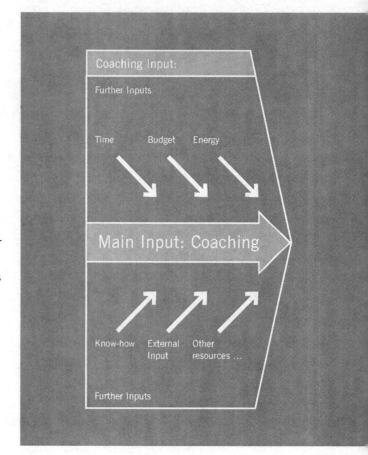

Time and budget are key inputs. Other input resources are energy and know-how provided by people. You may get internal and external support, so you also have external input. Finally, there are other resources you may think of (e.g. office space, intranet, technological devices).

Decisions on the level and kind of input will be informed by the resources available and a thorough cost-benefit analysis. The coaching value chain framework helps you gain greater clarity in this respect.

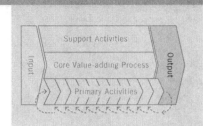
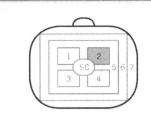

2. THE OUTPUT

Well-implemented coaching may provide enormous benefits (output) for the individual, the team, the organisation as well as potentially the wider society. Additionally, these benefits may reinforce and nurture each other. (See Key Success Factor 6 in Framework 1.)

Also, there is a chronological dimension to the benefits of coaching: Coaching may initiate a whole chain of outputs containing first, second, third, … tier benefits.

Any coaching programme is fundamentally meant to improve organisational performance and excellence overall.

The actual coaching output (benefits) may vary significantly depending on your company context and the specific purpose and design of your coaching programme.

Accordingly, develop a clear idea of what you want to achieve by coaching in your organisation specifically. What are the most important benefits you want to focus on and gain from coaching? Define your goals and objectives for coaching as appropriate for your purposes.

Typical benefits of coaching are listed below, including short and long term, direct and indirect benefits, at an individual, team, organisational and social level:

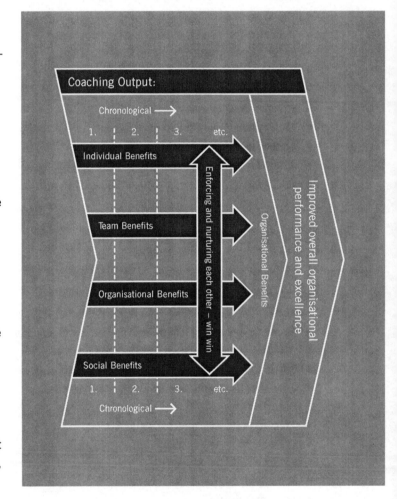

Benefits at the individual level

- Improved performance and excellence
- Higher motivation/commitment
- More effective management of change processes
- Faster mastery of new roles/tasks
- More accurate use of technologies & tools
- Enhanced leadership skills
- Improved communication and relationships
- Greater clarity in goals, strategy and process
- Better knowledge transfer
- Increased self-awareness and self-reflection
- Personal growth and development
- Greater agility and versatility
- Improved work life balance
- Optimal sustainability in all these areas
- etc.

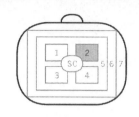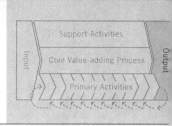

Benefits at the team level

- Improved team performance and efficiency
- Higher motivation/team spirit
- More effective management of change processes
- Better communication/team work/relationships
- Greater clarity in goal, strategy and process
- Creation of synergies
- Effective conflict management
- Team building, growth and development
- Greater agility and versatility
- Optimal sustainability in all these areas
- etc.

Benefits at the organisational level

- Improved organisational performance and excellence
- Improved organisational capability
- Higher profitability/return on investment/productivity/sales
- Greater agility and ability of the organisation to adjust to changing circumstances
- Buy-in to organisational values and behaviours
- More effective organisational structures, processes and operations
- More accurate use of technologies & tools
- Effective communication
- Higher creativity/innovation
- Better staff motivation and retention
- Less absenteeism
- Employer attractiveness for current and future employees, in particular for talent
- Open and productive organisational culture and climate
- Developing the learning organisation
- Sustainable form of learning and development
- Optimal sustainability in all these areas
- etc.

Benefits at the social level

- More successful company (with the associated benefits for society like more secure jobs, higher tax incomes, etc.)
- Positive role model for other organisations
- The positive atmosphere in the company can spread to its social environment.
- Increasing company contributions to the wider community/protection of the environment (more value-adding products, corporate social responsibility and sustainability initiatives)
- etc.

Ideally, in your coaching initiative, all levels of benefits reinforce each other – and finally feed into and nurture improved organisational performance and excellence overall.

Consider the chronological order of benefits you envisage gaining from coaching. Just to give a simple example illustrating this point: A one-to-one leadership coaching initiative may first of all be focussed on the leadership ability of the individual (first tier benefit), but will then – directly or indirectly – also have an impact on the team spirit and performance (second tier benefits), on its department and business unit (third tier benefits), thereby also on the overall organisational performance (fourth tier benefits) – and potentially also on the wider community (fifth tier benefits), which in turn may again have positive effects on the organisation (sixth tier benefits) (etc.).

Where you expect or identify negative outcomes/disadvantages from a coaching programme, do take these into account, but as an input. Inputs include all the investments, costs and losses stemming from a coaching initiative. The output of the coaching value chain is only about what you gain from coaching.

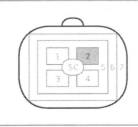
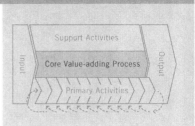

3. FROM INPUT TO OUTPUT: THE CORE VALUE-ADDING PROCESS

Despite the possible significant differences between existing coaching programmes, there is a common core value-adding process that applies to all coaching initiatives from input to output:

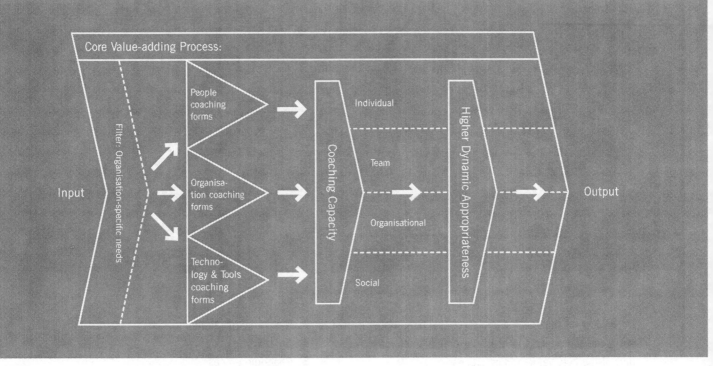

Let us have a look at each element of this process.

Step 1: Filtering

Starting from coaching (whatever you may actually understand by it at the beginning), it is firstly important to filter for your company-specific coaching needs and, on the basis of these, to approach and define coaching for your purposes. Just letting in coaching unfiltered may run the risk of taking away rather than actually producing value. (See Key Success Factors 1 and 2 in Framework 1.)

Step 2: Implementing/Optimizing suitable coaching forms

Building on the above, the next stage is to choose, implement and optimise the most suitable coaching form(s) for your organisation. There is a wide range of possible coaching forms available to you. See Key Success Factor 3 in Framework 1 where you find a very detailed explanation on each of these and how they may add value:

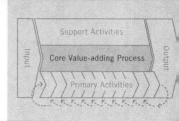

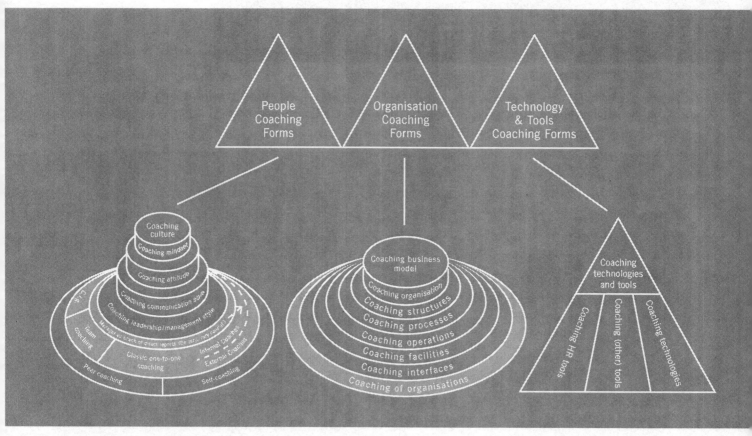

(The coaching forms marked in light blue require the use of professional coaches.)

Depending on the specific choice of coaching forms, different types and designs of coaching programmes may become part of the core value-adding process.

To give an example, any one-to-one coaching programme is classically based on and designed around the following six stages of a coaching intervention:

1. Availability of suitable coaches (Building a coach pool)
2. Request for coaching
3. Matching coach and coachee
4. Contracting
5. Coaching process
6. Evaluation

So if you want to implement 1:1 coaching successfully, these stages normally need to become part of your core value-adding process in some way. For other coaching forms, other aspects may gain relevance (see Key Success Factor 3 in Framework 1).

Request for coaching → Matching coach and coachee → Contracting → Coaching process → Evaluation

Availability of suitable coaches (Building coach pools)

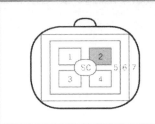
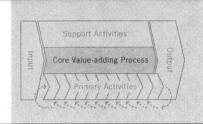

Step 3: Building coaching capacity

The next logical phase in the core-value-adding process is the emergence and reinforcement of coaching capacity as a result of the successful implementation and/or improvement of coaching forms.

Coaching capacity is the ability to actually achieve better/ optimal fit (i.e. achieve higher dynamic appropriateness) (for further information, see the coaching pyramid model in the book introduction and/or the coaching capacity building framework which is Framework 3).

Coaching capacity as such is quite intangible, tacit and abstract – and thus not too easy to grasp. What it actually means in practice only becomes concrete and visible in each context. At this point, we will work with the general term.

Coaching capacity may be built at the individual, team, organisational and/or social level and can have a more general and high-level or a context-specific focus.

You can view coaching capacity as only an intermediary stage of the process; or as a key benefit and output of the coaching value chain. In some coaching initiatives, developing coaching capacity is even the main objective.

Other terms for coaching capacity are coaching capability, coaching intelligence or coaching culture (in this context, the term culture then embraces not only the people, but all dimensions).

Step 4: Achieving better fit (higher dynamic appropriateness)

The next phase is that the actual use of the above successfully developed coaching capacity generates higher dynamic appropriateness – be it at the individual, team, organisational and/or social level – in your firm.

The approaches and solutions in your firm begin to show greater fit in the areas where coaching capacity has been built/enhanced.

Like coaching capacity, fit as a term is quite intangible, tacit and abstract. What it actually means in practice, is dependent on each specific case.

Also, you can view the optimised fit as only an intermediary stage of the process – or as a key benefit and output of the coaching value chain.

The above steps 3 and 4 are of central importance for any coaching initiative. The following questions may give you a first idea of key issues to take into account in this respect:

- What kind of coaching capacity is actually needed in your company?
- What kind of coaching forms are best suited to build it?
- How can the actual use of coaching capacity be best ensured?
- What does better fit mean in your specific context?
- What is the exact focus of each part of the coaching programme with regard to building and applying coaching capacity?
- Are the same or different people responsible for building and applying coaching capacity?
- Who finally decides what is to be deemed as appropriate and what must be done in what context?

(See Framework 3 – the coaching capacity building framework – which addresses coaching programmes in detail from the coaching capacity perspective.)

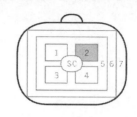

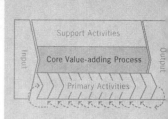

Step 5: Realisation of the output
(chain of benefits)

Achieving better fit (i.e. higher dynamic appropriateness) in the firm triggers the desired chain of benefits at the individual, team, organisational and social level – eventually resulting in improved organisational performance and excellence overall. This is the output of the coaching value chain.

In summary, the proper implementation and optimization of suitable coaching forms effects **three subsequent, necessary stages of outcomes**: The first is about building coaching capacity, the second about achieving better fit through its application, and the third about unfolding the various benefits resulting from this better fit.

So it is not only important to be clear on what you finally want to achieve by coaching, but also on how coaching is meant to work for your company to achieve these intermediary, necessary steps and targets.

www.frank-bresser-consulting.com

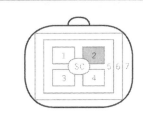
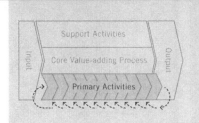

4. THE PRIMARY ACTIVITIES

The following are the classic, chronological steps to design, initiate, realize and optimize successful coaching programmes:

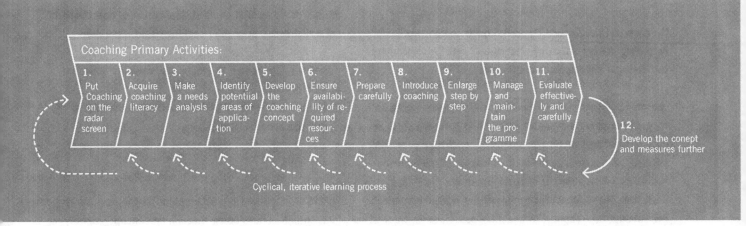

1. Put coaching (more) on the radar screen

The first step is to raise awareness of coaching and its various forms. This is essential to implementing or improving coaching in your firm.

The trigger to increase awareness of coaching can come from anywhere outside or inside your organisation. Even when you think you already know coaching very well, you may still come across new perspectives on and approaches to coaching, which may further widen your awareness of coaching.

So whether you are already highly experienced and skilled in making use of coaching in your company or whether you are new to coaching – coaching remains a learning journey. Your radar may become more sophisticated over time.

In order to raise your self-awareness, recall how you came across coaching for the first time. How may this have subjectively influenced and shaped your understanding and prac-

tice of coaching? Has your awareness of coaching changed over time? If yes – when, how and for what reasons? Reflecting on these kinds of questions will give you more clarity on your access to coaching.

2. Acquire (more) coaching literacy

You may be immediately delighted with the coaching that you have come across and which is on your radar screen, however do not rashly implement it; the initial enthusiasm may quickly disappear again. Your own critical reflection on coaching before implementation, will ensure you take appropriate action. For this purpose, you need to develop coaching know-how and enable yourself to properly assess its substance and potential.

You may decide to ask for the support of a coaching consultancy and/or coaching providers to design your coaching initiative more effectively. To do this responsibly, you first need

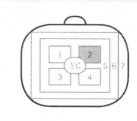

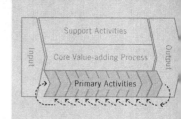

to build some coaching literacy yourself in order to be able to choose suitable, qualified coaching service providers. Look for those consultancies and providers who are committed to helping you develop your own coaching capability, and avoid those who – explicitly or implicitly – try to keep your coaching capacity low and make you dependent on them instead.

So once you have coaching on the radar screen, work on acquiring deeper coaching literacy and aim for continuous professional development in this area.

You may use many diverse sources to acquire coaching literacy. These may be available within your company (e.g. review of existing coaching programmes; exchange with other HR/OD/L&D colleagues in your company; coaching resources in your firm intranet) or outside your company (e.g. this and other books; coaching seminars and workshops; coaching consultancy; support by coaching associations; internet).

3. Analyse your organisation's needs thoroughly

The starting point of any HR/L&D/OD programme and of any coaching initiative should be your company-specific needs – not coaching itself. Coaching is a means, not an end.

Your analysis of your organisation's needs and objectives will inform what approaches, such as coaching, may be useful to actually meet your firm's needs.

4. Identify potential areas of application where coaching may add value

On the basis of acquired coaching literacy and the proper analysis of your organisational needs, the next step is to consider and narrow down whether and how coaching specifically may help meet your business goals/objectives/strategy.

This may require – besides the use of existing information – further coaching-specific research within your organisation. In particular, involve the potential stakeholders of coaching as early as possible to get their input and feedback on the current and potential future use of coaching. See this step as an evolving process and learning loop.

Identify the potential areas of application of coaching and get a first sense of where coaching could/should be ...

- newly implemented to create new value for your firm
- kept exactly as it is
- applied in a more effective way than in the past to add better value than before
- abandoned, where there seems to be no need for it any more.

This is an important pre-assessment for the next primary activity, which is developing a coaching concept. Identifying the potential of coaching for your firm is the most legitimate reason to explore further and develop a concrete coaching programme.

Coaching can be as a separate coaching programme and/or as part of a wider initiative.

5. Develop a company-specific coaching concept

Once you have come to the conclusion that coaching, or the optimization of an existing coaching programme, is likely to add substantial value for your business, the challenge is then to develop an organisation-specific coaching concept that is exactly tailored around your company's needs.

This may imply further research and further involvement of the stakeholders, which may expose that coaching (or its improvement) is not a suitable approach for now. Making pilots first or workshops to discuss coaching plans are very useful

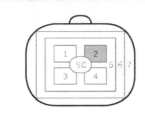 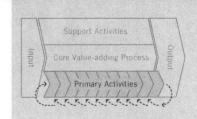

elements to get further clarity on the opportunity for coaching to add value for your firm.

The development of an appropriate high-quality coaching concept may be the most important and most challenging part in the process of implementing and/or optimizing coaching. It requires from you to think through the whole coaching value chain in advance: What is your envisaged output? What is your planned input? What is your intended core value-adding process from your input to your desired output? How will your primary and support activities need to look like to actually make all this happen? What is your actual organisation-specific coaching understanding and strategy as a basis of all this?

Developing a company-specific coaching concept lies at the centre of the whole coaching value chain, as it covers all its aspects and is the starting point for everything that follows. It is worth investing substantial time and effort in this step – it will pay off tremendously.

Creating a coaching concept means making decisions to get coaching into shape for your company-specific purposes:

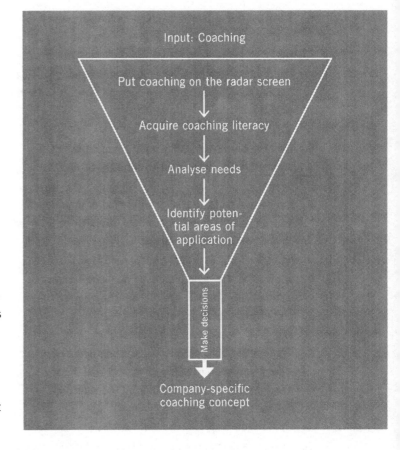

Your coaching concept needs to allow for a suitable balance of rigour and flexibility and reflect systematic planning, while remaining pragmatic and flexible. Revisit, review and possibly refine and adjust it on a regular basis.

The implementation and optimization of coaching is an evolving process; which demands responsiveness to the actual process as it evolves rather than a bureaucratic, rigid sequence of steps. Also, the more in advance you plan, the less concrete and detailed your planning can be. Very detailed planning is only possible for the next time frame and the less certain you are about how coaching will be received in your organisation, the more carefully you should proceed. (In this context, for example, making a pilot first may help reduce uncertainty and facilitate further planning.)

In order to develop a high-quality coaching concept for your context, the following **sequence of 15 steps** may be helpful:

1. Be clear on your role as HR/L&D/OD manager and the resources available.

2. Review the core of coaching which is dynamic appropriateness/best fit (see the coaching pyramid model in the book introduction).

3. Identify precisely the area(s) for the implementation and/or improvement of coaching in your company.

4. Clearly formulate your desired output (i.e. benefits) from coaching in this/each area.

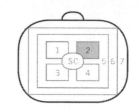
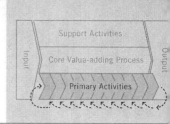

5. Consider the different coaching dimensions and forms that are available and choose – or develop yourself – the most appropriate one(s) that best suit your coaching purpose (see detailed explanations on all coaching forms and dimensions in key success factor 3 in Framework 1).

6. Develop a realistic plan of what could be the core value-adding process from input to output.

7. Conceive a realistic plan of what kind of primary and support activities you (and others involved) would need to make this actually happen.

8. Review the complete picture of your whole coaching value chain. Check it and make further amendments and changes as appropriate.

9. Confirm that the coaching value chain is realistic, consistent and in alignment with your overall business and development strategy. Further adjust your plan as needed.

10. Imagine a best and worst case scenario for your coaching concept, if it was put into practice in its current form. What do these scenarios tell you about the quality of your concept? Refine and develop your concept further as needed.

11. Identify the essence of your concept/coaching value chain: Formulate as precisely as possible your final company-specific definition of coaching. Ensure your concept provides elements to make this understanding very transparent and clear to all stakeholders.

12. Similarly, formulate as precisely as possible your company-specific coaching objectives, your coaching strategy and how all this fits within your company strategy. Make sure your concept contains measures to make these very transparent and clear to all stakeholders.

13. "Shake" your concept many times, i.e. examine and check it from different perspectives. Then let it rest for a while and pick it up again and have another check. When it remains the same, you are ready.

14. If you are happy with everything, break down your plan into further detail as appropriate and prepare a concrete, operational action plan.

15. Revisit, refine and adjust your concept on a regular basis.

These steps include involving and getting feedback from the (potential) stakeholders of coaching and potentially undertaking further coaching-specific research and using external support.

Depending on what **kind of coaching form(s)** you (plan to) implement and/or optimize, your concept will need to address very different aspects. (Please see Key success Factor 3 in Framework 1 setting out all coaching forms and key aspects regarding their implementation and improvement.)

For example, when it comes to **1:1 coaching**, the programme design classically needs to be tailored around the six key stages of a one-to-one coaching intervention (i.e. availability of suitable coaches by building a coach pool, request for coaching, matching coach and coachee, contracting, coaching process, evaluation).

In contrast, when developing a **coaching leadership style** in your firm, the following seven stages will inform your design:

1. Identify the nature of the coaching leadership/management style needed.
2. Develop a specific coaching skills training concept for the targeted managers/leaders.
3. Make sure very clear boundaries are set regarding other coaching forms (in particular regarding internal coaches/the manager as coach of direct reports).

www.frank-bresser-consulting.com

 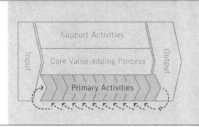

4. Recruit and familiarize suitable, qualified trainers/training providers (external and/or internal e.g. first external, then increasingly also internal).

5. Train the targeted leaders/managers.

6. Provide ongoing follow-up support for the trained leaders/managers to develop their skills further and keep standards high (e.g. building peer support networks; delivering advanced training; making relevant literature and other resources available).

7. Evaluate and continuously improve the measures.

As another example, developing a **coaching culture** (as a people coaching form) is handled differently. The coaching culture is a dynamic, flexible and highly scalable concept. The programme design and kind of measures to be taken may vary enormously depending on each case.

Here are some classic, possible elements of coaching culture initiatives:

• Programmes around one, more or all of the people coaching forms: self-coaching; peer coaching; one-to-one coaching by external/internal coaches; team coaching; coaching leadership/management style; leader/manager as coach; coaching communication style; coaching attitude; coaching mindset

• Workshops (and other formats like board meetings) to discuss the existing and desired culture, and/or develop a way to achieve a best fit culture

• Redesigning organisational processes and structures (e.g. decision-making processes, performance measurement systems, reward/appraisal systems, levels of hierarchy) in order to support the envisaged culture change

• Integrating coaching elements into already existing programmes (e.g. including more questioning techniques in traditional communication training)

• Other training on relevant topics like change, emotional intelligence (EQ), diversity, personal development, social skills, etc.

• Other, more informal means (e.g. spread the word, coaching success stories, networking, use of intranet and web 2.0; open days; events)

• Additional tools (e.g. mentoring programmes; 360 degree feedback, MBTI)

• Recruit/Bring in new employees with the coaching mindset

• etc.

So coaching concepts may vary hugely. When developing your own company-specific concept, in particular choices regarding the form(s) of coaching to be implemented/optimized are of central importance. (For more detailed information on coaching forms and dimensions, please see Key success Factor 3 in Framework 1.)

6. Ensure the availability of required resources

Before implementing any coaching concept, make sure you have the budget, the time and energy, the necessary support from the relevant stakeholders (e.g. top management) and also the organisational power to make it all actually happen. Or, if you don't have them yet, organize to get them in time. Resources may be available from within or outside your organisation (e.g. possible additional public funds for coaching/educational programs).

One important aspect regarding organisational power is where in your organisational structure to actually position coaching and the coaching programme. For people coaching forms, this is probably within the HR, L&D or OD function. Also, you may consider it to be a more general, strategic top management issue. What is the most appropriate position, will depend on the nature of your coaching initiative and your company's definitions of its functions.

Taking this further, reflect on who exactly is responsible for coaching in your organisation. Is there already a "coaching champion" or "coaching department/unit" in your firm? Does your own role and responsibilities cover the implementation of your planned coaching programme? Is there is a shared responsibility between roles and functions? Is there

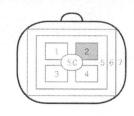 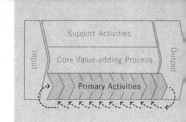

maybe a need to create a new role of a coaching champion, a new team or even a new function for coaching in your company? What organisational power and resources are needed to realistically implement your concept – and are these ensured?

Our experience and research show that coaching programmes (rather than one-off initiatives) benefit from having a coaching champion or specific coaching unit that is responsible for the implementation and improvement coaching and oversees the whole process. Advantages are better quality and consistency, clearer responsibilities, the provision of a central contact point and the development of a strong centre of coaching expertise and resources within the firm.

7. Prepare carefully

Once you have developed an appropriate coaching concept and find you have or can organize the required resources, the next step is to prepare and put everything in place to get started. This may last quite a time, but is key and needs to be done properly.

Classic tasks within this phase are, for example, the recruitment and selection of suitable coaches and/or coaching skills trainers; completing your information material for the various stakeholders and finalizing all required forms (e. g. coaching request/contracting/evaluation forms); coaching training and workshop agendas need to be completely worked out.

Part of this step may also be further research like making a test or pilot to see what works best in a specific area.

Prepare particularly thoroughly the introduction phase (see the next step), as it will set the tone and the course for everything that will follow and is the next upcoming time window.

8. Introduce coaching / the coaching programme properly

The start of your coaching initiative must be very appealing and professional – it will inform and shape how coaching (/its optimized form) is perceived and received by people in your firm.

Promote coaching as a positive, developmental tool and provide people with relevant information in a fresh and inspiring way. Clearly communicate the win-win benefits of coaching and make the coaching concept transparent and easy to grasp. Demonstrate the coaching spirit and aim to be a role model of what you want to see in your organisation. Be open to dialogue, feedback and further learning.

Consider having a special launch event to officially present, introduce and demonstrate coaching. An open coaching day, offering test coaching sessions or some coaching skills training for the coaching target group can work well. Arrange meetings where coaches and potential coachees (and/or coaching trainers and potential training participants) may meet and become familiar with each other and exchange information, experience and ideas.

Provide people with high-quality brochures/flyers on coaching. Maybe you also have a coaching logo and brand that people may identify with and buy into immediately. Spread the word throughout the organisation and communicate, communicate, communicate (e. g. by further presentations, announcements and articles in the company media). Use the language that people understand (by target group) and the information channels that are relevant to them.

Involve the top and get opinion leaders to officially promote coaching in your company. Ideally, you start the implementation and optimization of coaching from the top – with the top managers making effective use of coaching forms themselves and thereby becoming role models and a living demonstration for the whole organisation.

www.frank-bresser-consulting.com

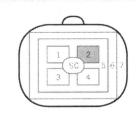
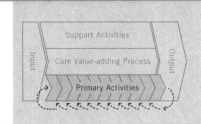

The coaching programme may show significant size at this stage already, or still be in a pilot phase only.

9. Enlarge your coaching initiative step-by-step

As the implementation and improvement of coaching is an evolving process, strive for an iterative step-by-step enlargement of coaching programmes, rather than for a massive one-shot coaching initiative right at the beginning.

With increasing coaching intelligence and certainty about the success of coaching initiatives, comes improved ability to explain the business case/actual benefits and to expand your programme further to meet the potential and thus justify the required resources for actually expanding the programme further.

Over time, you may also extend the variety of coaching forms used. A business may, for example, at first only have external coaches and later on graduate towards having their own internal coaches. Or it identifies, after having a 1:1 and team coaching programme, also a need and demand for having a coaching leadership style or coaching culture initiative.

Coaching may also be infectious and spread throughout the organisation beyond what was originally targeted by a coaching programme. For example, imagine a firm that implements a 1:1 coaching programme and after some time finds that a kind of coaching culture has emerged. So a step-by-step-enlargement can either be formally planned or emerge organically from an existing coaching programme. Consider also influencing the direction and control of this latter spread of coaching.

10. Manage and maintain the programme

While the programme is running, it is up to you to support and manage the process properly, keep integrity and quality standards high and intervene promptly where problems occur.

Keep your coaching initiative fresh and lively and respond to changing needs and circumstances by adjusting the programme accordingly. Keep people informed on the progress of the coaching measures on a regular basis. Spread coaching success stories and share issues of concern and learning around the coaching as well.

Connect people who are interested in coaching and/or are attending coaching initiatives. Establish and encourage the creation of peer groups and coaching networks and develop a coaching community within your firm.

Ensure the continuous development of the people involved in the delivery of your coaching programme (internal as well as external people). Identify their needs and provide them with a proper internal support and quality system.

You may for example give your coaches the opportunity (or make it compulsory for them) to join a peer learning group, get regular or on-demand supervision and attend further coach training.

Pay attention to the actual process as it evolves – and respond to it as appropriate without over-managing it. Remain open for dialogue, feedback and learning.

11. Evaluate your coaching initiative effectively and carefully

Measure the success and the quality of the process of your coaching initiative properly in order to track the outcomes achieved through coaching and be able to optimize the coaching programme on a continuous basis.

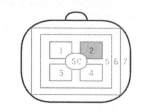

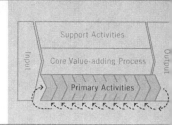

For detailed information on how to best evaluate coaching, see Key Success Factor 9 in Framework 1. At this point, we just want to highlight two central aspects of the evaluation of coaching:

On the one hand, there is a need for as valid and reliable results and data about the coaching process and outcomes as possible. Evaluation is an enabler and a continuous source of learning for everybody involved in the coaching programme. All this does require effective coaching evaluation.

On the other hand, the complex nature of the impact of coaching requires careful evaluation methods. Coaching is largely about people, their behaviours and attitudes, so there is a particular need for very careful methods of evaluation that respect people's privacy, foster buy-in and commitment and support the overall coaching processes and outcomes, rather than hinder them.

So evaluate effectively and carefully. Do this on a permanent basis, not only the formal evaluation methods used at certain points of the process, but also the continuous, informal evaluation through open dialogue and feedback.

12. Develop the concept and measures further (as part of the cyclical, iterative learning process)

On the basis of evaluation, develop your coaching programme further. This may mean very different things in practice, e.g. stopping, downsizing, re-launching, re-designing, changing, refining, keeping, extending or fully rolling out coaching measures.

Although the last of the 12 primary activities, developing your coaching initiative further is far from being the end of the process. It is this step which explicitly highlights and ensures the learning loop and opens the door to re-entering

the sequence of primary activities at any previous point as appropriate.

The implementation and improvement of coaching in organisations requires constant review and optimization and is an evolving, ongoing learning process. The optimal use of coaching in companies is thus an iterative, cyclical learning process. (See also Underlying Factor 2 in Framework 1.)

These were the primary activities. We now come to the support activities.

www.frank-bresser-consulting.com

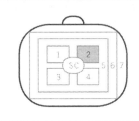
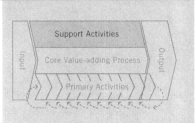

5. THE SUPPORT ACTIVITIES

The support activities – or better say support aspects – should be taken into account during all primary activities and are in principle valid for the whole coaching value chain. They don't represent chronological steps, but are recommended, underlying elements for any successful coaching initiative:

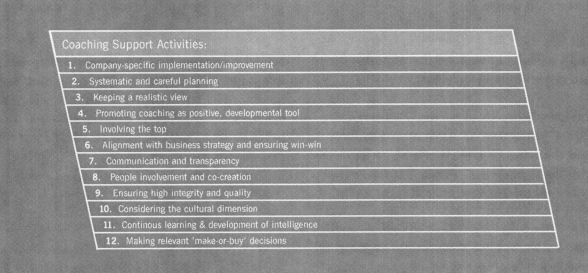

Coaching Support Activities:
1. Company-specific implementation/improvement
2. Systematic and careful planning
3. Keeping a realistic view
4. Promoting coaching as positive, developmental tool
5. Involving the top
6. Alignment with business strategy and ensuring win-win
7. Communication and transparency
8. People involvement and co-creation
9. Ensuring high integrity and quality
10. Considering the cultural dimension
11. Continous learning & development of intelligence
12. Making relevant 'make-or-buy' decisions

1. Implement and improve coaching in a company-specific way at any time

The term coaching may mean very different things to different people and organisations. In fact, there are several tenable ways of defining and using coaching – and the tricky point is that the same coaching approach and measure may work very well in one company, but poorly in another.

Therefore, at all times, make sure you have the kind of coaching definition and implement the type of coaching programme that are tailored around and best suit your company's needs specifically. (See also Key Success Factor 1 in Framework 1: Develop an organisation-specific understanding of coaching.)

2. Implement and optimize coaching systematically and plan carefully, while remaining flexible and pragmatic

The larger the size of coaching programme, the more critical is the need for systematic and careful implementation. But also in very small coaching initiatives, the number and complexity of issues to be addressed may be extensive. So never underestimate the sophisticated nature of a professional coaching programme. (See also Key success factor 2 in Framework 1: Adopt a systematic approach.)

Ad hoc solutions and improvisation may cover the lack of systematic planning for a while. Sooner or later, however,

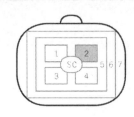
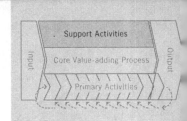

the point will come when these fail and a more systematic approach needs to be put in place. The question then is: How much damage has already been caused by not taking a systematic approach right from the beginning?

Having said this, a good coaching concept always needs to allow for a balance of rigour and flexibility and reflect systematic planning while remaining pragmatic and flexible. As was already said, the implementation/improvement of coaching is an evolving process.

3. Keep a realistic view on the opportunities and risks/limits of coaching

Keep coaching well-grounded and clearly linked to reality at all times. Neither over- nor under-estimate the value and potential of coaching. Coaching is definitely not a panacea and not "the only right way". Equally, it is also not just a buzzword and not "just about being nice to each other" either.

Coaching is a business tool, which, when properly applied, can produce a range of benefits and add value for your organisation and your people.

Be specific about the role and value coaching actually has in your context.. Also when evaluating the outcomes of your coaching programme, emphasize an honest and objective measurement in order to draw fair conclusions from the past for the future.

4. Approach, brand and market coaching as a positive, developmental tool

Adopt a positive 'coaching for excellence' approach that enables you to produce optimal commitment and readiness for coaching in your organisation and achieve quality results.

Coaching is about high performance and excellence, about optimal dynamic appropriateness and it is important to make sure people understand that. Whatever level of performance people are currently at, coaching is potentially able to add value – to weak as well as to peak performers.

When you encounter the opinion that coaching is just remedial, only a tool for weak performers or people with personal problems, a form of therapy and not a business tool, it is your responsibility to position coaching more accurately and positively.

In terms of communication, if you have something really valuable and attractive to offer, don't hide it – show it. Be proactive and bold in your offering. In this spirit, also consider developing a quality in-house coaching brochure or intranet site and coaching logo specifically designed for your company coaching programme.

(See also Key Success Factor 5 in Framework 1: Promote coaching as a positive developmental tool.)

5. Get the support of top management – and other important stakeholders – and implement coaching at the top as well (if possible and appropriate)

Strive for public affirmation from top management. This is to ensure the necessary organisational support and resources for the coaching initiative as well as strategic consistency throughout the organisation. It enhances the credibility of the whole coaching programme, makes things much easier, and is a good foundation for enlarging the coaching programme further in the future as and when required.

In addition, it is highly recommended to implement coaching at the top – with the top managers making effective use of coaching forms themselves and thereby becoming role models and a living demonstration of coaching for the whole organi-

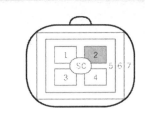
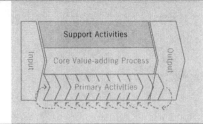

sation. This gives your coaching measures much greater credibility and authority in the firm and increases their appeal, making it likely that others will copy.

(See also Key Success Factor 4 in Framework 1: Involve the top.)

6. Ensure consistency/alignment of all coaching measures with corporate/ business/functional strategy – and create optimal win-win situations

Make sure that your coaching programme ties in with the other business activities and supports the overall organisational strategy to add value and sustain. This includes two aspects – firstly how you use and position coaching strategically, secondly how to ensure consistency between strategy and your coaching measures. (See also Key Success Factor 7 in Framework 1: Achieve full consistency of coaching with business strategy.)

Seek to create an optimal win-win value for all stakeholders through sustainable coaching measures (see also Key Success Factor 6 in Framework 1). It is in the nature of coaching that the interests of all stakeholders are adequately appreciated, acknowledged and balanced appropriately. Coaching fosters creative solutions that reconcile and integrate the various interests and thus encourages mutual support.

7. Communicate, communicate, communicate, and ensure transparency of your coaching concept

Work out the coaching concept and its governing rules very clearly in order that complete transparency is ensured; and communicate these adequately and continuously in a professional and succinct way throughout the organisation.

Where everybody has a precise idea of and clear expectations about the procedures and steps in place and the rationale behind these, coaching measures become trustworthy, well-understood and appealing.

This clarity encourages the people involved to take ownership and fosters their high-quality dialogue, making coaching a highly collaborative, common effort. You enable them to give well-informed feedback and make suggestions to help improve and further develop the coaching concept.

Make use of various relevant communication channels to convey your information as needed, e.g. include new technologies like the intranet, email-newsletters, Web 2.0, teleconferencing.

(Also see Key Success Factor 8 in Framework 1: Ensure complete transparency of the whole coaching concept.)

8. Involve people properly at all times and foster co-creation where possible

Take a coaching approach while implementing/improving coaching in your firm: The involvement of your people and the integration of co-creative elements are eligible ways to foster collaboration, integrate multiple stakeholder perspectives, raise receptiveness for the coaching programme, get ideas to optimize your coaching initiatives, achieve optimal fit and encourage people to take more ownership of coaching.

While there may be a specialized coaching champion (or coaching unit) mainly responsible for the coaching programme in a company, this doesn't mean this champion (or unit) holds all ownership and responsibility for coaching. The implementation of coaching is and remains a common effort. Everybody involved in the delivery of the programme or participating in a coaching measure is invited to buy into the process, take ownership and contribute in their area of influence.

www.frank-bresser-consulting.com

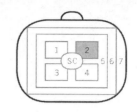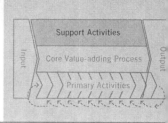

9. Ensure high integrity and quality at all levels

The best tool in the world doesn't add any value, if it is applied and used in an inappropriate way. Therefore coaching can only produce benefits and unfold its potential, if it is properly implemented and used. This, in turn, requires high integrity and quality at all levels of your coaching programme.

Having said that, be aware that high integrity and quality in coaching may mean different things in different contexts and initiatives. This is because both, integrity and quality, are mainly about "fit for purpose" and thus a matter of perspective and subjective.

Therefore make sure you identify and formulate your own integrity and quality standards from your own company-specific perspective. Do not just rely on the existing general and abstract quality standards and codes of ethics of the coaching industry.

(See also Key Success Factor 10 in Framework 1: Ensure high integrity and quality at all levels.)

10. Fully take into account the cultural dimension

Any coaching programme contains a cultural dimension and requires some kind of culture management/change.

One of your key tasks as manager responsible for coaching in your organisation is to take into account the existing culture in your company and design and implement your coaching plan accordingly. Also, you may need to develop and/or reinforce a positive culture and environment around a chosen coaching form in order to ensure its acceptance and successful use in your company. Finally, there are good reasons to take the perspective that all coaching programmes are – in some way or other – ambassadors

of some kind of a coaching culture and thus coaching culture initiatives.

This means considering the various dimensions of culture that may play a role in the context of coaching initiatives:

1. Culture (national, corporate, professional, generational, etc.) as the context and environment in which coaching measures are implemented and optimized and around which you need to tailor your coaching initiative (also see Underlying Factor 1 in Framework 1: Impact and importance of culture)

2. The current state and development of coaching in the world overall, in each continent, region and country (see also Extra Box 2 in Underlying Factor 1 in Framework 1)

3. Universality versus culture-specificity of coaching (see Underlying Factor 1 in Framework 1)

4. The appropriateness of the existing culture or whether culture change is needed in order to facilitate the smooth implementation of a coaching programme in the organisation (see the sections on coaching cultures in Key Success Factor 3 in Framework 1)

5. Coaching culture as a specific (or even overarching) people coaching form that you may choose to build and develop (see coaching cultures in Key Success Factor 3 in Framework 1).

6. Coaching culture as another term for overall coaching capacity which may apply to all coaching dimensions: the people, organisation and technology & tools dimensions (see Framework 3 in this book).

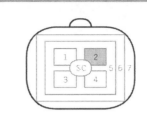
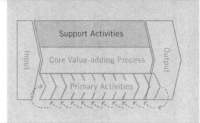

11. Learn on a continuous basis und build implementation and improvement intelligence

See the use of coaching in your company as an iterative, cyclical learning process. The success of coaching programmes is far from being a matter of simply applying pre-cast steps and frameworks. To generate ongoing value, the coaching experts also need to be committed to continuous learning and to building coaching implementation and improvement intelligence over time.

The effective use of coaching in organisations requires constant review and optimization and is an evolving process. So apply your coaching literacy with intelligence and vigilance in each specific case. View the experience you make as a valuable asset and learning opportunity.

Learning takes place in loops, so setbacks are a natural part of this process. However well prepared you may be in planning a coaching initiative, you cannot really avoid that you will also make some "mistakes", that you will find areas which you can optimize, that you will encounter and reach limits. This is all part of the process. So plan carefully, then have the courage to make things happen and get feedback, ensuring the organisation learns from the feedback and improves the coaching accordingly.

(See also Underlying Factors 1 and 2 in Framework 1: Continuous learning process & Coaching implementation and improvement intelligence.)

12. Make relevant "make or buy" decisions and get professional support as needed

Awareness of your limits of coaching literacy and coaching intelligence will allow you to get relevant external input and help as needed.

At any stage in the coaching value chain, feel free to develop things yourself or to consider getting external guidance and support from a coaching consultancy on how to implement and improve coaching in your company successfully (also see Framework 6: The coaching guidance and support framework.).

Please note that independent coaching consultancies advise you on the effective use of coaching in your firm and may – as one possible task among many – also help you find suitable coaches and coaching trainers for your organisation. However, they normally do not provide coaching or coaching training themselves, except where these constitute a necessary part of the coaching consultancy process (e.g. in order to develop an optimal company-specific coaching plan).

In terms of professional coaches, think about whether and to what degree external and/or internal coaches may be most suitable for your specific coaching programme and purpose (see External/Internal Coaches in classic 1:1 Coaching in Key Success Factor 3 in Framework 1).

Similarly, consider external as well as internal coaching trainers – or a combination of these – for your coaching initiative. Experience shows that it may sometimes be a very worthwhile option for external trainers to train internal people, who then operate as internal trainers, assist the externals and/or even take over the whole coaching training. Where key opinion leaders of your organisation are among your internal trainers, this may further enhance the credibility, quality and attractiveness of your programme.

For quality assurance reasons, the external trainers or a coaching consultancy may then still function as supervisors, review and assess the quality of the internal training on a regular basis and provide support and follow-up training to keep standards high.

When it comes to deciding on appropriate coaching tools/techniques or coaching evaluation methods, you may also

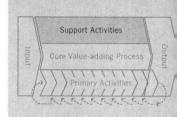

consider either using external or developing internal ones
(or maybe having internal ones specifically (co-)developed
by external providers).

Generally speaking, the "buy" option may particularly make
sense in areas of coaching initiatives where ...

• your company doesn't have the required skills and resources (and also cannot build these easily)
• special external expertise, a fresh perspective from outside or an independent, objective entity is needed
• timeliness is a requirement and external support is the
  only way to get things done in time
• the costs of external support are low relative to its benefits and when compared with the costs of the "make-
  yourself" option
• suitable, qualified providers are available in the market.

Whatever choice you make, your longer term goal should always be to build coaching capacity yourself. Therefore seek
external support that helps you develop your own coaching
intelligence, and avoid providers who – explicitly or implicitly
– try to keep your own coaching capacity low and make you
dependent on them.

These were the support activities – the fifth and last
element of the coaching value chain.

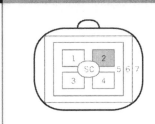
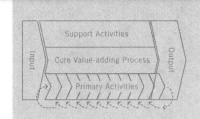

Summary:

COACHING VALUE CHAIN FRAMEWORK (FRAMEWORK 2)

We covered the complete Framework 2. Here is once again the whole picture of the coaching value chain:

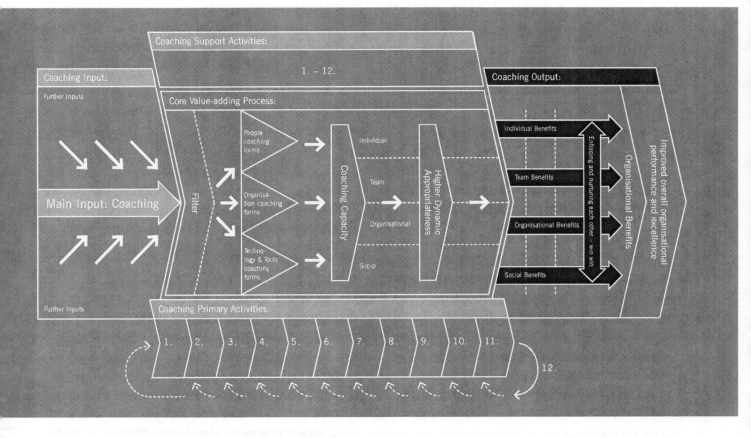

There are mainly two ways of making use of this management tool: On the one hand, it may serve you as a central thread and starting point to plan, design and implement new coaching programmes. On the other hand, you may use it as a measure and means to review and optimize existing coaching initiatives.

For further reflection and to integrate practice and theory, we invite you to apply the above framework to the next case study and/or to any of the other case studies included in this book. What is the value chain of coaching in each case study? What is the input, the output, the core value-adding process

and the company's primary and support activities? What has been done particularly well, and where do you see potential for further development and optimization?

Framework 3 (the coaching capacity building framework), which follows after the next case study, will introduce another approach and perspective on how to successfully implement and optimize coaching in organisations. Imagine looking at the above coaching value chain framework through a magnifying glass or microscope with increased precision and exploring more precisely what is going on within it. This is what Framework 3 is about.

EXCELLENT COACHING SOLUTIONS ↗   www.frank-bresser-consulting.com

Geographical focus: *Turkey in Europe/Asia*

CASE STUDY 19	AVEA, TURKEY

Company: *Avea İletişim Hizmetleri A.Ş.*

(Avea is the sole GSM 1800 mobile operator of Turkey)

www.avea.com.tr/index_en.shtml

Authors: *Aslı Barış Seyis/Hande Turna/Canan Arıcan*

Function: *Employee Development and Talent Management Director/Senior HR Account Manager/ Development & Assessment Projects Supervisor (based in Turkey, Istanbul)*

The Coaching Program in Avea

Avea, the youngest operator in Turkey was founded in 2004 and has a nationwide customer base of 11.8 million as of end of 2009. It is growing fast both in corporate and individual services with the brand "Avea" and constantly investing in technology and infrastructure as well as in its management and 2,592 employees. Having roaming agreements with 617 operators in 199 countries, the company continues to expand its roaming partnerships.

As Avea, to create a common management culture and support our managers with customized solutions, we decided to provide coaching for all our department managers and directors and launched the Leadership Coaching Program in 2008.

Our research showed that coaching is one of the most preferred career development tools in the world, helping to increase both individual and organizational performance. It provides long term, permanent and tailored solutions for individuals. We found that coaching is mostly used for three areas in organizations: increasing individual performance, increasing productivity and developing skills in the needed area.

We made some preparations before initiating the coaching program. We set the following selection criteria for the coaches: Business/management experience, an international coaching certificate, experience in executive coaching and positive references. One to one interviews were held with approximately 60 coaches and 15 were chosen for the program.

Using international applications as benchmark, the process was planned as consisting of 12 hours. But at the end, extra coaching hours were provided for the coachees on the basis of their development needs.

At the beginning of the process we organized a meeting with the coach and the coachee's manager to identify the coachee's strengths/development areas in order to set appropriate goals. After 6 and 12 hours had been completed, we arranged another meeting to get feedback on the coachee's development. At the end of the 12 hours we asked the coachees to complete an evaluation form also covering their level of satisfaction. The general coachee satisfaction was rated 4.42 out of 5.

During the program, 107 managers got individual coaching and 1340 coaching hours were provided in total. The program was successfully completed and it is considered as a unique coaching implementation in Turkey with its program design, number of coachees participating and coaching hours provided.

Geographical focus: *Turkey in Europe/Asia*

AVEA CASE STUDY: *The Coaching Program in Avea*

We conducted an online survey at the end of the process by an independent consultancy company to evaluate the effectiveness of coaching on the individual and organizational level as a development tool. The coachees who completed the survey, made the following main evaluations:

Statements of the participants	% of participants
Coaching program has been beneficial for Avea.	97%
Coaching program has positive impact on business results.	73%
Coaching program met my personal development needs.	94%
In general, it made a positive change on the work culture.	79%
Coaching is more effective than the other individual development tools.	89%
I would like to be an internal coach in Avea.	82%

In addition to this, we got further feedback from coaches, coachees and the coachees' managers. Some quotations are:

- "... coaching increased my awareness and helped me to develop my relationships with my manager and team. I noticed the areas I can develop and understood the importance of looking at different points of view. Coaching affected all my business life and it created an important change in terms of productivity, quality and communication ..." (One of the coachees)

- "... the most important characteristic of the coaching program in Avea is that it creates a communication platform and it focuses on the individual's needs. I observed the positive effects of coaching in Avea in all departments that's why especially in large organizations like Avea, coaching should be provided for the middle and upper management level ..."
(One of the coachees' managers)

- "... the coaching program in Avea was successful because it was effectively planned and implemented.

HR, the coaches and the managers of coachees' worked cooperatively in the process and the coachees were eager and ready to develop themselves ..." (One of the coaches)

The Coaching Program will also be carried out for the managers who are promoted to or directly recruited to department manager and director positions. As of 2010 the coachees (and the assessors of coachees) will be completing 360° questionnaires at the beginning and at the end of the process in order to even better measure the coaching effect of coaching on individual development.

To be able to cascade the coaching culture in Avea, we also launched an Internal Coaching Program to provide coaching for supervisors and line managers. The program started in July 2009 through a pilot study with participation of 12 internal coaches and coachees. Internal coaches were selected among department managers and directors who had experienced the coaching process as a coachee and volunteered to be an internal coach. After completing the training program, they started their coaching sessions and had supervision periodically with the participation of a professional

www.frank-bresser-consulting.com

Geographical focus: *Turkey in Europe/Asia*

AVEA CASE STUDY: *The Coaching Program in Avea*

coach. The pilot program is still running but the feedback we have got from the coaches, coachees and coachees' managers is very positive so far. The success that we have had, has motivated and encouraged us to continue the program with a broader reach in 2010 and we are planning to also support a coaching program around team coaching in order to achieve expected team goals and results.

Our key learning/Recommendation:
If you want to create and expand a coaching culture in your company, provide coaching for your top management first and then internal coaching for employees at further levels.

Questions and exercises for further reflection and to integrate practice and theory:

1. What is the business case for coaching in the company?

2. What coaching forms were implemented?

3. What is the input and output of the coaching programme(s)?

4. What is the core value-adding process from input to output?

5. What were the primary activities undertaken by the company?

6. What were the support activities?

7. What is your key learning from this case study?

www.frank-bresser-consulting.com

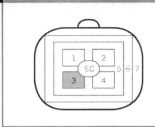

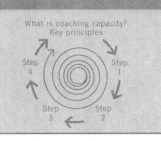

PART III

THE COACHING CAPACITY BUILDING FRAMEWORK

(also called: The high performance coaching culture framework)

This third management tool sets out another approach to and perspective on how to implement and improve coaching in organisations successfully.

This framework provides an integrated and deeper approach to the effective use of coaching by emphasizing the common aim of all coaching forms: developing or enhancing coaching capacity (also called: coaching culture, capability or intelligence) in companies. – Whether this is as a means to achieve something else or as an explicit asset and skill in the organisation.

In this chapter, coaching capacity is explicitly put at the centre of all considerations, so that the implementation of each single coaching form only becomes one possible means among many to build or reinforce it. Taking this perspective enables you to gain a deeper understanding of the heart of coaching and its dynamic nature, get a more integrated view of implementing coaching in business and make optimal use of the scalability and adjustability of coaching programmes.

This framework addresses what coaching capacity is, what the key principles around building it are, and the steps towards making it a reality.

Managers and directors responsible for the use of coaching in their organisations to strive for outstanding results and

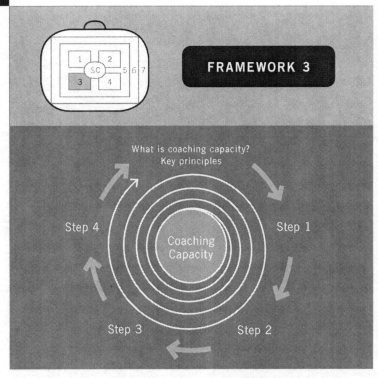

Framework 3: Coaching capacity building framework (simplified version)

excellence, may benefit enormously from taking a coaching capacity perspective and using this framework.

This management tool may stretch your thinking and be quite challenging at first. So do not necessarily expect to fully understand it immediately, but allow time to consider this framework in your context. The higher your coaching implementation and improvement intelligence, the more relevant its enormous reach and usefulness will be for you.

Actually, this framework is recommended for advanced and master level only. Beginners are advised to work through the first two frameworks of this book thoroughly before getting to this one.

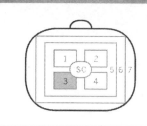

Here is the overview of the framework in full detail. We will have a closer look at each of its elements:

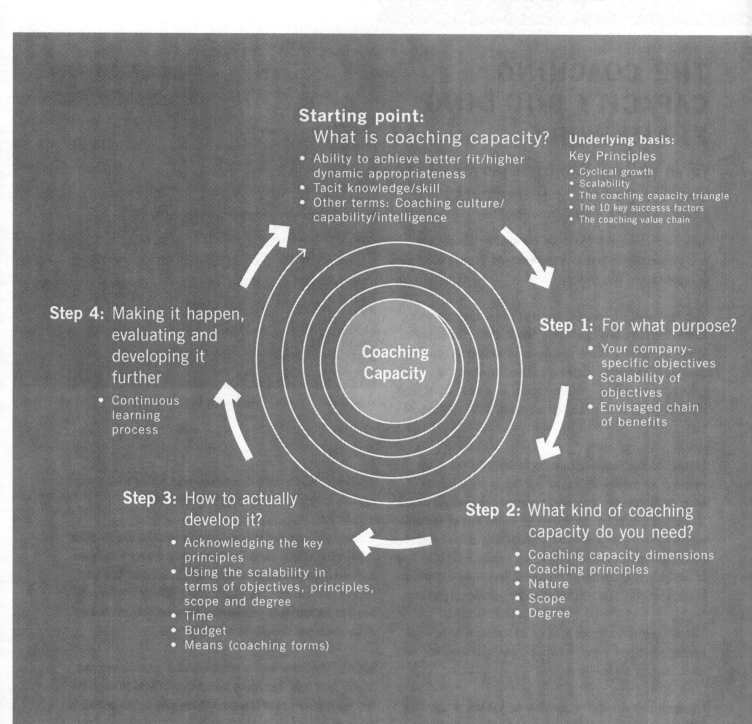

Starting point:
What is coaching capacity?
- Ability to achieve better fit/higher dynamic appropriateness
- Tacit knowledge/skill
- Other terms: Coaching culture/capability/intelligence

Underlying basis:
Key Principles
- Cyclical growth
- Scalability
- The coaching capacity triangle
- The 10 key successs factors
- The coaching value chain

Coaching Capacity

Step 4: Making it happen, evaluating and developing it further
- Continuous learning process

Step 1: For what purpose?
- Your company-specific objectives
- Scalability of objectives
- Envisaged chain of benefits

Step 3: How to actually develop it?
- Acknowledging the key principles
- Using the scalability in terms of objectives, principles, scope and degree
- Time
- Budget
- Means (coaching forms)

Step 2: What kind of coaching capacity do you need?
- Coaching capacity dimensions
- Coaching principles
- Nature
- Scope
- Degree

Framework 3: Coaching capacity building framework (High performance coaching culture framework) (detailed version)

FRANK BRESSER CONSULTING & ASSOCIATES

EXCELLENT COACHING SOLUTIONS ↗

www.frank-bresser-consulting.com

Starting point: What is coaching capacity?

- Ability to achieve better fit/higher dynamic appropriateness
- Tacit knowledge/skill
- Other terms: Coaching culture/capability/intelligence

Underlying basis:
Key principles for building coaching capacity

- Cyclical (progressive) growth of coaching capacity
- Using the scalability of coaching capacity initiatives
- The coaching capacity triangle
- The 10 key success factors (and their underlying factors)
- The coaching value chain

Step 1: For what purpose do you want to have or build coaching capacity?

- Your company-specific objectives
- Scalability of objectives
- Envisaged chain of benefits

Step 2: What kind and shape of coaching capacity exactly do you need?

- Possible coaching capacity dimensions
- Emphasized coaching principles
- Nature of coaching capacity
- Scope of coaching capacity
- Degree of coaching capacity

Step 3: How to actually develop and build coaching capacity?

- Acknowledging the key principles for building coaching capacity
- Making use of scalability in terms of objectives, principles, scope and degree
- Time
- Budget
- Means (coaching forms)

Step 4: Making it happen, evaluating and developing the programme further

- Continuous learning process

As with the first two frameworks, you may use this framework for purposes of coaching implementation or improvement: On the one hand, it may serve you as a central thread and starting point to plan, design and implement new coaching programmes. On the other hand, you may use it as a measure and means to review and optimize existing coaching initiatives.

www.frank-bresser-consulting.com

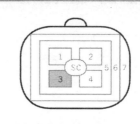
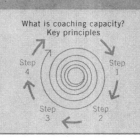

STARTING POINT: WHAT IS COACHING CAPACITY?

Ability to achieve higher dynamic appropriateness

Coaching capacity is the ability to actually achieve better/ optimal fit. It is about initiating and executing transformational processes resulting in higher dynamic appropriateness, which is the core of any existing coaching form in business. (For further information, see again the coaching pyramid model in the book introduction.)

It is about bringing together people, organisational and technology & tools requirements; about integrating and combining external and internal requirements – be it from an organisational, team, individual or other relevant perspective or a mix of perspectives.

Depending on each specific context, different coaching principles and coaching forms may gain importance and become elements and tools of a coaching initiative in order to achieve better fit and finally overall organisational (and people) performance and excellence.

There are many types of coaching capacity. For example, the focus may be more general and high-level or context-specific and concrete. It may be built at the individual, team, organisational and/or social level. It may develop within and through people, organisational structures and processes, as well as technologies and tools.

You may see the development of coaching capacity as only an intermediary stage to achieve subsequent benefits, or as a benefit and output of the coaching implementation and improvement process itself. In some coaching initiatives, building coaching capacity is even the main objective.

A tacit knowledge/skill

In terms of content and terminology, coaching capacity may at first appear quite intangible, tacit and abstract, when you come across it for the first time. Indeed, it is not too easy to grasp at the beginning. This is because what it actually means in practice, only becomes concrete and visible in each context.

Over time, things will increasingly become tangible, however, at this point, maybe just take the general term of coaching capacity as it is. This framework will help you fill the term with lifeblood for your own company-specific context.

Synonyms

The terms **coaching capacity**, **coaching culture**, **coaching capability** and **coaching intelligence** (coaching implementation and improvement intelligence) in principle mean the same thing when applied to the organisation and may be used interchangeably.

Regarding the term coaching culture, there is some detail on coaching cultures and the cultural dimension of any coaching programme in Key Success Factor 3 in Framework 1. Where we identified that there are good reasons to take the perspective, that the implementation and improvement of any coaching form is a kind of coaching culture initiative, whether deliberately envisaged or not. It spreads and promotes the principles of better fit etc. in the organisation in some way.

The main reason for this is that coaching and better fit are much more than a simple, superficial technique. They imply

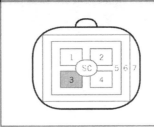
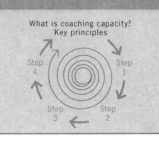

adopting some kind of a coaching attitude, i.e. thinking more in continuums and seeking dynamic solutions, rather than going for fixed solutions only and looking for "right/wrong" decisions. Genuine coaching capacity is exactly about this: It is a matter of attitude, of being, of culture.

Accordingly, this third management tool may also be called **"the high performance coaching culture framework"**. The term coaching culture here is meant in its broadest sense and not only embraces the people coaching dimension (as in Key Success Factor 3 in Framework 1), but also the organisation and technology & tools dimension.

UNDERLYING BASIS: KEY PRINCIPLES FOR BUILDING COACHING CAPACITY

The following points need to be taken into account during the whole process and all steps of developing coaching capacity.

Cyclical growth

Building coaching capacity is an evolving, iterative learning process which consists of learning loops, of revisits to previous stages, of progression and setbacks, of taking different perspectives on different/the same subjects, of continuously integrating practice and theory, of questioning, widening and deepening one's achievements. This process is far from being linear and one-dimensional.

What is more, this process never really stops, as things are in a steady flux and achieving and sustaining optimal fit is an ongoing process. Factor X may come into the equation – the unforeseeable complexity and coincidences of business and the human element. Also, coaching capacity exists within a system, i.e. your organisation, which itself is part of larger systems and contains smaller systems.

Therefore, strive for dynamic, organic growth of coaching capacity. For this to happen, involve people fully, have significant co-creative elements, give coaching proper space and time to grow, think systemically and remain attentive, responding to the actual process as it evolves rather than just sticking to a rigid sequence of steps.

Successful coaching initiatives evolve and learn over time and will adapt to circumstances to achieve best results, rather than seek to force through a plan that is not well received. You need a long term strategy, a rough plan for the possible phases of the initiative and responsive detailed planning for the next time window (e.g. the upcoming phase). So in developing and communicating your plan (also see Key Success Factor 2 in Framework 1) use it flexibly. The effective use of coaching is a lively, evolving process and your planning process needs to reflect this.

In this way, the coaching capacity developed may achieve best fit for your organisational context and optimal sustainability. This will allow it to survive even situations such as suspending or stopping a coaching initiative (e.g. because of budget limits).

Use coaching intelligence while building it, role model what you want to see in your firm. (Also consider getting suitable external support, where you don't yet have the coaching capacity to plan and realize such a coaching initiative properly.)

Scalability

The design of coaching programmes may differ enormously depending on the situation and needs of each company. Also within the same organisational context, the coaching

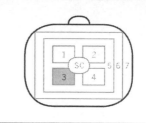

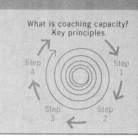

capacity concept is in no way fixed or narrow, but dynamic, flexible and highly scalable and adjustable. Coaching initiatives may start small or in a specific way and be easily extended and changed as needed to achieve the desired outcomes and benefits and respond to changing circumstances.

Building coaching capacity is highly scalable in terms of programme objectives, emphasized coaching principles, scope, degree, time, budget and means (coaching forms). Make use of this great scalability of coaching programmes to achieve easy implementation and best results. (Steps 1 to 4 in this framework will pick up this principle.)

The coaching capacity triangle

As a useful guideline, your coaching initiative should always be in alignment with and properly take into account the following three aspects:

1. The specific needs of your organisation
2. Your people's receptiveness
3. Where your company already is (in terms of optimal fit/ dynamic appropriateness)

Use this triangle as a navigator and always stay within it. If you find any of these three triangle elements gets neglected, check and correct your course, as otherwise your coaching capacity initiative may go astray.

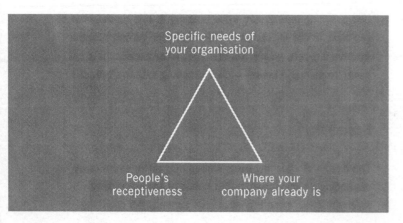

The 10 key success factors

In order to best develop coaching capacity in your firm, …
- define and use coaching in a company-specific way
- adopt a systematic approach
- choose an adequate level of organisational penetration of coaching
- involve the top
- promote coaching as a positive, developmental tool
- create an optimal win-win value for all stakeholders
- achieve full consistency of coaching with your business strategy
- ensure complete transparency of the coaching concept
- evaluate effectively and carefully
- ensure high integrity and quality at all levels.

(see Framework 1 in this book)

While doing this, take the cultural dimension of coaching fully into account, view the effective use of coaching as a continuous learning process and use coaching implementation and improvement intelligence.

The coaching value chain

Consider also the idea of the coaching value chain (see Framework 2 in this book) to create optimal coaching capacity for your firm. It may greatly help you work out what kind of coaching capacity to go for and in what way you may best develop it:

What is your input? What is your output? What is your core value-adding process from input to output, i.e. what specific coaching forms are needed in order to build appropriate coaching capacity, achieve better fit by its application and finally produce the various benefits resulting from this better fit?

How will your primary and support activities actually make all this happen? What is your actual organisation-specific coaching understanding and strategy as a basis of all this?

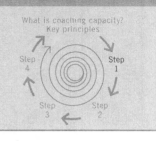

STEP 1: FOR WHAT PURPOSE DO YOU WANT TO BUILD COACHING CAPACITY?

Your company-specific objectives

What do you need coaching capability for? Developing it is not an end, but a means to achieve something else. It is only by applying coaching capacity that better fit actually happens and further benefits may result from this (see figure below).

Coaching capacity doesn't stand alone and is always built within a context – in your case in your specific organisational context. So what is the exact purpose for which you actually want and need to develop coaching capability in your firm?

You may formulate this purpose either broadly or narrowly as needed in order to give your coaching programme optimal fo-

cus and momentum. Your choice of objectives fundamentally determines the direction and nature of your whole coaching initiative.

The potential benefits of coaching programmes are enormous. See Key Success Factor 6 in Framework 1 (or the Output section in Framework 2) where you find a detailed list of the whole range of possible benefits on the individual, team, organisational and social level.

Identify and select the ones that are most needed and applicable to your firm. On the basis of these, formulate clear objectives that your coaching programme will be aimed at.

Coaching capacity ⟩ Application ⟩ Better fit ⟩ Leading to ⟩ Resulting Benefits ⟩ Improved overall organisational performance and excellence

Scalability of objectives

In principle, any coaching initiative may potentially produce a whole range of coaching benefits over time in some way. However, it is up to you to precisely choose the most suitable entry point and focus for your coaching interventions to best meet your specific needs.

In order to best prioritize your objectives and manage the process on a permanent basis, distinguish between primary objectives (the main reasons why you want to build coaching capacity in your company), secondary objectives (good reasons to have the programme, but ones which are not central),

marginal objectives (reasons with low importance) and dormant objectives (potentially good reasons in the future).

Your primary objective(s) should enable you to keep both appropriate focus and dynamism in your coaching initiative. Its specific content is highly scalable:

1. Where there is an obvious, striking need for coaching capacity with regard to a specific outcome, take this as the primary objective of the coaching initiative. Focus on the one specific objective (e.g. increase sales/leadership effec-

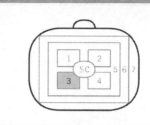

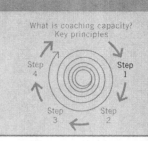

tiveness/attracting talent) that is most important for your organisation and only extend as appropriate over time.

2. In case you don't have one striking issue only, but a number of different important areas that need to be addressed by building coaching capacity, go for the achievement of a number of primary objectives at the same time right from the beginning.

3. Finally, if you don't have one, two or more burning reasons to develop coaching capacity, but find it is generally useful, e.g. as a basic skill and tool for your staff, then your primary objective will be to provide your organisation with this basic standard capability (e.g. through general people development) in order to fulfil its organisational mission and purpose.

In any case, be aware of overburdening the programme, especially at the beginning. Pay attention to defining your objective(s) in a particularly succinct and specific way where ...
• your company has little experience with coaching so far

• there is limited support from top management or your people's overall receptiveness towards coaching is still rather low
• you find there is an organisational requirement to evaluate programmes very meticulously.

In these cases, ensure your coaching initiative has a clear focus and tangibility and makes it easy for people who are not familiar with coaching to buy into the initiative. In this way, you also facilitate the evaluation of the programme, as the outcomes that need to be measured are more precisely defined.

Envisaged chain of benefits

With your primary objectives identified, break down and formulate suitable intermediary sub-goals, which you need to strive for to reach these objectives. Think through the first, second, third tier benefits in chronological terms. (See the output and core-value adding process in Framework 2.)

www.frank-bresser-consulting.com

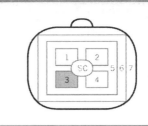 

STEP 2: WHAT KIND OF COACHING CAPACITY DO YOU NEED?

The range of possible types of coaching capacity is tremendous. It may take very different forms and shapes. However, in order to create and add real value, any coaching capability needs to be aligned with the organisation and tailored around its specific context. In fact, one kind of coaching capacity, which is successful in one company (or area), may not work at all in another.

So identify the kind of coaching capability that exactly suits your purpose. (While doing this, always work with and around the coaching intelligence that is already there in your firm.)

There are various choices available to you.

Possible coaching capacity dimensions

Identify the most appropriate pillar(s) for building coaching capability in your firm. Can the focus be on one pillar or across the pillars of People, Organisational structures & processes and Technology & tools?

Overall business coaching capacity		
Pillar 1: People Coaching Capacity	**Pillar 2:** Organisation Coaching Capacity (Structures and processes)	**Pillar 3:** Technology & Tools Coaching Capacity
Dynamic appropriateness/Better fit		

Actually, all three dimensions show different sides of the same coin. Naturally, there is significant overlap between the three, and each one will have immediate, direct impact on the other two in some way. (See also Key Success Factor 3 in Framework 1.)

Classically, many organisations start with the people coaching capacity dimension first. Over time, they also start to explicitly consider building coaching capacity through the other pillars.

This choice is influenced by whether you want to develop coaching capability at the individual, team, business unit and/or organisational level.

Emphasized coaching principles

Another key aspect to consider is how the coaching principles will inform your definition of the desired coaching capacity.

The most relevant and commonly found coaching principles (most of them are mainly related to the people dimension) are listed in order of importance below. Choose the most relevant ones for your specific context. You may either just focus on dynamic appropriateness, i.e. better fit as the core principle, or be more specific by adding or particularly emphasizing other principles:

Core principles
- Dynamic appropriateness/optimal fit: what fits best where and how
- Integrating people, organisational and technology & tools requirements
- Integrating external and internal requirements

www.frank-bresser-consulting.com

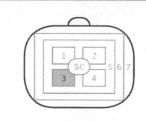

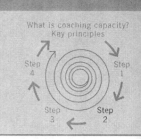

Basic coaching principles

- High performance and excellence
- Growing people and performance alike
- Purpose, awareness, responsibility and self-belief

Key coaching principles

- Empowerment and ownership
- Self-directed and life-long learning
- The learning organisation
- Trust, open communication and feedback
- Daring to make mistakes/no blame culture
- Collaboration and information sharing
- Mutual support and on-the-job staff development
- Respect and seeing people in terms of their potential

Emerging coaching principles

- Whole system approach
- Natural system approach
- Sustainability and corporate social responsibility

See detailed explanations on the coaching principles in the sections on coaching cultures in Key Success Factor 3 in Framework 1. Please note that the ideas behind the principles are more important than their above exact formulation. So feel free to reformulate or regroup them in a way that is most appropriate for your purposes.

It is worth highlighting that many of the listed coaching principles are linked with each other and mutually supportive. This means, when you focus on some of the coaching principles, others may implicitly also be supported, developed and reinforced over time.

The most appropriate mix of principles to choose for your coaching programme will depend on your specific organisational needs and situation. Therefore, as the process evolves, you may need to review and change your initial choice over time.

You may also build different types of coaching capacity within the same organisation – i.e. take different priorities regard-ing the principles to meet different needs in different areas of your firm. In this case, make sure you have a consistent, overall understanding of coaching capacity and can make this concept transparent and accessible to the stakeholders.

The choice of coaching principles as ingredients of coaching capacity is thus highly scalable and adjustable in various ways.

In this context, also consider (as above for the programme objectives) formulating primary, secondary, marginal and dormant coaching principles. In terms of selecting primary coaching principles, you may …

1. emphasize only the very core principle(s) of coaching, i.e. what fits best where and how. This option may make particular sense, where you are developing general coaching capacity in your firm.

2. focus on the core principle of coaching as above, but also explicitly support specific other coaching principles, which are especially relevant.

3. concentrate only on one coaching principle/area of principles (e.g. "trust, open communication and feedback"). This may be advisable where the chosen principle or area perfectly fits your needs; where you find a high receptiveness for it in your firm; and/or where there is a special requirement to make your initiative as sharp, tangible and straight-forward as possible.

4. ingrain a certain combination of coaching principles in your definition of coaching capacity, because exactly these work together very well in your context (e.g. a combination of optimal fit, high performance and excellence, awareness and responsibility, empowerment and ownership, self-directed and life-long learning and collaboration). Any combination is possible provided it is able to meet your needs.

5. see the whole set of coaching principles (or at least most of them) as a kind of general best practice culture you

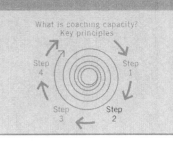

want to build in your firm. In this case, your envisaged coaching capacity will be designed to work as a general enabler of business performance.

Nature of coaching capacity

This is about the question of what you actually understand by the content of coaching capacity. There are three main ways of seeing it:

1. You may regard coaching capacity as a **driver and enabler of choice**. It is meant to encourage people to strive for optimal fit at all times and to seek, create and identify options from which to choose the most appropriate ones in any context. This understanding actively promotes choice and dynamic appropriateness, but doesn't give any answers on what options are finally the most appropriate. Finding this out is the task of the decision-makers.

2. Or you may understand coaching capacity to be the **spread and adoption of best practice recommendations** in your firm to foster optimal fit in a general area or specific context. This approach still embraces the whole range of options and makes concrete best practice recommendations. Here the coaching programme clearly provides input in terms of content, but does this in the form of recommendations.

3. Lastly, you may understand coaching capacity as a specific, rather fixed way of doing things considered to produce optimal fit in a certain context. It is thus seen as a clear request for people in the company to abide by this specific way in a specific area. So this view makes the choice around what is appropriate, and makes this obligatory in some way.

The above options address a central aspect of any coaching initiative: Who should finally decide what is to be deemed as appropriate and what is/must be done in what context? Who

actually decides? Who is meant to have final ownership of decisions?

As manager responsible for coaching in your organisation, where and to what extent do you aim to let people develop solutions themselves and where and to what extent may it be more suitable to provide people with some recommendations and solutions on what is commonly deemed to be appropriate?

This question is a matter of degree and balance, not of yes or no (right or wrong). In fact, no single approach exists in a 100% pure form in business. There is always some mix of letting others develop solutions and of providing answers in any coaching programme.

Who is actually meant to build what kind of coaching capacity? – Are the same or different people responsible for building coaching capacity on the one hand and applying it on the other hand? Your answers will inform the kind(s) of coaching capability to be developed.

In order to illustrate this point, take for example a coach and a coachee in a 1:1 coaching assignment. What kind of coaching capacity shall each of them actually have, develop and apply? There are various options available to you. Among these are:

1. You want the professional coach just to be a driver and enabler of real choice, not to give solutions him or herself on what is most appropriate. It is the coachee who is meant to use the coaching service in a self-directed way to develop solutions him or herself. In this case, you may require from the professional coach more generalist, content-free and non-directive coaching capability. At the same time, you would require the coachee to build a good understanding of what is coaching and how best to use it in a self-directed way (which is also some kind of coaching capacity). What is more, by using coaching in a self-directed way, the coachee actually

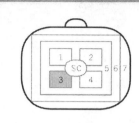

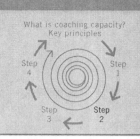

practises and further enhances his or her own coaching capacity.

2. You see the role of the professional coach not only in facilitating the coachee's decision-making process, but also in offering and providing suggestions, direction, advice and knowledge sharing as appropriate. Here the coach is also asked to partly be an expert coach, apply coaching capacity to the specific issue of the coachee and put this input at the disposal of the coachee. While the coachee may keep overall ownership of the process, there is less demand on his or her own coaching capacity.

3. You clearly want the professional coach to act as a directive expert coach and to actively lead the coachee towards most appropriate solutions. In this case, specialist coaching capability is required of the coach, as he or she is now expected to be an expert in the field, apply the expertise to the specific issue of the coachee and provide solutions. The coachee, in turn, is asked to follow, rather than to develop solutions him or herself. He or she needs little or no coaching capacity upfront and is given relatively low ownership of the coaching process. Through this process, the coachee may enhance very specific, but no general coaching capacity.

4. You may define the primary goal of 1:1 coaching as helping the coachee to develop general coaching capacity, i.e. a coaching attitude. In this case, you clearly intend the transfer of the coach's general coaching capacity to the coachee. The aim is that the coachee will ingrain it into his or her daily work and take full ownership of building and applying coaching capacity in the workplace. This transfer may happen in a more or less directive way, as appropriate or defined by you. The professional coach needs general coaching capability plus the skill to develop coaching ability in the coachee. This is a very different approach from seeing 1:1 coaching as a specific business tool with the professional coach keeping a rather exclusive position.

Professional coaching here may become more generally redundant in the future.

To give another example, think of coaching leadership style training. Do you want the trainers to let the training participants develop their optimal leadership style fully themselves? Or to what degree do you expect the trainers to suggest and provide clear advice and recommendations? Or would you rather want that they give the participants very clear direction and train them in a certain style of leadership that is thought to be the most appropriate?

So consider carefully what mix and balance between these approaches is most suitable for your purposes. Do you require ...
- more general or more specific coaching capacity?
- a purely professional or more integrated and ingrained coaching capacity?
- more external or more internal coaching capacity?

Scope of coaching capacity

This aspect refers to the question of where in your organisation you need what kind of coaching capacity.

Depending on your organisation's needs, you may build coaching capability in your entire business or only at a specific level, for a selected target group (e.g. high potentials in their first years in a company), in a certain business unit, division, department, area, group or team (or teams). See this scalability of the scope of coaching initiatives as a very useful precision tool to leverage the desired development in your organisation.

Especially at the beginning of a coaching initiative, when there is still a lack of experience with coaching and high uncertainty about how coaching activities will be received, it is recommended to start with a pilot with limited scope first, and then to extend the programme over time as appropriate.

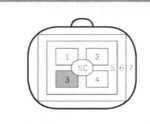
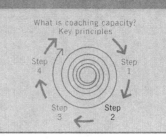

Another approach well worth considering is to build so-called "pockets" or "islands" of coaching capacity in your company at first. Beginning with developing coaching capacity precisely in those areas of the organisation where you know the management is open to this kind of approach can make the introduction easier and smoother. This creates strong pockets of coaching capacity which may serve as exemplary case studies and role models for the organisation as a whole.

Ideally, involve the top and start by developing coaching capacity in the company's boardroom (also see Key Success Factor 4 in framework 1: Involve the top). This can be leveraged to spread coaching culture easily throughout the organisation.

In determining the scope, make sure you keep on top of the game. Too many initiatives in your coaching programme can risk overwhelm, in which case it is recommended to first focus on one or a few areas only, where you feel fully comfortable. It is always better to start "small and good" than "big and bad". You can always extend the scope of the initiative as you progress.

Degree of coaching capacity

Part of defining the optimal kind of coaching capability is deciding what precise degree of coaching capacity you aim for in the chosen area(s). In principle, you may choose to build coaching capacity ...

- at a (very) low degree, so it only has very limited significance for people's daily work
- at a middle level, so that it becomes a substantial element with clear impact on people's daily work
- at a (very) high degree, so that it sets the basic tone and becomes the favoured way of doing things, possibly also implying and requiring a paradigm shift in the chosen area/your organisation.

Organisations may consist of plenty of sub-systems which may have very different needs and preferences. Therefore, think about the impact this has on the requirements of building coaching capacity in your chosen scope. Maybe you need to build different degrees of coaching capacity in different parts of the scope.

When developing coaching capability, build it up step-by-step. It is an evolving, continuous process, so focus on achieving the next level of degree only, before planning in detail the levels thereafter.

Where you have strong pockets of coaching capacity and can build a high degree of coaching capability in these, it may create real powerhouses of coaching. These may become strong role models and create momentum for developing coaching intelligence in wider areas of the organisation.

Starting from where your company already is on its journey in terms of coaching capacity, build your coaching programme to close the gap to the desired coaching capacity. Sometimes you just need to reinforce or further develop an already existing element in the organisation to achieve the desired degree of coaching capability.

Make sure you are on top of the process at any time: In order to keep the overview and manage the process, plan for a smooth development of coaching capacity. Always concentrate on what is most important and design the programme in a way that you feel comfortable with.

In summary, be clear on what kind and shape of coaching capacity you actually need to build to best achieve your set objectives. Make decisions regarding your preferred coaching capacity dimensions, emphasized coaching principles, nature of coaching capacity, its scope and degree.

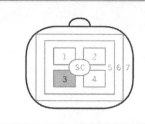 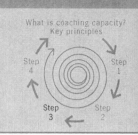

STEP 3: HOW TO ACTUALLY DEVELOP AND BUILD COACHING CAPACITY?

The **key principles for building coaching capability** which are cyclical growth, high scalability, the coaching capacity triangle, the 10 key success factors and the coaching value chain, represent an underlying basis and need to be taken into account at all times.

What **scalability of coaching programmes** actually means in terms of objectives, emphasized coaching principles, scope and degree of coaching capacity, was already set out above (see steps 1 and 2). When it comes to the 'how' of developing coaching capability, the following key aspects of coaching programmes come into play:

- Time (i.e. time period and pace)
- Budget
- Means (coaching forms)

Time

Within what time period and at what pace are you actually going to build coaching capacity in your organisation?

Formulate time schedules and objectives to work towards. However, acknowledging the iterative, evolving nature of coaching initiatives means you can't fix a detailed time-table far in advance.

Whatever plan you may have in the beginning, the initially envisaged time periods and pace may change over time, as the process evolves. Having said this, it remains vital to develop a strategy and plan to be able to embark on this learning process.

The final pace and time needed will depend on many factors, e.g. the level of quality of your coaching concept and the

people involved in its development and implementation; people's receptiveness towards coaching.

As to the **time period**, the smaller the gap between the current and the desired level of coaching capacity, the less time it may take to effect this change. The narrower the focus of your coaching initiative and the higher your people's receptiveness towards it, the quicker you may be able to achieve your programme objectives.

It clearly makes a huge difference whether you aim to build high coaching capacity throughout a company requiring a far-reaching paradigm shift, or just promote and reinforce an already existing coaching capacity element in a firm that is highly receptive towards coaching anyway. Massive coaching initiatives may sometimes take several years, while slim coaching programmes may be a matter of some days, weeks or months to achieve the objective.

So the time period is highly scalable in terms of your set objectives and size of the coaching programme. Time is also scalable in so far as you may suspend or stop a coaching initiative at any time (e.g. for budget reasons).

In terms of **pace**, accelerating the pace of your programme will not necessarily allow a more rapid build of coaching capacity. A rapid pace may significantly hinder the emergence of coaching intelligence and even lead to counter-productive results. Responsiveness to circumstances is important here, enhancing the pace only if the process as it evolves permits it. For example, where you find there is higher receptiveness towards coaching than expected, you may consider proceeding more quickly than initially planned.

If there is time pressure, but the process doesn't permit a faster pace, it is always better to rethink, redesign and

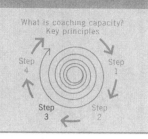

downsize a coaching programme, than over-stretch its pace.

When determining the optimal pace for your coaching initiative, keep the following general rules of thumb in mind:

- The higher the uncertainty about the impact of coaching and how it will actually be received in your company, the more carefully you should proceed and the slower the pace.

- Thorough analysis and preparation upfront (including feedback workshops/tests/pilots) may greatly help minimize uncertainty and allow for a faster pace.

- Better start "small and good" than "big and bad". It is preferable to choose a slow pace at first and then increase as the coaching initiative gains momentum, rather than try to be particularly quick and find the programme hits a dead end. Consider creating strong pockets of coaching capacity in a company first, which may serve as successful role models and speed up the pace of a subsequent roll-out of the coaching programme.

- The more you find out what really works, the more you can enhance the pace. As new uncertainties arise, slow down the pace again.

- The more receptive people are towards the coaching programme, the faster the pace may be. However, slow down the pace when people become too enthusiastic about coaching and start to see it as a panacea or "the only right way".

- Only proceed at fast pace (e.g. to create a momentum for change in the organisation) after considering and preparing such a step very well. Check people's receptiveness towards this high pace well in advance (e.g. by a pilot/workshop) and evaluate deeply and frankly afterwards.

Budget

The level of investment is equally scalable and may range from very small to very large budgets.

The greater the gap between the current and the desired state and the more massive you finally determine a coaching initiative to be, the more funds you will need to develop the desired coaching capacity.

Whatever your available budget, consider your investments carefully, i.e. they create real value for your firm. By investing in quality which hits the bull's-eye, you may achieve more with less time and effort and save a lot of money overall. Consider the full cost-benefits of any proposed investment to ensure you are making decisions that will deliver the required quality of coaching capacity. Save money by downsizing a coaching programme rather than by buying low quality services.

Having said this, there are many tricks and ways of saving costs without any trade-off in impact of the programme that you should be aware of:

- Use informal methods of enhancing coaching capacity that don't require any additional financial investment, e.g. pooling resources, knowledge sharing and networking with co-workers equally committed to building coaching capacity, spreading coaching success stories in the company, being a role model of coaching capability yourself.

- Develop a sense for when coaching capacity actively needs to be promoted in the organisation and when it may be better to let it spread more naturally. In this way, you can save a lot of money and, at the same time, allow for optimal cyclical growth of coaching intelligence.

- Good examples and role models of coaching (at best at the top of your company) make the development of coaching capacity not only easier, but also cheaper. Therefore,

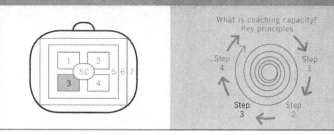

identify and involve key opinion leaders in your business – ideally also in the boardroom of your business – in contributing to the initiative.

- The more ownership people in your firm take for building coaching capacity themselves, the less formal coaching activities are needed and the less massive and costly your coaching programme will be over time. So actively involve people, support intrinsic motivation, provide significant co-creative elements to foster people's ownership of coaching. You thereby ensure that the benefits are sustainable, as people may carry forward their coaching capability themselves, even when you need to stop the programme.

- Continuously work on developing your own coaching intelligence further. Over time, you will increasingly find better ways to reach your coaching programme objectives with less investment of money, time and effort.

- Consider developing internal coaching capacity (e.g. internal coaching trainers or an internal coach pool) to replace external providers who may be more costly.

- When you only use coaching as a professional service provided by professional coaches, consider ingraining coaching capacity into your organisational life (e.g. by developing a coaching communication or leadership style). This encourages responsibility and people will support each other to solve relevant issues in the workplace. In this way, you may save a lot of money by making professional coaching services redundant.

Means (coaching forms)

Once you are clear on for what purpose and in what shape you want to build coaching capacity and what time and budget are in principle available, the final question is around the design and concrete elements of your coaching programme.

What kind of coaching forms will be part of your initiative in order to build the desired coaching capability and achieve the set objectives?

Not surprisingly, coaching initiatives are also highly scalable in this regard. The design of coaching programmes may range from the use of one external coach to massive, global coaching culture initiatives containing extensive activities around your people, your organisation structures & processes and your technologies & tools.

In the following figure (see next page), you find a **comprehensive overview of all three coaching dimensions and all coaching forms within each dimension** that you may decide to make part of your coaching initiative. (In Key Success Factor 3 in Framework 1, you get detailed explanations on each and how they may be implemented and improved successfully.)

At their core, all above coaching forms foster better fit and higher dynamic appropriateness. In fact, the various coaching forms may complement and mutually support each other very well, if properly implemented. However, each single coaching form has its own specific purpose, dynamics and entry point in organisations to develop coaching capacity.

You may focus on the implementation and optimization of one coaching form, combine two or more coaching forms at the same time or maybe even embrace all of them. Any combination is fine, as long as it is appropriate to build your specifically desired coaching capability.

Coaching initiatives are very adjustable: you can start very small and enlarge one step at a time. Implementing only one coaching form at first to test it out and gain experience, is a good idea, extending as appropriate over time. On the other hand, you may decide to reduce or remove a coaching form, when it is not needed any more or doesn't show the desired outcomes.

www.frank-bresser-consulting.com

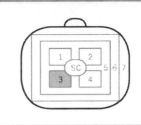

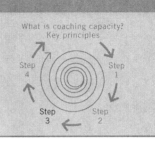

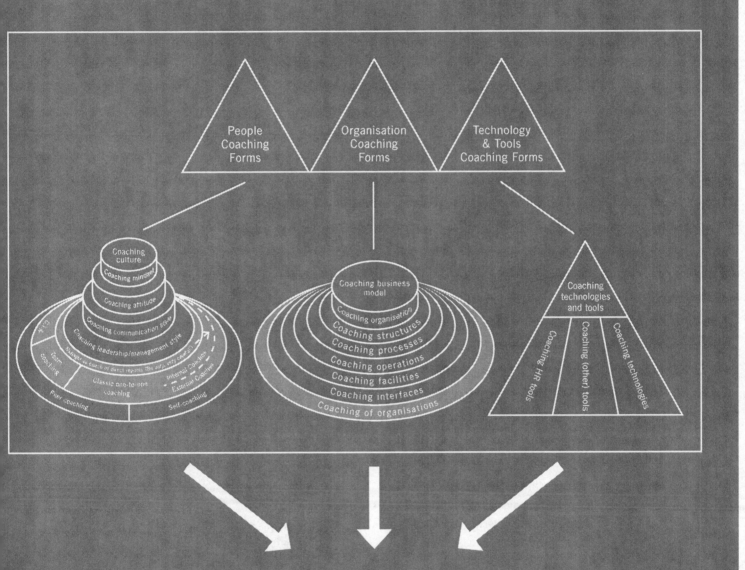

Building coaching capacity

The following seven implementation tendencies regarding the choice of coaching forms in organisations (see next pages) may be observed in business today. These may inspire you to make up your own mind on what choice and order of implementing coaching forms is most appropriate for your specific context.

www.frank-bresser-consulting.com

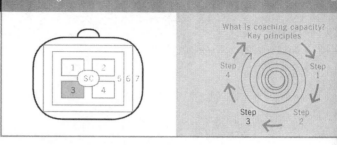

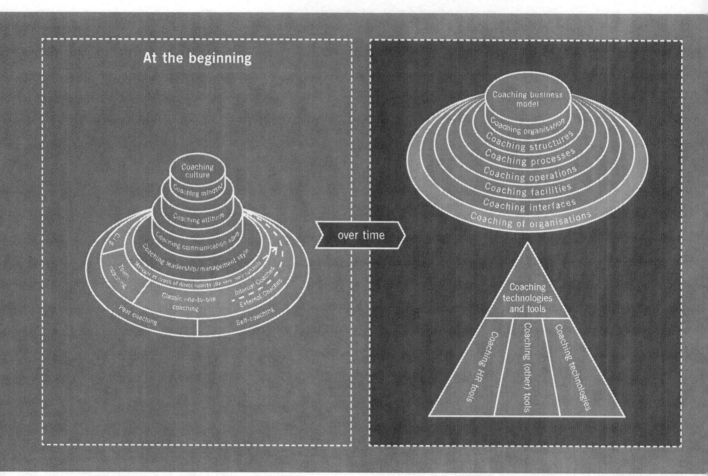

Figure: Tendency 1

Tendency 1: Starting with the people coaching forms –
only over time increasingly entering the
organisational and technology & tools
coaching dimension

Tendency 2: Within the people coaching forms: Starting
only with professional one-to-one coaching
(and maybe professional team coaching) –
then over time also increasingly implementing
the coaching forms ingraining coaching into
organisational life (e.g. coaching leadership/
management style, coaching communication
style, coaching culture)

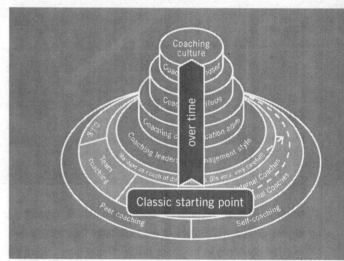

Figure: Tendency 2

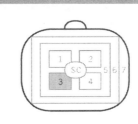

Tendency 3: Starting with professional external coaches (and/or external coaching trainers) – over time increasingly building an internal pool of coaches (and/or of coaching trainers)

Tendency 4: Starting with professional one-to-one coaching – over time increasingly implementing professional team coaching

Tendency 5: Interesting combinations of coaching forms that may increasingly be found in companies today, are for example:
- External coaching programme for the top management level & internal coaching programme for the levels down the hierarchy
- Coaching training & professional one-to-one coaching for the same target group
- Professional team coaching & one-to-one coaching for each of its members at the same time
- Coaching training & integrated peer coaching
- Professional one-to-one coaching after 360 degree feedback using the results in the coaching

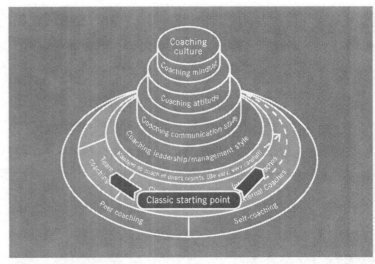

Figure: Tendencies 3 and 4

Tendency 6: With rising understanding and receptiveness for coaching in an organisation: At first, only integrating single coaching elements into existing programmes (if needed also without even mentioning the term "coaching"; e.g. including more questioning techniques in traditional leadership or communication training) – then using coaching more and more as an official business tool and/or service (coaching techniques; professional 1:1 coaching service; coaching leadership style) – finally reaching the understanding of coaching as an integrated way of doing business (and cultural orientation).

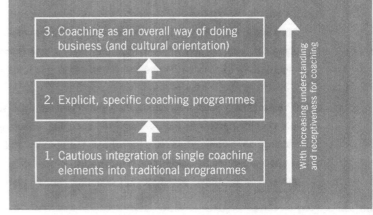

Figure: Tendency 6

Tendency 7: With increasing coaching literacy: Starting with a quite narrow understanding of coaching at first (i.e. being familiar with one coaching form only); then widening the understanding to other coaching forms step-by-step; then getting deeper to the core of coaching that is underlying all coaching forms and finally taking an integrated, overarching coaching capacity/coaching culture perspective.

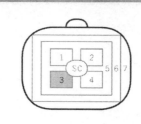
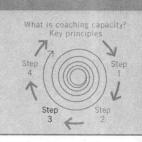

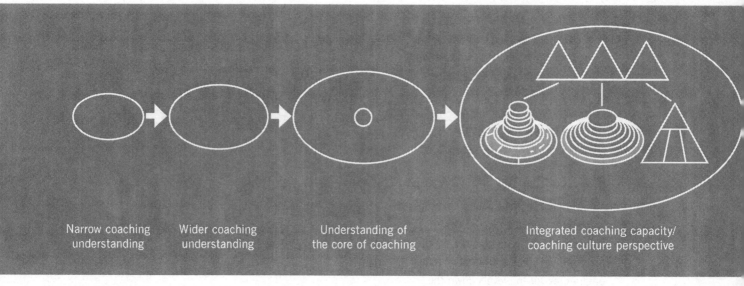

Narrow coaching understanding   Wider coaching understanding   Understanding of the core of coaching   Integrated coaching capacity/ coaching culture perspective

Figure: Tendency 7

So what is the best choice of coaching forms for your context? Once you have selected one or more coaching forms, make a plan of how to actually implement or improve each of these successfully. (See again Frameworks 1 and 2 in this book.)

When planning your programme, distinguish between the actual coaching activities (e.g. professional coaching, coaching training, coaching culture workshops) and the primary and support activities to make these happen (e.g. preparation and review meetings, recruiting and selecting people, com-

munication/briefing, management, evaluation, organisation and administration, reporting).

Develop a clear and detailed concept on what kind of coaching forms and other activities you are planning to make part of your coaching programme (and in what way). Plan in great detail for the next upcoming window (starting phase), but in less detail for the subsequent stages of the process. As the process evolves, you will need to review and accordingly refine, adjust and change your concept.

www.frank-bresser-consulting.com

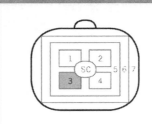
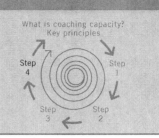

STEP 4: MAKING IT HAPPEN, EVALUATING AND DEVELOPING THE PROGRAMME FURTHER

After having worked out a comprehensive coaching plan, it is now time to put it all into practice and make it a reality. Start implementing and optimizing your coaching programme. Go for building your desired kind of coaching capacity and achieving your set objectives and always be aware that it is a **continuous learning process**.

Successful coaching initiatives evolve and learn over time and will adapt to circumstances to achieve best results. They are not forced on the organisation.

So use the high scalability of coaching initiatives to allow for optimal cyclical growth of coaching capacity and revisit, review, refine and adjust your concept as appropriate.

Be open for dialogue and feedback. Take resistance seriously and learn from it. Involve people, provide co-creative elements, be attentive and respond to the actual process as it evolves rather than sticking to a rigid sequence of steps.

Evaluate the programme (see Key Success Factor 9 in Framework 1: evaluate effectively and carefully) and develop it further on a continuous basis. Enter the learning loop and permanently work on improving your own coaching implementation and improvement intelligence.

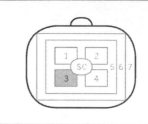
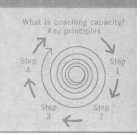

Summary:

COACHING CAPACITY BUILDING FRAMEWORK (FRAMEWORK 3)

We covered the complete Framework 3. Here it is once again in full detail:

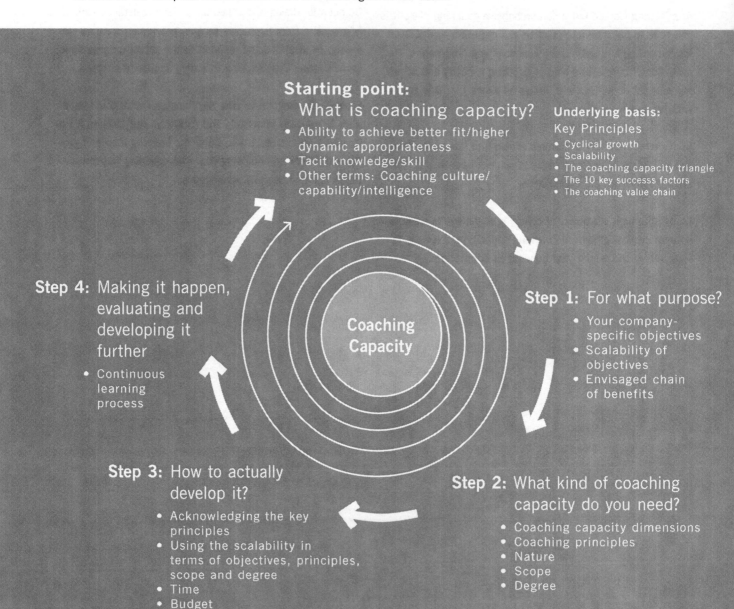

Starting point:
What is coaching capacity?
- Ability to achieve better fit/higher dynamic appropriateness
- Tacit knowledge/skill
- Other terms: Coaching culture/ capability/intelligence

Underlying basis:
Key Principles
- Cyclical growth
- Scalability
- The coaching capacity triangle
- The 10 key successs factors
- The coaching value chain

Step 4: Making it happen, evaluating and developing it further
- Continuous learning process

Coaching Capacity

Step 1: For what purpose?
- Your company-specific objectives
- Scalability of objectives
- Envisaged chain of benefits

Step 3: How to actually develop it?
- Acknowledging the key principles
- Using the scalability in terms of objectives, principles, scope and degree
- Time
- Budget
- Means (coaching forms)

Step 2: What kind of coaching capacity do you need?
- Coaching capacity dimensions
- Coaching principles
- Nature
- Scope
- Degree

www.frank-bresser-consulting.com

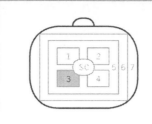
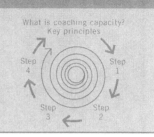

On the one hand, it may serve you as a central thread and starting point to plan, design and implement new coaching programmes. On the other hand, you may use it as a measure and means to review and optimize existing coaching initiatives.

For further reflection and to integrate practice and theory, we invite you to apply the above framework to the next case study (and/or any of the other case studies included in this book). Taking a coaching capacity perspective may be quite challenging at first, but is likely to pay off tremendously over time.

Framework 4 (the coaching change dynamics framework), which follows after the next case study, will introduce another perspective on how to successfully implement and optimize coaching in organisations. Imagine you look at the above coaching capacity building framework through a magnifying glass or microscope with increased precision and can now explore more precisely what is going on within it. This is what Framework 4 is about.

Geographical focus: *Estonia, East-/Northern Europe*

CASE STUDY 20	NORDEA BANK, ESTONIA

Company: **Nordea Bank, Estonia**

(Nordea's vision is to be the leading Nordic bank, acknowledged for its people, creating superior value for customers and shareholders.)

www.nordea.ee
www.nordea.com

Authors: *Jane Järvalt and Tiina Käsi*

Function: *HR (based in Tallinn, Estonia)*

From Good to Great through Coaching

Nordea values and leadership competencies

Nordea's story of coaching started when our three new values 'Great customer experiences', 'It's all about people' and 'One Nordea team' were introduced in 2007. Strengthening the implementation of values meant that we had to change the ways of working and behaviour in our organisation in all countries. We knew that our success in increasing performance and delivering great business results depended to a large degree on leadership. It became equally true about living our values. In order to be more customer- and people-oriented we introduced five leadership competencies directly linked to the values.

'It's all about people' from the leadership angle means that 'We coach and communicate' (see figure next page). Our managers at all levels are expected to show respect for others and act with integrity, understand and inspire commitment and initiative taking, create an atmosphere of open dialogue, nurture talent by coaching and offer opportunities for development. We believe that by keeping the focus on growing our people and developing the organisation we enhance employee commitment and customer satisfaction, thereby supporting sustainable organisational performance.

Nordea Group's top management full commitment is that all our leaders, i.e. several thousand people, throughout the

bank are expected to improve their coaching capabilities. The initiative has been cascading down all countries and units, including the New European Markets (Estonia, Latvia, Lithuania, Poland and Russia). There are a number of tailormade training programmes for different target groups in Nordea.

'Coaching Basics' is compulsory for all our current and future managers, whereas 'Coaching Experienced' and 'Team Coaching' are more advanced training for those who are willing to develop their coaching skills even further.

The practice of coaching in our country/region

In Nordea Bank Estonia we have been building our coaching culture for two years. We have taken Nordea 'coach-approach', which we have adapted into our local context.

All our managers have gone through a very practical training programme to understand what coaching is and to practise basic coaching skills. They use these in their daily leadership, but also in creating customer relationships. The performance and development dialogue, held once a year, is another excellent opportunity for managers to use their coaching skills towards employees. During this dialogue coaching is used to facilitate development and improve performance and satisfaction. Moreover, coaching has been

Geographical focus: *Estonia, East-/Northern Europe*

NORDEA BANK CASE STUDY: *From Good to Great through Coaching*

successfully used in other areas of people management: It is closely linked to talent management, career management and employer branding.

The practical coaching training also covers the GROW model and how to execute coaching sessions. In fact, each manager is supposed to conduct 10 formal coaching sessions with employees/colleagues/etc. in order to get some experience in giving coaching sessions (specially allocated time for coaching on particular issues, agreed between coach and coachee). Of course, the issues coached in this format are more limited than with external coaches. Usually the topics are very much work-related (e.g. improve performance, facilitate competence development,

solve problems and set targets, improve satisfaction and cooperation, create motivation).

After these ten coaching sessions, we ask the managers to reflect and write a report about their coaching experience. From this feedback, we have found out that managers have started to benefit from coaching as a leadership tool in even wider areas of their life, using coaching not only towards their colleagues and customers, but also towards family members and friends.

After the training, most managers keep coaching as an integrated part of their daily leadership/activities. But only some continue to also give a formal coaching session. Ma-

---

Making it possible

A great European bank
acknowledged for its people, creating
superior value for customers and shareholders

We create ambition, clarity and purpose

Great customer experiences	It's all about people	One Nordea team
We direct focus towards customers	**We coach and communicate**	**We team up and work together**

Profit orientation and prudent cost, risk and capital management

We drive to achieve

---

www.frank-bresser-consulting.com

Geographical focus: *Estonia, East-/Northern Europe*

NORDEA BANK CASE STUDY: *From Good to Great through Coaching*

nagers sometimes have professional coaches from outside Nordea – and we also have 3 people from HR providing formal coaching sessions.

Coaching has now become part of our everyday vocabulary.

Evaluation and outcomes of coaching

In order to keep our coaching culture alive, we need to measure how well we are doing. Therefore, we "take the temperature of the organisation" in our Employee Satisfaction Survey every year. Success through coaching is reflected in the scores of living the values, leadership competencies and overall satisfaction and motivation. Performance and development dialogues also provide an opportunity for us to measure the results of coaching, either through the quality and content of the dialogue reports or through direct evaluation of leadership competencies. We also follow up on our improvements by measuring the customer satisfaction index and its correlation with our business results.

Our success story of achieving remarkable results through coaching comes from our corporate banking: In two years, after we had launched the values and coaching concept, the same team with the same number of people doubled both the income as well as profit per employee. Although there were other factors that affected these great business results, living the values and coaching were important drivers.

Giving people the opportunity to take more initiative and responsibility, focusing on the future and personal growth played a major role. In Nordea it is crucial to know "what" we want to achieve, but it is equally or even more important "how" we do things. In the previously described case, the "how"-part has really made a difference.

Learning

There are several learning points from our coaching experience. First, we believe that the top management's full commitment at Nordea Group level and country level is a major prerequisite to develop our coaching culture. Secondly, we have noticed that over time and with more experience, coaching turns from a tool to a mindset. Managers need to practise it and consciously dedicate some time for it. Thirdly, the integration of the coaching concept into the values and leadership competencies has been the key to our success. Last, but not least, our experience has shown that coaching clearly supports us to achieve business goals on our way from a Good bank to a Great bank. Coaching is a vehicle for taking us in the direction we wish to travel – to Great Nordea.

Our key learning/Recommendation:
Coaching-based leadership creates great results – also in tough times.

Questions and exercises for further reflection and to integrate practice and theory:

1. What is the purpose/business case for building a coaching culture in the firm?
2. What exact kind of coaching capacity was/is needed?
3. How has it actually been developed (e.g. through what kind of coaching forms)?
4. What is the success of the coaching culture initiative? How was the process and its outcomes tracked/measured?
5. What is your key learning from this case study?

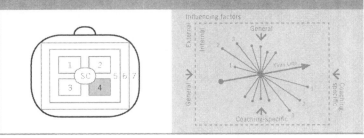

PART IV

THE COACHING CHANGE DYNAMICS FRAMEWORK

This fourth management tool approaches the successful implementation and optimization of coaching in organisations again from another perspective: It puts your coaching initiative into proper context and equips you with a sophisticated framework to design, configure and refine all coaching programme parameters in accordance with existing and changing business requirements. It emphasizes the need for mobility and flexibility of any coaching initiative within the continuously changing business environment.

This framework increases your awareness of existing or future influences and helps you adjust and make effective decisions around your coaching programme on a continuous basis. It explores in depth the scalability and adjustability of coaching initiatives as well as their dynamics and complexity.

The tool covers the coaching design variables of any coaching programme, the possible influences (internal and external; general and coaching-specific) as well as the best ways to configure the coaching variables.

Managers and directors responsible for coaching in their organisations and striving for outstanding results and excellence through coaching programmes, may benefit enormously from using this framework.

While the overall structure of this management tool may be easy to understand, its actual application in practice can be highly challenging and greatly stretch your thinking. The higher your coaching implementation and improvement intel-

FRAMEWORK 4

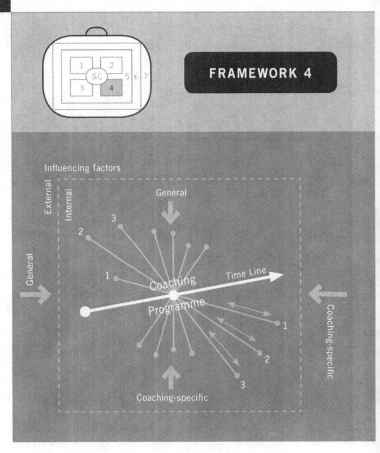

Framework 4: Coaching change dynamics framework (simplified version)

ligence, the more you will be able to use this framework in a highly sophisticated and effective way and leverage its full potential.

This management tool is recommended for advanced and master level practitioners. While beginners may also benefit from reading it, they are advised to work through the first frameworks of this book before getting to this one, as it builds on them in various ways.

Here is a more detailed overview of the framework and we will take a closer look at each of its elements:

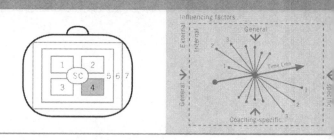

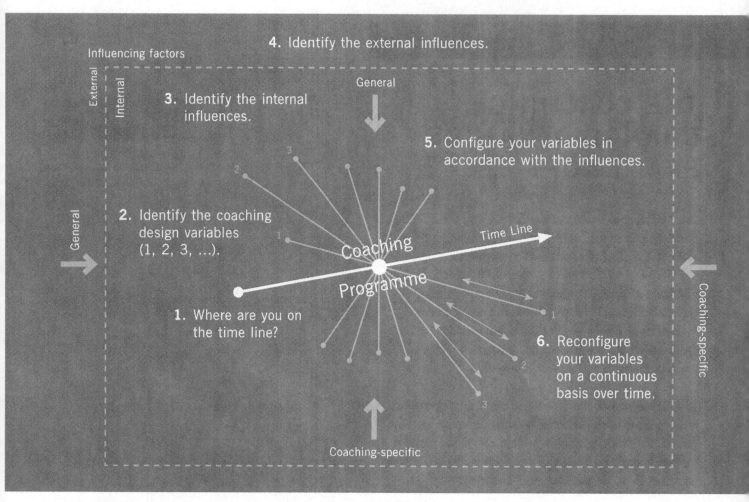

Framework 4: Coaching change dynamics framework (more detailed version)

1. Where is your coaching programme on the time line?

2. Identify the coaching design variables.
- Choice and thinking in continuums
- List of 30 classic variables
- Relationship between variables
- Importance and variability

3. Identify the internal influences.
- General internal influences
- Coaching-specific internal influences
- Coaching programme itself
- Importance and variability

4. Identify the external influences.
- General external influences
- Coaching-specific external influences
- Importance and variability

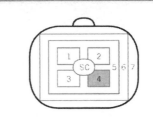
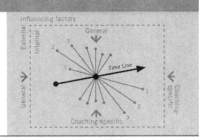

5. **Configure your variables in accordance with the influences.**
   - General guidelines
   - Typical configurations

6. **Reconfigure your variables on a continuous basis over time.**
   - Dynamic process of adaptation
   - Continuous learning process
   - Increasing coaching intelligence

As with the previous frameworks, you may use this framework for purposes of coaching implementation or improvement: On the one hand, it may serve you as a central thread and starting point to plan, design and implement new coaching programmes. On the other hand, you may use it as a measure and means to review and optimize existing coaching initiatives.

1. WHERE IS YOUR COACHING PROGRAMME ON THE TIME LINE?

Any coaching initiative has a time dimension: It starts at some point in a certain design and form, may evolve and be adjusted over time as needed, and finally stops at one point or is continued for an indefinite time.

So where is your coaching programme on its time line? Has it already started? For a current programme: how has it evolved in the past, and where is it exactly today? How long are you going to run it in the future?

Your points of departure for implementing or improving coaching are very different: When you plan to implement a new coaching programme from scratch, you, in principle, have all design options still available. Where you optimize and develop an existing programme – be it because you started it some time ago or because you took it over from

a colleague/predecessor – you need to work around and build upon the current programme design, so changing or replacing it may have significant implications.

The time line emphasizes the need for continuous learning and further development of your coaching initiative. However fantastic your coaching initiative may be at the beginning, if you just continue it as it is without keeping it up-to-date and in tune with your organisational needs, it may increasingly lose connection to what is actually needed, create less and less value and possibly even lead to counterproductive results. The effective use of coaching in organisations is a dynamic process that requires constant care and adjustment of your coaching programme.

www.frank-bresser-consulting.com

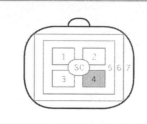
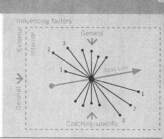

2. IDENTIFY THE COACHING DESIGN VARIABLES.

Successful coaching initiatives are characterized by being designed for their specific organisational context and purpose. The "one and only right way" of making use of coaching in business doesn't exist, but coaching programmes need to be designed in many different ways to meet the specific needs. While there are many do's and don'ts around coaching that clearly need to be observed, research and experience strongly suggest that many kinds of design may potentially add value and have a role to play depending on the circumstances of each case. The challenge for you is to always configure your coaching programme in exactly the way that best suits your organisation-specific needs and resources.

Choice and thinking in continuums

The scalability and adjustability of coaching programmes allow for flexibility in perfectly tailoring and designing your coaching initiative. This requires that you have a coaching attitude when implementing and improving coaching: Seek dynamic appropriateness, create choice and think in continuums (rather than in categories of right or wrong).

To give an example: Instead of seeing directive and non-directive coaching approaches as two mutually excluding, opposing schools of thought and assuming you would have to decide in favour of only one of these, regard the two approaches as end points of a whole continuum of options (see figure below), i.e. as a variable you may configure.

Interpreting the graphic: the closer you put the dot of one end of the continuum to the time line, the more emphasis shall be put on that approach. You may position this continuum bar more to the one side or the other, as appropriate for your programme.

The bar configuration in the below graphic (i.e. equal distance of both end dots to the time line) means that the coaching programme has an equal balance of both approaches: You may for example have coaches working with an integrated, equal mix of non-directive and directive elements. Or you have a coach pool with some coaches working in a highly directive way and others working in a highly non-directive way (e.g. to best meet the whole diversity of coaching requests coming in).

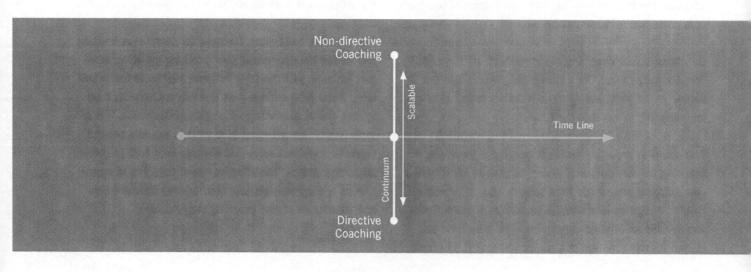

www.frank-bresser-consulting.com

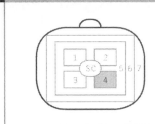
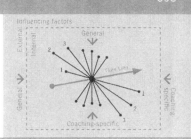

Two further examples of possible configurations of this bar are given as follows:

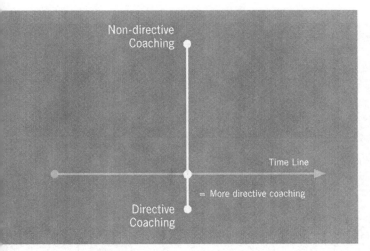

Example 2: More directive coaching

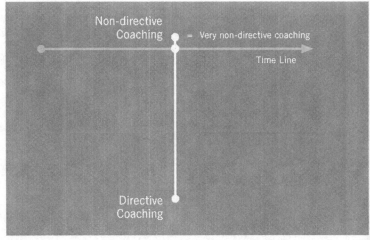

Example 3: Very non-directive coaching

What actually is the best choice in this regard for your coaching programme, is shaped by the internal and external environment and influences (see below) in your specific case.

You will typically start with one particular configuration of the coaching design variable at the beginning – and adjust and change it on a continuous basis over time in order to keep your coaching programme up-to-date.

List of 30 coaching design variables

The above example continuum bar (directive/non-directive) is just one dimension among many. In fact, there are plenty of scalable variables of a coaching programme. By adding further bars to the above graphic, a centred bundle of bars is generated. By configuring the various bars according to your context, it is possible to display the 'fingerprint' of your optimal coaching programme design.

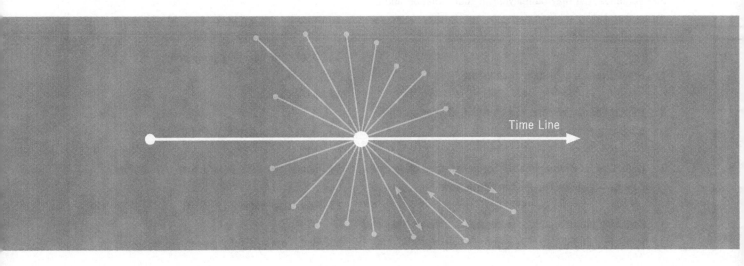

www.frank-bresser-consulting.com

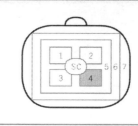
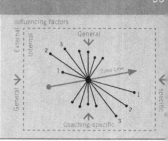

As the positioning of the continuum bars may be adjusted and change over time, the whole picture of the coaching programme may evolve – for example in the following way:

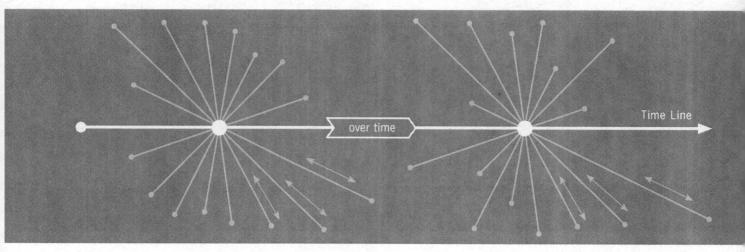

Please note that you may apply this continuum model not only to your programme as a whole, but also to any single part of it separately, as needed.

The following list of **30 common coaching design variables**, while not being exclusive, gives a useful overview of key options available when implementing and improving a coaching initiative. Each of these variables may add a continuum bar to the picture and facilitate the specific configuration and management of your coaching initiative. Add further variables that may be relevant in your situation and underline the ones that are of particular relevance for your specific context:

1. Broad/Narrow definition of coaching

2. Broad/Narrow purpose and objective of your coaching programme

3. High/Low level of organisational penetration of coaching (see Key Success Factor 3 in Framework 1)

4. Coaching forms requiring professional coaches/Coaching forms ingraining coaching into organisational life

5. Focus on external/internal coaching capability ('make/buy')

6. High/Low strategic integration of coaching

7. High/Low emphasis on the people/organisational/ tools&technology dimensions

8. Focus on business/people needs

9. Big/Small coaching programme

10. As a separate programme/part of a wider programme

11. One/many coaching programmes

12. Global/Local

13. High/Low investment and costs

14. Short/long term programme

15. Fast/Slow pace

16. High/Low structural power and resources

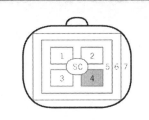 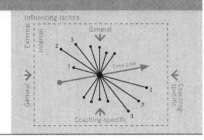

17. Top down/bottom-up implementation and improvement

18. Small/Large target group

19. Very high/Minimum required level of involvement and co-creation

20. Rigour/Flexibility (Stability/Change)

21. Growth/Retrenchment

22. High/Low level of standardization

23. Excellent/Minimum required level of quality (see Key Success Factor 10 in Framework 1: Ensure high integrity and quality at all levels)

24. Effective/Careful evaluation (see Key Success Factor 9 in Framework 1: Evaluate effectively and carefully)

25. Quantitative/Qualitative evaluation

26. Purely developmental/Includes remedial use of coaching

27. Focus on coaching as a specific business technique/as a matter of attitude

28. Directive/Non-directive; Provide solutions/Let develop solutions; Telling/Listening; Push/Pull; Compulsory/ Voluntary; Support/Challenge; Focus on knowledge and expertise/on facilitating processes

29. High/Low use of technology (e.g. web 2.0, phone, videoconferencing)

30. Using explicit coaching terminology/Using other terminology instead

Relationship between coaching design variables

Be aware that some variables may be highly interdependent. You need to examine the internal and external influences thoroughly first (see further below) in order to be able to assess the actual relationships between design variables.

For example, an invested higher budget in a programme may normally imply larger size and/or better quality, than a small investment. But this is not necessarily true, as it depends on many influences, e.g. a manager responsible for coaching with a huge budget, but low coaching intelligence, may not deliver the impact, reach and quality, that a manager with a small budget, but high coaching intelligence can.

Importance and variability

Identify the coaching design variables that are particularly relevant and/or tricky in your context and clarify the degree of volatility and uncertainty of each variable. What variables are easy to anticipate now? Which ones may be less foreseeable, require a higher degree of flexibility and adjustability from your side and possibly be particularly challenging at some point?

Make a list of the most relevant coaching design variables for your coaching programme.

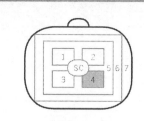 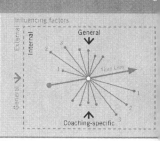

3. IDENTIFY THE INTERNAL INFLUENCES.

How to actually position the continuum bars in your coaching programme, is primarily a matter of context. It is therefore your task as HR/OD/L&D manager to scan your business environment properly and identify what substantial internal and external influences on the design of your coaching programme actually exist (or may be expected in the future). By being clear on these and configuring your variables according to them, you will achieve optimal fit with your coaching initiative.

Let us first focus on scanning the internal environment/influences. We distinguish between general and coaching-specific internal influences, which may inform and shape your coaching programme design.

1. General internal influences

These characterize the overall company situation, which impacts on the design of your coaching initiative. This list of general internal influences is not exclusive – add further items as appropriate and mark the ones that are of particular relevance in your context:

Your company's ...

- Mission statement and strategy

- Business model

- Size and geographical presence

- Organisational structure

- Strengths and weaknesses (e.g. core competencies, competitive advantage)

- Performance, financial and other (e.g. profitability, ROI, customer satisfaction)

- Identified specific organisational needs

- Management style

- Level of continuity of management

- Politics and other dynamics

- Culture and climate

- People's skills, attitude and needs

- Ethics, philosophy and history

- Organisational processes

- Programmes and initiatives

- Tools and technologies used/available internally

- Level of staff retention (employer attractiveness)

- Composition of staff (diverse or homogeneous)

- Role, credibility, acceptance, competence and financial strength of the HR/L&D/OD function

- Level of support/buy-in from the top for people and organisational development

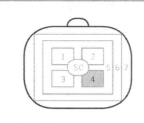

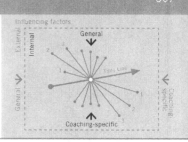

2. Coaching-specific internal influences

These describe the internal company environment regarding coaching specifically. You need to take these into account when configuring your coaching programme variables. Also here, add further items to the following list as appropriate and underline the ones that are particularly important for your context. Coaching-specific internal influences are:

Your company's ...

- Understanding/Definition of coaching (if there is one already)

- Already existing (or past) coaching programmes

- Their processes and outcomes

- Current level of organisational penetration of coaching

- Already identified coaching-specific organisational needs

- People's receptiveness towards coaching

- Already existing coaching capability (/capacity/culture/ intelligence)

- Level of demand for coaching

- Cultural preferences, taboos or reservations related to coaching

- Developmental/Remedial understanding of coaching

- Structural, organisational positioning and power of coaching (e.g. who is responsible for coaching in your company: the top, HR/L&D/OD, is there a coaching champion or specific coaching unit/department in your firm)

- Level of credibility, acceptance, competence and financial strength of the people responsible for coaching in your firm

- Level of support/buy-in from top management for coaching

The coaching programme itself

As the coaching initiative evolves, it also shapes its own design. When your first evaluation results provide information on how to best improve your coaching programme, you will, of course, take this into account in your programme design. Once you are implementing your coaching initiative, it also becomes part of your internal business environment and thus an internal influence on the programme design.

It is the purpose of any coaching programme to change the environment in some way. Its influence on other conditions thus influences your coaching initiative. For example, you may at first have low receptiveness towards coaching and low support from the top, but by planning and implementing a high-quality programme that turns out to be a huge success, you raise people's receptiveness and the top management support. Or imagine you solve a problem by the effective use of coaching, even making that programme redundant and allowing you to finish it.

So not only the environment has impact on the coaching programme design, also, vice versa, the programme has impact on the environment. It is an interconnected, two-way process of mutual influence.

Importance and variability

Identify all relevant internal influences in your context and assess them in terms of their levels of importance. Internal influences are also variable, i.e. they may change over time and can be seen as continuums (e.g. on a scale of very high to no support for coaching from top management, where is your company now?).

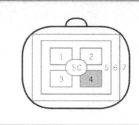
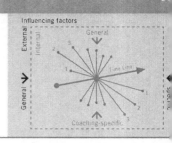

Identify how certain and stable each of the internal influences is: What influences are stable and easy to anticipate? Which ones may be less foreseeable, change significantly within a short time and require a particularly high degree of flexibility and adjustability from your side?

4. IDENTIFY THE EXTERNAL INFLUENCES.

The external influences on the design of your coaching programme are those coming from your company's external environment.

As above with internal influences, we distinguish between general and coaching-specific external influences as follows.

1. General external influences

These characterize the overall market drivers which impact on the configuration of your coaching design variables. Identify those relevant to your situation and add other items as needed:

- Customer/Market needs and trends

- Level of demand/request for your firm's products/services

- The overall economic, educational, political and legal situation

- Social, cultural, ethical and environmental aspects

- Competition in the market

- Existence of suitable suppliers/distributors

- Specific characteristics of/dynamics in the kind of business you are involved in

- Reputation of your brand and of your company overall

- Availability of suitable, qualified people/talent in the labour market

- Demands of qualified people/talent on the employer

- Existing business networks and bodies

- State of the technology and of know-how

- Level of availability of needed resources, e.g. fundraising, information, materials, energy

- Needs of your various company stakeholders (e.g. government, unions, company owners)

- State of business research and teaching

2. Coaching-specific external influences

These are those influences emanating from the external coaching industry and market. Paying particular attention to these is essential when designing your coaching programme. Coaching-specific external influences are:

- Current stage of development of coaching in business and society overall (locally and globally)

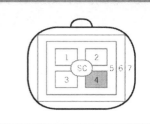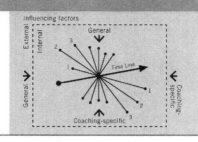

- Prevailing definition(s)/understanding/reputation of coaching outside your company

- Degree of development, quality and acceptance of the coaching industry

- Spread and success of the use of coaching in organisations so far

- Level of general acceptance/available evidence on the benefits of coaching for organisations

- Level of coaching capacity and capability available in the market in terms of quantity, quality and integrity regarding coaching consultancies, coaches, coaching trainers, etc. (in general and specifically for your needs)

- Nature of the body of acquired coaching knowledge already available

- Existing cultural preferences, taboos or reservations related to coaching

- Overall business receptiveness for coaching

- Kind of coaching networks and bodies available

- Specific characteristics of the coaching industry (e.g. trends, historical influences, particular dynamics and politics)

- State of coaching research and teaching

- Existing/Upcoming legislation related to coaching

Feel invited to add further points as appropriate and underline the ones that are particularly relevant in your case.

Importance and variability

As with internal influences above, clarify what each of the external influences actually means for your context and what impact they may have on the configuration of your coaching programme design variables. They are also not fixed, but variable (continuums) and may change over time. So how uncertain and volatile is each of the external influences in your case? What influences are stable and easy to anticipate? Which ones may be less foreseeable, change significantly and require a particularly high level of adjustability?

Compile a list of the most important external influences on your coaching programme design.

5. CONFIGURE YOUR VARIABLES IN ACCORDANCE WITH THE INFLUENCES.

By identifying all relevant coaching design variables and all critical internal and external influences on these on a continuous basis, you put yourself in the best position to design your coaching initiative in a way that ideally suits your context and creates optimal value for your company.

In working out what is the best configuration of the continuum bars for your coaching initiative, play through various alternatives, go through an iterative reflection process and feel free to challenge any 'accepted thinking'.

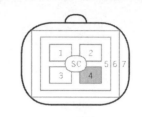
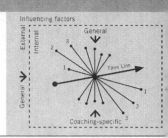

It is in the nature of such an undertaking that there is no easy off-the-shelf solution. It may require some time and effort to get to the point where you have identified a configuration that is consistent and coherent in the light of the internal and external influences and able to produce optimal fit.

In principle, the whole book – in particular Frameworks 1 to 3 above – provides you with detailed guidance and support on how to actually configure your coaching programme variables. Reading through the book and putting its contents into practice thus enables you to make concrete choices regarding the selection and positioning of relevant continuum bars.

General guidelines

Here are some general rules of thumb in order to facilitate your overall reflection process:

- Think your coaching initiative through to its end, before deciding on its concrete design and shape today.

- Factor the internal and external influences in properly (i.e. give each of these proper weight). Neither underestimate or ignore an influence, nor overemphasize or make an influence an absolute.

- Think thoroughly about what role each of the identified, relevant influences will actually play in the design of your coaching programme. For each influence, you may choose to …
    … adapt to it and aim for explicit conformity with it
    … be rather neutral and deal with it properly to avoid that it interferes with the coaching initiative
    … explicitly work towards diminishing/removing it, as this may be the purpose or inevitable necessity of your coaching initiative.

- Take into account the likely future development of internal and external influences when configuring your coach-

ing programme today. For example, in a company that is known for rather frequently replacing its top management and changing its HR/L&D/OD strategy, it may be advisable not to over-tailor the design of a coaching initiative around the specific preferences of a current board, but to make sure that the designed programme may sustain and add value under future managements. Also, where you have a significant budget for coaching, but expect it to be cut in a few years, design your coaching initiative accordingly, i.e. avoid massive long-term programmes and/or make sure that the developed coaching capability and achieved benefits may be carried forward by the people themselves after the programme end.

- Building on the above, acknowledge that the effective use of coaching is an evolving process. Accept the need to proceed with due caution and limit detailed planning to the next upcoming time window. Consider also formulating different possible scenarios, e.g. regarding the receptiveness for coaching activities, and configure your programme variables in a way that you can respond flexibly to whatever scenario will actually occur.

- Strive for optimal fit, but not necessarily for 100 % perfect fit: often you may need to address contradicting influences and interests. In these cases, despite all efforts to find innovative solutions and create win-win situations, you may discover there is no ideal, perfect way available, but some kind of trade-off becomes necessary. In which case, the most tenable approach is the "perfect one" for now.

Typical configurations

An infinite number of possible constellations of different variables and internal and external influences are thinkable. The final effort of working out the best configuration of the positioning of the continuum bars for your specific coaching programme and context is a task no global business guide

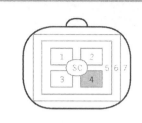

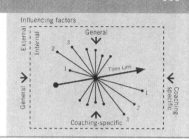

in the world may spare you. For this, you need to invest your own time and effort – or get appropriate, additional support as needed (also see Framework 7: Guidance and support framework).

We illustrate here a few examples of common internal and external influences with their resulting classic configurations of variables as a first inspiration. However, you need to check what is most appropriate in each specific case and context.

Example 1: High receptiveness for coaching by your people and also great support from the top may classically lead to higher organisational penetration of coaching, a more strategic integration of coaching, greater investment, more extensive structural power and resources, more top down implementation, a wider scope of the programme, a faster pace, a larger target group and a more explicit use of coaching terminology.

Example 2: A lack of external coaching capability in the market, that would be required to meet your company-specific coaching needs, normally fosters the development of internal coaching capability and makes a rather slow and cautious pace (at least at first) advisable.

Example 3: A more traditional, authoritarian management style in a company classically tends to foster a more narrow definition and use of coaching at first, a higher focus on expertise and knowledge, less top down implementation, a higher level of standardisation, rigid evaluation and very careful use of coaching terminology.

Example 4: A very volatile business environment and company situation may typically lead to a broader definition and use of coaching, greater emphasis on coaching as an attitude, higher focus on ingraining coaching into organisational life and a higher level of overall programme flexibility.

6. RECONFIGURE YOUR VARIABLES ON A CONTINUOUS BASIS OVER TIME.

Let us consider the time line of the coaching programme. At any point in time, you may decide to keep or change the positioning of the continuum bars in your coaching initiative. The effective use of coaching in organisations is a **lively, dynamic process of adaptation** that requires constant care and adjustment of your coaching programme.

As you gain more and more experience and knowledge on what works and what needs further improvement, you can optimize the programme over time. As time progresses, the initiative also evolves. The next time window for which to plan in full detail moves on and the environment (with its resulting influences) may change – sometimes even fundamentally. For all these reasons, the further development of

your coaching programme is a business requirement and **continuous learning process**.

Make sure you keep your coaching initiative fresh, up-to-date and in tune with your organisational needs at all times. Rescan the coaching environment and reconfigure your coaching design variables on a regular basis as you move along the time line.

The higher your **coaching intelligence**, the more you will discover the enormous possibilities of positioning and moving the continuum bars and the more you will enhance your ease and intuition in configuring your coaching programme design.

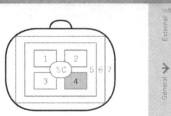
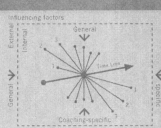

Summary:

COACHING CHANGE DYNAMICS FRAMEWORK (FRAMEWORK 4)

Here is the overview of Framework 4:

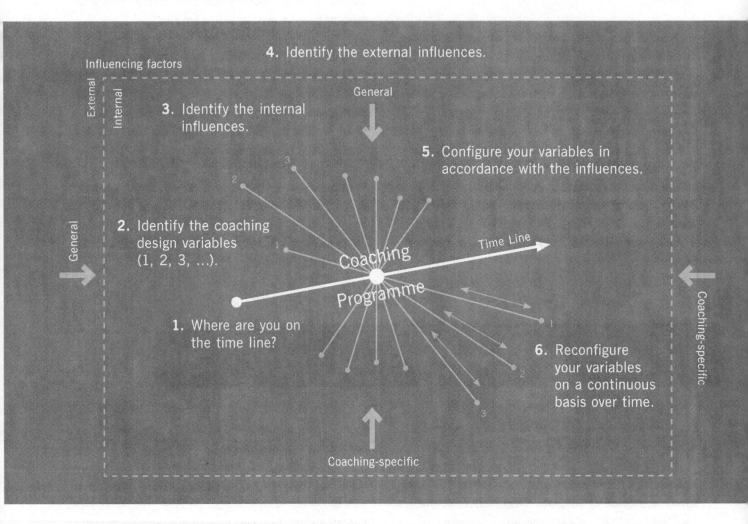

4. Identify the external influences.

Influencing factors

External / Internal

3. Identify the internal influences.

General

5. Configure your variables in accordance with the influences.

General

2. Identify the coaching design variables (1, 2, 3, …).

Coaching Programme

Time Line

1. Where are you on the time line?

Coaching-specific

6. Reconfigure your variables on a continuous basis over time.

Coaching-specific

On the one hand, this management tool may serve you as a central thread and starting point to plan, design and implement new coaching programmes. On the other hand, you may use it as a measure and means to review and optimize existing coaching initiatives.

For further reflection and to integrate practice and theory, we invite you to apply the above framework to the next case study (and/or any of the other case studies included in this book). What are the relevant coaching design variables in each case study? What are the internal and external influences? How was the coaching initiative configured at the beginning, and how has this configuration changed over time? What has been done particularly well, and where do you see potential for further development and optimization?

www.frank-bresser-consulting.com

Geographical focus: *Bulgaria in Europe*

CASE STUDY 21	EOS MATRIX OOD, BULGARIA

Company: *EOS Matrix OOD*

(With over 250 employees EOS Matrix OOD is the leading debt management company in Bulgaria and is part of EOS Group – one of the world's largest financial services companies with over 30 years of experience, 40 subsidiaries in 20 countries, over 4000 employees and 20 000 customers worldwide.)

www.eos-matrix.com

Author: *Rayna Mitkova-Todorova*

Function: *Managing Director, based in Sofia*

Building Resilience in the Process of Organizational Transformation

The challenge

Prior to the coaching engagement in late 2007, EOS Matrix was already a market leader. The debt management industry was becoming increasingly competitive, though. The Managing Director Mrs. Rayna Mitkova became aware that to preserve its position, EOS needed to start laying the ground for a long-term growth. Also, in 2007 her managing partner abruptly left the firm and the situation challenged the CEO's leadership capacity.

At the time, coaching and executive coaching in particular was (and still is) not a widely used tool for spurring corporate growth and leadership development in Bulgaria. EOS had no prior experience with coaching and turning to it was more of an intuitive decision.

Objectives

The initial goal of coaching was to support the planning and execution of the following objectives (1st stage of the coaching program):

1. Co-creating and aligning the team toward the EOS Matrix strategic direction – the vision, mission, values and strategic goals while meeting short-term ones
2. Preserving the firm's leading market position
3. Developing leadership skills (e.g. confidence, delegating, giving feedback, work-life balance)

Then, pressured by the looming crisis in 2009, EOS was striving for clearer direction. So in the course of the coaching program (2nd stage) and through extensive in-house work the objectives gradually evolved to:

1. Building a path and capacity for creating a sustainable growth while meeting short-term goals in the midst of the crisis (organizational level)
2. Developing the capacity to lead authentically (CEO level)

The coaching program
(a whole span and blend of coaching formats)

Starting with an individual executive coaching for the CEO at first, the coaching initiative quickly evolved to a three stage coaching program (see figure) encompassing the

Geographical focus: *Bulgaria in Europe*

EOS MATRIX OOD CASE STUDY: *Building Resilience in the Process of Organizational Transformation*

whole organization and covering a whole blend of coaching forms:

- Individual executive coaching (for focus & execution and authentic communication)
- Executive board coaching (team and individual)
- Larger management team coaching (1-2-day off-site events)

- 'Strategy in Action' Initiative – systematic larger management team coaching (CEO, 5 executive board members and 14 key mid-level managers, all given a choice to participate) (2 sessions twice a month)
- Two advanced leadership trainings with a coaching approach
- Use of organizational leadership coaching ('leadership' denotes a systemic perspective of the organization based on the most advanced leadership models)

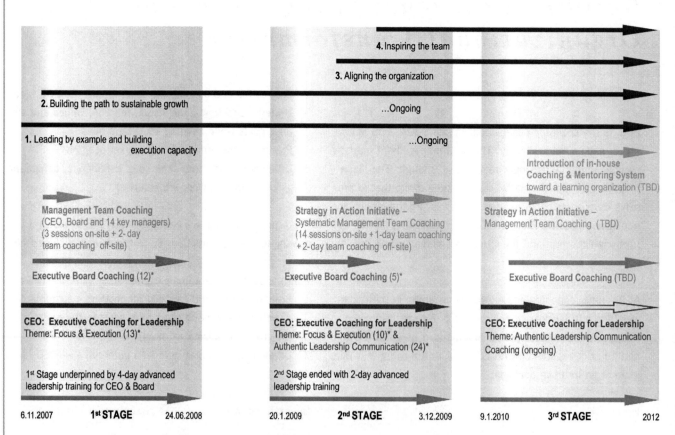

Figure: A Three-Stage Coaching Program at EOS Matrix OOD aimed toward creating a learning organization and sustainable growth.

The number in parenthesis shows number of coaching sessions.
The coaching program is provided by external coaches. Internal coaching capability is to be introduced within the company in the future.

Geographical focus: *Bulgaria in Europe*

EOS MATRIX OOD CASE STUDY: *Building Resilience in the Process of Organizational Transformation*

The thinking that led to undertaking the 'Strategy in Action' intensive team coaching in a financially strained 2009 was, "If coaching doesn't help, there is nothing that can help". It was considered not an expense, but 'the required minimum' and 'a safe bet'. It was based on coach selection criteria ensuring credibility and acceptance, which were professional expertise, organizational experience, trust, inspiring, being an honest mirror and honestly admitting they do not know vs. pretending to know it all.

The coaching programme is led by the CEO who, besides coaching, has also explored other avenues for building leadership capacity, including completing an EMBA program and personal development work. In late 2009 the CEO was selected among the Top 10 Managers of Bulgaria in a national competition.

The outcomes

With the coaching program ongoing, the key reported benefits are:

1. Helped Create a Clear Path to Sustainable Growth

Clear Strategic Direction

- A clear strategic direction and transformation road map by 2014 ensures flexibility in turbulent times. Participants reported, "We are no longer willing to do things just to fix the budget. We also want them to have meaning, bring us closer to where we want to go and to enjoy them". To that end, we had to drop a few short-term profits, which was painful, especially in 2009, they admit.
- The team is now regarded as one of the strategically most prepared within the EOS Group which led to stronger backing from the mother company.

Team Ready and Engaged

- The employee engagement has increased from 29% in 2007 to 41% in 2008 (Hewitt research). "Coaching contributed 100% for this result", Mrs. Mitkova recognizes.
- The management team shares a common understanding of the EOS strategic direction vs. the past when the CEO imposed it. The result: a faster and easier decision making process. Management team members report to be 'much more conscious and responsible, believe more in themselves, have a stronger bond and hope for the future'.
- Specifically, the Strategy in Action coaching initiative 'dragged the team out of a state of lethargy and they engaged in co-creating the basis for long-term growth'.

2. Helped Build Resilience in the Transformation of Challenges

- Coaching supported the management team to build resilience, not stress, by transforming a number of challenging experiences. Strained communication, abrupt departures of team members, financial and ethical issues literally brought them to the edge in 2009. The difference is that the team now feels 'ready', not burned out.

3. ROI

- The ROI from coaching was 433% in the first stage of coaching. That stage was a resource of crucial importance to meet the crisis, the team assessment showed.
- The ROI was 315% for 2009.
- In the midst of financially challenging 2009 the firm met its financial target.

Geographical focus: *Bulgaria in Europe*

EOS MATRIX OOD CASE STUDY: *Building Resilience in the Process of Organizational Transformation*

The future

The company is planning to provide external coaching for the executive board members and roll out a coaching and mentoring program with internal coaches for the middle management.

Our key learning/Recommendation:

Coaching reinforces/helps develop ownership, resilience and confidence in a company.

Questions and exercises for further reflection and to integrate practice and theory:

1. What is the business case for coaching in the company?

2. What are the key variables of the coaching programme design – and how have these evolved in their configuration over time?

3. What are the internal influences on the coaching programme design – and how have these evolved over time?

4. What are the external influences on the coaching programme design – and how have these evolved over time?

5. What are the coaching outcomes?

6 . What is your key learning from this case study?

www.frank-bresser-consulting.com

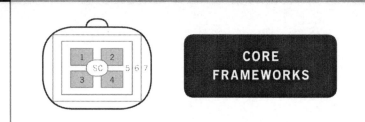

CORE FRAMEWORKS

Review:

THE CORE FRAMEWORKS (FRAMEWORKS 1 TO 4)

We covered all 4 Core Frameworks for the successful implementation and improvement of coaching in organisations.
Here is once again an overview of the management tools:

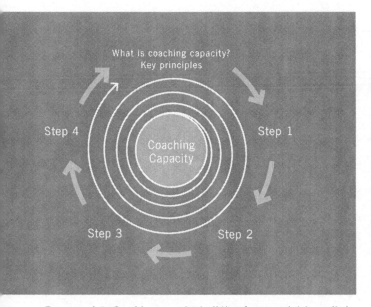

Framework 1: Coaching success factors framework
(also called: 10 key success factors framework)

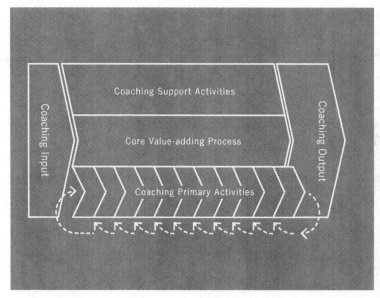

Framework 2: Coaching value chain framework

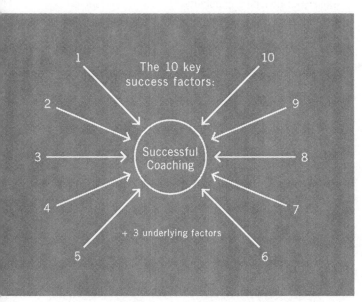

Framework 3: Coaching capacity building framework (also called:
High performance coaching culture framework)

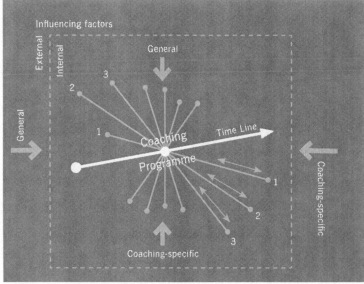

Framework 4: Coaching change dynamics framework

www.frank-bresser-consulting.com

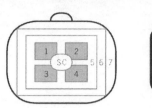

CORE FRAMEWORKS

Depending on your specific needs and personally preferred learning style, you may use just one, more or all of these tools.

Please note that at the end of this book (see Coaching Integration Framework 7) you will find additional guidance on how to fully integrate the four tools and use them in a com-

plementary manner. Having said this, each framework can also stand alone and be used separately.

For the time being, we come to the Embedding Frameworks 5 and 6 in the following chapters, which help you further raise your coaching capability.

**THE 2 EMBEDDING
FRAMEWORKS**

The 2 Embedding Frameworks

Frameworks 5 and 6 are more general than the previous four core frameworks. They provide you with an overall idea of how to make effective use of coaching in your organisation. While, in part, they embed the application of the previous frameworks, they can also stand alone and be used separately.

Framework 5: **Coaching growth and maintenance framework**

Framework 6: **Coaching guidance and support framework**

PART V

THE COACHING GROWTH AND MAINTE- NANCE FRAMEWORK

(also called: The coaching gardening metaphor framework)

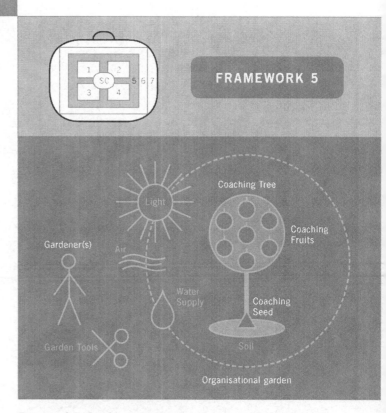

FRAMEWORK 5

*Framework 5: Coaching growth and maintenance framework
(simplified version)*

This fifth management tool gives you a different perspective on the implementation and improvement of coaching: Through a coaching gardening metaphor, this framework enables you to get a deeper sense of the right balance between organic and control management of coaching programmes. You may also improve your systems thinking regarding coaching and better understand the requirements of continuous management of coaching initiatives and the need for patience and calm.

Finally, the gardening metaphor addresses the emotional part of your brain and will help you integrate and see more links and complex relationships.

Speaking within the metaphor, this framework leads you through the process of planning your organisational garden, being and/or choosing good gardeners, and growing and cultivating thriving coaching trees successfully.

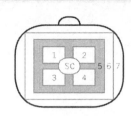
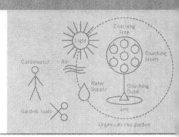

Managers and directors responsible for coaching in their organisations and striving for outstanding results and excellence through coaching programmes may benefit enormously from internalizing this framework.

Having said that, this framework works through a metaphor, is not that linear and straightforward, and not conveying the explicit messages that the other management tools in this book do.

That is not the purpose of this tool. Its main purpose is to give you another kind of access to the implementation and improvement of coaching that particularly supports your

natural senses, as these are very important for the effective use of coaching as well.

We acknowledge that people's receptiveness will differ. For some it will resonate and inspire, yet others may wonder why it is in the book. Either response is fine. We invite you to take the opportunity to give it a try and find out for yourself whether it triggers anything positive in you. If it does, the framework may unfold its potential and significantly raise your coaching capability.

Here is the more detailed overview of the framework. We will take a closer look at each of its elements.

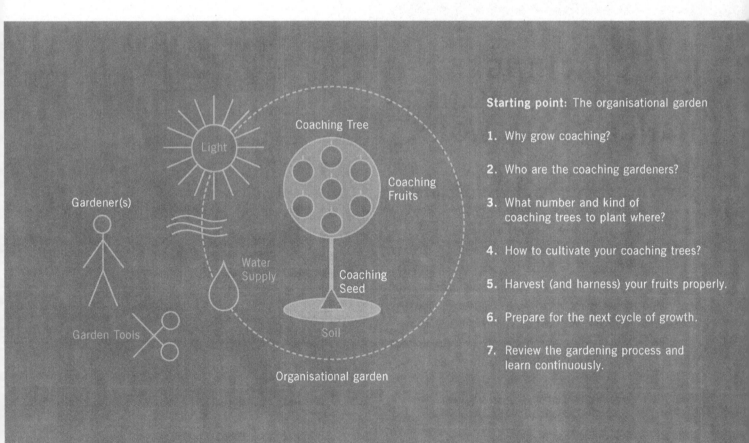

Starting point: The organisational garden

1. Why grow coaching?

2. Who are the coaching gardeners?

3. What number and kind of coaching trees to plant where?

4. How to cultivate your coaching trees?

5. Harvest (and harness) your fruits properly.

6. Prepare for the next cycle of growth.

7. Review the gardening process and learn continuously.

Framework 5: Coaching growth and maintenance framework (detailed version)

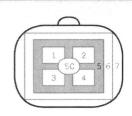
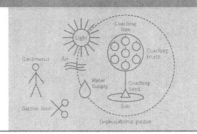

STARTING POINT: THE ORGANISATIONAL GARDEN

In this metaphor, see your company as an organisational garden, where you will cultivate and produce fruit. A garden is a highly organic ecosystem with complex structures and levels of interconnectedness. Trees, bushes, plants and grasses all grow organically in a cyclical way having their own circadian and seasonal rhythms. The same is true for the human and organic element in any firm and for coaching. In order to keep a garden in a desired shape, a systemic view and continuous care are needed.

A garden is more than the ground on which the trees and fruit grow. It is also a work place and social environment at the same time. The classic tasks of organisational gardeners are therefore to ...

- produce an optimal harvest
- provide an engaging, productive environment for the people working in the garden (or visiting it)
- sustain an ecological balance within the garden and in its relationship to the larger ecosystem it belongs to

It is the proper cultivation of coaching (to keep things simple and tangible, we talk about 'coaching trees' in this metaphor) that delivers the above – an optimal harvest, environment and ecological balance. The art of coaching gardening is to know what coaching tree(s) to grow where, when and how, i.e. to achieve optimal fit. Well planned, designed and implemented coaching initiatives are the precision tools of this discipline of coaching gardening.

Coaching gardeners acknowledge that they (as well as any other people working in or visiting the garden) are part of the ecosystem, and work with and around the conditions they find. They may be able to change and improve some conditions, while others they acknowledge they cannot change. The current environment, possibilities and limits may also change and evolve over time.

When tending a garden, coaching gardeners regularly need to make choices about to what extent they let the garden grow naturally, i.e. without any intervention, and to what extent they actively support and control the direction of its growth. In fact, there always needs to be a **proper balance between natural spread and control mechanisms** to allow for optimal development. Both approaches have a role to play and need to take into account the organic dimension of people and organisations. It is important to see the two approaches in a pragmatic, complementary way, and not to overemphasize or stigmatise either of them. Indeed, as a manager responsible for coaching in your organisation, you will provide people with proper information, input, guidance and support regarding coaching on the one hand, and also let things develop very naturally on the other hand, as appropriate.

1. WHY GROW COACHING? FOR WHAT PURPOSE?

The overall purpose of planting coaching may be to achieve improved conditions for the garden to produce an optimal harvest, environment and ecological balance. The specific purpose may vary tremendously. For example, by growing coaching trees you may focus on ...

www.frank-bresser-consulting.com

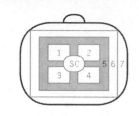
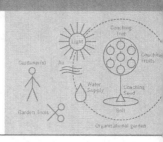

- enhancing the quality of your fruits
- increasing the quantity of your fruits
- making the garden fresher, more friendly, beautiful and lively
- using the shadow of the coaching trees to allow other plants to grow better
- using the tree trunk wood or its branches for further processing
- making the garden's soil more resistant to erosion
- using the trees as lookout points
- improving the quality of the air
- using the trees to overcome obstacles (e.g. a rock/river)

- providing living space for animals that are wanted/needed
- using trees as a border, meeting point or screen from view
- creating new top soil through natural composting
- giving people protection against rain and excessive sun
- creating a space for physical and mental refreshment, inspiration and regeneration

The first step is to clarify what you want to achieve by cultivating coaching in your organisational garden. Beforehand, identify what coaching trees you already have in your garden and what purposes these fulfil.

2. WHO ARE THE COACHING GARDENERS?

In organisational gardens, you normally have different types and hierarchies of gardeners. It is the company board who are the top gardeners deciding on the overall design and envisaged development of the garden. Only as far as they ingrain coaching themselves or see the cultivation of coaching as a strategic top management issue within their direct responsibility, do they also become and act as coaching gardeners more specifically.

Classically, the HR, L&D or OD function is given the task of growing coaching (i.e. to implement and improve coaching forms). However, other areas or functions may also integrate coaching elements and become coaching gardeners in their specific field.

In larger gardens, you may also have explicit, specialized coaching gardeners responsible only for coaching (a coaching expert/champion, team, unit or department).

In addition, you may use the support of professional coaching gardeners, be they external or internal: coaching consultants, coaches and/or coaching trainers may help your firm

grow coaching. Also, you can buy full-grown coaching trees from external coaching gardeners and plant them at suitable places in your garden.

In some gardens, everybody in a firm may be educated/trained to take over the role of a coaching gardener in their position and sphere of influence in some way (shared coaching gardening). This may occur in one or more of the following ways:

- Growing coaching in one's own allocated garden plot (e.g. as a leader of a team)
- Taking over and fulfilling coaching gardening tasks beyond one's own plot (becoming a part-time internal coach/coaching trainer/coaching contact point and information resource)
- Taking co-responsibility by notifying the main coaching gardeners of any perceived poor condition of coaching trees
- Removing smaller problems concerning coaching within one's capability, when one comes across them (removing dead wood and rubbish from a coaching tree)

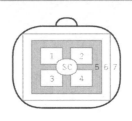
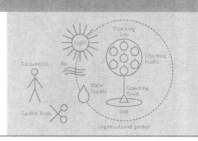

- Abiding by the governing coaching gardening rules at any time (e.g. respecting beds of small coaching trees)

As manager responsible for coaching in your organisation, you probably have the task of identifying and selecting suitable coaching co-gardeners with proper integrity and quality suited for your purposes.

How many people, and who exactly to appoint as main and co-gardeners for coaching depends on ...

- what level of (strategic) importance coaching is given in your company
- where coaching is positioned in your organisation
- how much coaching capability already exists in your firm, where and by whom precisely
- what is the organisational structure, e.g. how hierarchical or flat it is
- what is the specific purpose, nature and size of each coaching initiative

- the culture in the organisation and level of receptiveness for coaching

In your decision making, ensure an appropriate balance between centralized and decentralized gardening. While the first approach has the classic advantages of high consistency and alignment and avoids fragmentation, the latter facilitates necessary local adjustments, quick actions and response times and local ownership.

Provide your appointed co-gardeners with the needed training and promote continuous further development and knowledge sharing.

All coaching gardeners are bound by the hierarchy of strategies, i.e. any coaching gardening activity needs to be done in alignment with corporate, business and functional strategy. Where coaching is made an explicit, inherent part of strategy, this needs to be respected down the hierarchy.

3. WHAT NUMBER AND KIND OF COACHING TREES TO PLANT WHERE?

As a gardener, it is important to adopt a systematic and systemic approach. After formulating your purpose for growing coaching in alignment with the business gardening strategy, think through thoroughly where and in what variant(s) exactly you need to plant coaching trees.

3.1. Aim for a proper level of spread of coaching

What space should coaching actually take in your garden? A whole range of possible options is available. Depending on your organisation-specific needs, you may decide for example to ...

- add one or two single coaching trees in a specific area of the garden
- grow a number of coaching trees spread over various areas of the garden
- plant a few or many coaching trees at one point of the garden (coaching pocket)
- grow and arrange a certain number of coaching trees in a specific constellation/way (e.g. one tree every 100 yards or at every fork)
- have coaching trees everywhere in the garden as a minor/important/dominant element
- plant a pure coaching garden, i.e. a garden only with coaching trees/plants.

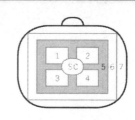 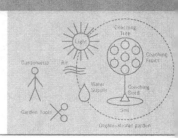

Equally, consider removing, transplanting or cutting back existing coaching trees. Identify what coaching trees you already have in your garden and review their actual state and fit.

As the implementation and improvement of coaching is an evolving, cyclical learning process, plan in stages of development. Be clear on where you need to grow coaching in each phase of the process. The garden will inevitably evolve over time, so include the dynamic factor and allow for a level of uncertainty in your garden planning.

3.2. Choose suitable coaching seeds/trees

There is a whole range of types of coaching seeds and trees with different characteristics available. Grow and plant the kind of coaching that is most appropriate for your purposes and gardening conditions. As required, plant various, different types of coaching trees at different points in the garden.

While the core of all coaching variants is the same (i.e. dynamic appropriateness: what fits best where and how), the number of different, existing types and forms is high (see Key Success Factor 3 in Framework 1 setting out all coaching dimensions and forms). Also, with proper coaching capability, you may be able to breed new coaching plants for your specific purposes, e.g. by combining or developing existing coaching forms further. Coaching gardening initiatives are scalable and adjustable in many ways.

The types of coaching trees/seeds to choose from differ mainly by their...
- size
- level of robustness and durability
- speed and cycles of growth
- types of fruits (in terms of quantity and quality)
- requirements on the environment
- impact on the environment
- ways of reproducing and spreading further

- special function in the ecosystem
- compatibility with other plants
- degree of difficulty of cultivating them, i.e. the level of time, effort, skills and resources needed by gardeners
- specific characteristics, e.g. particular wood, special healing effect, immunity against certain vermin, risk of deteriorating soil and air by planting too many/large coaching trees of a specific kind (typical example: the manager/leader as coach of his or her direct reports).

Any coaching trees you grow need to find the right conditions to be able to survive and thrive. When the conditions are not right, improve them, choose a more suitable type of coaching seed/tree, or abandon the idea of planting this type of coaching tree at this place.

3.3. Optimize the conditions

It is your job as a coaching gardener to work with and around the conditions that you find. Part of this is also to change and improve the existing conditions by the use of gardening tools in order to help coaching thrive. While doing so, you will also necessarily encounter limits of what is possible.

A professional one-to-one coaching or coaching leadership style training programme for example can only be successful, if it can take place in an environment that is sufficiently receptive towards it. If this is not the case, you need to change the conditions beforehand by creating a positive atmosphere around the programme first. If you find this is not feasible, do not start the initiative at least in this form at this place. Implement another, more suitable coaching programme, or choose another, more receptive place in the organisation to run it.

Key elements determining the gardening conditions are the existence/characteristics of the ...
- soil
- light

www.frank-bresser-consulting.com

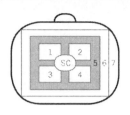 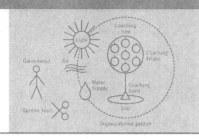

- water
- air
- already existing plants
- animals
- gardeners and other people (e.g. workers, guests, passersby)
- weather
- other geographical circumstances

In your organisation these equate to the overall business and market situation, the culture and climate, existing programmes and initiatives, the level of coaching capability, the support from the top, available resources (e.g. budget, staff), the receptiveness for coaching and many other aspects.

In order to improve the conditions, you may ...

- replace soil by higher quality soil or add fertiliser
- provide more and/or better water (or hold back too much water)
- ensure better air by reducing pollution, growing plants that produce good air, ensuring the desired air temperature and characteristics through using a greenhouse
- have optimal light by arranging the trees/plants towards the sun in a suitable way, growing plants in a certain way so that some may protect others against too much light, using gardening lamps
- make sure that other plants are compatible with coaching (and remove plants that are not, e.g. weeds)
- keep all trees/plants in proper shape, so that optimal conditions are sustained on a permanent basis
- give the coaching trees special, positive treatment
- install devices to support and direct the optimal growth of coaching (e.g. stakes to stabilize young trees)
- support/add animals that foster the ecosystem (and reduce/remove those damaging it, e.g. vermin)
- omit interventions and behaviours which have a negative impact on the climate

Whether and to what extent you may actually be able to change existing conditions in a positive way, depends on ...
- the scope of your role and responsibility as a gardener
- your available gardening tools
- your level of gardening skills
- the quality of cooperation with the other responsible gardeners
- the nature and power of natural developments and internal dynamics within the garden ecosystem
- the nature and power of fundamental external influences on your ecosystem

Whatever measure you plan to take, consider its impact on the whole ecosystem upfront and weigh up its advantages and disadvantages. For example, you may discover that providing more water may serve some plants, but damage others. Where you don't have clear knowledge yet, be very careful to avoid harming the overall ecological balance – and the impact may be much more complex than you might have initially expected. This is in particular true for the use of non-organic (e.g. chemical) elements in gardening interventions. Run extensive pilots/tests beforehand to find out more in a controlled environment in order to make the impact reasonably and sufficiently foreseeable.

Coordinate your measures well with the other responsible gardeners. Make sure all gardening activities are in alignment with the overall gardening strategy. Share your insights, learning and needs to allow other gardeners (also the top gardeners) to refine and improve their gardening strategies accordingly.

3.4. Consider the time dimension properly

Getting the timing right for planting coaching seeds/trees as well as for optimizing the conditions is essential and can create significant momentum and a boost for coaching. Where you are too early or too late, coaching may need more time to grow or even die off just because of the disadvantageous timing.

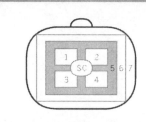
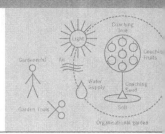

Gardening is an evolving, cyclical learning process, and at each point the environment and the gardening conditions may change in some way. Keep these dynamics in mind at all times and adjust your planning as required.

Have a long term vision and strategy and plan in stages of development. Think about at what stage you need to plant what kind of coaching tree where over time.

4. HOW TO CULTIVATE YOUR COACHING TREES?

Once you have sown the coaching seed in the soil or have planted a new, already fuller-grown coaching tree in the garden, pay attention to how you cultivate it.

Maintain and optimize the conditions for your coaching trees to thrive on a continuous basis, and keep a good balance between natural spread and control mechanisms as appropriate to allow for optimal development.

Get a sense for what is needed and for what is possible and what not. Have patience in growing your coaching trees. Work with what is there and what is possible. Support and challenge, but do not try to force anything into something it is not and may never become. Where things do not develop as you wish or anticipate, integrate the findings. It is great learning.

Be a true gardener and observe, listen to, experience and 'feel' the garden with its coaching trees. Keep coaching and the conditions in good shape and support each stage of the coaching development properly. Respond to local changes

and problems (e.g. emerging illnesses, vermin, weeds), changes of the overall circumstances (e.g. upcoming difficult weather conditions) and changing gardening strategies up the hierarchy. Work on improving the conditions continuously.

Where you find coaching trees grow too much or wildly, intervene by limiting and/or directing and controlling their growth (e.g. cutting trees back, installing cultivation frames). In principle, do the same with other plants harming the coaching trees. However, it is not always obvious which tree or plant actually needs to be given priority, and whether you are allowed to make this intervention. Therefore, make sure you always respect the limits of your gardener role and coordinate your actions with other responsible gardeners. Strive for fair compromises and innovative win-win solutions where different plants, while both being desired, hinder each other's optimal development.

Appoint co-gardeners and have them trained properly as appropriate (see 2. above). Advise other people in the garden to behave in a way that the garden can be kept in a good state.

5. HARVEST (AND HARNESS) YOUR FRUITS PROPERLY.

Once a coaching tree carries fruits, make sure these develop well. Get the timing right to harvest them, i.e. neither too early (so they can't be used/eaten) nor too late (so they are rotting).

In order to ensure good timing, not only check the fruit maturity on a regular basis, but also prepare your harvest carefully:

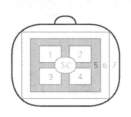
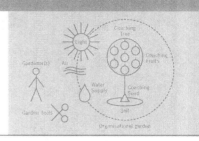

- Know exactly in advance what to do with the fruits once they are picked from the trees (e.g. leaving them in their current form or processing them to make something else of them; using them for internal consumption within the garden or for external distribution and/or sale; giving them a required treatment).

- Have the right number of properly qualified people available to pick the fruits from the trees carefully and quickly enough.

- Have the right means to pack/store/process and transport the fruits to their envisaged destination.

- As needed, inform the receivers of the fruits beforehand on how to best prepare and eat the fruits.

- Have provisions on how to proceed, if fruits cannot be harvested in time or have been harvested too early.

- Determine which and how many fruits may be harvested in what way to allow for an optimal, sustainable development of the trees, the harvest and environment.

So besides the harvest itself, also plan the optimal flow, processing and logistics of the harvested fruits. Coordinate your actions well with the other responsible gardeners. Be aware that different types of coaching trees may carry different kinds of fruits, so also know in advance what fruits have priority for the case that a harvesting bottleneck and overload occurs.

It is important to highlight that not only the actual tree fruits may be harvested. Also other components like the tree wood, roots, bark or leaves may potentially provide useful by-products and thus represent some kind of 'fruits' to be harvested and used.

6. PREPARE FOR THE NEXT CYCLE OF GROWTH.

Ensure optimal, sustainable development of the coaching trees, its harvest and environment. Finishing one cycle is already the beginning of the next. So while picking the coaching fruits and processing, packing, storing and transporting them to their destination, pay attention to keeping the garden in a proper shape. Once the harvest is complete, tidy up and remedy all damage that may have occurred.

Prepare properly for the next cycle of growth, e.g. by removing disturbing/ill branches or by giving the trees or the soil a special, regenerating treatment. In this way, you make sure you only farm your garden and do not exploit it.

 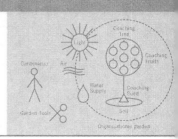

7. REVIEW THE GARDENING PROCESS AND LEARN CONTINUOUSLY.

Coaching gardening is a cyclical learning process. With increasing experience, you enhance your coaching capability and get a more and more refined sense for what is actually needed to make your organisational garden thrive in terms of coaching.

Constantly review and evaluate your gardening process accordingly, draw appropriate conclusions and learn for the future. Foster knowledge sharing across the garden and help build a common coaching knowledge base for coaching gardening in your organisation. Co-create and be part of external and/or internal coaching gardener networks/communities.

Summary:

COACHING GROWTH AND MAINTENANCE FRAMEWORK (FRAMEWORK 5)

Here is again the detailed overview of Framework 5:

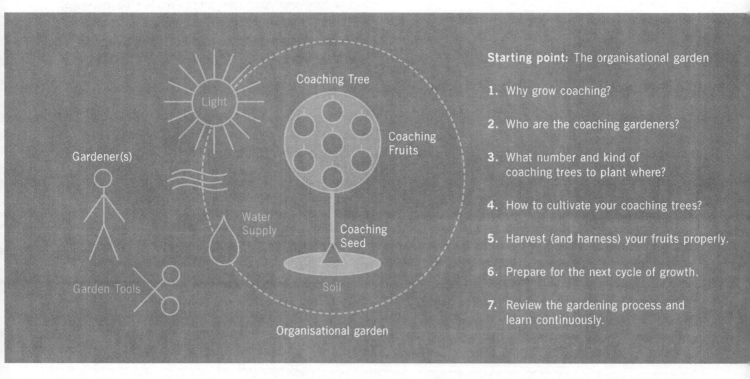

For further reflection and to integrate practice and theory, we invite you to apply the above gardening metaphor to the next case study(/ies) (and/or any of the other case studies included in this book). You may significantly deepen your coaching understanding and your sense for what is actually needed to implement and improve coaching successfully in your organisation.

www.frank-bresser-consulting.com

Geographical focus: *Kenya*

CASE STUDY 22	FRONT ROW VENTURE LIMITED, KENYA

Company: *Front Row Venture Limited*

(sports management – organizing and marketing sports in Kenya; non-profit)

www.frontrowkenya.wordpress.com
(provisional)

Author: *Karanja Simon*

Function: *General Manager, based in Nairobi*

Recovery coaching for optimal team performance

Background

Sports in Kenya is a neglected sector. Front Row is non-profit, having only very limited resources to pursue its goals, e.g. enabling each division in Kenya to experience football.

So our personnel strategy couldn't (and wasn't meant to) be to employ costly high-end professionals. Instead we engaged young employees with some experience, who had undergone difficult times and had been forced to quit their previous jobs for various reasons (we excluded ethical or fraudulent reasons).

As a result, the team faced issues like cynicism, lack of motivation and disillusion, partly also of serious financial situations.

The management was aware of the challenges such a team implied and engaged a coach to deal with/solve the issues. The title of the coaching module that was run was "Recovery Coaching Model". Its purpose was to enable the team to accept the individually experienced losses, move on to create a better future for themselves, and perform well as part of the organisation.

Design of the coaching program

First, the coach was introduced to the team. Together they determined the scope of the coaching intervention, and developed a coaching plan: The team was educated on coaching – its limitations, possibilities and application. The team members were asked to identify what to expect at the end of and during the coaching process – their answers were written down and submitted for the record. The team was also asked to jot down their limitations that they felt might impede their progress.

The coaching initiative contained two kinds of coaching interventions:
- Team sessions (live sessions with 8 participants, once a week for twelve weeks)
- One-to-one coaching (individual tele-sessions, every fortnight for twelve weeks)

Team sessions

Firstly, the team members sat down together with the coach to explore their individually experienced corporate issues of the past that may affect their performance and delivery these days. Bearing in mind the bitterness and disappointment from previous employment, the team had half the lesson dealing with grieving, loss and breakaways. But then, the other half was dedicated to the future which is where the team members could exert influence, be active and have at least some sort of control. The team coaching process contained the following four stages:

FRONT ROW VENTURE LIMITED CASE STUDY: *Recovery coaching for optimal team*

1. Break-ups
When a piece of wood breaks, it splints, glass does too, and so do many other inanimate objects. When we break a bone, it hurts: and so, leaving an employer, no matter what the circumstances, is both painful and some parts are lost.

Sometimes we can fix a break, sew it, glue it, or wait for time to heal it: and this basic principle did apply to the unique situation of this team. There was a need to be open and ready to heal, and accept that nothing is permanent.

The team got there and was committed to moving on to the next step.

2. Healing/Joining/Gluing
Cynicism borne out of bitter pasts can affect our output. Whatever the reason for the break/layoff, we must accept the situation, as it is, and give time to heal.

Various healing exercises from compartmentalization to forgiveness were done with the team. Members were also asked to identify their roles in situations, and with less bitterness, it became possible to realize the magnitude of these roles.

Once the team took responsibility over their issues, we moved on to the next and final step of the coaching.

3. Moving on
This was an exercise the team went through for three weeks. We made amends with our past, especially regarding family members and friends, but also forgave ourselves. The team created new motivation, rather than blaming themselves and losing focus any more. We set up future team goals and en-rolled each other, to remind one another of the steps we had taken to be here, and why we should not return.

4. Celebration and acceptance
At the end of twelve weeks, the team met with the coach for one final session to celebrate the lifetime of the program. There was also evaluation of the whole sessions, and a report from the coach on individual matters. The team was awarded a medal and commissioned to move on, in gratitude for another chance to realize their life goals.

One-to-one coaching

Every two weeks, the coach had a telephone session with each member of the team, to analyse their tasks and set out a personal agenda derived from the team agenda. Most of the personal issues covered were motivation, career development and personal responsibility.

Together with the coach, each individual was thus encouraged to formulate and pursue personal goals that would supplement the team effort and corporate output. Individuals also took this opportunity to address personal problems, which may not be corporate-oriented directly, but affected their general output.

Our key learning/Recommendation:
It is possible to use coaching to effectively deal with loss and grievances in the work-place. It not only works great to enhance the team morale, but also lifts the general output of the team.

Questions and exercises for further reflection and to integrate practice and theory:
1. What is the business case for coaching in this organisation?
2. What coaching forms were implemented? What are the outcomes?
3. In what way(s) does the aspect of organic growth of coaching capability come through in this case study?
4. What has actually helped the team and each individual grow and perform better?
5. What is your key learning from this case study?

Geographical focus: *Czech Republic*

CASE STUDY 23	CSOB, CZECH REPUBLIC

Company: *Československá obchodní banka a.s. (CSOB)*
(CSOB is a key player in the Czech banking sector)
www.csob.cz

Author: *Jan Pešek*
Function: *Senior HRM Coach, Prague*

The ČSOB Coaching centre

Introduction

Our CSOB Coaching centre functions as a coaching provider, gives advice on choosing a proper coach, supports the definition of coaching contracts, and governs the implementation of coaching in accordance with the CSOB rules. We believe coaching helps to change our stereotypes in thinking or manners and to look for more effective solutions, which are not so easily evident. Therefore the CSOB Coaching centre is aimed at creating an effective system and tool for enhancing employees´ motivation, self-reliance and corporate readiness to cope with permanent changes and new challenges of the economical environment.

How we define coaching

In CSOB, we are focusing on business coaching resulting in performance/competence enhancement and also on career coaching for top talent. On the other hand, most of the internal coaches are also able to do personal coaching bringing benefits in increased motivation. Our internal coaches are well selected HRM specialists or CSOB managers with verified prerequisites, who have completed the basic training for coaches, develop themselves continuously and actively coach within CSOB. Since 2009 internal coaching has been offered to all CSOB staff, but middle and line managers and talent with clear managerial potential still remain the main target groups. Our external coaches are professional suppliers of individual or group coaching chosen from a list of pre-selected, well established and experienced coaches in the market. External coaches are recommended to CSOB Senior Management.

Main outcomes and trends in CSOB

The CSOB journey towards a „coaching culture" started in 2005, when our CEO Mr. Kavánek came with a wish and goal to reinforce strongly the level of leadership within the CSOB management style. Over the next couple of years, all CSOB managers went through the „Leadership Academy", where group coaching was part of the program. Some of our top & middle managers hired external (professional) coaches and completed their first coaching contracts. At the same time (2006-2007), we also had our first internal coaching contracts.

In 2009 there were 10 managers (15 in 2008) coached by external professionals, and 60 managers or talented staff (32 in 2008) making use of internal CSOB coaches. This shows an increasing trust in the internal coaches within CSOB and of course, the interest in the optimal use of internal resources. By the way, in the last 2 years CSOB people have increasingly requested to become an internal coach. Through all this, a developing „coaching culture" contributes to the enhancement of the level of leadership in the CSOB Group, which is still the main objective.

Geographical focus: *Czech Republic*

CSOB CASE STUDY: *The ČSOB Coaching centre*

Key milestones overview

CSOB Coaching Centre figures	2003 - 05	2006 - 07	2008	2009	2010
Internal	7 coaches; 10%	25 coaches; 40%	32 coaches; 70%	42 coaches; 85%	50 coaches; ???
External	90% of coaching	60%	30%	15%	???
Key issues	First coaching contracts; screening of the market and suppliers (tasting of coaching) + training of internal coaches	Group coaching in the LA program; internal coaching only as a cure for low performers – be careful!	Setting the principles and rules for the CSOB Coaching Centre (e.g. Ethics Code); staff asking to become a coach	Internal coaching open for all CSOB staff; coaching resources in the CSOB intranet	Search for coaching efficiency + NEW program launch – internal mentoring; coaching culture as a base for leadership

Key learnings

* Internal coaching is a highly motivating tool both for the coachees and even more for the coaches
* Well defined goals for coaching at the beginning account for more than 50% of success at the end
* Coaching can't stand alone as a cure-all approach and must be followed by other aspects (manager's care, processes, social environment and other motivating factors). We also experienced a few coachees, who left the organization as a result of coaching (higher self-awareness)

Speaking from experience, here are a couple of tips for those who are considering coaching:

* Do you wanna change someone else? Forget about coaching!
* Does the goal come from your inside? Then coaching can help you a lot!
* Are you ready to be straight talking, first of all to yourself? Then the coaching can be successful!
* Are you afraid of uncomfortable questions? Then coaching is unlikely to succeed, as this is what coaching is largely about!

Our key learning/Recommendation:
Always have internal coaching linked with a motivational benefit – do not use it as a cure or manipulation tool.

Questions and exercises for further reflection and to integrate practice and theory:

1. What is the business case for coaching in the company?
2. Which of the 10 key success factors (and 3 underlying factors) of Framework 1 are particularly relevant in the context of this case study? (Apply Framework 1.)
3. What is the core value chain of this coaching programme? (Apply Framework 2.)
4. What kind of coaching capacity has been developed, for what purpose and how, through this coaching programme? (Apply Framework 3.)
5. What are the relevant change dynamics happening in this case study? (Apply Framework 4.)
6. Why, how and with what harvest was coaching grown in the company? (Apply Framework 5.)
7. What is your key learning from this case study?

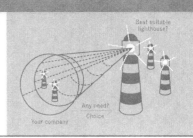

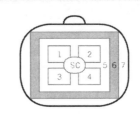

PART VI

THE COACHING GUIDANCE AND SUPPORT FRAMEWORK

(also called: The coaching lighthouse metaphor framework)

FRAMEWORK 6

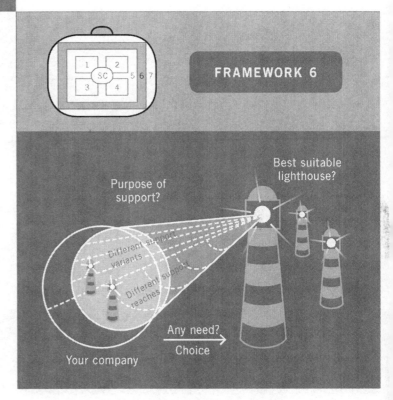

This sixth management tool provides you with an easy-to-use framework to assess your own limits of coaching literacy, identify your exact needs for further external input (beyond this publication), make appropriate 'make-or-buy' decisions and get suitable external guidance and support on the implementation and optimization of coaching in your company, if required.

Through the use of a coaching lighthouse(s) metaphor, this framework helps you reach higher precision, confidence and assertiveness in identifying and sourcing external support on the use of coaching. It addresses how to identify and arrange your needs, when to use external support (and when not), what kind of support is available in the market, and how to achieve the best fit.

Framework 6: Coaching guidance and support framework (coaching lighthouse metaphor) (simplified version)

This tool is equally suitable for beginners, advanced and master level. Any manager and director responsible for the use of coaching in their organisation is well advised to consider this framework and use external guidance and support as needed.

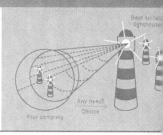
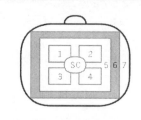

Here is an overview of the framework in detail. We will have a closer look at each of its elements:

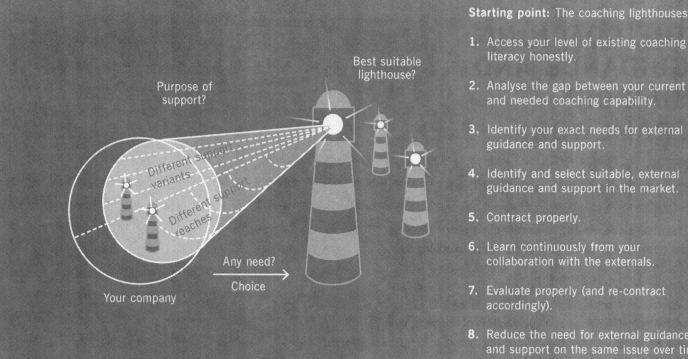

Starting point: The coaching lighthouses

1. Access your level of existing coaching literacy honestly.

2. Analyse the gap between your current and needed coaching capability.

3. Identify your exact needs for external guidance and support.

4. Identify and select suitable, external guidance and support in the market.

5. Contract properly.

6. Learn continuously from your collaboration with the externals.

7. Evaluate properly (and re-contract accordingly).

8. Reduce the need for external guidance and support on the same issue over time.

Framework 6: Coaching guidance and support framework (coaching lighthouse metaphor) (detailed version)

STARTING POINT: THE COACHING LIGHTHOUSES

In your role as manager/director responsible for coaching in your company, you specifically need coaching implementation and improvement intelligence. This kind of coaching capability aimed at the successful, systematic use of coaching in organisations has a pure management perspective and is very different from, for example, the coaching know-how of a professional coach or coaching trainer.

It is the sources and centres of this managerial coaching implementation and improvement intelligence specifically

that we call **'coaching lighthouses'** for the purposes of this framework. Such lighthouses may be individuals, teams, units or departments, be internal or external.

As manager responsible for coaching in your firm, you should be (or aim to be) the – or one of the – 'coaching lighthouses' in your company. At the same time, you should also be able to make proper use of other internal as well as external coaching lighthouses, as and when required.

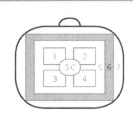 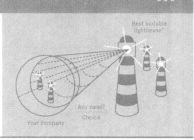

Distinguish management from delivery

Your management task is very clearly to be distinguished from the actual delivery of coaching interventions (e.g. professional coaching delivered by coaches/coaching training provided by trainers). Management and delivery are two separate disciplines and responsibilities.

People involved in the delivery of coaching may also become ambassadors and multipliers of coaching in their sphere of influence. However, it is the high-level management of coaching initiatives that sets the overall frame and direction of coaching within a company and provides the central basis for successful coaching in the organisational context.

It may well happen that as manager responsible for coaching in your firm, you also consider taking on one or more delivery tasks in the course of a coaching initiative that is managed by yourself. This may make sense for example because you want to ...
- ensure highest consistency of the whole initiative
- experience coaching and the people getting involved as closely as possible

- enhance your own coaching capability
- keep your investment/costs low

However, consider this step very thoroughly beforehand and if you do take on any delivery tasks, do it in such a way that you can make sure (and also credibly communicate) that these ...
- are compatible with and in support of your manager role
- are compatible with each other
- are made fully transparent by you at any time
- can be delivered in the required quality with proper integrity
- do not produce any insurmountable conflicts of roles and problems of confidentiality
- do not hinder the professional/unbiased evaluation of the whole initiative, i.e. also your own delivery elements

We recommend you aim to always role model what you want to see in your firm. This means ingraining coaching principles into your management (and leadership) style, i.e. into the way you lead, plan and manage coaching programmes. This is something that takes place within the limits of your manager role (see Key Success Factor 3 in Framework 1).

1. ASSESS YOUR LEVEL OF EXISTING COACHING LITERACY HONESTLY.

Firstly, get a realistic idea of the nature and degree of your own coaching implementation and improvement intelligence. Answering for yourself some or all of the following questions in an honest and frank way may help you:

- What qualifies you to be a manager responsible for coaching in your company?

- What experience do you already have in the field (or in relevant related fields)?

- What relevant training/education have you undertaken?

- What coaching (or related) bodies and associations do you belong to?

- What relevant characteristics/natural talents do you bring in?

- What are your key strengths and weaknesses in terms of implementing and improving coaching?

www.frank-bresser-consulting.com

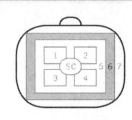
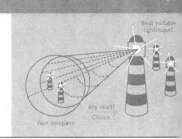

- What is the breadth of your coaching capability? For example: What coaching forms and management tasks in the coaching context are you familiar with?

- What is the depth of your coaching capability? Do you have specific knowledge or specialisation around a certain type of coaching programme (e.g. professional 1:1 leadership coaching initiatives) or around particular steps of implementing coaching (e.g. development of coaching programmes/evaluation)?

- How would you describe the nature of your coaching implementation and improvement intelligence in one sentence?

- On a scale of 1 to 10 (10 = very high; 1 very low), what degree of coaching implementation and improvement intelligence do you have?

- Where do you feel very comfortable and where do you see objective limits to your current coaching capability?

- How committed are you to enhancing your coaching intelligence further?

- What do you actually do at the moment to develop it further?

- What other measures can/could you take to raise it further?

- Where do you want/expect your coaching intelligence to be in 1/5/10 years? What factors does this depend on, and how may you influence these factors in a positive way?

- Speaking within the lighthouse metaphor, what kind of light are you already able to send out as coaching lighthouse in your firm?

Likewise, also assess the existing coaching capability of your whole team (if you have one), of the whole HR/L&D/OD function and of your organisation. Identify all coaching lighthouses within your company (and other potential sources of internal coaching capacity) that may potentially help you implement and improve coaching successfully. For example, maybe you have a number of managers responsible for coaching in different geographical units/subsidiaries of your company.

2. ANALYSE THE GAP BETWEEN YOUR CURRENT AND NEEDED COACHING CAPABILITY.

As a first step, establish your organisation-specific coaching needs and the resulting coaching implementation and improvement intelligence requirements on your firm (and on your role specifically).

2.1. Question of analysis competence

A very tricky point in this context is that in order to figure these things out, you already need substantial coaching ca-

pability. Without it, various possibilities, opportunities and needs, but also the risks and pitfalls of coaching in a company, may not be identified.

Even in very small coaching initiatives, the number and complexity of issues to be considered may be extensive. Where a manager doesn't recognize the actual potential of coaching for his or her organisation or rashly assumes everything is easy and manageable by him or her, the point will definitely come – sooner or later – when the coaching

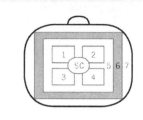
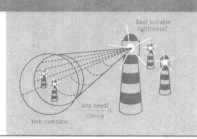

initiative will stumble into trouble. The question then is: How much damage has already been caused?

In order to ensure best practice in coaching and prevent avoidable pitfalls right from the beginning, it is worth considering getting external support to make a professional needs analysis and assessment of the qualifications needed by you to implement and optimize coaching successfully.

Alternatively, think about taking adequate measures (e. g. the participation in suitable external training) to develop your own coaching capability up to the point where you find you can make an appropriate analysis yourself.

Managers who have the required analysis competence can use this book to help them in conducting that analysis. (In case you are not sure about your level of competence, but cannot or don't want to invest money in getting proper professional support, be aware of the risk you are taking and proceed more carefully.)

2.2. Compare your existing with the needed coaching capability

Examine to what extent your current coaching implementation and improvement intelligence includes the level and kind of coaching capability required (gap analysis, see the figure below). Is there partial or full coverage? Is the coverage just sufficient, good or ideal? Where you can identify gaps, what kind of gaps are these exactly?

It is all about fit: In what way does your existing coaching capability actually fit the requirements of your task as manager responsible for coaching? (In the event there is no gap, but ideal coverage, skip the following steps, as there is obviously then no need for external guidance and support.)

In business today we find that managers and directors responsible for coaching in their firms are quite often not sufficiently qualified to fulfil their roles properly. The possible reasons for this are many, e. g.:

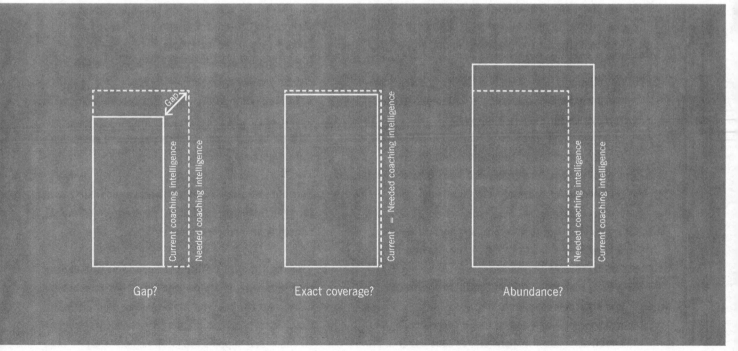

www.frank-bresser-consulting.com

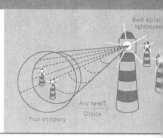

- Coaching, and in particular its systematic implementation, is still a young discipline, so it is often still seen as a rather experiential field of improvisation (learning by doing only).
- The coaching industry itself has been – and today for the most part still is – unable to really provide managers with proper, systematic guidance and support in the field.
- The managers responsible for coaching often have a whole range of tasks to accomplish, one of which is coaching.
- Coaching and the proper qualification of the responsible manager are sometimes still given low importance by companies.

2.3. Find optimal ways of filling your identified gap(s)

Having identified a gap is one thing. Deciding whether and how to fill it is another. Actually, there are various possible ways of dealing with a lack of coaching capability:

1. Filling the gap internally
e.g. **a.** by improving company-wide knowledge sharing, mutual support and synergies among all people involved in coaching
b. by gathering, integrating and making the existing coaching know-how accessible in an easy-to-use, appropriate format in the intranet
c. by reorganizing your firm in terms of coaching and for example establishing the position/authority of a specialized coaching champion, team, unit or centre responsible for coaching only

2. Using external guidance and support to develop your coaching capability up to the needed level
e.g. **a.** by reading this book
b. getting training on the successful implementation and improvement of coaching
c. receiving coaching and/or consulting on being an effective manager responsible for coaching in a firm

3. Hiring properly qualified personnel to raise your company's internal coaching implementation and improvement intelligence as needed
e.g. by employing one or more suitable coaching experts/consultants/managers (depending on circumstances, you may also explicitly recruit another person to take over your role as coaching manager)

4. Having external guidance and support to assist you while planning, implementing and improving coaching programmes (and to grow your own coaching capability)
e.g. by contracting a coaching consultancy to provide you with proper advice and coaching during the actual management process

5. Asking for external expert opinions as additional back-ups
e.g. asking a coaching consultancy to assess the quality and consistency of your planned coaching programme as a double-check to make sure you are on track

6. Delegating/Outsourcing specific management tasks to qualified externals
e.g. **a.** getting a coaching consultancy to make a coaching needs analysis
b. to work out a new or optimized coaching programme concept
c. to recruit and select suitable coaches and coaching trainers
d. to evaluate a coaching initiative

7. Full outsourcing: Have an external coaching consultancy or manager appointed to the role of managing coaching in your company

8. Leaving the gap unfilled for now and proceeding very carefully at a slow pace in order to learn by doing and fill the gap step-by-step over time
e.g. because there is no budget or adequate external guidance and support available in the market

www.frank-bresser-consulting.com

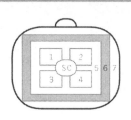
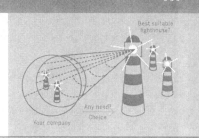

9. Picking out and starting with only those areas where you already have suitable coaching capability (and defer the other areas)
e.g. starting with a 1:1 coaching programme first, but postponing a coaching culture initiative indefinitely until you know more and feel more sure about it

So what is the best approach for your identified gap(s)? As appropriate, choose one or more of the above options.

As shown, getting external guidance and support is just one way of addressing an existing gap, and can take very different forms.

Making use of external guidance and support is particularly worth considering where …

- your company cannot easily build required coaching implementation and improvement intelligence itself
- special, unique external coaching expertise is only available at a specific external 'lighthouse'
- you seek a fresh perspective from outside/an independent, objective view
- you find external support simply makes things much easier and more effective
- timeliness is a requirement and external support is the only way to get things done in time
- the costs of external support are low when put into relation to its benefits and when compared with the costs of the "make-yourself" option
- suitable, qualified providers are available at a reasonable price in the market
- you have a need to delegate/outsource coaching management tasks because of high workload within your firm

Speaking within the lighthouse metaphor, possible purposes for using external coaching lighthouses are to …

a. Be guided by the lighthouse light towards the optimal use of coaching

The lighthouse sends out a light for you/your organisation that leads and directs you to suitable coaching approaches and solutions. You follow it, because you checked it and trust in its high competence.

b. Have a useful, additional light orientation for checking your own decision-making around implementing and improving coaching
You in principle trust in your own orientation, but also take into account the information from the lighthouse. The external light serves as a second opinion to complement yours in order to review and confirm or amend your chosen course.

c. Get proper lighting to see better and more clearly
The main value of the external light in this variant is to give light, i.e. to illuminate your company and its environment in terms of coaching. You use this light like a torch or lamp to see better. It allows you to get a clearer view of what is going on around you, of the needs, the actions to take, and options available to you, in order to implement and improve coaching most successfully in your company.

d. Be enlightened yourself to grow your own coaching capability
The focus of the light from the external lighthouse is on you, i.e. on enhancing your coaching implementation and improvement intelligence (be it yours only or also that of others responsible for coaching in your company). Light can give direction or illuminate an area, and also has a warming, dynamising and vitalising effect. It can transform in a positive way what it is shining on. You use the external lighthouse to become a greater, internal coaching lighthouse yourself.

Whatever choices you make in this context, keep ownership of the process as a whole and find a suitable mix of external and internal coaching capability for your purposes.

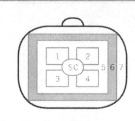
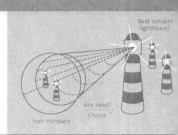

Where you come to the conclusion that the best solution to fill an existing gap is by internal means only, skip the following steps, as there is no need for external guidance and support then.

3. IDENTIFY YOUR EXACT NEEDS FOR EXTERNAL GUIDANCE AND SUPPORT.

Once you have determined there is a need for an external light, formulate your need as clearly and precisely as possible. Be clear in particular on what shall be the focus, variant and reach of the external light(s):

3.1. Different, possible focuses of the light

In what area(s) do you need the services of an external coaching lighthouse?

1. **Mainly for the enhancement of your own coaching capability and/or for the successful realization of a specific coaching programme?**

2. **For the successful implementation of a new programme – or the optimization of an already existing coaching programme?**

3. **For the effective use of what specific coaching form (one, more or all of them)?**
   e.g. one-to-one coaching by internal/external coaches, team coaching, manager/leader as coach, coaching management/leadership style, coaching communication style, coaching mindset, high performance caching culture, organisational coaching forms, technology & tools coaching forms (see also Key success factor 3 in Framework 1)

4. **For what stage(s) of implementing/improving coaching (one, more or all of them)?**
   e.g. needs analysis, acquisition of coaching literacy, planning and design of a coaching concept, preparation, intro-duction, step-by-step enlargement, maintenance, evaluation, learning and further development of the concept (see also Framework 2)

5. **For what support activity around a coaching initiative (for one, more or all of them)?**
   e.g. develop an organisation-specific understanding of coaching, adopt a systematic approach, choose an adequate level of organisational penetration of coaching, involve the top, see coaching as a positive developmental tool, achieve full consistency and alignment with business strategy, ensure transparency, consider the cultural dimension, ensure high integrity and quality (see Frameworks 1 and 2 in this book)

3.2. Different, possible variants of getting light

What ways of receiving external light are most suitable to meet your specific needs?

- Support and assistance/Guidance and leadership/Delegation (deciding instead of you within a clearly defined frame)

- Formats: Consulting/workshops/seminars/coaching/working materials/tools/concepts/speeches/...

- Emphasis on knowledge and expertise or on process and self-reflection

www.frank-bresser-consulting.com

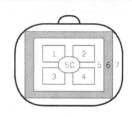
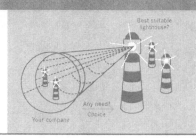

- Face-to-face (local)/Online, remote (e.g. email/phone/internet)

- One-off/on demand/regular/continuous light

- Company-wide/selected parts/only one part of the firm

- Local/national/regional/global

- Short/medium/long term

- For beginners/advanced/master level

3.3. Different, possible reaches of the light cone

What type of reach and thus penetration of your company by the external light do you actually need? – You may either visit an external lighthouse to benefit from its conventional, existing standard light, or you may ask the lighthouse to send out a particular light specifically for your organisation. On the basis of this thought, we may differentiate between 5 possible levels of reach of external light cones:

Level 1
You receive general best practice coaching know-how from a lighthouse accessible by a wider audience at the same time. (E.g. reading this book; attending training which may be tai-lored only to a certain degree around the specific needs of a single participant; public keynote speeches; internet resources)

Level 2
A lighthouse makes up a special light cone only for you. While you provide information about your organisation (online or by a visit) to be illuminated in the cone, you still don't let the light physically enter your organisation. The lighthouse can only work with the information you give. (E.g. you send your coaching concept/plan online to an external consultancy

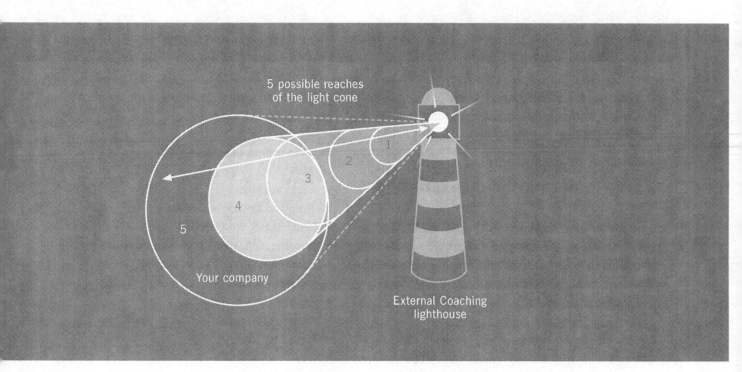

www.frank-bresser-consulting.com

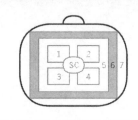 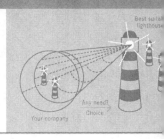

to have it reviewed and checked in terms of consistency and best practice; you get a consulting service or coaching by phone or face-to-face at a remote place outside the company)

Level 3

Like level 2 above, but in addition, you also allow the light to enter into your organisation to some degree. So there is some element of local presence and analysis by the external in the organisation that permits the light to generate and examine first hand information. (E.g. by permitting interviews with people in your firm or the observation of company meetings or workshops)

Level 4

You explicitly request the external lighthouse to examine your company and its environment, gain first hand information

and experience and have impact on your people and the organisation by its light
(E.g. a coaching consultancy makes extensive research within your company to develop or optimize a major coaching programme; it runs one or more workshops in your firm to train the people responsible for coaching in your firm/to co-develop ways of implementing and improving coaching)

Level 5

You want and allow the lighthouse to light up and analyse the whole company and develop/optimize and implement a comprehensive, company-wide coaching plan.

So in fact, the use of external guidance and support is highly scalable and adjustable. Formulate your needs as exactly as possible, and choose from the above range of possible options the one(s) that are most suitable for your context.

4. IDENTIFY AND SELECT SUITABLE, EXTERNAL GUIDANCE AND SUPPORT IN THE MARKET.

This contains the following aspects: Identify a suitable coaching lighthouse profile, scan the market accordingly, and select the most suitable lighthouse(s).

4.1. Establish a coaching lighthouse profile

Once you are clear about your exact need, use this information to develop a lighthouse profile as precisely as possible, setting out the specific characteristics and qualifications required to meet your specific need. Use these as orientation and selection criteria.

Give the criteria different weightings, as appropriate. Also, differentiate between minimum requirements on the one hand

and additional wishes/ideal characteristics and qualifications on the other hand.

Consider and develop relevant lighthouse selection criteria in terms of ...
• Key competences
• Types and formats of services offered
• Reputation in business
• Formal qualifications (e.g. education and training received)
• Independence (in terms of objectivity/bias)
• Experience
• Geographical reach
• Price/Fee range
• etc.

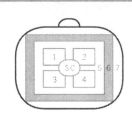
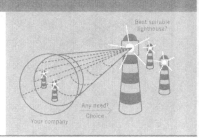

(See also Key success Factor 10 in Framework 1: Ensure high integrity and quality at all levels.)

4.2. Scan the market and select the most suitable lighthouse(s)

As a general statement, the number of independent coaching consultancies specializing in the systematic implementation and improvement of coaching is minimal today.

What you can find very easily in the coaching industry these days, are plenty of people and organisations specializing in the delivery of specific coaching services (e.g. professional coaching or coaching training). However, these normally don't focus on taking and supporting your management perspective specifically.

Where these coaching providers have started to also provide guidance and support for the effective use of coaching in organisations, there is a concern of quality as well as of bias, as they normally have an interest in selling their delivery services to you.

Traditional management consultancies are increasingly picking up the topic of coaching and integrating it as part of their overall company consultancy. They are also not specialists in supporting you as manager or director responsible for coaching in your firm specifically. Due to this background, the coaching approaches used are often very specific and only cover a small part of the whole coaching story.

Coaching consultancy for the management of coaching programmes is in its infancy and needs to grow and raise its quality in order to enable businesses to best leverage the full potential of coaching for their purposes. At present the quantity and *average* quality of the coaching consultancy market is still low.

One key reason for this is that the systematic implementation and improvement of coaching in organisations – and thus

also the offering of external guidance and support in the field – is a quite new discipline within the field of coaching, which is only a young discipline itself. Experience must therefore still be quite limited when compared with that in more traditional business fields.

Another very important reason is that it is simply a difficult area. It takes a considerable amount of time to really think through the implementation and improvement of coaching in organisations in all its aspects thoroughly, and to develop a comprehensive, systematic coaching management (and consultancy) concept.

In this context, as part of the market overview, we have to emphasize that the frameworks presented in this book *are* leading-edge. As was said in the book introduction, this publication is filling an enormous gap. There is nothing comparable out there in business and the coaching industry today. (Please note that Frank Bresser Consulting is the only consultancy licensed to officially provide services on the basis of these frameworks.). Only a very small number of specialized coaching lighthouses currently exist in the market.

But make up your own mind: Scan the market of external coaching lighthouses properly. Since the writing and publication of this book, further coaching lighthouses may have emerged. Use for example the following sources:

- Word-of-mouth/references/networking
- Lists and search engines from coaching bodies, business registers, magazines and/or other institutions and portals
- Public advertising/public bids
- Coaching or consultancy conferences and congresses
- Tracking authors of relevant literature
- Searching consultancy websites or using coaching information portals in the internet
- Getting external support for scanning the market

Where there are no suitable external coaching lighthouses within your geographical reach, ...

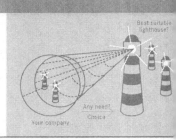

- consider getting effective online support, e.g. by email or phone (which can take place independently of geographical distances)
- review your qualification requirements in terms of minimum versus additional, ideal qualifications
- consider and check again other possible ways of addressing a lack of coaching capability (see again 2.3. above)

Always accept existing, objective limits of feasibility, and do not compromise on the required quality of the lighthouse. It is better to do less, confident of the quality, than run a bigger programme with questionable quality.

When you have your final list of promising coaching lighthouses, contact and check thoroughly each of them and select the best one(s). (See also Key success Factor 10: Ensure high integrity and quality at all levels.)

5. CONTRACT PROPERLY.

Confidence and assertiveness in using external guidance and support will make a difference to the suitability of the solution. Contract exactly and only what you really want and need, and this at a reasonable price.

Keep an element of flexibility for the future and ensure an atmosphere of constructive collaboration. A professional coaching lighthouse will seek to enhance your coaching capability, so that it makes itself redundant as much and as early as possible. Where you sense that the consultancy is patronizing you or putting you under pressure, this doesn't meet the role modelling expectations and is unacceptable.

The contract should create a real win-win for the consultancy and your company and foster the growth of your coaching implementation and improvement intelligence.

Depending on your organisation-specific needs and the quality and quantity of external guidance and support available in the market, you may choose to contract one or more lighthouses. As appropriate, you can use more than one for the same subject, for different elements or at different stages of the management process.

Normally, it is advisable to consider starting with a smaller contract to test things out at first. Enlarge the collaboration step-by-step as mutual trust and familiarization grow.

6. LEARN CONTINUOUSLY FROM YOUR COLLABORATION WITH THE EXTERNAL PROVIDERS.

Your knowledge of your company and your own coaching capability are invaluable for the optimal development and improvement of any coaching programme in your orga-

nisation. Therefore, strive for a high level of collaboration and coordination between you and any external consultancy.

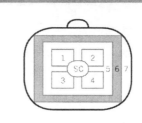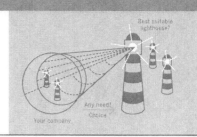

As the reason for having external lighthouses is that they have a level or kind of coaching capability that you don't have, there is a lot for you to learn from them.

If external guidance and support is explicitly aimed at enhancing your own coaching implementation and improvement intelligence (e.g. this book, seminar, coaching, consulting), your learning is the goal anyway. But also where, for example, you ask a coaching consultancy to develop a complete coaching plan for your company, it is not only the finally output that you can learn from. You can also learn from your interaction with the consultancy and by observing their whole process of getting to the solution – the how.

There are limits: It is essential to respect the lighthouse copyright, any other legal regulations and in particular your contractual agreements.

The amount you learn will depend on the quality and approach of your external lighthouse. Where you find you are dealing with stuff you already know, you can also take something important out of it – higher awareness and appreciation of your own existing level of coaching implementation and improvement intelligence.

7. EVALUATE PROPERLY (AND RE-CONTRACT ACCORDINGLY).

Evaluating coaching initiatives effectively and carefully is critical. Continuous monitoring and measuring the quality and outcomes of external guidance and support is an important element of this. (See Key Success Factor 10 in Framework 1 for all details on effective and careful evaluation.)

Good evaluation is essential to find out whether and where you are on track and what needs further improvement. It allows you to make informed decisions about the appropriate level of further use of external coaching lighthouses. You may extend the collaboration with a lighthouse, keep it as it is, refine or change it, reduce or stop it.

The initial selection of external coaching lighthouses (see 4.2. above) is just the first gateway passed. After an induction and familiarisation phase, when the coaching consultancy becomes active in your company, it needs to undergo permanent further assessment and evaluation and continue to prove its suitability. This is important, as only in practice can you actually find out how credibly and effectively an external coaching lighthouse works.

Re-contracting also becomes necessary, where the internal or external business environment evolves in such a way, that your needs for external coaching lighthouses change as well.

www.frank-bresser-consulting.com

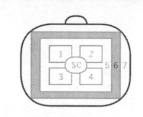
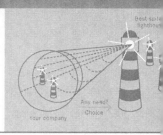

8. REDUCE THE NEED FOR EXTERNAL GUIDANCE AND SUPPORT ON THE SAME ISSUE OVER TIME.

Continuously work towards improving your own coaching implementation and improvement intelligence. In this way, your need for external guidance and support on the same subject should naturally decrease. Also, as already mentioned, a professional, external coaching lighthouse will seek to enhance your coaching capability, so that it makes itself redundant as much and as early as possible.

Having said this, there may also be good reasons to increase the use of external coaching lighthouses over time, e.g. in the following cases:

- Because of the satisfactory, high-quality work of an external lighthouse, you widen the collaboration with it.

- With rising coaching literacy, you discover new fields to use coaching in your business and therefore ask for more external guidance and support in these new areas.

- Changes in the internal or external business environment may suddenly require from you a more intensive use of external lighthouses (e.g. the new CEO wants to have a company-wide coaching culture programme implemented as soon as possible)

- As HR/L&D/OD manager you may need to concentrate on other tasks than coaching. If you have an increasing workload, you may consider delegating more coaching tasks to external lighthouses.

At all times, ensure a proper mix of external and internal coaching capability for your specific purposes. It is important not to stigmatise either, but to use both as appropriate.

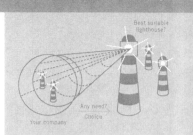

Summary:

COACHING GUIDANCE & SUPPORT FRAMEWORK (FRAMEWORK 6)

We covered complete Framework 6. Here is again the detailed overview:

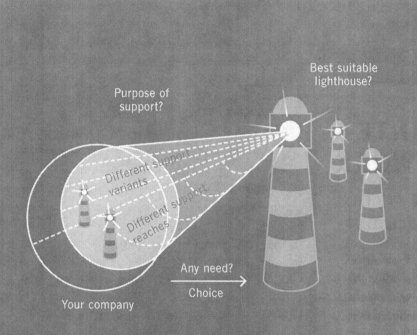

Starting point: The coaching lighthouses

1. Access your level of existing coaching literacy honestly.

2. Analyse the gap between your current and needed coaching capability.

3. Identify your exact needs for external guidance and support.

4. Identify and select suitable, external guidance and support in the market.

5. Contract properly.

6. Learn continuously from your collaboration with the externals.

7. Evaluate properly (and re-contract accordingly).

8. Reduce the need for external guidance and support on the same issue over time.

For further reflection and to integrate practice and theory, we invite you to apply the above framework to your own company and/or to any of the company case studies included in this book. This will help you to reach higher precision, confidence and assertiveness in making a most effective use of external support for the successful implementation and improvement of coaching in your business.

We covered all core frameworks (1 to 4) and embedding frameworks (5 and 6). Last but not least, we now come to the seventh, the activating framework.

The 1 Activating Framework

This last management tool aims to fully activate and integrate all previous frameworks and unite them. You may also apply the core idea of it to any other context or coaching approach you want to integrate. This framework can equally stand alone and be used separately, i.e. independently of the previous ones.

PART VII

THE COACHING INTEGRATION FRAMEWORK

(also called: The coaching microchip and powerhouse framework)

The seventh and final management tool equips you with a synergizing framework helping you bring any (or all) of the previous frameworks into optimal flow and make them one. You will find that the various tools will become much more manageable, clear and easy to use, as they will transform into one integrated toolkit.

This last framework provides you with a still deeper understanding of the effective use of coaching in organisations. The integration of the various frameworks will put you on the path to excellence and produce the best results. Leveraging the full potential of this framework for optimal coaching implementation and improvement is the master discipline of this book.

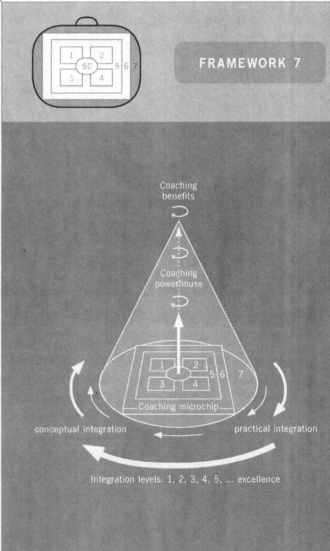

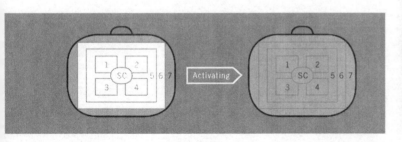

Framework 7: Coaching integration framework (coaching microchip & powerhouse metaphor) (simplified version)

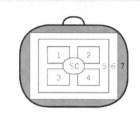
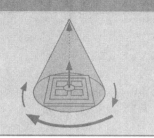

Through an energetic coaching 'microchip and powerhouse' metaphor, the framework sets out how to bring the frameworks into real movement, how to achieve increased conceptual and practical integration of them, and what levels of integration are needed to achieve true excellence.

Any manager responsible for coaching and striving for outstanding results and excellence through coaching programmes, may benefit enormously from internalizing and using this framework.

To use this management tool effectively, you need to have already acquired some coaching implementation and improvement know-how, which you want to integrate further using this framework (i.e. you worked through one, more or all of the previous 6 frameworks and/or bring acquired coaching literacy).

Here is a more detailed overview of the framework. We will have a closer look at each of its elements:

Starting point:
The high-power coaching microchip

1. Choose the main components of your microchip.

2. Activate it!

3. Spin it!

4. See the effect of (and on) your spinning microchip becoming a powerhouse.

5. Continuously optimize your microchip/powerhouse!

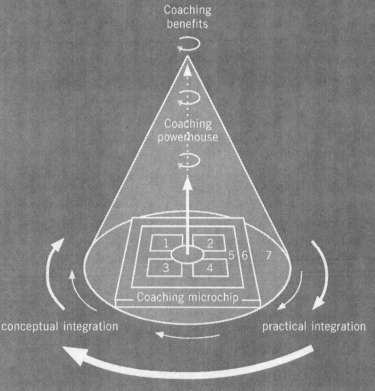

Framework 7: Coaching integration framework (coaching microchip & powerhouse metaphor) (detailed version)

www.frank-bresser-consulting.com

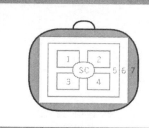
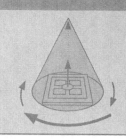

STARTING POINT: THE HIGH-POWER COACHING MICROCHIP

When you have a look at the part of the toolbox that includes the first 6 frameworks, its form reminds you somehow of a microchip, doesn't it?

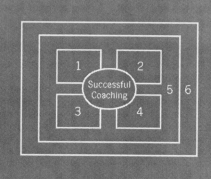

Now imagine it is a microchip and that the frameworks are components installed on it (with the dot in the middle being the microchip centre.) Look at the coaching microchip from the side, and you can see its flat, three-dimensional form:

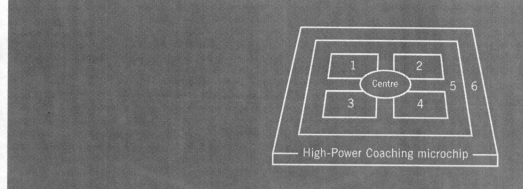

Figure: The high-power coaching microchip

Imagine it is a high-power coaching microchip – a very special microchip with extraordinary features. What this means, will be discussed in this chapter. At this point, we just want to reveal that the centre of the microchip contains a sophisticated motor.

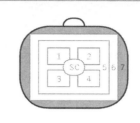

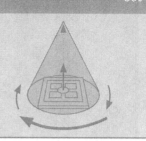

1. IDENTIFY THE MAIN COMPONENTS OF YOUR MICROCHIP.

There are 6 standard pre-installed, main components of the high-power coaching microchip. These are the 4 core frameworks and the 2 embedding frameworks:

The 4 Core Frameworks

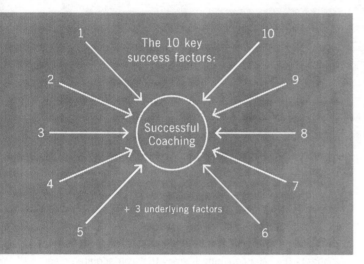

Framework 1: Coaching success factors framework (also called: 10 key success factors framework)

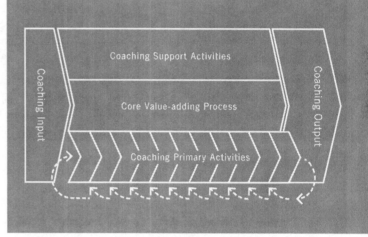

Framework 2: Coaching value chain framework

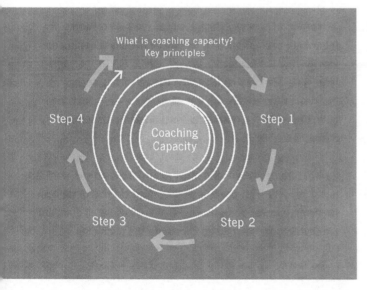

Framework 3: Coaching capacity building framework (also called: High performance coaching culture framework)

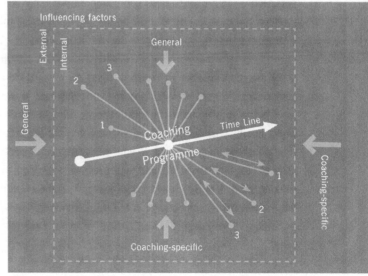

Framework 4: Coaching change dynamics framework

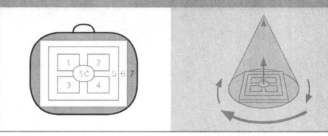

The 2 Embedding Frameworks

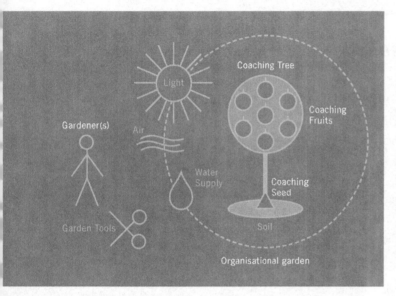

Framework 5: *Coaching growth and maintenance framework*
(simplified version)

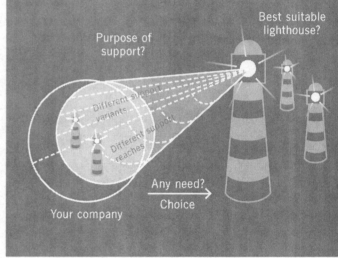

Framework 6: *Coaching guidance and support framework*
(coaching lighthouse metaphor) (simplified version)

These 6 frameworks constitute a fully integrated, sophisticated unit. They are complementary, providing different perspectives, building on each other in different ways and constitute an integrated toolkit. The ability to use all six perspectives in a coordinated, complementary manner will produce the best results for your organisation. By using this seventh framework, you will learn how to acquire this ability.

If you feel comfortable with each of these six pre-installed components, do not uninstall any of them. However, it is always better to use one framework properly, than all frameworks poorly. Quality of application is much more important than quantity. So depending on your specific needs, existing level of coaching capability and your personal learning and working style, feel free to start with just one, some or all of the frameworks as components of the microchip (and remove the others, until you feel skilled enough to include them).

It is also possible for you to link or add other main components (i.e. any coaching literacy that you acquired elsewhere) to the above frameworks and co-install them on the microchip.

Be careful in how you change any of the 6 frameworks or the overall configuration of the microchip. Have confidence in adjusting the microchip to your needs, but at the same time make sure you consider the impact of any change of the system thoroughly. Do not damage any key cables required to make the microchip function and produce the desired benefits.

So what frameworks – and other know-how – do you want to install on your high-power coaching microchip? (For demonstration purposes, let us assume that you choose all standard pre-installed frameworks to constitute the microchip.)

www.frank-bresser-consulting.com

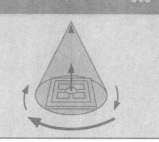

2. ACTIVATE YOUR MICROCHIP!

After the proper confirmation/installation of your selected components, press the centre of the microchip, i.e. the Power/On button, in order to activate the whole chip.

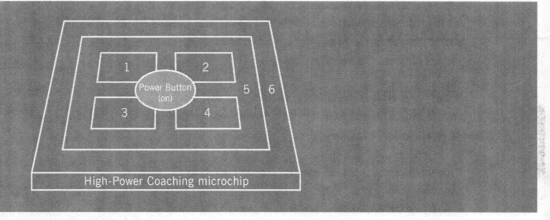

The sophisticated motor embedded in the centre of the microchip now becomes active for the first time and extends a linear device through the microchip centre, so that the microchip now looks like a spinning top, when seen from the side. Also, it creates a basic energy field around the chip that keeps the microchip stable, i.e. prevents it from falling to one side, though it is not spinning yet.

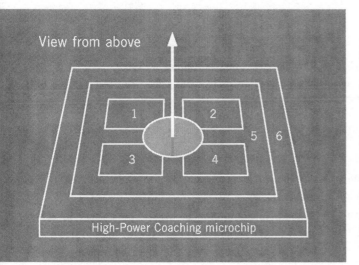

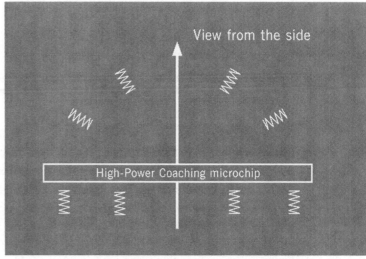

Activating your microchip corresponds to a real commitment and decision to work with the selected components. Therefore, press the power button only if you have really checked and are comfortable with your chosen elements.

www.frank-bresser-consulting.com

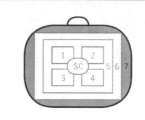
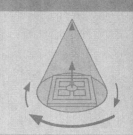

3. SPIN YOUR MICROCHIP!

After successfully activating your microchip, cause it to move and make it rotate. Start spinning slowly at first and increase speed over time while keeping control and sustainable resources to continue spinning. Please note that speed here means level of integration and quality, not the speed of coaching implementation and improvement.

Actually, you achieve this spinning through your own thoughts and actions, i.e. by going through the processes of the following two (successive) steps:

- Conceptual and practical integration of all microchip components
- Applying the microchip in and to your company in reality (and thereby again enhancing conceptual and practical integration)

The better you succeed in these areas over time, the quicker you will be able to rotate the microchip.

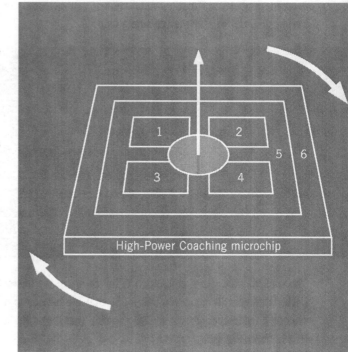

High-Power Coaching microchip

3.1. Conceptual and practical integration

This takes place at 5 levels:

Level 1: Understanding each component as such

Refresh and deepen your understanding of each single framework included in your microchip. In order to bring each component into its proper state and flow, review the framework chapters one-by-one and consider the following questions for each individual component:

- What is its core idea and purpose?
- What are its elements?
- In what areas do you feel (very) sure/less or not sure?

- How can you further enhance your understanding?
- Do you have a proper learning attitude?
- What questions do you still have – and how can you best get the answers?

Think about:

- Are there opportunities to discuss with other people, e.g. colleagues?
- Is there a need to practise the framework more by applying it to further company case studies (e.g. in this book)?
- Have you already applied it to your own company context (as exercise only, i.e. without impact on real decision-making yet)?
- Is there a need for external guidance and support?

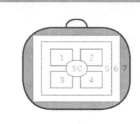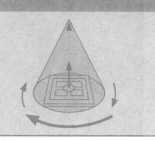

Level 2: Discovering existing links between the microchip components

The 6 frameworks are complementary, building on each other and constitute an integrated toolkit. So uncover, understand and internalize this synergistic interconnectedness. Identify and establish the links and connections between the various frameworks.

One useful exercise is to search and identify elements of one framework in all others, e.g.:

Framework 1: Take any of the 10 key success factors (e.g. KSF 4: Involve the top) or of the 3 underlying factors (UF 1: Importance of culture). Where can you find these factors in the other 5 frameworks?

Framework 2: The idea of the coaching value chain is also reflected in all other frameworks – where and how? Take any of the primary or support activities and identify their reflection in other frameworks.

Framework 3: To what extent is the coaching capacity concept (or elements of it like the scalability of coaching programmes) also included in other frameworks?

Framework 4: Where can you find the idea of change dynamics, of continuum thinking and variables, of internal and external influences in other frameworks?

Framework 5: How is the idea of gardening (or of elements of it like the organic growth of coaching) reflected in other frameworks?

Framework 6: At what points in the various frameworks do you find the aspects of assessing your own level of coaching literacy realistically and of seeking needed external guidance and support?

Another, practical exercise is to apply more than one framework at the same time (for example to the case studies included in this book).

Level 3: Seeing each microchip component as a specific part of the bigger entity

This requires from you to develop and watch out for answers to questions like:

- What *is* the specific role or function of each framework within the whole set of frameworks?
- Where and when does which framework gain particular importance?
- What are the strengths and weaknesses of each framework within the toolkit?

As a useful exercise, apply the whole set of frameworks to the same company case studies and get a sense for when you prefer what kind of framework and how these actually complement each other.

Level 4: Experiencing the microchip as an entity (into which the single frameworks fully merge)

Increasingly approach and use the microchip as a whole, being more than the sum of its single components. Experience the full, sophisticated nature, dynamics and synergies of this integrated unit. Think about:

- What is the common base and essence of all frameworks?
- What are the synergies of using all frameworks in a concerted way?
- What new information is created at a meta level?

As an exercise, apply the microchip as a whole to company case studies regularly.

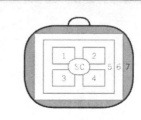 

Level 5: Development of intuition in making use of the whole tool

Practise, practise, practise in order to use all frameworks as one tool more and more intuitively over time, and to learn to juggle and play with its elements properly and with increasing ease. You will thereby enable yourself to take full ownership of the microchip and adjust and optimize all configurations as appropriate.

Going through these 5 levels is an evolving, ongoing learning process. As and when required, get external guidance and support to achieve the desired quality in using the microchip and the resulting benefits.

3.2. Application to your company in reality

Only after achieving a high level of conceptual and practical integration, should you start to apply the microchip for actually implementing and improving coaching in your company, i.e. to make real decisions and take real actions on its basis in your organisation.

Applying the frameworks in real life – versus in a theoretical setting only – makes a huge difference. This is when you can really find out how well you have understood the frameworks and are able to use them for your company-specific context.

You need to prove that you can use them in a dynamically appropriate way, with intelligence and vigilance for optimal fit in each case; that you see the implementation and improvement of coaching as an evolving, learning process; that you are able to fully tailor the application of the frameworks around your organisation-specific needs.

This is how you can develop the required company-specific coaching implementation and improvement intelligence. At the same time, you also significantly enhance your overall conceptual and practical integration of the microchip. Assess your own level of coaching capability realistically on a regular basis and get external guidance and support as required.

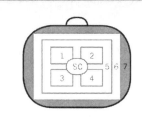
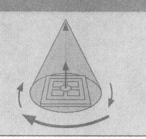

4. SEE THE EFFECT OF (AND ON) YOUR SPINNING MICROCHIP BECOMING A POWERHOUSE.

When you spin your microchip quite slowly at first, there is no real, significant change. But the faster the spinning over time, the more the silhouettes and forms of the various microchip components get into movement and become less separate from each other. Also, the quadratic form of the microchip increasingly morphs into a circle:

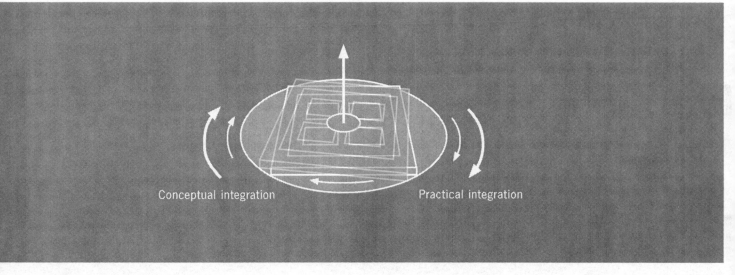

Conceptual integration   Practical integration

At high speed, the whole microchip may finally even merge into one integrated, full circle. This corresponds to uniting and making all frameworks one:

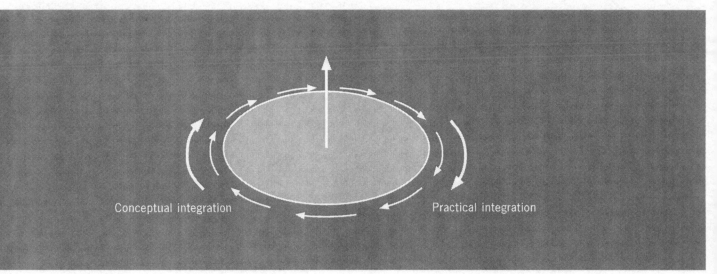

Conceptual integration   Practical integration

FRANK BRESSER CONSULTING & ASSOCIATES

EXCELLENT COACHING SOLUTIONS ↗

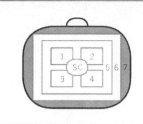
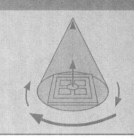

The longer you rotate the microchip over time at a certain level (or higher), the easier it becomes to keep that speed and the more time it takes the microchip to slow down again, if – for whatever reason – you need to pause the spinning. To make it stop immediately (e.g. to replace a component), you can just press the microchip centre which is now the 'Power off' button.

The powerhouse effect

After achieving a good spinning speed, you can start to apply the microchip in your company – with the following effects:

By spinning (in the real context), all relevant information from the environment is absorbed and energy is increasingly generated by the coaching motor within the centre of the microchip.

The microchip starts to become a powerhouse: By processing both – the information and the energy – it is able to create an energy field of better/optimal fit specifically for your organisation. This in turn produces various benefits at the individual, team, organisational and social level, which again lead to overall improved organisational performance and excellence.

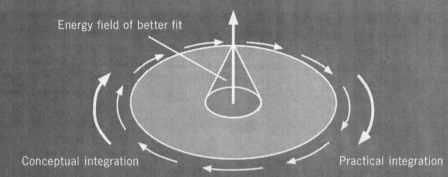

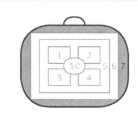
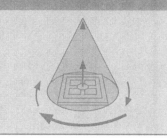

The higher your achieved spinning speed, the more this energy field of modern, dynamic appropriateness and its resulting, organisational benefits grow:

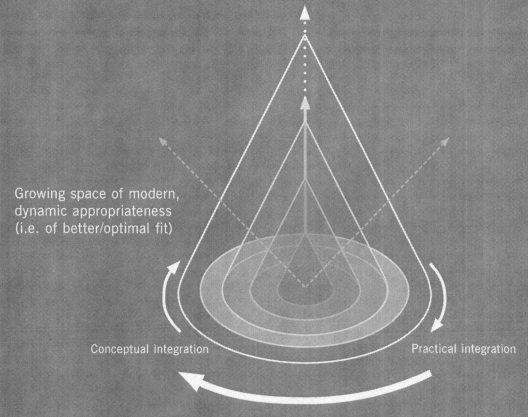

Growing organisational benefits

Growing space of modern, dynamic appropriateness (i.e. of better/optimal fit)

Conceptual integration

Practical integration

Spinning levels: 1, 2, 3, 4, 5, ... excellence

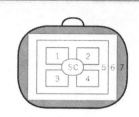
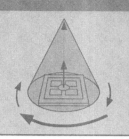

5. CONTINUOUSLY OPTIMIZE YOUR MICROCHIP/POWERHOUSE!

The speed of spinning and thus the size of the energy field can be further increased at all times. There always remains room for learning, whether you are a beginner or at advanced or master level. Always aim to get to the limit that is feasible and appropriate in and for your situation. Mastery/excellence is the ability to keep the speed extraordinarily high on a continuous basis.

Don't take any achieved level of speed for granted. Keep working, otherwise the microchip may again slow down, the energy field disappear and no further benefits created. It is a learning process, which never really ends – a goal to work for day-by-day. As required, get external guidance and support. The successful implementation and improvement of coaching is an evolving, ongoing learning process.

Review the choice of microchip components, their configuration and the spinning speed on a regular basis. Evaluate thoroughly the process and the outcomes, and continuously develop your coaching microchip/powerhouse.

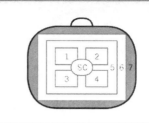
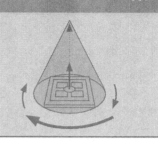

Summary:

COACHING INTEGRATION FRAMEWORK (FRAMEWORK 7)

We covered the complete Framework 7. Here is the detailed overview:

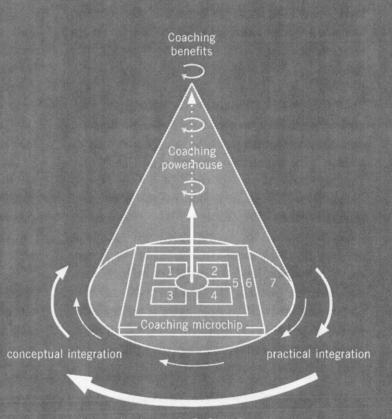

Starting point:
The high-power coaching microchip

1. Choose the main components of your microchip.

2. Activate it!

3. Spin it!

4. See the effect of (and on) your spinning microchip becoming a powerhouse.

5. Continuously optimize your microchip/powerhouse!

Leveraging the full potential of this seventh framework for optimal coaching implementation and improvement is the master discipline of this book.

We have come to the end of this book. We close by giving a final, short 'Conclusion and future perspective'.

www.frank-bresser-consulting.com

CONCLUSION AND FUTURE PERSPECTIVE

This book has provided you with 7 cutting-edge management tools to structure the implementation and improvement of coaching in its various forms in your organisation.

It has covered all existing coaching forms in the business context, and critically examined and identified the most suitable ways of using coaching – rather than promoting and assuming a specific coaching form as the only correct one or naively assuming the value of coaching under all circumstances.

The 7 frameworks are complementary, providing different perspectives, building on each other in different ways and constitute an integrated toolkit. In fact, the more tools you are able to use and combine properly, in principle the better: The ability to use all seven perspectives in a coordinated, complementary manner will produce the best results for your organisation.

However, it is always better to use one framework properly than all frameworks poorly. Quality of application is much more important than quantity. So depending on your company-specific needs and your own personal learning and working style, feel free to use just one, some or all of the presented management tools. Each of them can also stand alone and be used separately.

Managers or directors responsible for coaching in the organisation will hopefully find this guide an invaluable resource for their daily work in this area. Also CEO's, board members, directors, coaching providers or consultancies involved in coaching programmes will hopefully benefit enormously from their newly acquired coaching know-how.

If you want to learn more about the frameworks and/or need external guidance and support to implement and improve coaching successfully in your company, please get in touch. Alternatively, see www.frank-bresser-consulting.com for more information on our consulting services, workshops, online offers (etc.).

It will be very interesting to see how coaching in business develops in the future. Everything is in flux. New coaching forms may emerge. A greater cultural diversity of coaching approaches may develop across the globe (e.g. in Asia) within the next years and decades.

The coaching forms ingraining coaching into organisational life (e.g. coaching leadership/management style, coaching communication style, high performance coaching cultures) are likely to gain further importance in the future. The same is also expected to be the case for the organisational and the technology & tools coaching forms. (All of these are set out in detail in Key Success Factor 3 in Framework 1).

In times of increased globalisation, a faster changing business environment, a more pluralistic and diverse society, of rising questioning and break-up of traditional values and systems, of increasing complexity in all aspects of our work and life, the core coaching principle of better/optimal fit (i.e. what fits best where and how/dynamic appropriateness) can only gain in significance and become/remain a universal principle with high validity.

I very much hope and believe that this book will add real value to the implementation and improvement of coaching in businesses across the globe. I welcome any feedback on this book, any stories about how your firm is applying the tools, as well as any enquiries about working together to implement and improve coaching successfully in your organisation.

www.frank-bresser-consulting.com

Your Notes:

www.frank-bresser-consulting.com

Your Notes:

FRANK BRESSER CONSULTING & ASSOCIATES

EXCELLENT COACHING SOLUTIONS ↗

www.frank-bresser-consulting.com

Lightning Source UK Ltd.
Milton Keynes UK
UKOW01f0108161013

219131UK00005B/94/P